# SCHOOL LAW
## for K-12 Educators

*To Frank, Danielle, and Frankie, whose future*

*gives meaning to the past*

# The SEI Series in Software Engineering

ISBN 0-321-46108-8

ISBN 0-321-22876-6

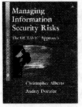

ISBN 0-321-11886-3

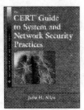

ISBN 0-201-73723-X

ISBN 0-321-50917-X

ISBN 0-321-15495-9

ISBN 0-321-17935-8

ISBN 0-321-27967-0

ISBN 0-201-70372-6

ISBN 0-201-70482-X

ISBN 0-201-70332-7

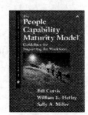

ISBN 0-201-60445-0

ISBN 0-201-60444-2

ISBN 0-321-42277-5

ISBN 0-201-52577-1

ISBN 0-201-25592-8

ISBN 0-321-47717-0

ISBN 0-201-54597-7

ISBN 0-201-54809-7

ISBN 0-321-30549-3

ISBN 0-201-18095-2

ISBN 0-201-54610-8

ISBN 0-201-47719-X

ISBN 0-321-34962-8

ISBN 0-201-77639-1

ISBN 0-201-73-1134

ISBN 0-201-61626-2

ISBN 0-201-70454-4

ISBN 0-201-73409-5

ISBN 0-201-85-4805

ISBN 0-321-11884-7

ISBN 0-321-33572-4

ISBN 0-321-51608-7

ISBN 0-201-70312-2

ISBN 0-201-70-0646

ISBN 0-201-17782-X

Please see our web site at informit.com for more information on these titles.

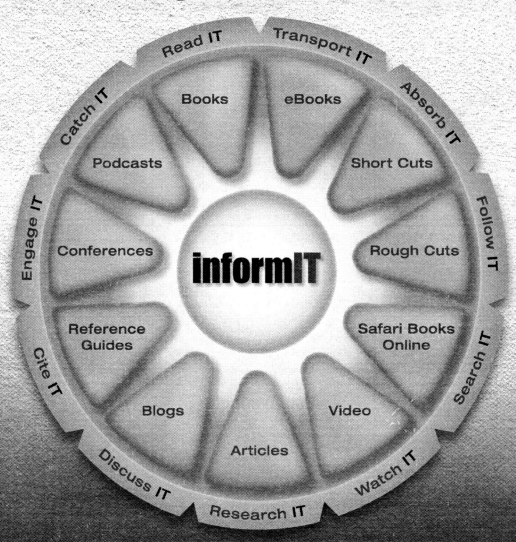

# SCHOOL LAW
## for K-12 Educators
### CONCEPTS and CASES

## FRANK D. AQUILA

*Cleveland State University, Ohio*
*McGown & Markling co., LPA*

**SAGE Publications**
Los Angeles • London • New Delhi • Singapore

*For information:*

Sage Publications, Inc.
2455 Teller Road
Thousand Oaks, California 91320
E-mail: order@sagepub.com

Sage Publications Ltd.
1 Oliver's Yard
55 City Road
London EC1Y 1SP
United Kingdom

Sage Publications India Pvt. Ltd.
B 1/I 1 Mohan Cooperative Industrial Area
Mathura Road, New Delhi 110 044
India

Sage Publications Asia-Pacific Pte. Ltd.
33 Pekin Street #02-01
Far East Square
Singapore 048763

Printed in the United States of America

*Library of Congress Cataloging-in-Publication Data*

Aquila, Frank D.
School law for K–12 educators: Concepts and cases / Frank D. Aquila.
    p. cm.
Includes bibliographical references and index.
ISBN 978-1-4129-1386-7 (cloth)
ISBN 978-1-4129-6030-4 (pbk)
    1. Educational law and legislation—United States—Cases. I. Title.

KF4118.A68 2008
344.73'071—dc22                    2007025409

This book is printed on acid-free paper.

07  08  09  10  11   10  9  8  7  6  5  4  3  2  1

| | |
|---|---|
| *Acquisitions Editor:* | Diane McDaniel |
| *Editorial Assistant:* | Ashley Plummer |
| *Production Editor:* | Diane S. Foster |
| *Copy Editor:* | Diana Breti |
| *Typesetter:* | C&M Digitals (P) Ltd. |
| *Proofreader:* | Taryn Bigelow |
| *Indexer:* | Will Ragsdale |
| *Cover Designer:* | Candice Harman |

# Brief Contents

# Detailed Contents

## PART I: POLICY ISSUES

## 1 SCHOOL DESEGREGATION   3

## PART II: STUDENTS' RIGHTS

 **4** School Attendance    85

**5** Student Conduct and Discipline    103

# PART III: TEACHERS' RIGHTS

## 9   TEACHERS' RIGHTS AND CONCERNS    191

# PART IV: LEGAL ASPECTS OF SCHOOLS

## 13   Local School Boards and Contract Liability   279

# 14 TORT LIABILITY OF SCHOOL DISTRICTS, OFFICERS, AND EMPLOYEES    307

# 15 FINANCING PUBLIC SCHOOLS AND USE OF FUNDS    335

# 16 SCHOOL VIOLENCE AND INTERNET ISSUES   361

# Additional Case Briefs Available Online at http://www.sagepub.com/aquilacasebriefs

1. **School Desegregation**

   Arthur v. Nyquist, 712 F.2d 816 (2nd Cir. 1983)
   Brown v. Board of Education of Topeka (Brown II),
      349 U.S. 294, 75 S. Ct. 753 (1955)
   Columbus Board of Education v. Penick, 443 U.S. 449, 99 S. Ct. 2941 (1979)
   Dayton Board of Education v. Brinkman (Brinkman I),
      433 U.S. 406, 97 S. Ct. 2766 (1977)
   Dayton Board of Education v. Brinkman (Brinkman II),
      443 U.S. 526, 99 S. Ct. 2971 (1979)
   Milliken v. Bradley (Milliken II), 433 U.S. 267, 97 S. Ct. 2749 (1977)
   Plessy v. Ferguson, 163 U.S. 537, 16 S. Ct. 1138 (1896)
   Washington v. Seattle School District
      No. 1., 458 U.S. 457, 102 S. Ct. 3187 (1982)

2. **Church-State Interaction000**

   Agostini v. Felton, 117 S. Ct. (1997)
   Allen v. Casper, 622 N.E.2d 367 (Ohio App. 8 Dist. 1993)
   Board of Education of Central School District
      No.1 v. Allen, 392 U.S. 236, 88 S. Ct. 1923 (1968)
   Board of Education of Kiryas Joel Village School
      District v. Louis Grumet et al., 114 S. Ct. 2481 (1994)
   County of Allegheny v. ACLU, Greater Pittsburgh Chapter,
      492 U.S. 573, 109 S. Ct. 3086 (1989)

Dick-Friedman ex rel. Friedman v. Board of Education
   of West Bloomfield, 427 F.Supp.2d 768 (E.D. Mich. 2006)
Epperson v. State of Arkansas, 393 U.S. 97, 89 S. Ct. 266 (1968)
Illinois ex rel. McCollum v. Board of Ed., S.D. 71,
   Champaign County, Ill., 333 U.S. 203, 68 S. Ct. 461 (1948)
Lee v. Weisman, 112 S. Ct. 2649 (1992)
Lemon v. Kurtzman; Early v. Dicenso, 403 U.S. 602, 91 S. Ct. 2105 (1971)
Mitchell v. Helms, 530 U.S. 793 (2000)
Mueller v. Allen,  463 U.S. 388, 103 S. Ct. 3062 (1983)
Resnick v. East Brunswick Township Board of
   Education, 77 N.J. 88, 389 A.2d 944 (1978)
Rosenberger et al. v. Rector and Visitors of
   University of Virginia et al., 515 U.S. 819, 115 S.Ct. 2510 (1995)
Santa Fe Indep. School District v. Doe, 120 S. Ct. 2266 (2000)
School Dist. of Abington Township v. Schempp;
   Murray v. Curleti, 374 U.S. 203, 83 S. Ct. 1560 (1963)
School District of the City of Grand Rapids v. Ball, 473 U.S. 373 (1985)
U.S. v. Bd. of Educ. of School D. of Philadelphia, 911 F.2d. 882 (3rd Cir. 1990)
Zorach v. Clauson, 343 U.S. 306, 72 S. Ct. 679 (1952)

## 4. School Attendance

Allen v. Casper, 622 N.E.2d 367 (Ohio App. 8 Dist. 1993)
Beeson v. Kiowa County School Dist.,  567 P.2d 801 (Colo.App. 1977)
Bishop v. Colaw, 450 F.2d 1069 (8th Cir. 1971)
Davenport v. Randolph County Bd. of Ed., 730 F.2d 1395 (1984)
Eisner v. Stamford Board of Education, 440 F.2d 803 (2d Cir. 1971)
Guzick v. Drebus, 431 F.2d 594 (6th Cir. 1970)
Martinez v. Bynum, 461 U.S. 321, 103 S. Ct. 1838 (1983)
Massie v. Henry, 455 F.2d 779 (4th Cir. 1972)
Tate v. Bd. of Ed. of Jonesboro, Ark., Special Education District,
   453 F.2d 975 (8th Cir. 1972)
Trachtman v. Anker, 563 F.2d 512 (2d Cir. 1977);
   cert. denied, 435 U.S. 925, 98 S. Ct. 1491 (1978)
Warren v. National Assn. of Secondary Sch.
   Principals, 375 F. Supp. 1043 (1974)

## 5. Student Conduct and Discipline

C. J. v. School Board of Broward County, 438 So.2d 87 (1983)
Davenport v. Randolph County Bd. of Ed., 730 F.2d 1395 (1984)
Goetz v. Ansell, 477 F.2d 636 (2d Cir. 1973)
Ingraham v. Wright, 430 U.S. 651, 97 S. Ct. 1401 (1977)
S. V. Board of Education, San Francisco Unified Sch.
   Dist. App., 97 Cal.Rept. 422

Tibbs v. Bd. of Ed. of the Township of Franklin, 276 A.2d 165 (NJ Super. Ct. 1971)
Vernonia School District v. Acton, 515 U.S. 646 (1995)

## 6. Student Records

Fay v. South Colonie Central School District, 802 F.2d 21 (2d Cir. 1986)
Van Allen v. Mccleary, 211 N.Y.S.2d 501 (N.Y. Sup.Ct. 1961)

## 7. English Language Learners

Castaneda v. Pickard (Castaneda II) (Unpublished)
Serna v. Portales Municipal Schools, 499 F.2d 1147 (10th Cir. 1971)

## 8. Education of Students With Disabilities

Bevin H. v. Wright, 666 F. Supp. 71 (W.D. Pa. 1987)
Brookhart v. Illinois State Board of Education, 697 F.2d 179 (7th Cir. 1983)
Chalk v. U.S. District Court, Central District of California,
   840 F.2d 701 (9th Cir. 1988)
Clarke v. Shoreline School District No. 412,
   King County, 729 P.2d 793 (Wash. 1986)
Clyde v. Puyallup School District No.3, 35 F.3d 196 (9th Cir. 1994)
Dellmuth, Acting Secretary of Education of Pennsylvania
   v. Muth, 491 U.S. 223, 109 S. Ct. 2397 (1989)
Doe v. Dolton Elementary School District
   No. 148, 694 F. Supp. 440 (N.D. III. 1988)
Grube v. Bethlehem Area School District, 550 F. Supp. 418 (1982)
Hurry v. Jones, 734 F.2d 879 (1st Cir. 1984)
Kruelle v. New Castle School District, 642 F.2d 687 (3rd Cir. 1981)
Max M. v. Illinois State Board of Education, 629 F. Supp. 1504 (N.D. Ill. 1986)
Mitchell v. Helms, 530 U.S. 793 (2000)
S-1 v. Turlington, 635 F.2d 342, 347 (5th Cir. 1981)
School Board of Nassau County, Florida v. Arline,
   480 U.S. 273, 107 S. Ct. 1123 (1987)

## 9. Teachers' Rights and Concerns

Board of Regents of State Colleges v. Roth, 408
   U.S. 564, 92 S. Ct. 2701 (1972)
Boring v. Buncombe Board of Education, 136 F.3d 364 (4th Cir. 1998)
Clarke v. Shoreline School District No. 412,
   King County, 729 P.2d 793 (Wash. 1986)
Dike v. School Board of Orange County, Florida,
   650 F.2d 783 (5th Cir. 1981)
East Hartford Ed. Assn. v. Board of Ed., 562 F.2d 838 (2d Cir. 1977)
Fisher v. Snyder, 476 F.2d 375 (8th Cir. 1973)

Fowler v. Board of Education of Lincoln County, 819 F.2d 657 (6th Cir. 1987)
Geller v. Markham, 635 F. 2d 1027 (1980)
Givhan v. Western Line Consolidated School District, 439 U.S. 410 (1979)
O'Connor v. Ortega, 480 U.S. 709, 107 S. Ct. 1492 (1987)
Phelps v. Bd. of Education of Town of West New York,
    300 U.S. 319, 57 S. Ct. 483 (1937)
Schafer v. Board of Public Ed., 903 F.2d. 243 (3rd Cir. 1990)
Stroman v. Colleton County School District, 981 F.2d 152 (4th Cir. 1993)
Wilson v. Chancellor, 48 F.Supp. 1358 (D. Or. 1976)

## 10. Teacher Certification, Licensure, and Contracts for Employment

Amador v. New Mexico State Board of Education,
    80 N.M. 336, 455 P.2d 840 (1969)
Ambach v. Norwick, 441 U.S. 68 (1979)
City of Richmond v. J. A. Croson Co., 488 U.S. 469, 109 S. Ct. 706 (1989)
Martin v. Wilks, 490 U.S. 755, 109 S. Ct. 2180 (1989)
Oklahoma ex rel. Thompson v. Ekberg,  613 P.2d 466 (1980)
Univ. of Pennsylvania v. Equal Employment Opportunity
    Comm'n, 493 U.S. 182, 100 S. Ct. 577 (1990)

## 11. Collective Bargaining

Chicago Teachers Union v. Hudson, 475 U.S. 292, 106 S. Ct. 1066 (1986)
City of Madison v. Wisconsin Employment Relations
    Commission, 429 U.S. 167, 97 S. Ct. 421 (1976)
Dike v. School Board of Orange County, Florida,
    650 F.2d 783 (5th Cir. 1981)
East Hartford Ed. Assn. v. Board of Ed., 562 F.2d 838 (2d Cir. 1977)
Knight v. Board of Regents of University of State of New York,
    269 F. Supp. 339 (1967), affd 390 U.S. 36 (1968)
Nat'l Gay Task Force v. Bd. of Education of
    Oklahoma City, 729 F.2d 1270 (10th Cir. 1984)
O'Connor v. Ortega, 480 U.S. 709, 107 S. Ct. 1492 (1987)
Phelps v. Bd. of Education of Town of West
    New York, 300 U.S. 319, 57 S. Ct. 483 (1937)
Pinsker v. Joint District No. 28J of Adams and
    Arapahoe Counties, 735 F.2d 388 (l0th Cir. 1984)
Schafer v. Board of Public Ed., 903 F.2d. 243 (3rd Cir. 1990)
Skinner v. Railway Labor Executives Assn.,
    489 U.S. 602, 109 S. Ct. 1402 (1989)

## 12. Teacher Dismissal, Retirement, and Discrimination in Employment

Board of Regents of State Colleges v. Roth,
    408 U.S. 564, 92 S. Ct. 2701 (1972)

## 13.  Local School Boards and Contract Liability

## 14.  Tort Liability of School Districts, Officers, and Employees

Texas State Teachers Assn. v. Garland Independent School Dist.,
777 F. 2d 1046 (5th Cir. 1985)

## 15. Financing Public Schools and Use of Funds

Resnick v. East Brunswick Township Board of Education,
77 N.J. 88, 389 A.2d 944 (1978)
Revell v. Mayor of Annapolis, 81 Md. I, 31 A. 695 (1895)

# Preface

After nearly 20 years of teaching school law to teachers who were preparing to become school administrators, my frustration with the difficulties students had studying the complex law cases—and the tedious legal language in our school law textbooks—triggered my attempt to write a different type of law book. First, I wrote a case notes style of book, similar to books used as a supplement in law school classes. To an extent, this helped to improve student comprehension, especially when supplemented with personal materials. However, even with improvements in later editions, I was still not satisfied. Somewhat out of desperation, I decided to devise a blended version, with short case briefs as well as brief—but solid—concept sections and case studies to stimulate classroom discussion about key issues. Field tests with my aspiring school administration students led me to believe that this version is a move in the right direction.

While my intent was to provide a useful text for prospective school administrators, I decided to expand the content and approach so that undergraduates as well as graduate students in other disciplines could also use this book.

I believe that the most compelling feature of this book is that it does not contain the complex legal discussions found in traditional legal texts. At the same time, I have tried to provide enough background information to help those without legal training to comprehend complex legal arguments. Each chapter contains an Overview, which provides the context for that chapter; two Case Studies with discussion questions; an outline of Important Concepts; a Conclusion summarizing the chapter; and a series of short-form Case Briefs, including major cases that explicate the concepts discussed in the chapter. Additional Case Briefs are provided to supplement the chapter material and provide deeper understanding. This material can be found on the SAGE Web site: http://www.sagepub.com/aquilacasebriefs.

## ACKNOWLEDGMENTS

In acknowledging those most helpful in the completion of this law book, I would be remiss if I did not thank Karen Majeski for her patience, humor, and generous support. Also deserving thanks are those who assisted with the research and organizational support. Those who deserve recognition include Kristen Vance, for her outstanding organizational skills; Kelly Hedberg, who conducted extensive early research; and Shawn Romer and Heather Banchek, who provided later research and editing. The Sage team composed of Diane McDaniel, Ashley Plummer, Diane S. Foster, and Diana Breti provided both personal support as well as exceptional technical assistance.

The following reviewers generously provided their time and insight:

Barbara Abbott Allbright, Texas State University

Bradley Vance Balch, Indiana State University

David J. Blacker, University of Delaware

Mark W. Clark, University of Wisconsin, Eau Claire

Susan G. Clark, University of Akron

Audrey M. Clarke, California State University, Northridge

Boyd E. Dressler, Montana State University

Ellen Eckman, Marquette University

Richard Fossey, University of Houston

Jan Hammond, State University of New York

Philip Huckins, New England College

Leslie Jones, Nicholls State University

Cheryl L. Kelsey, University of Central Oklahoma

Richard A. King, University of Northern Colorado

R. Stewart Mayers, Southeastern Oklahoma State University

Cynthia McDaniels, Southern Connecticut State University

Joseph R. McKinney, Ball State University

Gloria Jean Thomas, Idaho State University

David P. Thompson, University of Texas, San Antonio

Christine Villani, Southern Connecticut State University

# Introduction to the Legal System and Legal Research

## OVERVIEW OF THE LEGAL SYSTEM

The heart of the body of knowledge commonly identified as education or school law is statutory and **case** law. The material included in this book, whether case briefs, outlines, or textbook/treatise reference information, provides a summary of the most important aspects of the law regarding education.

Statutory law is made up of criminal and civil laws, or **statutes**. Statutes are enacted by a governmental body authorized to pass such laws. For example, Congress enacts federal statutes; state legislatures enact state statutes; and local elected bodies, such as city councils, enact municipal **ordinances**. Case law refers to the body of written decisions that have been rendered at the conclusion of lawsuits, or cases, that come before various courts.

Two types of courts with which you will need to be familiar are trial courts and appellate courts. A **trial court** renders two types of decisions: decisions based on law and decisions with respect to facts. Trial court decisions made on the basis of law are usually made by a judge; a jury makes findings of fact. An **appellate court** generally reviews the decisions of trial courts in order to determine whether proper procedures were followed and whether the correct law was applied. Usually, only appellate courts render decisions that, when published, become case law.

Another way to categorize courts is by the nature of the disputes that particular courts consider. In civil law, legal disputes arising between two or more parties usually occur in a particular state or are based on state law principles. Such suits are properly filed in state courts. On the other hand, matters that arise in or involve more than one state (**diversity jurisdiction**) or that specifically involve the federal government, federal laws, or federal **constitutional** issues are filed in **federal courts**.

In the state court system, a case is first heard by a trial court. An **appeal** "of right" to the state appellate level is available, while the state supreme court has discretion to either grant or deny further review on appeal. This discretionary review is called **certiorari**, or sometimes, "granting cert." Figure I.1 shows a typical state court (in this case, Ohio) judicial structure.

## State Court System

The process is similar in the federal court system (see Figure I.2). A federal case is first filed in a federal district court, the "trial court" of the federal system. On appeal, the case will be heard in the federal court of appeals in the particular circuit in which proper **jurisdiction** is established (see Figure I.3). The highest federal court, sometimes referred to as the "court of last resort," is the U.S. Supreme Court. Again, an appeal to the Supreme Court is discretionary; the court may either grant or deny certiorari.

## Federal Court System

Finally, with respect to education law in particular, a little background about the educational system in this country is in order. In the United States, education is the responsibility of each state government. Despite the manner in which local school board members are appointed or elected, they are state, not local, officials.

Obviously, state legislatures cannot foresee (and therefore cannot legislate with respect to) every important education-related issue that may arise. For this reason, local school boards have been granted **implied** authority to set policies and resolve problems as they arise. The exercise of such powers is permitted so long as local school board actions do not conflict with state or federal laws and regulations. This grant of implied authority was actually developed by the courts (and, hence, is a product of case law) as an efficient method of granting authority to local school board actions that appear educationally sound. When school board actions are not sound, litigation between the aggrieved parties (the **plaintiff**) and the school board (**defendant**) may be, and often is, initiated.

Before a lawsuit is tried, the parties must assess their positions in light of both existing statutes and case law—the "building blocks" upon which lawsuits are initiated and defended. Below is a closer look at the nature of case law.

# CASE LAW

*Precedent.* A written court decision in a specific area of law establishes a **precedent**. Reliance on precedent is often referred to as the **doctrine** of **stare decisis** (Latin for "let the decision stand"). Precedents guide future courts as they **decide** certain issues and thereafter write their own concise rules of law with respect to the issues before them. Other state and federal trial courts will then rely on the appellate decisions rendered in their jurisdiction, unless a "compelling case" indicates that the precedent should not be followed, but instead overruled. Compelling cases are court decisions from outside the jurisdiction that are used to influence a decision. For instance, an Ohio court could decide whether to find an Illinois appellate decision compelling, but that same Ohio court would *have* to follow a valid case previously decided in its own jurisdiction. Thus, the only court that can change a precedent is the court that set it or one of higher authority.

The **majority opinion** is written by a **justice** from the majority. This holding establishes the precedent. A justice who agrees but may have used different reasoning may include a

**Figure I.1**   Ohio State Court System

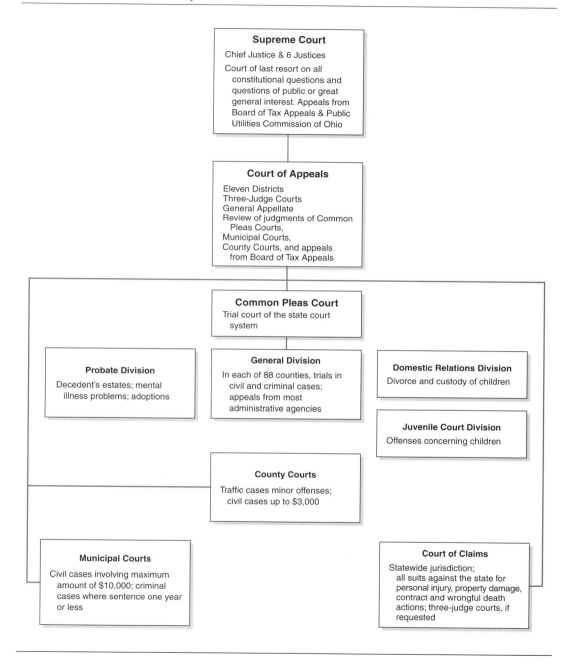

**Figure I.2** The Federal Appellate Circuits

| 1st Circuit | 2nd Circuit | 3rd Circuit | 4th Circuit | 5th Circuit | 6th Circuit | 7th Circuit |
| --- | --- | --- | --- | --- | --- | --- |
| Maine | Connecticut | Delaware | Maryland | Louisiana | Kentucky | Illinois |
| Massachusetts | New York | New Jersey | South Carolina | Mississippi | Ohio | Indiana |
| New Hampshire | Vermont | Pennsylvania | North Carolina | Texas | Michigan | Wisconsin |
| Rhode Island | | | Virginia | | Tennessee | |
| | | | West Virginia | | | |

| 8th Circuit | 9th Circuit | 10th Circuit | 11th Circuit | D.C. Circuit | Federal Circuit | |
| --- | --- | --- | --- | --- | --- | --- |
| Arkansas | Alaska | Colorado | Alabama | Washington, D.C. | Washington, D.C. | |
| Iowa | Arizona | Kansas | Georgia | | | |
| Minnesota | California | New Mexico | Florida | | | |
| Missouri | Hawaii | Oklahoma | | | | |
| Nebraska | Idaho | Utah | | | | |
| North Dakota | Montana | Wyoming | | | | |
| South Dakota | Nevada | | | | | |
| | Oregon | | | | | |
| | Washington | | | | | |

**Figure I.3** Geographic Boundaries of Unites States Courts of Appeals and United States District Courts

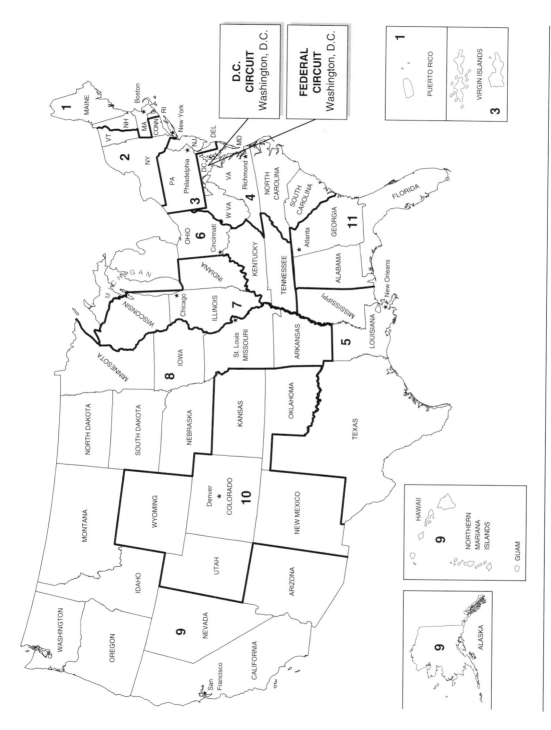

SOURCE: http://www.uscourts.gov/images/CircuitMap.pdf

**concurring opinion**. Further, in many cases, a justice from the minority may issue a **dissenting opinion** in order to provide an alternative rationale. This can be important, especially when a similar issue reaches the court at a later time.

*Citation*. A **citation** is used to locate case law in published law reports. It includes the name of the case; the name, volume, and page number of the law report; and the year of the decision. For example, in the student rights and regulations case *Goss v. Lopez,* the official citation is *Goss v. Lopez,* 419 U.S. 565 (1975).

The "U.S." in the citation refers to a collection of bound volumes known as the *United States Reports,* or *U.S. Reports,* the official repository of U.S. Supreme Court decisions. One can find the full text of the *Goss* decision in volume 419 of the *U.S. Reports,* at page 565. The citation also lets us know that the case was decided by the Supreme Court in 1975. When you review a court decision, there will always be a majority decision written by a justice on the majority side. In some more complicated cases, there may also be a concurring **opinion** written by a justice of the majority who wishes to emphasize different reasoning for concurring. Similarly, a case may be important enough that a dissent will be written by one or more justices from the minority side.

*Parallel Citations*. In most cases, a decision may also be referred to by a parallel citation. Each parallel citation leads the reader to the same opinion but in a different set of volumes (i.e., a different reporter system).

For example, the full citation for *Goss v. Lopez* is as follows: *Goss v. Lopez,* 419 U.S. 565, 95 S. Ct. 729, L.Ed. (1975).

"S. Ct." refers to the *Supreme Court Reporter,* an unofficial set of volumes, or reporter series, which parallels the official *U.S. Reports* series. Similarly, "L.Ed." refers to the unofficial reporter series known as the *United States Supreme Court Reports, Lawyers' Edition* (hereinafter, *Lawyers' Edition*).

*Goss v. Lopez* may now be located in any one of these three publications: the *U.S. Reports,* the *Supreme Court Reporter,* and the *Lawyers' Edition.* As "public documents," official court decisions are not subject to copyright law; private publishing companies may thus copy them and reprint them in any format.

*Court Reports*. Court **reports** are volumes that contain reported appellate decisions and opinions from various geographical jurisdictions. There are reports for every appellate jurisdiction, including the U.S. Supreme Court, the federal courts of appeals, and state appellate courts. An "official" publication is one that is published by or for a branch of government. For example, the *U.S. Reports* series, the official collection of U.S. Supreme Court decisions, is published by the U.S. Government Printing Office. The term "reporter," as in *Supreme Court Reporter,* usually refers to unofficial versions of decisions published by private publishing companies.

## PUBLICATION DESCRIPTIONS

*United States Reports*. As discussed above, the *United States Reports* series (abbreviated "U.S.") is the official Supreme Court publication by the U.S. Government Printing Office. The *U.S.*

*Reports* series citation is used when citing U.S. cases in the U.S. Supreme Court and other federal courts. The official citation should always precede a parallel or unofficial citation.

*Lawyers' Edition.* The *Lawyers' Edition* (abbreviated "L.Ed.") is an unofficial publication of the Lawyers Cooperative Publishing Company. The official texts of cases, as published in the *U.S. Reports,* are published in this series. The L.Ed. (first series) includes volumes 1 through 351 of the *U.S. Reports;* the L.Ed.2d (second series) contains volumes 352 et seq. of the *U.S. Reports. Lawyers' Edition* features parallel citation references to the official *U.S. Reports* printed on the spine of each of its volumes (both editions). Also, within each volume, further parallel citations to the *U.S. Reports* are printed at the beginning of or within each case.

*Supreme Court Reporter.* The *Supreme Court Reporter* (abbreviated "S. Ct.") is unofficially published by West Publishing Company. As with *Lawyers' Edition,* the same cases that are officially published in the *U.S. Reports* are unofficially published in the *Supreme Court Reporter.* This series also provides parallel citation references to the official *U.S. Reports.* Such citations appear on the spine of each S. Ct. volume and at the beginning of each case, at the top of the page. For citation accuracy, S. Ct. text pages must correspond to the official *U.S. Reports* pages. Therefore, each S. Ct. page includes a cross-reference to the corresponding page in the official *U.S. Reports* version of the case. Obviously, the unofficial reporters are published with these pagination features so that citations to the *U.S. Reports* series can be made without actually having to refer to the corresponding *U.S. Reports* volume for a specific page number.

*United States Law Week.* The *United States Law Week* (abbreviated "U.S.L.W.") is an unofficial publication of the Bureau of National Affairs (BNA). It is a loose-leaf, two-volume set that is published weekly. The material is sent to the publication's subscribers in loose-leaf form, hole-punched so that it can easily be placed in the volume's three-ring binder. This service affords a subscriber quick access to newly released U.S. Supreme Court opinions. Newly released opinion texts are mailed to subscribers on a weekly basis; other reporter series generally require 6 to 8 weeks' lead time prior to publication. Citations to this unofficial publication are permitted when U.S., L.Ed.2d, and S. Ct. citations are not yet available. Recently, Web sites with legal information have reduced the usefulness of U.S.L.W.

*Federal Court Reporters.* Federal court cases are published by private publishing companies in the following series:

*Federal Reporter.* The *Federal Reporter* (abbreviated "F.") is the only reporter series in which all U.S. Courts of Appeals cases are published. The set contains two series; the first series contains volumes 1 to 300, with published cases from nine federal circuit courts of appeals and the D.C. circuit. The second series (abbreviated "F.2d") contains all of the published decisions from the same federal circuits as well as several new federal circuits and the U.S. Court of Claims, the Court of Customs and Patent Appeals, and the Temporary Emergency Court of Appeals. When you **cite** a circuit court case, the circuit from which the case originated is always included, for example, 729 F.2d 1270 (10th Cir. 1984).

*Federal Supplement.* The *Federal Supplement* (abbreviated "F. Supp.") is also an unofficial publication of the West Publishing Company. This set contains cases decided in the federal district courts, which are subdivisions of the federal judicial appellate circuits. Every state has at least one federal district court; larger states have several federal district courts. Similar to federal courts of appeals decisions, there is no "official" publication for federal district court decisions. The *Federal Supplement* contains only those cases that are selected for publication and is the exception to the rule that only appellate court cases, and not trial court cases, are published. Federal district court judges have discretion as to whether or not a decision will be published. Usually the cases released for publication are those the trial court considers unique or that offer guidance on a significant issue that has not previously been litigated. Citations in this set should include the federal district in which the case originated, for example, 348 F.Supp. 866 (D.C. 1972).

*Regional Reporters.* The National Reporter System (NRS) is a network of reporters that includes seven regional reporters containing all published state appellate court decisions. For example, the *North Eastern Reporter* (abbreviated "N.E." or "N.E.2d") includes state appellate cases from the states of Illinois, Indiana, and Ohio. If a state publishes its own "official" appellate reports, citations should include both the official report citation and the regional reporter citation.

*Addendum.* It would be remiss to not mention the tremendous changes the Internet has created regarding informal legal research. Education law students now have statutes and other enactments as well as case law at their fingertips. Statutory amendments are accessible through state legislature Web sites as well as state department of education Web sites. All federal cases are available through various Web sites. One of the Web sites most often used by school law students is http://www.findlaw.com, which provides easy access and is reasonably simple for nonlawyers to navigate. Other effective Web sites include, but are not limited to, the following:

Constitutional documents: http://www.lawinfo.com/links/federal/constitution.html

Congressional Record: http://thomas.loc.gov/home/r110query.html

Constitution Law Links: http://www.law.emory.edu/LAW/refdesk/subject/const.html

Cornell Law School: http://www.law.cornell.edu/

Council of School Attorneys: http://www.nsba.org/cosa/

EDLAW Center: http://www.edlaw.net/

Federal Register: http://www.gpoaccess.gov/fr/index.html

THOMAS: Legislative information from the Library of Congress: http://thomas.loc.gov/

National Law Net: http://www.lawsites.com/

U.S. Department of Education: http://www.ed.gov/

U.S. DOE Special Education and Rehabilitative Services: http://www.ed.gov/offices/OSERS/IDEA/the_law.html

U.S. Supreme Court Opinions: http://lawinfo.com/supremesearch.html

*Westlaw/LexisNexis.* Most practical legal research is now conducted through one of these two online legal databases. The major difference between Westlaw and LexisNexis is that Westlaw includes entire cases published by the West Regional National Reporter System, including summaries and headnotes. In contrast, LexisNexis entries consist of the opinions as published by the various courts, without summaries and headnotes. Both are commercial services from which the companies profit, and users are billed for each search. Researchers primarily use these databases to find cases by citation. However, the services also feature "keyword" and other search processes. One can also research secondary sources, such as legal digests and encyclopedias. These services have become popular because of the practical ease in allowing the researcher to quickly find cases without needing to go to a law library and search through a reporter series.

## THE COMPONENTS OF CASE BRIEFS

Each case brief in this book contains the following parts:

*Case Caption.* This is the official citation, with parallel citations where appropriate. By referring to this citation, the reader may obtain a copy of the full text of the case from any law library.

*General Rule of Law.* The general rule of law is the court's legal resolution of the issue. It is the generally accepted rule that arises based on the facts at hand. The rule of law may be derived, in whole or in part, from previously decided cases in the same or other jurisdictions or higher courts. Please note, however, that in many cases, the decision may change or alter precedent if the court believes it necessary.

*Procedure Summary.* This section identifies the party who initiated the **action** (the plaintiff); the party who, in response to the plaintiff's lawsuit, has been forced to defend itself (the defendant); and all lower court decisions up to but not including the final disposition of the instant case.

*Facts.* This section explains the factual background, including why the case was initiated and/or appealed to a higher court. Prior court rulings have again been included for a cursory review of lower court decisions.

*Issue.* The issue is the legal question the court is trying to resolve. Although many issues may be present in any given case, most courts usually narrow in on the one or two that are most crucial.

*Holding and Decision.* The holding is the answer to the question the legal issue presents. It is the ruling on the case by the last or final court that heard it. The judge's name (when available) appears in parentheses at the beginning of this section.

*Comment.* This section includes our editorial analysis of the case, where appropriate, and the case's implications for or applicability to your roles as students, educators, and administrators in the field of education.

*Discussion Questions.* Following each case is a list of questions for student discussion in small groups or, alternatively, by the entire class.

# RELATED LEGAL ISSUES

## Common Law

**Common law,** which is also called judge-made law, has been described as "natural" or "discovered" law, in contrast to statutory law as enacted in constitutions and legislation. The American or Anglo-American system of jurisprudence has developed out of English common law. In fact, early in our history we adopted the common law precedents of England, which traced back to 1066 AD. Both legal systems follow the doctrine of stare decisis; courts tend to follow earlier decisions (precedents). Our common law traditions concerning torts, contract, land management, and related concepts were originally adopted from English common law.

The English tradition expanded the concept of the common law to include **equity** law. The early common law courts eventually became operationally difficult in many situations because of the dependence and reliance on case precedents. This often led to seemingly unfair and unjust outcomes in certain situations. The King eventually created a system of equity courts to provide relief apart from the common law. Equity courts did not as strictly adhere to precedent, but rather tried equity remedies based on broader principles of justice. Equity remedies tried to protect plaintiffs from unjust harm. Examples of equity court actions include **injunctions** and protective court orders as well as contempt of court citations.

## U.S. Constitution

Without doubt, the most important statutory enactment is the Constitution of the United States, the law of the land. All federal, state, and local enactments, including the enactments of the local school board, are subordinate to and subject to the Constitution as interpreted by the Supreme Court. This authority was established in *Marbury v. Madison* (1803).[1] Interestingly, while education is not mentioned anywhere in the Constitution, it was a major concern of our founding fathers: An early federal enactment, Northwest Ordinance of 1787, had an education focus that encouraged schools and the means of education.

Our country has operated most effectively using what is called the separation of power doctrine, whereby each of our three branches of government—executive, legislative, and judicial—operates independently, and the branches are of relatively equal power and authority. The executive branch, led by the President, implements laws adopted by the legislative branch, composed of senators in the Senate and representatives in the House of Representatives, while the laws and actions of government are reviewed and scrutinized by the Supreme Court. While some strict constructionalists argue that the review power was not in the Constitution but assumed through the *Marbury v. Madison* (1803) case, there is little argument that this tripartite system of government has operated effectively for over 200 years. Similarly, the balance between state and federal government has been respected and recognized through the application of the comity principles of the Eleventh Amendment.

Each of our original amendments, called the **Bill of Rights,** deals with a specific freedom or concern. Because education is not mentioned in the Constitution, it is a state responsibility as delineated by the reserve **clause** of the Tenth Amendment: "The powers not delegated to the United States by the Constitution, nor prohibited by it to the States, are reserved to the States respectively, or to the people." Other amendments dealing with personal rights usually have the most impact on schools. Some constitutional provisions also have more application, especially Article I, § 8 (to provide for the general welfare) and § 10 (to regulate commerce). Among the amendments most used in litigation are the First, Fourth, Fifth, and the Fourteenth.

## Associated Issues

The assumed power of the Supreme Court to review the constitutionality of decisions or enactments of the legislative and executive branches is fundamental to the operation of government. This is part of our separation of powers doctrine; the three branches of government check and balance each other in our constitutional system. The presumption is that the actions of another branch are constitutional. The judicial branch, when it does intervene, has several specific judicial purposes. First, it settles controversies by applying legal principles to a specific fact situation. Second, it **construes** or interprets legislative enactments. Finally, it determines the constitutionality of legislative enactments or executive actions. Essentially, the courts settle conflicts that involve actual cases and controversies, as required by Article 3 of the Constitution. It cannot provide advisory opinions. Of course, what determines a case or controversy is left to the judgment of the court.

At the trial level, a jury (or the judge, in what is called a "bench" trial) issues **findings** of fact after evaluating evidence, including witness statements and exhibits. A judgment and decree are issued, establishing the outcome of the litigation. This ruling is actually the beginning of common law regarding the issue. Appeals are then available from the trial court to a higher court, usually called a court of appeals. The party appealing the ruling is called the **appellant** and the opposing party the **appellee**. An appellant court may only review for **error** (e.g., ineffective counsel, admission of improper evidence, misinterpretation of testimony, or use of improper exhibits). It may not hear new evidence, hear witnesses, or consider any issue not raised in the trial court. Common law principles hold that decisions in one state are not binding precedent on courts in another state, but they may be persuasive (nonbinding) for similar fact patterns. In the federal system, there is only one correct answer to any question (i.e., a ruling by the U.S. Supreme Court). That Court grants an extraordinary writ, called certiorari, accepting only a few cases each **term**. If the Court refuses to grant certiorari, then the decision of the appellate court becomes binding on that specific jurisdiction. Finally, after the U.S. Supreme Court (or the highest court in a state on issues not involving federal issues) makes a decision, that ruling becomes **res judicata**, a matter settled.

## NOTE

1. Marbury v. Madison, 5 U.S. (1 Cranch) 137 (1803).

# Part I

# Policy Issues

# 1

# School Desegregation

*In view of the Constitution, in the eye of the law, there is in this country no superior, dominant, ruling class of citizens . . . . Our constitution is color-blind, and neither knows nor tolerates classes among its citizens.*

—John M. Harlan
*Plessy v. Ferguson* (1896)

## OVERVIEW . . . . . . . . . . . . . . . . . . . . . . . . . . . . . . . . . . . . . . . . . . . .

Few would question that there is perhaps no single area of school law in which the federal court system, particularly the U.S. Supreme Court, has been as active in dictating policy and supporting change as that of public school desegregation. Essentially, the body of law that has developed regarding desegregation is concerned with rectifying discriminatory practices and violations of minority students' equal educational opportunities. The legal basis underpinning school desegregation is the equal protection clause of the Fourteenth Amendment of the U.S. Constitution.

The famous dissent of the elder Justice Harlan in *Plessy v. Ferguson* (1896)[1] clearly states the constitutional basis, as well as the moral standard, that was later adopted in *Brown v. Board of Education of Topeka (Brown I)* (1954).[2] The slow development of the principle of racial equality from a minority and socially unacceptable dissenting opinion to a majority view has been ineradicably linked to public education. Possibly because racial injustice is most visible in our schools, the white racial discrimination that legally infected education and sustained segregation was the logical focus to remedy legally contrived discrimination.

Though the Court could establish in 1954 a doctrine of equality, full implementation of this doctrine was still a distant goal. The court system became inextricably entwined with this American dilemma. In trying to impede the racial prejudice that permeated the fabric of American society, the Supreme Court may have thought that it was only addressing state-created segregation. This was, of course, far from reality; the underlying issue of institutionalized

3

private and social discrimination created chaos in our country, and it was played out in America's public elementary and secondary schools. Using federal statutory and constitutional law, the Court created unitary school districts (school districts in which **de jure** forms of segregation were eliminated) while also trying to eliminate the vestiges of past discrimination.

This chapter demonstrates the evolution of judicial thinking from formal recognition to prohibition of discriminatory federal and state statutes. Also considered is how the courts addressed the more subtle prejudicial educational treatment of African Americans as the courts resolved to preserve individual rights and freedoms.

The doctrine of "separate but equal" was first enunciated in a pre-Civil War state court case, *Roberts v. City of Boston* (1849).[3] Five-year-old Sarah Roberts was forced to walk past five nearby all-white elementary schools in order to attend Smith Grammar School, a school for African American children. Civil rights activist and later U.S. Senator Charles Sumner established that Smith Grammar was in poor condition. Sumner expounded many of the same arguments that eventually prevailed 100 years later. Using arguments that segregated schools were not equal and violated the Massachusetts Constitution, the court announced the separate but equal doctrine. Reflecting the racial attitudes of the times, this court unfortunately held that race was a legitimate segregating classification.

The Fourteenth Amendment was ratified in 1868. The second sentence of the third clause said, "Nor shall any State . . . deny to any person within its jurisdiction the **equal protection of the laws**." Effectuating the meaning of these words would take many years. Its application was limited because the Fourteenth Amendment does not apply to private entities who choose to discriminate. Further, a Mississippi statute requiring segregated train cars was upheld because it applied only to in-state transportation. This circumvented the protections of the equal protection clause and legitimatized state-enforced segregation based on race. "Jim Crow" laws soon translated private discriminatory practices into state law through Southern reactionary judgments. The landmark case legitimatizing segregation was *Plessy v. Ferguson* (1896), which established the Roberts principle of "separate but equal" as the national standard. Separate but equal accommodations for the races were not unconstitutional because state legislatures had wide discretion in promoting peace and good order. Further, and not surprisingly, the courts also separated a Mongolian child from Caucasian children and required the child to attend a school for African American children.[4]

The National Association for the Advancement of Colored People (NAACP) began a legal initiative to overturn *Plessy*. The initial approach was to attack segregation when supposedly equal facilities were obviously inadequate. The first major case was *Missouri **ex rel**. Gaines v. Canada* (1938),[5] which concerned a Missouri law prohibiting African Americans from entering the University of Missouri Law School. African Americans who did not want to go to a law school out of state had no available law school within Missouri. The court held that requiring a specific classification to attend an out-of-state law school and not providing an equivalent facility in-state resulted in an equal protection violation. This, of course, did not overturn *Plessy,* but merely **distinguished** (qualified) it.

World War II slowed the NAACP's legal challenges. However, in 1950, a Texas case dealt with establishing an in-state law school. This was an attempt to address *Gaines's* having precluded forcing African Americans to attend an out-of-state law school. The issue was how to provide an equal facility within a state. In *Sweatt v. Painter* (1950),[6] the Court ruled that the law school that Texas built for African Americans would not be equivalent. The Court further ruled that the University of Texas Law School had to admit African Americans because a new law school could never be equivalent to a long-established state law school. Further, in a case released on the same day, *McLaurin v. Oklahoma State Regents for Higher Education* (1950),[7] the Court held that the College of Education at the University of Oklahoma could not segregate within the college. McLaurin, an African American doctoral student, had been required to sit and study in an area designated for African Americans while in a classroom and other areas. These cases were combating segregation in higher education, but they did little, if anything, to address the issues in public elementary and secondary schools. Only a full-scale assault on the separate but equal doctrine could address these injustices.

*Brown v. Board of Education of Topeka (Brown I)* (1954)[8] was the case that opened the door to confronting the racial discrimination that permeated American society. While it dealt with elementary and secondary education, it had even farther-reaching societal effects. First, *Brown I* opened the door to a tsunami of litigation in all areas of education. Before *Brown I,* an education law professor could say that she or he knew every decided federal case involving education, and could possibly be correct. To say that after *Brown I* is absurd. Second, the *Brown I* rationale has been used in various other arenas to deal with inequities. Probably the most litigious of these is special education, although litigation on behalf of non-English-speaking minority groups is significantly increasing. *Brown I*'s rationale and legal basis has especially supported those defending the rights of children with special needs.

*Brown I* was initially before the Court in December, 1952. Several justices felt that a 6–3 passage, as indicated by a straw vote, would have led to an even more contentious situation than that which resulted from the eventual 9–0 vote. A change in the chief justice and the retirement of another justice restructured the Court, and the timing was right. *Brown I* was actually a combination of five cases from Kansas, South Carolina, Virginia, Delaware, and the District of Columbia, which attempted to present the full range of possible arguments so the rationale for the Court's decision would be clear even to those on the losing side—and so that alternative legislative approaches would be unsuccessful. In *Brown I*, the Court overturned the separate but equal doctrine, rendering it unconstitutional. *Brown v. Board of Education of Topeka (Brown II)* (1955) dealt with the appropriate remedy to make the plaintiffs whole, which required providing a unitary school district.[9] Federal district court desegregation cases after *Brown I* rendered the verdict and devised the remedy in the same case. In *Brown II,* the Court ruled that desegregation must occur "with all deliberate speed." Unfortunately, this standard was unenforceable because it was ambiguous. Little progress toward developing adequate remedies resulted in any states. District court judges fashioned remedies and maintained jurisdiction as plaintiffs tried to obtain a unitary status in the segregated school districts. Defendants simply refused to implement adequate remedies with deliberate speed. Finally after 15 years, in 1969, the Court completely discarded its "all deliberate speed" criterion for evaluating school desegregation and instead decided that "the obligation of every school district is to terminate dual school systems at once and to operate now and hereafter only unitary schools."[10] Even with this change, most desegregation efforts met with intransigence or resistance. Not surprisingly, there were over 100 districts still under federal district oversight at the beginning of the new millennium. This meant that federal district court judges were still effectively in charge of school district operation as it related to the implementation of a constitutional remedy to the violations found at trial. Of course, this number has drastically decreased as federal district courts find that school districts have eliminated the vestiges of prior segregation to the greatest extent practical.

Now that the decades have lessened the impact, many do not even realize the unrest and danger that our nation faced as it tried to deal with the implementation of the concept of equality. Discrimination permeated our society, and its poison was hard to eliminate. In 1958, President Eisenhower had to send in the National Guard and federal troops to ensure that African American children could enter a Little Rock, Arkansas high school. Dissenters used old Civil War arguments of nullification and interposition, among other tactics, in defense of their refusal to obey federal court orders. More blatantly, in the early 1960s in Prince Edward County, in the shadow of our national capital, the public schools were closed and private schools operated with state and county support. Sadly, while many of the legal issues have been adjudicated, the social issues underpinning school desegregation remain unresolved social ills.

## Case Study

### Correcting an Inequity or Taxation Without Representation

After an extensive trial in your court, both the state and the largest urban school district in the state have been found guilty of committing numerous Fourteenth Amendment violations resulting in segregation in the urban school district. During the remedy phase, a desegregation plan was accepted and is being implemented. Over the past few years, you, as a federal court judge, have been monitoring the state and school district's efforts to create a unitary school district. To implement the plan, large sums of money are needed to improve the school buildings and facilities as well as pay for general school expenses. The state has regularly paid its share of the desegregation costs, but the school district has failed to pass seven consecutive levies that were intended to pay for the school district's share of the desegregation costs. The plaintiffs have filed a **brief** arguing that you, as a federal district court judge overseeing a school desegregation case, have the remedial power to order a tax increase to provide the funds necessary to implement a plan that will ensure that the plaintiff children are provided with sufficient resources. You realize that if you implement such an order (and it is supported by the Supreme Court), it will cause great unrest. During the hearing, there were numerous references to "taxation without representation."

What should you do? Why?

### Discussion Questions

1. What are the arguments of the plaintiffs? Are they valid?

2. What are the arguments of the defendants? Are they valid?

3. How should you rule? Why?

# IMPORTANT CONCEPTS

- **Segregation implicates students' rights to equal protection of the laws:** State-sponsored discrimination against a particular group implicates the equal protection clause of the Fourteenth Amendment to the U.S. Constitution.

- **No absolute right to equality:** There is no **absolute** right to equality of treatment at the hands of the government. In most cases, only classifications that are not supported by sound governmental purposes are forbidden.

- **Laws affecting race are strictly scrutinized:** However, under the **strict scrutiny** test, courts will invalidate all race-based classifications unless they support a compelling governmental interest and are instituted in the least restrictive manner possible.

- **"De jure" defined:** Segregation that results from classifications that have been instituted or permitted by state law is termed de jure segregation.

- **Races treated separately but equally:** At one time, state-sponsored racial segregation was permissible under the "separate but equal" doctrine.

- **U.S. Supreme Court strikes down segregation:** In the landmark *Brown v. Board of Education of Topeka* (1954) decision, the U.S. Supreme Court declared that racially segregated schools were "inherently unequal" and therefore unconstitutional.

- **Role of the courts in implementing desegregation:** After the *Brown I* decision and its progeny, federal courts were faced with the twofold task of (1) determining whether official action or inaction had created segregated schools and (2) fashioning an appropriate remedy that would lead to a unitary school system.

- **Criteria for identifying unlawful segregation:** The existence of state-imposed segregation can be determined by looking to the quality of buildings and equipment, construction or abandonment of buildings, the racial composition of teachers and staff, and the quality and extent of activities offered.

- **Court-imposed remedies for segregation:** Acceptable remedies for state-imposed segregation include redrawing attendance zones, reassigning teachers, using racial quotas, and busing.

- **School districts have an affirmative duty:** At present, where unlawful segregation exists, school districts have an affirmative duty to rectify it.

- **"De facto" defined:** Segregation that results "naturally," that is, not by reason of official action, is termed **de facto** segregation.

- **No obligation to correct:** A school district has no obligation to correct common forms of de facto segregation, such as segregation resulting from the uniform application of local zoning ordinances.

*(Continued)*

(Continued)

- **Power to correct:** In most cases, school officials are empowered to eradicate de facto segregation if they so choose.

- **Race-based teacher assignments unconstitutional:** Assigning teachers on the basis of race denies students equal educational opportunities and is therefore unconstitutional.

- **Goal of teacher desegregation:** The U.S. Supreme Court has **affirmed** desegregation plans that seek to achieve the same ratio of African American and white teachers within a particular school as exists in the district as a whole.

- **Multi-district remedies inappropriate:** Multi-district remedies, which occur when more than one school district is involved in remediating a constitutional violation, are not proper if de jure segregation is found in only one district and if there is no finding that the other districts failed to operate unitary school systems.

- **Judicial action to release:** The recent trend has been for federal district courts to release school districts from federal control. The federal courts have held that these school districts have achieved unitary status (are no longer segregated). In the mid-1990s, there were more than 200 school districts under federal district control because of segregation. At the time of this writing, only a few dozen school districts are still controlled by a federal district court.

## CONSTITUTIONAL AND STATUTORY UNDERPINNINGS

### U.S. Constitutional Right Implicated by Segregation

The primary constitutional safeguard against state-sponsored group discrimination is the equal protection clause of the Fourteenth Amendment. The equal protection clause does not guarantee absolute equality of treatment. Rather, it protects individuals from adverse treatment that cannot be justified by a sound governmental purpose. The U.S. Supreme Court has enunciated three different standards for determining which group classifications are justified and which are not.

1. *Rational basis test:* Under this standard, laws promoting classifications that do not infringe fundamental rights or adversely affect protected minorities will be upheld if they serve reasonable governmental purposes and use reasonable means to achieve those purposes. If such is the case, incidental adverse effects on groups of individuals are permissible.

2. *Intermediate scrutiny test:* Under this standard, laws promoting classifications that discriminate based on gender will be upheld so long as they serve important governmental objectives and are substantially related to those objectives.

3. *Strict scrutiny test:* Under this standard, laws promoting classifications based on race or infringing fundamental rights are deemed suspect classifications. Such classifications

are presumed to be unconstitutional and will be invalidated unless the government is able to prove that the classifications serve compelling governmental interests and employ the least offensive means of carrying out those interests. The government rarely meets its burden under this test.

## Statutory Remedies for Discrimination

The Fourteenth Amendment implicates official (i.e., state-sponsored) discrimination only. Only state and federal legislation can outlaw private discrimination. Furthermore, there is no right to sue for monetary damages under the U.S. Constitution. The right to sue for damages based on unconstitutional discrimination must therefore be provided by statute. Federal and state civil rights statutes have been enacted to provide stronger legal remedies for discrimination.

# CHALLENGES TO STATE-FOSTERED (DE JURE) SCHOOL SEGREGATION

## De Jure Segregation

Segregation that results from classifications instituted or permitted by state law is termed de jure segregation and is unconstitutional. However, this was not always the case. De jure segregation exists only if the following elements are present:

1. *Government action:* The segregation in question must have been instituted or supported by the state;

2. *Intent to discriminate:* The segregation must have been instituted with an actual intent or motive to discriminate; and

3. *Net increase in segregation:* The net effect must be the creation of segregation or an increase in segregation that already exists.

## Separate but Equal: The Law Prior to *Brown v. Board of Education of Topeka*

In *Plessy v. Ferguson* (1896), the U.S. Supreme Court interpreted the equal protection clause as permitting state-sponsored racial segregation by holding that the U.S. Constitution did not require racial integration so long as African Americans and whites were treated equally. The Court subsequently extended the separate but equal doctrine to the public schools in *Gong Lum v. Rice* (1927).

## *Brown v. Board of Education of Topeka* and the End of the Separate but Equal Doctrine

In *Brown I,* **supra,** the U.S. Supreme Court held that racially segregated schools were "inherently unequal," thereby repudiating its "separate but equal" interpretation of the equal protection clause. A year later, the Supreme Court decided *Brown II,* in which it declared that segregated, dual school districts must be converted to integrated, unitary districts with "all deliberate speed." In attempting to adhere to the mandates of *Brown I* and *Brown II,* lower federal courts have faced a dual task: determining whether official action or inaction has created or perpetuated unlawful segregation in violation of the equal protection clause and, if a violation is established, fashioning an appropriate remedy. Because the *Brown* decisions neglected to set forth their view of the specific conditions that contributed to the unconstitutional segregation of students, lower courts were at a loss when it came to fashioning segregation remedies. Some courts held that their constitutional obligations were satisfied so long as remedies were provided that removed all barriers to integration, that is, so long as the state remained "neutral" to integration.

*Slow Pace of Desegregation.* Because *Brown II* had not set a specific deadline for the implementation of the *Brown I* mandate, the pace of desegregation dragged on in the decade that followed. In 1964, the Court declared that the time for "deliberate speed" had run out—a clear indication that vindication of the constitutional rights of schoolchildren was long overdue.[11]

*"Deliberate Speed" Not Speedy Enough.* Finally, in 1969, the Court completely discarded its "all deliberate speed" criterion for evaluating school desegregation. It decided instead that "the obligation of every school district is to terminate dual school systems at once and to operate now and hereafter only unitary schools."[12] Mere state neutrality toward integration was no longer acceptable. After *Alexander v. Holmes County Bd. of Ed.* (1969), many lower courts issued orders requiring that school districts take affirmative action with regard to the slow pace of school desegregation.

*Characteristics and Remedial Actions Taken.* In the landmark case of *Swann v. Charlotte-Mecklenburg Bd. of Ed.* (1971), the U.S. Supreme Court for the first time identified the characteristics of a segregated school system and some of the steps that may be required to bring about a unitary system.[13] The existence of state-imposed segregation can be determined by looking to the quality of buildings and equipment, construction or abandonment of buildings, the racial composition of teachers and staff, the quality and extent of activities offered, and the like. Acceptable remedies for state-imposed segregation include the redrawing of attendance zones, the reassignment of teachers, use of racial quotas (even though it is not a requirement that every school in a district reflect the racial composition of the district as a whole), and, in some circumstances, busing. In *Swann,* the Court also discussed the continuing role of the federal courts in correcting de jure violations. It concluded that "no fixed . . . guidelines can be established as to how far a court can go, but it must be recognized there are limits." A host of considerations must be taken into account in identifying and remedying unconstitutional segregation, including demographics, financial resources, geographical considerations, and student welfare.

# CHALLENGES TO NONPURPOSEFUL (DE FACTO) SCHOOL SEGREGATION

## De Facto Segregation

Segregation that results "naturally" (i.e., not as a result of official action intended to bring it about) is de facto segregation. True de facto segregation is not unconstitutional.

De facto segregation looks similar to de jure segregation; in a common example, it is characterized by a school that is populated by a large majority of students who are of a racial minority.

## Case Law Pertaining to De Facto Segregation

In 1973, the Supreme Court considered for the first time allegations of unconstitutional segregation within a school district outside of the South. Because the City of Denver had no statutory dual system to begin with, the Court concluded that to prevail, the plaintiffs would have to prove both the existence of segregation and that the segregation was a product of "intentional state action" (i.e., it was maintained with a discriminatory motive).[14] Without an underlying discriminatory motive, what might appear to be unconstitutional de jure segregation is actually permissible de facto segregation. Most federal courts have passed on the issue of whether a school district has an obligation to correct common forms of de facto segregation, such as segregation caused by a uniform application of local zoning ordinances. In failing to address the issue, the courts have concluded that no such obligation exists. While no obligation to correct de facto segregation exists, school officials are empowered to make corrections if they so choose.

Legal challenges may arise from those who consider such remedial measures inappropriate under the notion of a "color blind" Constitution (insofar as these remedial measures are clearly based on race, yet are not constitutionally required). Such challenges rarely prevail. In the past, some state legislatures have attempted to thwart the voluntary efforts of local boards to prevent de facto segregation. Federal courts generally do not permit such actions if they interfere with lawful plans designed to protect the constitutional rights of students.

## Multi-District Remedies

Multi-district remedies are often proposed when a single-district remedy is inadequate to accomplish desegregation.[15] Prior to *Milliken v. Bradley* (1974), the federal district court had held that Detroit was segregated on the basis of de jure racial policies and practices. The district court concluded that a multi-district plan for remedying racial violations was proper.

*The Issue Considered.* The question that the Supreme Court sought to answer was whether a multi-district remedy was proper when de jure segregation was found in only one district and when there was no finding that the other districts failed to operate unitary school systems.

*Present Court Position.* Based on the *Milliken* decision, a multi-district remedy is only permissible where de jure segregation is found in each and every school district involved in the remedy. Clearly, there is a nexus between intentional acts of segregation and the existence of segregation. Further, the extent of the remedy should be limited by the extent of the de jure violations proven (i.e., the more violations, the greater the potential scope of the remedy).[16]

# DESEGREGATION OF TEACHERS

## Faculty Integration Designed to Protect Students' Constitutional Rights

Because the assignment of teachers on the basis of race violates the equal educational opportunities of students, it is an appropriate subject for court-ordered desegregation plans. In *Bradley v. School Bd. of the City of Richmond* (1965), the U.S. Supreme Court first passed on addressing the issue of teacher desegregation.[17] They noted that race-based faculty assignments affected students' rights. In *United States v. Montgomery County Bd. of Ed.* (1969), and later in *Swann,* the Court affirmed desegregation plans that sought to achieve the same ratio of African American and white teachers within a particular school as existed in the district as a whole.[18] In some school districts, the consolidation of dual systems into unitary systems, pursuant to court-imposed desegregation plans, has resulted in a reduction of teaching personnel. In the leading case of *Singleton v. Jackson Municipal Separate School Dist.* (1970),[19] the U.S. **Court of Appeals** for the Fifth Circuit set forth staff reduction criteria in order to prevent African American teachers from bearing a greater burden under these consolidation efforts than their white counterparts:

1. *Elimination of the race factor:* Hirings, firings, promotions, demotions, and assignments may not be made on the basis of race; and

2. *Development of objective standards:* Reductions in teaching staff must be based on objective criteria developed by the local school board prior to the institution of any reductions.

3. *Impairment of seniority rights:* Lower courts have held that even teacher seniority rights may be impaired. Of course, when a district court limits statutory or contractual rights of teachers, it must do so narrowly.[20]

**Note:** The *Singleton* criteria apply only to those districts that have not attained unitary status. Because most districts are no longer segregated, the *Singleton* criteria are rarely relied on in connection with staff reduction lawsuits.

## The Effect of Faculty Integration on Teachers' Rights

In some cases, efforts to achieve racially balanced teaching staffs (pursuant to desegregation orders aimed at vindicating students' rights) have violated the rights of teachers. Recent lawsuits have focused on the rights of teachers who have suffered in the wake of hiring and promotional preferences aimed at achieving racially balanced teaching staffs. Such preferences have been upheld when their use has contributed to the elimination of unconstitutional school segregation. Still, other recent lawsuits have focused on the seniority rights of nonminority teachers who have been laid off in order to protect minority teachers (and thereby achieve racial balance).

*Permissible in Most Cases So Long as Segregation Is Still in Place.* Some courts have upheld race-based preferences in teacher layoffs when the districts in question had not attained unitary status.

*Not Permissible Where No Desegregation Plan in Effect.* In *Wygant v. Jackson Bd. of Ed.* (1986), the U.S. Supreme Court struck down a school board's attempt to protect its minority teachers from layoffs under these circumstances because the district in question was not operating under a court-ordered desegregation plan.[21]

## RECENT COURT ACTIVITY

### Cost of Desegregation Remedy

*Educational Programs.* A federal district court may require a state to bear the cost of educating students who have been subject to past acts of de jure segregation.[22]

*Ordering a Tax Increase to Fund Desegregation Costs.* In the Kansas City (Missouri) School District, tax levies aimed at supporting the court-imposed desegregation plan were consistently voted down. The federal district court ordered a property tax increase. The Supreme Court held that a federal district court may not order a tax levy to fund (in part) a desegregation plan. This was an abuse of discretion and violated principles of federal-state comity. Nevertheless, the district court may require that the levy be increased to an amount adequate to fund the school district's portion of the plan, but it may not itself increase the levy.[23]

*Continuing Duty to Eradicate Effects of Segregation.* A school board has a continuing duty to eradicate the effects of segregation brought about by its former operation of dual systems. Thus, a school board must do more than abandon past discriminatory acts; it must actively ensure that the negative effects of its past policies are not perpetuated.[24]

*State Removal of Decision-Making Power Over Racial Issue.* A state may not abrogate a local district's decision-making power in connection with a racial issue. Thus, a local district that wishes to provide more extensive equal protection guarantees may do so without fear of a state initiative removing that guarantee.[25]

*District Court Relinquishing Control Incrementally.* In the course of supervising a desegregation plan, a district court has the authority to relinquish supervision and control of a school district in incremental stages, that is, before full compliance has been achieved.[26]

## Case Study

### Providing Plaintiffs With an Effective Remedy or Judicial Activism

You are president of the school board in a large urban school district that was found guilty of segregation on the basis of race as a result of official policies of the state as well as of the board of education. The victorious plaintiffs' attorneys now seek to implement a plan to effectively desegregate the urban school district. The federal district court found that various actions and policies

*(Continued)*

(Continued)

of your school board as well as the action of the state did, in fact, constitute de jure segregation of the schools; the court ordered that an urban district-only desegregation plan be submitted and that the board also submit plans covering multiple districts that were not parties to the action. The district court thereafter ruled that consideration of the multi-district plans was proper because the urban district-only plans were inadequate to accomplish desegregation. It seems clear that your school district, which is already more than 60% minority, will become almost all African American if an urban district-only plan is implemented. The court of appeals affirmed. Both the school board and the state sought review, alleging that the implementation of a multi-district plan was improper because there was no finding that the other districts had also practiced de jure segregation or failed to maintain unitary school systems. You are now beginning to wonder whether the plaintiffs are correct about the fact that your urban school district will become almost all African American, thus effectively making desegregation impossible as there will be no white students whom you can integrate into the student population. You now have some questions.

### Discussion Questions:

1. Do plaintiff children receive an effective remedy for the unconstitutional segregation that they suffered for many years if there is no attempt to desegregate the white suburban districts abutting the segregated urban district?

2. If it is incontrovertible that the segregated urban district will eventually become all African American due to white flight after the urban district-only remedy is implemented, would your answer to the first question be different?

3. Is a multi-district remedy proper when de jure segregation is found only in the urban district and there is no finding that the suburban districts failed to operate unitary school systems?

4. If the court refused to implement a multi-district remedy (absent findings of segregative acts) and your urban district becomes all African American, can any further legal action be taken to remedy the failure to provide an adequate remedy?

# CONCLUSION . . . . . . . . . . . . . . . . . . . . . . . . . . . . . . . . .

The cases included in this chapter as well as those on the Web site[27] clearly demonstrate the transition from a segregated school system to a unitary system. The cases below begin with *Brown I*, which found state laws allowing separate but equal policies unconstitutional. *Brown II* addressed remedial approaches and allowed the states to correct the constitutional violation with "all deliberate speed." *Swann v. Charlotte-Mecklenberg Bd. of Ed.* (1971) approved various remedies to desegregate, including redrawing attendance zones; reassigning teachers; using racial quotas; and, in some circumstances, busing students from one zone to another.

In *Keyes v. School District No. 1* (1973), desegregation cases left the South (where segregation had been established by state law and policy) when a Denver, Colorado, school district was found guilty of unconstitutional de jure segregation.[28] It should be noted that de facto segregation, while appearing to be unconstitutional, is actually constitutional absent an underlying discriminatory motive. The critical issue of implementing a multi-district remedy when a single-district remedy is inadequate to accomplish desegregation was the issue in *Milliken v. Bradley* (1974). After Detroit was found guilty of illegal de jure segregation, the plaintiffs presented no evidence of guilty acts in any of the 50-plus districts surrounding Detroit. The rationale was that only through a multi-district remedy could the plaintiffs in *Milliken* be made whole. The Court held in a 5–4 decision that a multi-district remedy is only possible when de jure segregation is found in each and every school district involved in the remedy. Essentially, there must be a nexus between intentional acts of segregation that resulted in actual segregation. Further, as the Court explained, the extent of the remedy should be limited by the extent of the de jure violations proven, that is, the more violations, the greater the potential scope of the remedy.

In *Missouri v. Jenkins* (1990), the Court held that a federal court could require the taxing authority to levy taxes in excess of statutory limits in order to fund the court-ordered desegregation remedies. This taxation without representation situation caused unrest and disagreement, as did a later decision to require remedies that would alleviate the individual learning effects and deficiencies caused by segregation.

The Court in *Freeman v. Pitts* (1992) held that the federal district court had the discretion to order the incremental or partial withdrawal of its supervision and control over the remedial process. In recent years, the federal district courts have been withdrawing from supervision of desegregation suits in declaring the school districts to be unitary.

The final case, *Parents Involved in Community Schools v. Seattle School District No. 1 et al.* (2007), deals with whether assigning children to different public schools based solely on their race violates the Fourteenth Amendment's equal protection guarantee. This case involves the controversial issue of affirmative action and the applicability of taking affirmative steps to implement a race-conscious standard in the assignment of students to schools.

While studying this topic, stay mindful of the year in which each case takes place so you can fully grasp the evolution of the desegregation cycle. As you progress through this chapter, you will see the various facets of education that the desegregation decisions of *Brown I* and *Brown II* have impacted. After reading the cases, you should better grasp the progression of desegregation and the Court's evolving reasoning.

# CASE BRIEFS · · · · · · · · · · · · · · · · · · · · · · · · · ·

## BROWN V. BOARD OF EDUCATION OF TOPEKA (BROWN I) 347 U.S. 483, 74 S. CT. 686 (1954)

**GENERAL RULE OF LAW:** Segregated public school systems violate the equal protection clause of the Fourteenth Amendment.

**PROCEDURE SUMMARY:**

**Plaintiff:** Brown (P), an African American student

**Defendant:** Board of Education of Topeka (Board) (D)

**U.S. District Court Decision:** Held for Board (D), finding separate but equal school systems permissible

**U.S. Court of Appeals Decision:** Reversed

**U.S. Supreme Court Decision:** Affirmed

**FACTS:** The Board (D) operated 22 elementary schools: 18 for white students and 4 for African American students. The schools were operated under the separate but equal doctrine announced by the Supreme Court in *Plessy v. Ferguson* (1896). Brown (P), an African American student, filed suit, claiming that the schools were not equal because the minority schools were inferior to the white schools in physical facilities, curricula, teaching resources, and student personal services, among other items. Brown (P) argued that this segregation, along with its accompanying inequalities, violated the equal protection clause of the Fourteenth Amendment. The district court, relying on *Plessy,* in which the Supreme Court declared separate but equal school systems permissible, found the facilities comparable and not in violation of the Constitution. The court of appeals **reversed**, and the U.S. Supreme Court granted review.

**ISSUE:** Does a school system's operating segregated schools violate the equal protection clause of the Fourteenth Amendment of the Constitution?

**HOLDING AND DECISION:** (Warren, C. J.) Yes. Segregated school systems are a violation of the equal protection clause of the Fourteenth Amendment. Even when all-minority and all-white schools are equal with respect to tangible factors such as facilities and curricula, there are intangible factors that prevent children in all-minority schools from truly receiving an equal education. Separating minorities from others of similar age and qualifications solely because of race generates a feeling of inferiority in students. Thus, separate facilities are inherently unequal. Affirmed.

**COMMENT:** *Brown I* unanimously overruled the separate but equal doctrine announced in *Plessy* by alluding to the intangibles that minority students were denied. However, the Court did little to define what these intangibles are and based its finding of inherent inequality principally upon social science and empirical evidence, for which it drew criticism. Regardless, *Brown I* is important in that it set the mandate for integrated public education by adopting the argument put forth by the first Justice Harlan in his eloquent dissent in *Plessy*. *Brown I* was actually a consolidation decision including four other cases, three from different states challenging different aspects of the separate but equal doctrine and the other from the District of Columbia (where a Fifth Amendment **due process** argument was used instead of a Fourteenth Amendment argument because D.C. is not a state). The reason for accepting five cases was so that the Supreme Court's decision could not be questioned on technical grounds—all types of separate but equal school statutory applications were analyzed. In addition to being the most important court case in education law, *Brown I* also had another impact in that it opened the door to public scrutiny and challenge of public education. Since 1954, legal challenges have been raised in almost every conceivable educational area, including discipline, gender equity, finance, and teacher rights. This public scrutiny of public schools has been persistent and will certainly continue.

## Discussion Questions

1.  Did the *Brown I* case violate the equal protection clause of the Fourteenth Amendment? If so, how?

2.  What significance did *Plessy v. Ferguson* have to *Brown I*?

3.  Did *Brown I* set a precedent for other cases? If so, what types of cases?

# SWANN V. CHARLOTTE-MECKLENBURG BOARD OF EDUCATION 402 U.S. I, 91 S. CT. 1267 (1971)

**GENERAL RULE OF LAW:** The district courts may fashion remedies eliminating public school segregation when school authorities fail to fashion such remedies themselves.

**PROCEDURE SUMMARY:**

**Plaintiff:** Swann (P), an African American student

**Defendant:** Charlotte-Mecklenburg Board of Education (Board) (D)

**U.S. District Court Decision:** Ordered the adoption of a plan that paired and grouped elementary schools

**U.S. Court of Appeals Decision:** Vacated

**U.S. Supreme Court Decision:** Reinstated district court order

**FACTS:** The Board (D) operated a school system with more than 84,000 students. Approximately 24,000 of these students were African American, of whom 14,000 attended schools that were 99% African American. Swann (P), an African American student, brought suit for relief requiring the Board (D) to produce a plan to take further steps to eliminate state-imposed segregation from its public school system. The district court ordered the Board (D) to provide a desegregation plan for elementary schools. The court found the plan submitted by the Board (D) unsatisfactory and appointed an expert to provide such a plan. The court ordered adoption of the expert's plan, but the court of appeals vacated the order in fear that the plan's pairing and grouping of elementary schools unreasonably burdened the Board (D) and pupils. The U.S. Supreme Court granted review.

**ISSUE:** May district courts fashion remedies eliminating public school segregation when the school authorities fail to fashion such remedies themselves?

**HOLDING AND DECISION:** (Burger, C. J.) Yes. District courts may fashion remedies eliminating public school segregation when the school authorities fail to fashion such remedies themselves. Such power is fully consistent with this Court's mandate in *Brown v. Board of Education* (1954), in which state-imposed segregation in the public schools was found constitutionally impermissible and district courts were ordered to use their equitable powers to decree its elimination. Furthermore, Title IV of the Civil Rights **Act** of 1964 does not restrict or abridge these powers but was merely designed to ensure that it was not interpreted as expanding these equitable powers. The district court order was correct. Order of the district court reinstated.

**COMMENT:** Apart from instructing district courts on the extent of their powers to fashion remedies, *Swann* also set forth the test for determining when remedial action is warranted: School boards may not be ordered to adjust the racial composition of any school unless there has been a finding that there was intentional, or de jure, segregation, as opposed to de facto segregation. *Swann* further clarified what were permissible means of implementing a desegregation plan, which included busing, rezoning of attendance zones, and limited use of racial quotas. However, it should be noted that *Swann* does not require that each and every school meet a specific racial balance. In fact, a one-race school can be accepted as part of a comprehensive desegregation plan, but the court will carefully scrutinize this seemingly inappropriate action.

## Discussion Questions

1. Were federal courts constitutionally authorized to oversee and produce remedies for state-imposed segregation?

2. To what extent should racial balance or racial quotas be used to implement a remedial order to correct a previously segregated system?

3. Should every all-African American and every all-white school be eliminated as an indispensable part of the remedial process of desegregation?

4. Are there any limits on the rearrangement of school districts and attendance zones as a remedial measure, or the use of transportation facilities to correct state-enforced racial school segregation?

5. Should every school in every community reflect the racial composition of the school system as a whole?

6. Should the school authorities or district courts be constitutionally required to make year-by-year adjustments of the racial composition of student bodies once the affirmative duty to desegregate has been accomplished and racial discrimination through official action is eliminated from the system?

# KEYES V. SCHOOL DISTRICT NO.1 413 U.S. 189, 93 S. CT. 2686 (1973)

**GENERAL RULE OF LAW:** When a policy of intentional segregation has been proven with respect to a significant portion of the school system, the burden is on school authorities to prove that segregation in other portions of the system is not also the result of such an intent.

**PROCEDURE SUMMARY:**

**Plaintiff:** Keyes (P), parent of a student

**Defendant:** School District No.1, Denver, Colorado (District) (D)

**U.S. District Court Decision:** Held for District (D), that it need not desegregate certain segregated schools but merely provide equal facilities

**U.S. Court of Appeals Decision:** Affirmed in part; reversed in part

**U.S. Supreme Court Decision:** Reversed and remanded

**FACTS:** Keyes (P), parent of a student, filed suit seeking the desegregation of Park Hill area schools in Denver. After the district court granted Keyes (P) relief as to those schools, Keyes (P) expanded the suit to include the remaining schools within the District (D). The district court denied relief to the remaining District (D) schools. It held that proof of segregation policy as to the Park Hill schools did not constitute proof of such a policy as to other schools within the District (D). It also held that Keyes (P) would have to prove de jure segregation for each additional Denver school area. The court then held that because there was no proof of such an intentional segregative policy, the District (D) need not desegregate the schools but must merely provide equal facilities. The court of appeals reversed the portion of the order mandating the provision of equal facilities, but affirmed that the proof offered of intentional segregation as to the Park Hill schools was insufficient to grant relief as to the remaining schools. The U.S. Supreme Court granted review.

**ISSUE:** When a policy of intentional segregation has been proven with respect to a significant portion of a school system, do school authorities have the burden of proving that segregation in other portions of the system is not also the result of such a policy?

**HOLDING AND DECISION:** (Brennan, J.) Yes. When a policy of intentional segregation has been proven with respect to a significant portion of a school system, school authorities have the burden of proving that segregation in other portions of the system is not also the result of such a policy. Proof that school authorities have pursued an intentional policy of segregation in a substantial portion of the school district will, without more, support a trial court's finding of a dual system. The lower court's rulings were incorrect because Keyes (P) did not have to prove that de jure segregation occurred in every school. He merely had to prove that it occurred in a substantial portion of the schools. Remanded to determine sufficiency of proof.

**COMMENT:** *Keyes* reaffirms that relief may only be granted for de jure, or intentional, segregation. However, it amends this rule by adding that a finding of de jure action in one part of a school district can create a **prima facie** case of such action in the entire district. This shifted an important burden of proof to the school boards. In order to rebut prima facie proof of a dual system, the school board would have to show that the part of the district found to be intentionally segregated should be viewed as separate and unrelated to the other parts of the district. Also, *Keyes* held that Hispanics should be considered with African Americans in such desegregation actions because they suffered from the same educational inequalities. The proper handling of Hispanic children as part of a comprehensive desegregation plan has caused some concern. Each U.S. District Court has adopted its own policy regarding the legal status of Hispanics and other minority children. Classification of Hispanics as either African American or white can have a tremendous impact on their involvement in the student transportation plan.

## Discussion Questions

1. Based on the Court's opinion, if there is one racial class that is in the majority, is this segregation?

2. What were the signs of segregation the Court looked at?

3. What actions can a state take to desegregate its surrounding school districts? What are actions a state can take that show intentional segregation?

4. Does the Court seem to ask whether there could have been a possibility of intentional segregation?

# MILLIKEN V. BRADLEY (MILLIKEN I) 418 U.S. 717, 94 S. CT. 3112 (1974)

**GENERAL RULE OF LAW:** A multi-district remedy is improper when de jure segregation is found in only one district and there is no finding that the other districts have failed to operate unitary systems.

**PROCEDURE SUMMARY:**

**Plaintiff:** Bradley (P), a class representative of parents and students

**Defendants:** Milliken (D), Governor of Michigan, and the Detroit Board of Education (Board) (D)

**U.S. District Court Decision:** Held for Bradley (P), ordering the Board (D) to submit a multi-district desegregation plan

**U.S. Court of Appeals Decision:** Affirmed

**U.S. Supreme Court Decision:** Reversed and remanded

**FACTS:** In 1970, Bradley (P), representing a class of parents and students, filed suit alleging that the Detroit public school system was segregated on the basis of race as a result of official policies of Milliken (D), the Governor of Michigan, and the Board of Education (D). Bradley (P) sought the implementation of a plan desegregating the system. The district court found that various actions and policies of the Board (D) did, in fact, constitute de jure segregation of the Detroit schools and ordered it to submit Detroit-only desegregation plans. The Board (D) was also ordered to submit plans covering multiple districts that were not parties to the action. The district court thereafter ruled that consideration of the multi-district plans was proper because the Detroit-only plans were inadequate to accomplish desegregation. The court of appeals affirmed. The Board (D) sought review, alleging that the implementation of a multi-district plan was improper because there was no finding that the other districts had also practiced de jure segregation or failed to maintain unitary school systems.

**ISSUE:** Is a multi-district remedy proper when de jure segregation is found in only one district and there is no finding that the other districts failed to operate unitary school systems?

**HOLDING AND DECISION:** (Burger, C. J.) No. A multi-district remedy is not proper when de jure segregation is found in only one district and there is no finding that the other districts failed to operate unitary school systems. In fashioning a desegregation remedy, the court may not casually ignore school district lines. The multi-district remedy at issue could extensively disrupt and alter the structure of the Michigan school system by requiring, in effect, the consolidation of 54 independent school districts. Before a court may properly require such a monumental effort, it must be shown that there has been a constitutional violation within one district that produces a significant segregative effect in another district. Or, in other words, it must be shown that racially discriminatory acts of the state or local district have been a substantial cause of inter-district segregation. The district court erred in fashioning the multi-district remedy because there was no showing of significant violation by any district other than the Detroit district, and there was no evidence that the segregation in the Detroit district had any segregative effect on the other districts. Reversed and remanded.

**COMMENT:** On **remand**, the district court limited the order requiring that only the Detroit school district take desegregation measures. *Milliken I* illustrates how narrowly the Court intended to interpret its finding of de jure segregation. The Court clearly sees the rule as requiring some clear nexus between particular intentional acts of segregation and the existence of segregation. For the Court, the obligation of the state is clearly different when segregation is intentional and when segregation is merely the result of personal living choices. In the former, the state's obligation is **mandatory**; in the latter, action is discretionary. Based on *Milliken I*, the Court perspective is that the extent of a desegregation remedy is limited by the extent of the de jure violations proven. Although a mid-1970s case, *Milliken I* is the last major position taken by the Court regarding school desegregation. While there have been Court decisions regarding staff development programs, funding, unitary status, and release from district court supervision, the school districts still under court monitoring and supervision are still bound by the positions established by the cases up to and including *Milliken I*.

## Discussion Questions

1. Does this case seem to shed light on whether all races need to be equally distributed in every school?

2. What needs to be proven for the Court to impose an inter-district remedy?

3. Can one school district claim to be affected by segregation in hopes of gaining some Court-appointed relief?

# MISSOURI V. JENKINS 495 U.S. 33 (1990)

**GENERAL RULE OF LAW:** A federal district court may not order a tax levy increase of a specific percentage to partially fund a desegregation plan.

**PROCEDURE SUMMARY:**

**Plaintiff:** Jenkins (P), a taxpayer

**Defendant:** The State of Missouri (State) (D)

**U.S. District Court Decision:** Held for the State (D), declining to enjoin enforcement of a court-ordered local property tax levy increase

**U.S. Court of Appeals Decision:** Affirmed

**U.S. Supreme Court Decision:** Reversed

**FACTS:** In a separate action the Kansas City (Missouri) School District was found to have been operating a segregated school system. As a result, the district court ordered the creation of a desegregation plan and detailed the financing necessary to implement the plan. The court ordered the school district to pay a portion of the cost of the plan, but it was found to have exhausted all available means of raising additional revenue to pay its portion of the cost. The court, therefore, ordered that the school district's tax levy be increased by a certain percentage to pay the cost, despite the fact that state law prevented such an increase. Jenkins (P), a taxpayer, sought to enjoin the court-ordered tax increase. He contended that the district court abused its discretion in fashioning this remedy. The court of appeals disagreed and affirmed the tax increase but with the caveat that in the future, the district court could not set a percentage. The U.S. Supreme Court granted review.

**ISSUE:** May a district court order a tax levy increase of a specific percentage to partially fund the cost of a desegregation plan?

**HOLDING AND DECISION:** (White, J.) No. A federal district court may not order a tax levy increase of a specific percentage to fund, in part, a desegregation plan. Such an order is an abuse of discretion and violates principles of federal-state comity. Local authorities have primary responsibility for assessing and solving problems of desegregation, including the financing of desegregation. Though the district court may require that the levy be increased to an amount adequate to fund the school district's portion of the plan, it may not itself increase the levy, especially where the court has failed to consider permissible alternatives. The local officials should have been given the opportunity to come forward and present such alternatives. Reversed.

**COMMENT:** Justice White held that a federal court may set aside state laws prohibiting any further tax increase and order the local government to impose the tax increase, but the court may not increase the levy itself. Thus, the district court abused its discretion by directly imposing the tax increase because its action violated the principles of comity (respect by the state for federal action and vice versa). Some commentators argue that this is a distinction without any true difference. Nevertheless, the case demonstrates just how expansive the Court views district courts' power to effectuate their desegregation decrees. The recurring cry heard by Kansas City residents was "taxation without representation." This was, and remains, an extremely sensitive situation. Nevertheless, it is a clear indication of the remedial power of a federal district court.

## Discussion Questions

1. Explain what is meant by "federal-state comity" in the *Missouri v. Jenkins* case.

2. The Supreme Court permitted the district court decision but stated that the principles of federal-state comity had been violated. What was the court referring to and what constitutional amendments are relevant to this issue?

3. Do you feel that the cost of a desegregation plan for a school district such as the Kansas City School District will tap resources to the point that the district will inevitably offer a lower-quality education program to its students?

# FREEMAN V. PITTS 503 U.S. 467, 112 S. CT. 1430 (1992)

**GENERAL RULE OF LAW:** A district court that has supervision and jurisdiction over a school district under a desegregation decree can relinquish its remedial control in areas of compliance while maintaining remedial control over areas of noncompliance.

**PROCEDURE SUMMARY:**

**Plaintiff:** Freeman (P) and other officials of De Kalb County, Georgia, School District (DCSS)

**Defendant:** Pitts (D), representative of a class of African American schoolchildren and parents

**U.S. District Court Decision:** Held for defendant, in part

**U.S. Court of Appeals Decision:** Reversed

**U.S. Supreme Court Decision:** Reversed, for DCSS, permitting the court to relinquish partial control

**FACTS:** In De Kalb County, Georgia, an Atlanta suburb, a 1969 court-ordered school desegregation decree placed the De Kalb County School System (DCSS), represented by Freeman (P), under the supervision and jurisdiction of the U.S. District Court for Northern Georgia. In 1986, Freeman (P) filed a motion for final dismissal. At the time, DCSS served approximately 73,000 students, ranging from kindergarten to high school. Finding that DCSS had achieved desegregation in four of six categories delineated by *Green v. New Kent County School Board* (1968),[29] the district court relinquished remedial control in regard to those categories in which unitary status (i.e., compliance) had been achieved. At the same time, the court retained its supervisory control over those areas not yet in full compliance. The Eleventh Circuit Court of Appeals reversed the district court's ruling, holding that the district court had to "retain full remedial authority over a school system until it achieves unitary status in six categories at the same time for several years." The U.S. Supreme Court granted review.

**ISSUE:** Can a district court relinquish its supervision and jurisdiction over areas of a school system in which desegregation compliance exists, even though other areas in the system remain noncompliant?

**HOLDING AND DECISION:** (Kennedy, J.) Yes. In the course of supervising a desegregation plan, a district court has the authority to relinquish supervision and control of a school district in incremental stages before full compliance has been achieved in every aspect of school operations. The duty and responsibility of a school district once segregated by law is to eliminate all traces of the unconstitutional de jure system. The court's goal, on the other hand, is to remedy the violation and to return a school district that is operating in compliance with the Constitution to local control. Local autonomy of school districts is a vital national tradition because only those school districts that are making decisions on their own, without judicial supervision, can be held accountable to citizens, courts, and the political process.

Partial relinquishment of judicial control, when justified by the facts of the case, is within the court's discretion and can be a significant step in fulfilling the court's duty to return control to local authorities. Furthermore, by partially withdrawing control, a court can better concentrate its resources (and the resources of the school district) on the areas in which discrimination has not yet been eliminated. In ordering partial withdrawal, the court should consider whether (1) there has been full compliance in those aspects of the system from which supervision is to be withdrawn, (2) retention of judicial control is necessary to achieve compliance in other facets of the system, and (3) the school district has demonstrated a good faith commitment to the equal protection guarantees of the Constitution. DCSS "has traveled the often long road to unitary status almost to its end." DCSS is a unitary (i.e., desegregated) system with regard to student assignments, transportation, physical facilities, and extracurricular activities. But in those areas in which compliance has not been achieved, namely, teacher and principal assignments, resource allocation, and quality of education, DCSS has neither acted in bad faith nor engaged in further acts of discrimination. Therefore, the court of appeals erred in holding, as a matter of law, that the district court could not permit DCSS to regain control over areas in compliance with the desegregation decree. Reversed and remanded.

**COMMENT:** This decision does not break new ground in the area of school desegregation litigation, but it does provide federal district courts with greater latitude when working with a school district. The Court has avoided any major decisions in this area in recent years. Nevertheless, the holding in this case should provide greater flexibility in the desegregation cases in which federal courts still retain authority over school districts.

## Discussion Questions

1. Do school districts need to be completely desegregated before a court will relinquish control over the districts? Or may a school just propose procedures for a court to relinquish control over the districts?

2. How many areas are school districts required to desegregate? What were the individual categories needing a district's attention?

3. Does the Court want to control the school districts indefinitely?

# PARENTS INVOLVED IN COMMUNITY SCHOOLS V. SEATTLE SCHOOL DISTRICT NO. 1 ET AL. NO. 05-908 DECIDED JUNE 28, 2007

**GENERAL RULE OF LAW:** The equal protection clause of the Fourteenth Amendment precludes the assignment of children to different public schools based solely on their race unless a compelling government interest is served.

**PROCEDURE SUMMARY:**

**Plaintiffs:** An organization of Seattle parents (Parents Involved) (P) and the mother of Joshua, a Jefferson County. (Kentucky,) student

**Defendants:** Seattle School District No. 1 and the Jefferson County, (Kentucky,) School District (D)

**U.S. District Court Decision:** Summary judgment finding that the plan survived strict scrutiny on the federal constitutional claim because it was narrowly tailored to serve a compelling government interest

**U.S. Court of Appeals Decision:** Affirmed in both ninth and sixth circuits

**U.S. Supreme Court Decision:** Reversed and remanded

**FACTS:** This decision includes two cases in which respondent school districts have implemented student assignment plans that rely on race to determine which schools certain children can attend. In the case of the Seattle School District (D), there was no history of segregation and the district had never operated legally segregated schools. In contrast, the Jefferson County School District (serving Louisville, Kentucky) (D) had once operated a segregated school system; it had been released from court supervision in 2001 after having eliminated the vestiges of prior segregation to the greatest extent practicable. In 2001, Jefferson County adopted its plan, classifying students as black or "other" in order to make certain elementary school assignments and to rule on transfer requests. In Seattle, the district instituted a racial tiebreaker, which was instituted only when children sought to enroll in a high school that was oversubscribed and integration-positive. Respondent school districts in both school districts voluntarily adopted student assignment plans using race as a factor, asserting that their student assignment plans were narrowly tailored to meet a compelling government interest.

**ISSUE:** Does assigning children to different public schools based solely on their race violate the Fourteenth Amendment's equal protection guarantee?

**HOLDING AND DECISION:** Yes. The school districts have not carried their heavy burden of showing that the interest they seek to achieve justifies the extreme means they have chosen, namely, discriminating among individual students based on race by relying upon racial classifications in making school assignments. Because racial classifications are simply too pernicious to permit any but the most exact connection between justification and classification, the equal protection analysis that must be used in the review is the highest standard of strict scrutiny. Therefore, the school districts must demonstrate that their use of such classification is "narrowly tailored" to achieve a "compelling" government interest. Although remedying the effects of past intentional discrimination is a compelling interest under the strict scrutiny test (see *Freeman v. Pitts*, 1992), that interest is not involved here because the Seattle schools were never segregated by law nor subject to court-ordered desegregation, and the desegregation decree to which the Jefferson County schools were previously subject has been dissolved.

**COMMENT:** These cases continue the trend of recent Supreme Court decisions to move away from more liberal positions regarding school desegregation and race-based job preference and affirmative action. Here, the impact of the decision is limited. The school districts either no longer had a desegregation plan in effect or had never implemented a desegregation plan. Essentially, a plan utilizing racial classifications must be narrowly tailored to further a compelling government interest. This has been and remains the standard.

## Discussion Questions

1. Is it important that the decision concerns a school district that had never been under a desegregation decree as well as a district that had been released from court supervision under a desegregation order?

2. Do these cases mean that a school district may never use a student assignment plan that uses race to determine which school a child may attend?

3. What impact does this case have on the traditional concept of affirmative action?

Additional case briefs can be found on the SAGE Web site at the following address:
http://www.sagepub.com/aquilacasebriefs

## NOTES

1. Plessy v. Ferguson, 163 U.S. 537 (1896).
2. Brown v. Board of Education, 347 U.S. 483, 74 S. Ct. 686 (1954).
3. Roberts v. City of Boston, 59 Mass. 198 (1896).
4. See Gong Lum v. Rice, 275 U.S. 78 (1927).
5. Missouri ex rel. Gaines v. Canada, 305 U.S. 337 (1938).
6. Sweatt v. Painter, 340 U.S. 846 (1950).
7. McLaurin v. Oklahoma State Regents for Higher Education, 339 U.S. 637 (1950).
8. Brown v. Board of Education of Topeka, 347 U.S. 483, 74 S. Ct. 686 (1954).
9. Brown v. Board of Education of Topeka, 349 U.S. 294, 75 S. Ct. 753 (1955).
10. Alexander v. Holmes County Bd. of Ed., 396 U.S. 19 (1969).
11. See Griffin v. County School Bd. of Prince Edward County, 377 U.S. 218, 84 S. Ct. 1226 (1964).
12. Alexander v. Holmes County Bd. of Ed., 396 U.S. 19, 90 S. Ct. 29 (1969).
13. Swann v. Charlotte-Mecklenburg Bd. of Ed., 402 U.S. 1, 91 S. Ct. 1267 (1971).
14. See Keyes v. School District No.1, 413 U.S. 189, 93 S. Ct. 2686 (1973).
15. See Milliken v. Bradley, 418 U.S. 717 (1974), which established case law regarding multi-district remedies.

16. See Milliken v. Bradley, supra; see also Dayton Board of Education v. Brinkman, 433 U.S. 406 (1977).

17. Bradley v. School Bd. of the City of Richmond, 382 U.S. 103, 86 S. Ct. 224 (1965).

18. United States v. Montgomery County Bd. of Ed., 395 U.S. 225, 89 S. Ct. 1670 (1969).

19. Singleton v. Jackson Municipal Separate School Dist., 419 F.2d 1211 (5th Cir. 1970), *cert. den.*, 396 U.S. 1032, 90 S. Ct. 612 (1970).

20. See Arthur v. Nyquist, 712 F.2d 816 (2nd Cir. 1983).

21. Wygant v. Jackson Bd. of Ed., 476 U.S. 267, 106 S. Ct. 1842 (1986).

22. See Milliken v. Bradley (Milliken II), 433 U.S. 267 (1977).

23. See Missouri v. Jenkins, 495 U.S. 33 (1990).

24. See Dayton Board of Education v. Brinkman (Brinkman II), 443 U.S. 526 (1979); see also Columbus Board of Education v. Penick, 443 U.S. 449 (1979).

25. See Washington v. Seattle School District No.1, 458 U.S. 457 (1982).

26. See Freeman v. Pitts, 503 U.S. 467 (1992).

27. Additional case briefs can be found on the SAGE Web site at the following address: http://www.sagepub.com/aquilacasebriefs.

28. Keyes v. School District No.1, 413 U.S. 189, 93 S. Ct. 2686 (1973).

29. Green v. New Kent County School Board, 391 U.S. 430 (1968).

# 2

# Church–State Interaction

*Congress shall make no law respecting an establishment of religion or prohibiting the free exercise thereof.*

—First Amendment,
U.S. Constitution

## OVERVIEW . . . . . . . . . . . . . . . . . . . . . . . . . . . . . . . . . . . . . . .

From the latter half of the twentieth century until the present, church-state relationships have provided the most volatile battleground for Supreme Court activity as well as public controversy. Whether it was the intent of the framers of the Constitution to sever religious and civil activities or merely to prohibit state-supported religion or discrimination is open to debate. That debate will undoubtedly continue. The most recent debate, beginning in the 1940s, has been over the proper interpretation of the establishment and free exercise clauses. Now, at the start of the new millennium, the issue remains controversial, with litigation continuing to expand and emotions growing more heated.

There has been a long history of religious debate, controversy, and atrocities. This can be traced back to the treatment of the Christians during the Roman Empire, the Jews historically (especially during the time of the Crusades), and the more recent Russian pogroms and the Holocaust. Our daily newspapers recount conflicts in Northern Ireland, Bosnia, and Kashmir to document our recent religious intolerance. The ongoing conflict between the Christian West and the Muslim East remains the defining intolerance of our time. Arguably, even Turkey's noninclusion in the European Economic Union may be traced to its large Muslim population. Clearly, religious intolerance remains a troubling issue worldwide and hinders almost all efforts for world peace.

*Everson v. Board of Education* (1947) concerned the first major intrusion of religion into public schools.[1] This was the first time the Court took an attenuated view of the First

Amendment's establishment clause and free exercise clause prohibitions. (Remember that the incorporation clause of the Fourteenth Amendment applied the Bill of Rights' protection to the states.) *Everson,* through its "child benefit doctrine," allowed for the provision of selected services to religious institutions and began the slow but steady erosion of the *Reynolds v. United States* (1879) "wall of separation."[2] The Court reasoned that when funds were expended for the benefit of the individual child rather than for religious purposes, these expenditures did not disturb First Amendment concerns. Later, the Court reasoned that because private schools serve a public purpose and perform a secular as well as a sectarian function, the expenditure of public funds is not unconstitutional.

In *Lemon v. Kurtzman* (1971), the Supreme Court first applied the tripartite test to determine the constitutionality of establishment clause issues.[3] Essentially, the *Lemon* test mandated that government action must have a secular purpose, have a primary effect that neither advances nor impedes religion, and not foster excessive government entanglement with religion. This test was applied consistently until 1992, when the Court began its present practice of not repudiating the *Lemon* provisions while quietly avoiding referencing them. *Lee v. Weisman* (1992) applied the coercion test, which finds an abridgement of the establishment clause if there has been direct or indirect governmental coercion.[4] Other justices support a "nonendorsement" test, which invalidates legislation that has the purpose or effect of *endorsing* religion by seemingly favoring a particular religious belief. In light of these shifting trends, it appears that the *Lemon* provisions, while still constitutional, are on shaky ground. Whether they will remain a "useful guideline" or something more will be determined in future cases.

The free exercise clause has usually involved the Supreme Court using a balancing test that determines whether a sincere and legitimate religious belief has been limited by the government's action. While this is a less volatile arena than the one surrounding the establishment clause, there has been significant activity. When an impairment of free exercise is established, the Court must first determine whether the state action serves a compelling purpose justifying the burden placed on the exercise of religion. Second, even when such a compelling interest is established, the government must reach its objective through the means least burdensome to affected free exercise rights.

The best known free exercise case was *Wisconsin v. Yoder* (1972).[5] Here, the Court excused Amish children from compulsory school attendance after their successful completion of the eighth grade. While extolling the primary importance of an educated citizenry, the Court found that the parents' right to practice their legitimate religious beliefs outweighed the state's interest in the enforcement of a state's compulsory education law. Of course, this free exercise ruling in support of the Amish was based on their historic tradition of providing vocational services to their followers, who usually enter their sequestered religious community rather than mainstream society.

Several cases have somewhat limited the extent of these free exercise balancing test provisions. The effect has been to limit the need to demonstrate a compelling government interest. Eventually, Congress enacted the 1993 Religious Freedom Restoration Act, which reestablished the need for the government to have a compelling justification to substantially burden a person's religious exercise. This statute will certainly play a major part in future free exercise clause litigation.

This expanding arena of Supreme Court litigation has left most school people somewhat confused, if not dazed. Often, public school officials have adopted simple procedures to avoid conflict and potential difficulties when dealing with religious concerns. For example, the practice of declaring school holidays on Christian holidays while not closing schools for Jewish, Muslim, and other non-Christian holidays could have led to extensive litigation. By utilizing a policy of reasonable accommodation (e.g., allowing the use of personal days and undetermined sick days), schools have provided release time and thereby avoided most conflicts.

Issues of school choice, such as home schooling, tax credits, postsecondary options, charter schools, or voucher programs, have grown significantly in recent years. For example, voucher programs have been introduced in both the federal legislature and various state legislatures. Voucher plans provide students with a specified amount of money that can be used at authorized public and private schools. Currently, no extensive voucher program has been instituted at the state level, although statewide voucher initiatives have been on the ballot in Washington, Oregon, California, and Colorado.

Whether a voucher system will eventually survive a Supreme Court **challenge** remains debatable. Court decisions seem to indicate it will. For example, state tax deductions that primarily benefited parents of religious school students were found not to violate the establishment clause. The **dicta** in *Zobrest et al. v. Catalina Foothills School District* (1993) also supported vouchers.[6] The argument will eventually be whether voucher initiatives could be considered religiously neutral legislation. The Ohio case *Zelman v. Simmons-Harris* (2002) provides further strong support for the constitutionality of voucher programs.[7] To support the parents of children in the failing Cleveland Municipal School District, the Ohio legislature authorized a limited voucher program that authorized funds for tuition at private and parochial schools. Using a neutrality or nonpreference rationale, the Court allowed participation of all schools, religious and nonreligious. This was the position even though 46 of the 57 participating private schools were religious schools. Clearly, the current Court will probably not strike down many government aid programs to church schools absent blatantly religious provisions.

## Case Study

### Equal Access or School Support of Religion?

Consider the following scenario involving the formation of a new Christian Club in a local public secondary school, Happy Hearts High School. After reading this chapter, you will be able to answer the questions that directly follow this case study.

Martin Luther King, Jr., High School is a public secondary school that receives federal financial assistance. As a practice, MLK High School allows its students to join any number of recognized non-curricular groups and clubs (limited open forum). Many of these groups meet after school hours on school premises.

Several students have asked the principal for permission to form a Christian Club that would operate with the same rights, responsibilities, terms, and conditions as other MLK student groups. They believe that the federal Equal Access Act guarantees them the right to form their club. The

(Continued)

(Continued)

Equal Access Act passed by Congress in 1984 prohibits public secondary schools that receive federal assistance and maintain a "limited open forum" from denying "equal access" to groups of "religious, political, philosophical" natures. Others argue that the establishment clause prohibits the government from passing laws that aid a religion or prefer one religion over another. These students prefer having no faculty sponsorship, although several faculty members have indicated an interest in the Christian Club's intention of prayer and religious contemplation.

Is your denial of their request appropriate in light of establishment clause concerns? Or, does the Equal Access Act apply to forbid discrimination against the Christian Club because of its religious content?

## Discussion Questions

1. Is there a problem if the Christian Club is assigned a staff member as sponsor and that sponsor attends the meetings? If so, why?

2. What is the concern regarding the existence of a "limited open forum"? How would the outcome change if the school in question had not established a "limited open forum"?

3. Could all clubs and noncurriculum groups in a school be denied the right to form and meet?

4. What is meant by the term "content discrimination"? Does it have application here?

# IMPORTANT CONCEPTS

- **Government must remain neutral toward religion:** The First Amendment establishment clause prohibits government from passing laws that aid a religion or prefer one religion over another.

- **Government must not interfere in religious practices:** The First Amendment free exercise clause prohibits government from interfering with legitimate religious practices.

- **Direct government financial aid to parochial schools is not supported:** Most attempts to provide financial support to parochial schools for the general educational needs of parochial students are unconstitutional because they result in an "excessive entanglement" between church and state. This violates the establishment clause.

- **Direct government financial aid should be to students:** Generally, the government may provide financial and material assistance directly to parochial school students (as opposed to the parochial school or the parents of parochial school students) without running afoul of the establishment clause.

- **Distribution/posting of religious literature is not allowed:** Religious literature may not be distributed and religious sayings may not be posted in public schools.

- **Public school on-campus religious instruction is prohibited:** Public school students may not be released from their regular classes to attend religious classes held in public schools, but they may be released from school to attend such classes if they are held off campus.

- **Prayer in public school is not allowed:** Bible reading, prayer, student-led prayer groups, and silent meditation conducted in public schools (in class or at school ceremonies) violate the establishment clause.

- **Nonreligious general study of the Bible is allowed:** The Bible may be studied as part of a general educational program.

- **Flag salute/pledge of allegiance requirements may be limited:** Students may not be required to salute the American flag or pledge allegiance if doing so offends their sincerely held religious beliefs.

- **Religious dress for teachers is not supported:** Public school teachers may not wear religious dress or insignia in public schools.

## THE KEY PRINCIPLE: GOVERNMENT MUST REMAIN NEUTRAL TOWARD RELIGION

The separation of church and state is governed by the establishment clause, which is in the First Amendment to the U.S. Constitution, and the legal precedents interpreting that clause. The clause states that government must remain *neutral* toward religion. This means that the government must not act or must refrain from acting in a manner that advances or inhibits religious expression. This maxim is easier said than observed. For the most part, the obligation to educate a state's school-age children rests with state legislators and local school boards. This includes ensuring that parochial school students, like public school students, receive an acceptable degree of general (nonreligious) education in addition to their religious studies.

Sometimes, when legislators attempt to assist parochial schools and their students in satisfying state-mandated general educational criteria, the legislators unconstitutionally aid the religious institutions themselves. At other times, actions to accommodate the religious practices and beliefs of students at public schools may, in effect, "advance" religion in the public school classroom.

The U.S. Supreme Court has developed a three-part test for determining whether government support of parochial schools and their students is constitutionally acceptable (often called the *Lemon* provision). The test ensures that government support does not advance religion. Similarly, the Supreme Court has developed a balancing test for determining whether it is appropriate for school authorities to limit or restrict the religious practices of students in public schools. What follows is a discussion of these principles that the courts have developed over the years as they have attempted to apply these tests in observance of the distinction between church and state.

## The Issue

The First Amendment to the U.S. Constitution states in part that "Congress shall make no law respecting an establishment of religion or prohibiting the free exercise" of religion. The incorporation clause of the Fourteenth Amendment makes the First Amendment applicable to the states.

## Establishment of Religion: The Excessive Entanglement Test

The U.S. Supreme Court has determined that the establishment clause prohibits states and the federal government from passing laws that aid a religion or prefer one religion over another.[8] In other words, government must remain neutral toward religion; it may not advance or hinder any religion. The Court has devised the excessive entanglement test, a three-part test for determining whether a particular government action withstands an establishment clause challenge.[9] The *Lemon* tests are as follows:

1. *Secular purpose:* The action must have a nonreligious, or secular, purpose;

2. *Neither furthers nor impedes:* Viewed in its totality, the action must not further or impede religious practice; and

3. *High degree of involvement prohibited:* The action must not result in too high a degree of involvement between government and religion.[10]

## Free Exercise of Religion

The free exercise clause prohibits the government from interfering with legitimate religious practices. However, an intrusion into the sphere of religious practice is sometimes justified by an important government interest. To make this determination, the U.S. Supreme Court applies a balancing test in order to determine whether government intrusion is lawful:

1. *Impairment of religious practices:* First, practices dictated by sincere religious beliefs must have been impaired by some kind of government action;

2. *Compelling interest:* If this is the case, the action will be justified only if it serves a compelling interest (i.e., one that is more critical than the exercise of the religious beliefs in question); and

3. *Least burdensome means:* Finally, the action in question must also represent the least burdensome means of achieving the government's objective.

## Tension Between the Establishment and Free Exercise Clauses

Complete government neutrality toward religion is not easily maintained. As stated above, the establishment clause requires the government to remain neutral toward religion. On the other hand, the free exercise clause prohibits the government from interfering with religious expression. For example, religious displays on school property can be viewed as religious expression that cannot be interfered with under the free exercise clause. However, these same religious expressions may be advancing a religious belief that runs afoul of the school's neutrality toward religion.

*Improper Advancement.* Sometimes, what appears to be a reasonable accommodation of free exercise rights is actually an improper advancement of religion in violation of the establishment clause. The Court has had to prohibit public schools from sponsoring daily prayer and Bible reading as a violation of the establishment clause, even though student participation might have been voluntary.

*Unnecessary Limitations.* Conversely, efforts to guard against state sponsorship of religion may result in unnecessary limitations on free exercise rights. An example of overzealous guarding of establishment clause protections was the prohibition of student prayer before and after school. This was held to be an unnecessary limitation of free exercise rights. The Equal Access Act attempted to clarify this student school prayer issue by authorizing school prayer when a school provided a limited open forum during noninstructional time. Schools felt that denying devotional clubs' requests to meet after school hours was acceptable even though the school allowed co-curricular clubs (e.g., scuba and chess clubs) to meet on school grounds. The Court, however, declared that this was an unnecessary limitation that denied the students equal access based on the content of their speech.

*Tension Remains.* The Supreme Court has not expressed a preference for the freedoms guaranteed by one clause over those guaranteed by another. While no preference for the establishment clause over the free exercise clause has been announced by the Supreme Court, there have been significantly more establishment clause issues before the Court. Allowing schools to provide accommodation for religion has been a somewhat standard position. While denying clergy the right to provide religious training to public school students in school settings during the school day, the Court has provided an accommodation by allowing students to obtain religious training off school grounds.[11]

## GOVERNMENTAL SUPPORT AND REGULATION OF PAROCHIAL EDUCATION

Even though the U.S. Constitution calls for what Thomas Jefferson termed "the separation of church and state," the Supreme Court has more recently permitted state and local governments to provide various forms of assistance to parochial schoolchildren. Since *Everson,* the traditional position is that government assistance must directly benefit parochial students rather than the religious institutions that educate them. This principle is sometimes referred to as the child benefit doctrine. An alternative supportive position—not as well-received—was that government should provide benefits directly to parochial schools or to parents of parochial schoolchildren, as a means of furthering the general welfare through the creation of an "educated citizenry." While supporting the child benefit doctrine, with few exceptions, the Court has determined that other forms of direct aid violate the First Amendment and are, therefore, impermissible.

*Everson* has established that the state may extend general benefits to all without regard to religious conviction, comparing the benefits a child would receive to other public services for all—such as police, fire, and health protection. Remember, the child benefit **theory** allows the state to provide service to religious schools, but it does not mandate such services. Thus, a state may refuse to provide services and benefits to parents and students in religious programs. The refusal would be based on state constitutional strictures that do not allow state-funded textbooks, transportation, and so on for religious institutions. Missouri's constitution, for one, will not even allow the delivery of Title I services to religious institutions using Missouri school district personnel to provide Title I math and reading support. Bypass provisions must be instituted through private providers to ensure that children in religious schools receive necessary Title I services.

The concern that services must meet the standard of a "legitimate state purpose" derives from the child benefit rationale. Public services, such as police and fire, are provided as a public benefit. The parallel logic is that similar services provided to religious schools do not violate establishment clause provisions because of the legitimacy of their purpose.

State financial aid to parochial schools varies from state to state. On a per capita basis, Ohio provides more support to religious schools than does any other state. The term "parochiaid" has been coined to describe this panoply of state-provided services. Because of the opinions of their citizens as expressed through their state legislatures, states like Ohio and Pennsylvania are very supportive of religious education and provide more parochiaid. Others, such as Missouri and Hawaii, provide almost no support.

## Child Benefit Doctrine

The child benefit doctrine holds that it is permissible for the state to provide materials to parochial school students if they are the same as those provided to public school students and the materials are necessary for an equal, nonsectarian, nonreligious education. In *Wolman v. Walter* (1977), the Court dealt with questionably permissible materials as well as services.[12] An Ohio law was upheld that allowed the use of public school funds to purchase reusable workbooks and manuals for loan to private schools. Providing record-keeping and testing services and therapeutic services (performed off school grounds) to private schools was also permissible.

*Basis of Support.* Support for this doctrine was based somewhat generally on the federal Constitution as opposed to specifically on the establishment or free exercise clauses of the First Amendment. For example, the Supreme Court held that the use of a state's severance tax to supply textbooks free of charge to all students in the state of Louisiana did not violate the Louisiana State Constitution nor any provision of the United States Constitution.[13] The Court concluded by saying that the textbooks supplied to the children of public schools were the same textbooks as those provided to parochial schoolchildren.

*Minority View.* Some state courts (e.g., Missouri) have interpreted their state constitutions as prohibiting some aspects of the child benefit doctrine. The Missouri Supreme Court held that the distribution of federal funds pursuant to Title I of the Elementary and Secondary Education Act of 1965 to benefit parochial schools was unconstitutional.[14] The Missouri court stated that federal funds deposited in the state treasury for public school purposes implicates both Article I, § 7 and Article IX, § 8 and, pursuant to these provisions, cannot be distributed to parochial schools. In order for underprivileged children to benefit from Title I funding, the state would need to funnel these funds to private independent contractors who would distribute services that benefit children of parochial schools. This practice is generally referred to as a "bypass procedure," and it creates many problems in order to ensure that Title I services are provided to eligible youth in parochial schools.

## Legitimate Public Purpose

Under the establishment clause of the First Amendment, a state-provided service to religious schools that serves a legitimate public purpose will generally be upheld by the courts.

*Equal Access to Nonsectarian, Nonreligious Education.* A state-provided service serves a legitimate public purpose if it in some way provides all students in public and private schools equal access to a nonsectarian, nonreligious education. For example, once a limited public forum (public property opened for a limited purpose) has been created, a student group cannot be denied equal access to it based on the content (religious or otherwise) of its meetings. Similarly, a university's allocation of funds for student group publications must include those who publish material with religious viewpoints.[15]

*Restrictive State Constitutions.* Some state constitutions are more restrictive of church-state relations than the First Amendment.

*NonMandatory State Services.* If a state-provided service is permissible but not mandatory, many state courts will not allow the state to continue to provide the service to parochial schools because it amounts to the use of public funds for sectarian purposes (i.e., in support of a religious **sect**). For example, the court invalidated a Michigan school district's extensive "shared time" program, in which the school district rented space from 40 parochial schools to offer a variety of enrichment and remedial courses to students enrolled in the religious schools.[16] Instructional services in these parochial school buildings had the effect of allowing a "direct and substantial advancement of the sectarian enterprise."

*Effect of Equal Protection.* The equal protection clause of the Fourteenth Amendment provides that states must treat similar classifications of people the same under the law. Nevertheless, there are some limitations on the application of this federal protection. The equal protection clause does not require that all individuals be treated the same in all respects; sometimes the pursuit of a legitimate public goal justifies treating similarly situated individuals differently. For example, when a state constitution requires absolutely no interaction between church and state, similarly situated public and private school students will receive different services unless there is proof of a compelling need (a higher equal protection standard). Thus, students in religious schools in almost every state may receive specialized services delivered through state education agencies, while similarly situated religious school students in Missouri, for example, will not receive these services in a direct fashion, but instead receive them from a nonschool source.

## State Financial Aid to Parochial Schools (Parochiaid)

Since 1947, there has been a significant increase in involvement between public elementary and secondary schools and religious schools. With the child benefit theory opening the door, there has been a steady increase in educational services being provided to private religious schools. Support has varied, from traditional services such as textbooks, transportation, and remedial services, to the more unusual services, such as required immunizations, income tax benefits, and even religious prohibitions against dancing. The term "parochiaid" has developed into a catch-all term that includes all the various sources of funding that states provide to parochial schools. The amount and specific areas of state financial aid vary from state to state based on legislative willingness and state statutory requirements. The Supreme Court decides the constitutionality of a state action regarding religious schools in its state. Unless that action is held to be mandatory (which is rare), another state does not need to implement a similar program of services to support religious schools. In fact, a state will often find that specific actions or services may violate state law regarding church and state interaction.

Nevertheless, many areas of parochiaid have been clearly delineated through court action and state practices. For example, the provision of textbooks has become a standard practice in many states. The only issue that raises concern is whether the books provided are appropriate, and this is usually handled by issuing a list of state-approved texts. Transportation has been litigated numerous times, especially in the 1950s and 1960s. Now, it is common practice for students who attend parochial schools to be transported on yellow school buses or receive the same public transit tickets that public school students receive. Religious schools may generally be reimbursed for costs related to standardized testing and scoring, so long as the public schools draft and score these tests. Through this process, there is little chance of advancing religious education.

The loan of instructional materials, such as periodicals, library books, computers, television sets, tape recorders, and computers, has been far more contentious than the textbook issue. It appears that the present Court will allow loan of instructional materials because the instructional material is based on neutral secular concerns that neither favor nor disfavor religion.[17] Obviously, the landscape is far from smooth, but there are some mile markers slowly being developed. For example, *Mitchell v. Helms* (2000) has explicated this position using a neutrality argument to allow instructional materials when services are provided in a neutral manner such that they neither favor nor disfavor religion.

*Provision of Textbooks to Parochial Students by State or Local Governments.* Building upon the earlier decision in *Cochran,* the Court upheld the constitutionality of a state statute that required local school boards to loan textbooks to parochial schoolchildren. It found that doing so benefited the interest of a quality education for all.[18]

*Provision of Transportation Services.* In an initial application of the establishment clause to the education context, the Supreme Court approved the use of public funds to provide bus service to children attending parochial school. A New Jersey school board's authorization of reimbursements to parents for costs related to parochial school bus fares was upheld because it extended a general service to all, not unlike police or fire protection. Thus, reimbursing parochial school parents satisfied a legitimate public purpose: that of helping all parents provide school transportation for their children, regardless of their religious affiliations.[19]

*Equal Protection Claims.* With regard to transportation services for parochial school students, most state courts have rejected equal protection challenges. In rejecting these challenges, the courts gave parochial students access to transportation services.

*Permissible, Not Mandatory.* In some cases, parents of children who have not been provided with publicly funded transportation services have sued local school districts. The parents claim that this is a violation of their equal protection rights. Because the Supreme Court held that public funding of parochial bus fares is permissible but not mandatory, several state courts have determined that this practice is constitutionally impermissible.

*Provision of Remedial Education Services by Public School Teachers to Parochial Students on Parochial School Grounds.* The Supreme Court first decided in 1985 that providing remedial service by public school teachers on parochial school grounds was unconstitutional.[20] Subsequently, the Supreme Court has reversed itself in a case arising from the same facts.[21] The Court upheld the general principles used to evaluate whether government aid violates the establishment clause, but it abandoned the presumption that placement of public employees on parochial school grounds inevitably results in an impermissible state sponsoring of religion. The court also abandoned the presumption that all government aid that directly benefits the educational function of religious schools is invalid.

*Purchase of Nonreligious Educational Services for Parochial Schools and the Provision of Salary Supplements to Parochial School Teachers for Teaching Nonreligious Subjects.* Purchase of nonreligious educational services and provision of salary supplements are intended to provide financial support to parochial schools for the general educational needs of their students. In the first instance, the state "purchases" secular (nonreligious) educational services on behalf of the parochial students being served by reimbursing parochial schools for teachers' salaries, textbooks, and instructional materials. In the second instance, the state pays a salary supplement directly to parochial school teachers for teaching secular subjects to parochial students.

*Landmark Opinion.* A state provided money to parochial schools to provide nonsectarian instruction and to supplement the salaries of parochial school teachers. In a landmark decision, the Supreme Court considered the constitutionality of both forms of aid and concluded that neither was permissible under the First Amendment. Both resulted in government expenditure of time and resources to ensure that the services being purchased from parochial sources satisfied secular requirements. This, in and of itself, promoted an excessive entanglement between church and state, regardless of the state's secular motivation for providing the support in the first place.[22]

*Promoting a Secular Legislative Purpose.* A state may provide aid to parochial schools if its provision promotes a secular legislative purpose while not principally or primarily advancing or inhibiting religion or fostering excessive government entanglement with religion.

Therefore, the provision of books, standardized testing and scoring, and diagnostic and therapeutic services was held to be constitutional. However, providing instructional materials and field trip transportation was unconstitutional.[23]

*Creation of a Special School District to Permit a Religious Community's Handicapped Children to Receive Financial Assistance.* In *Board of Education of Kiryas Joel Village School District v. Louis Grumet* (1994), the Supreme Court concluded that a New York state statute that created a special school district within the boundaries of a religious community violated the establishment clause.[24] A state may not delegate its civic authority to a group that is chosen according to religious criteria. Further, the state, while possibly not actually supporting one religion over another, clearly gave the appearance of doing so in creating a special school district for a fundamentalist Jewish sect.

## School Vouchers

The voucher controversy is closely related to the school tuition reimbursement controversy. Vouchers have had a mixed history, with recent Court support. Wisconsin upheld vouchers for students who attended religious schools, while a Florida appellate court struck down vouchers because the vast majority of students participating in the voucher initiative were in sectarian schools.[25] The Ohio Pilot Project Scholarship Program (OPPSP), designed to assist children in Cleveland's failing public schools, has apparently resolved this issue. In *Zelman v. Simmons-Harris* (2002), the Supreme Court abandoned the reasoning of *Committee for Public Education v. Nyquist* (1973) to uphold the constitutionality of the OPPSP, even though almost all participating schools were religiously affiliated.[26] It appears that the Court believes that it is advancing true private choice that directs benefits to needy private individuals.

*Provision of Income Tax Benefits.* In *Committee for Public Education v. Nyquist* (1973), the Supreme Court found that providing parents with income tax benefits in recognition of the cost of parochial school tuition violated the First Amendment. Of course, if a state legislature authorized income tax deductions for education-related expenses for all parents of schoolchildren, then parents who send their children to religious schools could participate. Further, such a statute would benefit, almost exclusively, parents sending their children to religious schools because public school parents have few, if any, deductible expenses.

*Government Encouragement Prohibited.* The Court reasoned that the tax benefit program rewarded parents for sending their children to parochial school and thus improperly advanced their respective religions.

*No Analogy to Property Tax Exemptions.* Interestingly, the Court refused to analogize the tuition-related tax benefit scheme to tax exemptions that historically have been provided for church-owned property.

*Education Tax Deductions Allowed.* The Court has since distinguished *Nyquist* by determining that a state legislature may provide income tax deductions for the cost of education-related expenses to parents of all schoolchildren, not just to parents with children who attend parochial schools.[27]

# RELIGIOUS INFLUENCES IN PUBLIC SCHOOLS

How far can public school officials go in accommodating free exercise rights before they run afoul of the establishment clause? This has always been a difficult distinction. In 2000, the Supreme Court, in a close decision, held that a policy permitting student-led prayers prior to high school football games violated the establishment clause.[28] In *Santa Fe Independent School District v. Doe* (2000), the Court used the endorsement test (rather than the psychological coercion test of *Lee v. Weisman*, 1992) to determine whether the purpose of the government action was to endorse or approve of a religion or religious activity. Here, it held that the policy permitting student-led prayers was such an intrusion. Furthermore, it held that there was no First Amendment concern, nor was the prayer a neutral act.

## Religious Instruction of Public School Students

As a rule, public school students may not be excused from their regular instruction to attend religious classes held in public school classrooms. However, local school boards are free to excuse students to attend religious classes that are held off campus.

*No Religious Instruction in Public Schools.* The Supreme Court is opposed to religious instruction in public schools for two reasons: dissemination issues and benefit issues. Dissemination in public settings benefits religious education, and instruction involving the dissemination of religious material in a public setting is a clear violation of the church-state separation principle. With regard to the benefit issues, the religious sects that sponsor the instruction benefit from the state's compulsory education requirements insofar as attendance records are kept for all classes, and therefore students who choose to attend must attend. This amounts to an advancement of religion because it assists the religious school's student attendance.[29]

*Off-Campus Religious Instruction.* A policy that allows the release of public school students so that they might attend religious instruction off campus neither establishes a religion nor denies free exercise rights. Actually, it accommodates freedom to worship without providing tangible support (such as access to public school classrooms or financial aid).[30]

## The Bible and Prayer in Public Schools

The Supreme Court has held that Bible reading and prayer in public schools violate the establishment clause.

*Bible Reading in Public Schools.* In considering the permissibility of Bible reading in public schools, the Court paraphrased two parts of the three-part *Lemon* test that it had enunciated several years earlier as a means of assessing establishment clause violations:

1. *Secular purpose:* What is the purpose of the governmental action?

2. *Primary effect:* What is the primary effect of the action?

*Result of Purpose-Effect Test.* If the purpose is anything other than secular, or if the effect is such that religion is either advanced or inhibited, then the action is constitutionally impermissible.[31] In *School Dist. of Abington Township v. Schempp* (1963), Bible reading was viewed as religious (not secular) in purpose. The fact that it took place on public property under the supervision of public school teachers further suggested an effect that advanced religion. It is important to note, however, that the Court distinguished ceremonial Bible reading from the study of the Bible (or religion) as part of a general educational program. The latter would not violate the establishment clause.

*Ceremonial Prayer Recitation.* The ceremonial recitation of prayer in public schools amounts to state sponsorship of religion, whether or not participation is compulsory and whether or not it occurs in class or at school ceremonies. Voluntary, student-led prayer conducted on the public school campus prior to or at the end of classes appears to be constitutionally permissible. The Supreme Court has also indicated that state laws calling for a daily period of silent meditation violate the establishment clause if they were passed as a means of circumventing school prayer restrictions.

## Miscellaneous Religious Influences

*Wearing Religious Dress or Insignia.* While the Supreme Court has not considered the issue, several state courts have upheld legislation that prohibits public school teachers from wearing religious dress or religious insignia. Such legislation does not violate a teacher's right to the free exercise of her religion because these restrictions are aimed at the *act* of wearing religious dress as opposed to the *underlying belief* that motivates the act.

*Distribution of Religious Literature.* The distribution of religious literature to public school students is generally viewed as unconstitutional because it appears to favor one religion over another. Even if students may only obtain the literature upon submission of a parental permission slip, the fact that all children are provided with blank slips may result in pressure to return them. The effect is thus considered to advance religion.

*Display of National Motto.* The display of the national motto of the United States, "In God We Trust," is permissible in a public school classroom. The posting of the Ten Commandments is not because the first requirement of the three-part establishment clause test is not met in this case: There is no valid secular reason for posting these religious principles.

*Observance of Religious Holidays.* Religious holidays may be observed in public schools so long as they are tied to a secular-oriented instructional program. This is accomplished by discussing the cultural and historical (i.e., secular) significance of the holidays. It would be wise to discuss Christian and non-Christian religious holidays as part of that review. Public displays of religious holiday symbols are permissible as long as they do not advance or inhibit religion. Even winter choir concerts must be careful to include non-Christian religious musical selections as well as nonreligious selections.[32]

*No Invocations or Benedictions by Clergy at Graduation.* A school may not invite clergy to perform invocations or benedictions at public secondary school graduation ceremonies.

Likewise, the state may not prepare or allow official prayers, even those purporting not to favor one religion over another. Such actions amount to the creation of a state religion. This is forbidden by the establishment clause.[33] Student-led observances have not encountered the same opposition as state-led ceremonies.

## RELIGIOUS OBJECTIONS TO PUBLIC SCHOOL PRACTICES

Sometimes, parents have sought to have their children excused from activities that conflict with their religious beliefs. Here, a balancing of competing interests must take place—the parents' interests in guiding the religious upbringing of their offspring versus the state's interest in providing for an educated citizenry. In this balancing of interests test, religious concerns have often been supported by the courts.

In *West Virginia v. Barnette* (1943), children with strong religious beliefs were not required to recite the Pledge of Allegiance.[34] Interestingly, teachers are likewise not required to recite the pledge if they do not wish to do so. Saluting the American flag also may not be required, and there is no requirement that the student must stand or be forced to leave the room. *Wisconsin v. Yoder* (1972) was a landmark ruling supporting a religious group's right to not educate their children in a public high school.[35] Of course, home schooling is also an option when there is an objection to a curriculum on religious grounds; such home schooling must meet the state's home schooling requirements.

*Landmark Case.* The landmark *Wisconsin v. Yoder* (1972) case established the First Amendment religious right of the Amish to educate their high school-age children. Their free exercise argument was supported because of their long tradition of self-sufficiency and Jeffersonian simple values.

*Saluting the American Flag.* The Supreme Court has determined that students may not be required to salute the American flag if doing so offends their religious beliefs. The Court was guided by evidence that suggested that refusal of students to participate in flag saluting would not interfere with the rights of others to do so and would not disrupt their doing so.

*Pledging Allegiance.* Students and teachers have a First Amendment (freedom of speech) right to refuse the ceremonial Pledge of Allegiance. Put another way, freedom *from* speech is protected under the First Amendment as well. In effect, a student may have the right to remain silent when called upon to speak the pledge if there is sincere objection.

*Exemptions From Offensive Curricula.* Public school officials may not force students to pursue studies that conflict with their sincerely held religious beliefs.

*Alternative Programs.* In an unusual logical twist, officials may run the risk of impermissibly advancing religion if public school officials accommodate those who object by providing students with alternative programs. The solution, according to some federal courts, is to permit the children in question to receive instruction at home.

## Case Study

### Free Speech or Supporting Christianity?

Stonewall High School is very involved in the local community. The high school is a new structure that was built with a "community center" concept in mind, to incorporate local organizations into the daily routine of the high school. The City of Stonewall is a diverse community, and the high school's clubs include the Hispanic Club, the Chess Club, the Gay and Lesbian Alliance Club, and the Environmental Club. Student groups and clubs have always been allowed to promote their meetings and events at school. There are bulletin boards specifically for club flyers and brochures. Some clubs are even allowed to place projects, art, and other artifacts in display cases in the hallway. However, after the Bible Club placed some Christian books in a display case, some teachers complained to the principal. The school board's attorney suggested that the display be removed. District officials took the display down because they felt that the display gave the impression that the school was endorsing Christianity. The Bible Club claims that not allowing them to place items in a display case violates their free speech rights and equal access rights. District officials respond that the Bible Club has always been allowed to place material on the bulletin boards, so the district is not violating their limited free speech rights.

### Discussion Questions

1. What are the legal issues presented in this case?

2. What cases support the district's position? What cases support the Bible Club's position?

3. Would your opinion of this case be different if this action took place in a middle school? An elementary school?

## CONCLUSION · · · · · · · · · · · · · · · · · · · · · · · · · · · · ·

Although the contentious nature of interactions between religion and public education has a long history, Supreme Court involvement has increased since the middle of the twentieth century. Even though these decisions have created a curious and somewhat shifting path, there appear to be some basic guideposts that provide direction to educators trying to navigate through what many consider a field strewn with land mines.

A public school district may permit schoolchildren to attend off-campus religious instruction during school hours. If such a program requires no state financial support, a release time policy (allowing students to leave before the end of the school day for religious instruction) is not counter to First Amendment prohibitions because it does not create or establish a religion, nor does it deny the free exercise of religion.

Beginning a class day with readings from religious texts is not authorized under the establishment clause. This is not acceptable whether it is conducted by teachers or students, or even if it is a voluntary initiative. The issue of silent meditation is still hotly debated: Resolution of this issue may depend on the language of applicable statutes and the intent of the framers.

Of course, studying about religion is constitutional as long as that study is part of a curriculum that includes all religions. This includes historical study as well as music, architecture, and literature classes. Even the Bible may be studied as part of a general educational program that includes the study of other great books such as the Torah and the Koran.

Students and teachers have a First Amendment right to refuse to recite the Pledge of Allegiance. Essentially, the right to remain silent when ordered to speak is as guaranteed as the right to speak when ordered to remain silent. Saluting the flag may not be required if the objection is based on religion or as a matter of conscience.

"Parochiaid" refers to the various sources of funding that states provide to parochial schools. Remember, the Supreme Court decides the constitutionality of a state action regarding religious schools. Unless that action is held to be mandatory (which is rare), another state does not need to implement a similar program of services to support religious schools. A state will often find that specific actions or services violate state law regarding church and state interaction. Nevertheless, many areas of parochiaid have been clearly delineated through court action and state practices. For example, the provision of textbooks to religious schools has become a standard practice in many states. It is now common practice for students who attend private and parochial schools to receive the same benefits as public school students. There is no longer much argument regarding the reimbursement of costs related to standardized testing and scoring services, as long as the public schools draft and score these tests. By limiting religious involvement in this manner, there is little chance of advancing religious education.

The loan of instructional materials, such as periodicals, library books, computers, television sets, tape recorders, and computers, while upheld, has been far more prevalent than the textbook issue. The Court will allow such loaning based on a neutrality argument—the instructional material is based on neutral secular concerns that neither favor nor disfavor religion.[36]

The *Lemon* provisions are under attack and may soon be revised or even overturned. Nevertheless, they remain good law. The tripartite *Lemon* provisions hold that a state may provide aid to parochial schools if the provision (1) promotes a secular legislative purpose, (2) does not principally or primarily advance or inhibit religion, and (3) does not foster excessive government entanglement with religion. While avoiding referencing the *Lemon* provisions, a new test was applied in *Lee v. Weisman* (1992): It involved a coercion test in which either direct or indirect government coercion would trigger a violation of the establishment clause. Other justices support a "nonendorsement" test: Government action will be struck down if it has the purpose or effect of endorsing religion by seemingly favoring a particular religious belief. Obviously, the *Lemon* provisions, while still constitutional, are on shaky ground. One justice merely referred to them as a "useful guideline." With such a great change in the Court in recent years, future cases will provide clarification.

Reasonableness appears to be the standard that is being adopted in regard to many establishment clause and free exercise clause conflicts. School districts often allow teachers to take personal leave for their non-Christian religious holidays, although districts are not required to pay for such leave. Usually, reasonable accommodation of a teacher's religion is the norm, so long as there is no excessive hardship to the district. A reasonableness analysis is also applied to the permissibility of religious displays during the holidays. For example, it appears that so long as a specific religious display is simply a part of a larger display celebrating the cultural diversity of a secular holiday season, it will be found permissible.

Although subject to argument, the reasonableness principle, I suggest, resulted in the reversal of *Aguilar v. Felton* (1985) by *Agostini v. Felton* (1997). The Court held that a federally funded program providing supplemental, remedial instruction to disadvantaged children on a neutral basis was not invalid under the establishment clause when such instruction was provided on the premises of sectarian schools. *Aguilar* had forced the New York schools to spend upwards of $100 million to rent vans for use as classrooms, merely to prevent public school teachers from setting foot in religious schools (which supposedly gave children the impression that the government supported the specific religious institution). Some now argue that in adopting this reasonableness position, *Agostini* erodes the principle underlying the establishment clause while favoring the free exercise clause.

One area certain to create future difficulty is the provision of federal programs in religious schools. The Individuals With Disabilities Education Improvement Act (IDEIA) services for the disabled have been upheld when the government program's benefits are provided in a neutral manner and without reference to religious classification. Such programs are not readily subject to an establishment clause challenge simply because sectarian institutions may also receive an attenuated financial benefit. In *Zobrest et al. v. Catalina Foothills School District* (1993), the sign language interpreter neither added to nor subtracted from that environment. Hence, the establishment clause did not bar the provision of such assistance.

Predicting what will happen regarding issues of religion and public education remains a difficult, if not impossible, task. With the recent changes in the composition of the Court, this will become even more problematic because it is likely that there will be new interpretations of the First Amendment's clauses related to religion. Change is the only constant.

# CASE BRIEFS ...................

# Lamb's Chapel et al. v. Center Moriches Union Free School District et al. 508 U.S. 384, 113 S. Ct. 2141 (1993)

**GENERAL RULE OF LAW:** Control over access to a nonpublic forum can be based on subject matter and speaker identity as long as the distinctions drawn are reasonable in light of the forum's purpose and are viewpoint-neutral.

**PROCEDURE SUMMARY:**

**Plaintiffs:** Lamb's Chapel (P), an evangelical church in the community of Center Moriches, and its pastor John Steigerwald (P)

**Defendants:** Center Moriches Union Free School District (D), et al.

**U.S. District Court Decision:** Granted **summary judgment** for defendants/respondents, rejecting all of the church's claims

**U.S. Court of Appeals Decision:** Affirmed the judgment of the district court in all respects

**U.S. Supreme Court:** Reversed, permitting the exhibition of the film series on school property as not violating the establishment clause's tripartite Lemon tests.

**FACTS:** Local school boards were authorized under New York Education Law § 414 to adopt reasonable regulations for the use of school property for 10 specified nonschool purposes. The permitted uses included holding social, civic, and recreational meetings and entertainment and other uses pertaining to the welfare of the community. A specific limitation was that meetings, entertainment, and other permissible uses had to be nonexclusive and open to the general public. Additionally, the list of permitted uses excluded meetings for religious purposes. Earlier, a New York appellate court, in *Trietley v. Board of Ed. of Buffalo* (1978), ruled that local boards could not allow student Bible clubs to meet on school property because "religious purposes are not included in the enumerated purposes for which a school may be used under section 414."[37] In *Deeper Life Christian Fellowship, Inc. v. Sobol* (1991), the Court of Appeals for the Second Circuit accepted *Trietley* as an authoritative interpretation of state law.[38]

Petitioners were Lamb's Chapel, an evangelical church in the Center Moriches community, and its pastor John Steigerwald. Twice, the church applied to the school district for permission to use school facilities to show a six-part film series containing lectures by Dr. James Dobson. The District (D) denied the first application, saying that "this film does appear to be church related and therefore your request must be refused." The second application—for permission to use school premises to show a film described as a family-oriented movie from the Christian perspective—was denied using identical language. The church brought suit in district court, challenging the denial as a violation of the freedom of speech and assembly clauses, the free exercise clause, and the establishment clause of the First Amendment, as well as the equal protection clause of the Fourteenth Amendment.

**ISSUE:** Is the free speech clause of the First Amendment (made applicable to the states by the Fourteenth Amendment) violated when a church is denied access to school premises to exhibit for public viewing and for assertedly religious purposes a film dealing with family and childrearing issues faced by parents today?

**HOLDING AND DECISION:** (White, J.) Yes. The complete ban on using school district property for religious purposes can survive a First Amendment challenge only if excluding this category of speech is reasonable and viewpoint-neutral. Rule 7, denying access to school premises for religious purposes, was not correctly applied here.

The court of appeals thought that the application of Rule 7 in this case was viewpoint-neutral because it had been and would be applied in the same way to all uses of school property for religious purposes. That all religions and all uses for religious purposes are treated alike under Rule 7, however, does not answer the critical question: whether, on the basis of viewpoint, to permit school property to be used for the presentation of all views about family issues and childrearing except those dealing with the subject matter from a religious standpoint.

There was no evidence suggesting that the lecture or film about childrearing and family values did not constitute a use for social or civic purposes otherwise permitted by Rule 10. This subject matter is not one that the District (D) has placed off-limits to any and all speakers. Nor is there any indication in the record that the application to exhibit the film was or would have been denied for any reason other than the fact that the presentation was to have been from a religious perspective. Therefore, denial on that basis was plainly invalid under *Cornelius v. NAACP Legal Defense and Education Fund* (1985), which held that "although a speaker may be excluded from a nonpublic forum if he wishes to address a topic not encompassed within the purpose of the forum . . . or if he is not a member of the class of speakers for whose special benefit the forum was created . . . the government violates the First Amendment when it denies access to a speaker solely to suppress the point of view he espouses on an otherwise includible subject."[39]

**COMMENT:** In this case, concerns of an establishment clause violation were unfounded (i.e., the film would not have been shown during school hours; would not have been sponsored by the school; and would have been open to the public, not just to church members). Furthermore, the school district had previously opened its facilities to two religious groups: the Southern Harmonize Gospel Singers and "Mind Center," a New Age religious group. Permitting school district property to be used to exhibit the film in this case would not have been an establishment of religion under the three-part *Lemon* test, either. Here, the challenged government action (permitting Lamb's Chapel to use school facilities) has a secular purpose, does not have the principal or primary effect of advancing or inhibiting religion, and does not foster an excessive entanglement with religion. Justice Scalia, in his concurring opinion, draws an interesting metaphor in his ongoing attack on *Lemon:* "Like some ghoul in a late-night horror movie that repeatedly sits up in its grave and shuffles abroad, after being repeatedly killed and buried, *Lemon* stalks our establishment clause jurisprudence once again, frightening the little children and school attorneys of Center Moriches Union Free School District. Its most recent burial, only last term, was, to be sure, not fully six feet under: Our decision in *Lee v. Weisman,* 505 U. S. 577 (1991) (slip op., at 7) conspicuously avoided using the supposed test but also declined the invitation to repudiate it."

## Discussion Questions

1.  Based on Justice Scalia's concurring opinion, is the *Lemon* test still valid? For how long?

2.  Could the school district have denied all requests from any religious groups to use its facilities?

3.  Is a church allowed to use school property to hold religious services?

# Everson v. Board of Education of the Township of Ewing 330 U.S. 855 (1947)

**GENERAL RULE OF LAW:** A state may reimburse the cost of transporting children to sectarian schools if it does not support the schools and such aid is provided without regard to a particular religion.

**PROCEDURE SUMMARY:**

**Plaintiff:** Everson (P), a New Jersey taxpayer

**Defendant:** Board of Education of the Township of Ewing (D)

**State Supreme Court Decision:** Held for Everson (P); the statute was unconstitutional because the state legislature lacked power to authorize reimbursement under the state constitution

**State Court of Errors and Appeals Decision:** Reversed; the statute was constitutional and violated neither the state nor federal constitutions

**U.S. Supreme Court Decision:** Affirmed (with respect to validity under the federal Constitution)

**FACTS:** New Jersey enacted a statute authorizing local school districts to make rules regarding the transportation of children to and from school. Ewing's Board of Education (D), pursuant to the statute, authorized reimbursement to parents of bus fare incurred transporting their children by public transit. Some parents received reimbursement for fares incurred sending their children to parochial schools. Everson (P) filed suit, arguing that reimbursement of parochial school fares violated both the state and federal constitutions. The trial court held that the state lacked authority to enact such a statute. The state court of appeals reversed, upholding the statute. The U.S. Supreme Court granted the appeal as to the federal question under the U.S. Constitution.

**ISSUE:** May a state reimburse the cost of transporting children to parochial schools if it does not support the schools and reimbursement is provided without regard to a particular religion?

**HOLDING AND DECISION:** (Black, J.) Yes. A state may reimburse the cost of transporting children to parochial schools if it does not support the schools and provides reimbursement without regard to a particular religion. The establishment clause is founded upon the framers' desire to prevent state aggression toward and interference with the free exercise of religion. It at least means that neither a state nor the federal government can create a church or pass laws that aid one religion or all religions or prefer one religion over another. Here, the state contributed no money to the parochial schools. It was not supporting them; rather, it merely was assisting parents to provide their children, regardless of their religion, with an education—a legitimate state interest. This does not violate the establishment clause. Affirmed.

**COMMENT:** *Everson* was one of the first cases to address whether public funds could be provided to parochial schools for secular purposes. Though only addressing the issue with respect to transportation reimbursement, it created the basic framework within which the Court later addressed the issue in other contexts. Most important, *Everson* made it clear that the establishment clause of the First Amendment applied to the states through the Fourteenth Amendment. This doctrine is called the child benefit doctrine: A state action providing a benefit to a parochial school is valid if it benefits the child and not the parochial school.

## Discussion Questions

1. What reason(s) did the court give for not striking down the law that allowed payments for transportation to public schools?

2. Do you have any examples of allowable reimbursements from a public school district to a religious school?

3. How would the Court have ruled if the parents receiving payment were parents of children attending a for-profit charter school?

---

# Lemon v. Kurtzman; Early v. Dicenso
# 403 U.S. 602, 91 S. Ct. 2105 (1971)

**GENERAL RULE OF LAW:** A state may not enact a system of assistance to parochial schools.

**PROCEDURE SUMMARY:**

**Plaintiffs:** Various individual taxpayers/citizens of Rhode Island and Pennsylvania

**Defendants:** Various state officials responsible for executing the educational assistance laws

**U.S. District Court Decision:** Action dismissed in Pennsylvania; motion to dismiss denied in Rhode Island

**U.S. Court of Appeals Decision:** Certiorari taken directly to Supreme Court; no court of appeals decision

**U.S. Supreme Court Decision:** Finding both programs unconstitutional, the Court held for the plaintiffs

**FACTS:** Rhode Island enacted an educational assistance program to aid private education, including parochial schools. The law provided for supplemental salaries, including supplements for parochial school teachers. Pennsylvania enacted a statute with a similar goal: to aid the purchase of supplies and textbooks in secular subjects. In both states, the vast majority of schools subject to the programs were religious, with church-affiliated personnel often providing instruction. Several citizens of each state brought actions in U.S. district courts in their respective states, in which they sought a declaration that the programs violated the First Amendment's separation of church and state. The district court in Pennsylvania dismissed the action filed there; the court in Rhode Island found the law of that state unconstitutional. The U.S. Supreme Court granted a direct **petition** for certiorari.

**ISSUE:** May a state enact a system of assistance to parochial schools?

**HOLDING AND DECISION:** (Burger, C. J.) No. A state may not enact a system of assistance to parochial schools. The First Amendment not only prohibits the passing of a law establishing religion, but it also prohibits the passing of a law even respecting such establishment. Therefore, for a law not to violate the

First Amendment, it must (1) have a secular purpose, (2) neither advance nor inhibit religion, and (3) not excessively entangle church and state. In regard to the Rhode Island law, it cannot be disputed that parochial schools constitute an integral part of the church's sweeping mission. A state cannot assume that a church-affiliated teacher will not indoctrinate his or her religious beliefs into pupils, even if the subject matter is secular. To supplement such a teacher's salary constitutes an unacceptable entanglement. As to the Pennsylvania law, the requirement that books and supplies be used for secular subjects necessarily implies surveillance and control. Such surveillance and control is precisely the kind of entanglement that the First Amendment prohibits. In view of this, the programs must be held to violate the First Amendment. The Rhode Island ruling is affirmed; the Pennsylvania ruling is reversed.

**COMMENT:** The separation of church and state in the First Amendment has always been one of the more problematic areas of constitutional law. On the one hand, a state cannot establish religion; on the other hand, it cannot abridge the right to worship. These two mandates are often at odds, and the Court has often had difficulty reconciling them. This particular case is one of the more important ones dealing with church and state. The three-part test described above has been the standard for establishment clause decisions since 1971.

## Discussion Questions

1. In *Lemon,* Pennsylvania and Rhode Island were found to be in violation of the establishment clause of the U.S. Constitution. What does the establishment clause say about government and religion?

2. Describe the three-part test established in *Lemon.*

3. How does the excessive entanglement test described in *Lemon* open the door for other types of government financial aid to parochial schools?

# Wolman v. Walter 433 U.S. 229, 97 S. Ct. 2593 (1977)

**GENERAL RULE OF LAW:** A state may provide aid to parochial schools if its provision promotes a secular legislative purpose while not principally or primarily advancing or inhibiting religion or fostering excessive government entanglement with religion.

**PROCEDURE SUMMARY:**

**Plaintiff:** Wolman (P), a resident taxpayer

**Defendant:** Walter (D), Ohio state superintendent

**U.S. District Court Decision:** Held for Walter (D), finding all provisions of the challenged statute constitutional

**U.S. Supreme Court Decision:** Reversed in part and affirmed in part

**FACTS:** Ohio enacted a statute that authorized the provision of books, instructional materials and equipment, standardized testing and scoring, diagnostic services, therapeutic services, and field trip transportation to private school pupils. An equal amount of funds was to be provided to public schools. Also, the amount expended per pupil in private schools could not exceed the amount expended per pupil in the public schools. Wolman (P) filed suit, contending that the provision of such aid violated the establishment clause. The district court held all the provisions constitutional, and Wolman (P) appealed.

**ISSUE:** May a state provide aid to parochial schools if such aid promotes a secular legislative purpose while not principally or primarily advancing or inhibiting religion or fostering excessive government entanglement with religion?

**HOLDING AND DECISION:** (Blackmun, J.) Yes. A state may provide aid to parochial schools if its provision promotes a secular legislative purpose while not principally or primarily advancing or inhibiting religion or fostering excessive government entanglement with religion. The provisions at issue—books, standardized testing and scoring, and diagnostic and therapeutic services—are constitutional. Wolman's (P) argument that the textbook provision was unconstitutional because it allowed for book substitutes lacks merit. The statute's separate provision defining instructional material and the stipulated definition of the term "textbook" both guard against abuse of this provision. The standardized testing and scoring serve a legitimate state interest by measuring student progress in only secular subjects. No private school personnel are involved in either drafting or scoring the tests, thereby eliminating the need for state supervision and excessive entanglement. Diagnostic services have little educational content and are not susceptible to ideological views. Therapeutic services, provided away from private facilities, do not advance religion or risk excessive entanglement because the services are provided by public employees only. Providing instructional materials, however, has the primary effect of advancing sectarian education and thereby supports the religious goals of the private schools. Further, providing transportation for field trips is impermissible because the schools, not the children, receive the aid and would require excessive supervision to ensure that the aid is used for secular purpose.

**COMMENT:** The fundamental issue for providing services, whether on or off the parochial school premises, is whether the government can provide the services in a neutral manner. Though the issue can be stated simply, it is clearly not as easily resolved. This has been evidenced by the approaches espoused by individual justices of the Supreme Court. Justice Brennan argued that simply the amount of state money being provided by the statute was sufficient excessive government entanglement to find the program impermissible. Justice Marshall proffered that the provision of therapeutic services was impermissible simply because it improved the performance of the parochial school students. On the other hand, Justice Stevens believed that providing transportation was permissible.

## Discussion Questions

1. Does the Ohio law in question meet the three-part *Lemon* test?

2. What is the relationship between the *Lemon* provisions and the decision in this case?

3. What impact does this decision have on private schools in regard to the use of state-funded materials? What safeguards are usually in place to ensure that the aid is used solely for secular purposes?

# Board of Ed. of the Westside Community Schools v. Mergens 496 U.S. 226, 110 S. Ct. 2356 (1990)

**GENERAL RULE OF LAW:** The Equal Access Act constitutionally prohibits limited open forum schools from denying student groups use of school premises based on the religious content of the groups' meetings.

**PROCEDURE SUMMARY:**

**Plaintiff:** Mergens (P), a Westside High School student

**Defendant:** Board of Education of the Westside Community Schools (Westside) (D)

**U.S. District Court Decision:** Held for Westside (D); the Equal Access Act did not apply to Westside (D), and Westside's (D) denial of Mergens' (P) request to use school premises was constitutional

**U.S. Court of Appeals Decision:** Reversed for Mergens (P), finding that the Act constitutionally prohibited Westside (D) from denying Mergens' (P) request

**U.S. Supreme Court Decision:** Affirmed

**FACTS:** Congress enacted the Equal Access Act, which prohibited public secondary schools (public forums by nature) from discriminating against students who wish to conduct meetings in the forum on the basis of the religious content of the meetings. Mergens (P) petitioned Westside (D) for permission to conduct a religious meeting on the Westside High School premises. Contending that the meeting would violate the establishment clause, Westside (D) denied the request. Mergens (P) filed suit and alleged that the denial of her request violated the Equal Access Act. Westside (D) responded that the Act did not apply to the school and was unconstitutional. The district court held for Westside (D) and upheld the denial. The court of appeals reversed, holding that the Act was constitutional and permissibly prohibited Westside (D) from denying the request. The U.S. Supreme Court granted review.

**ISSUE:** Does the Equal Access Act constitutionally prohibit open forum public schools from denying student groups use of school premises because of the religious content of the group's meetings?

**HOLDING AND DECISION:** (O'Connor, J.) Yes. The Equal Access Act constitutionally prohibits a limited open forum public school from denying a student group's request to use school premises on the basis of the religious content of the group's meetings. The Act grants equal access to both secular and religious speech. The Act also limits school official participation in religious meetings and requires that such meetings occur at noninstructional times. The Act thereby creates little risk of government endorsement of or coercion toward a particular religion. Further, the Act does not create a substantial risk of excessive entanglement of government and religion because it prohibits faculty participation in the meetings. The Act therefore satisfies the three-pronged test established in *Lemon,* and is constitutional on its face. Affirmed.

**COMMENT:** In *Widmar v. Vincent* (1981), the Court struck down a state university's action denying student groups access to university facilities for purposes of religious worship and teaching.[40] The Equal Access Act, enacted three years later, represented Congress's decision that an equal access policy serves a secular purpose and that high school students are not so immature as to make *Widmar* inapplicable in the high school context.

## Discussion Questions

1. In *Mergens,* the student group did not have a faculty adviser. Could the district have denied the group access to school facilities due to a lack of a faculty adviser instead of on religious grounds?

2. Under *Mergens,* can the building principal deny the student group access to the daily announcements to read an inspirational scripture passage each day?

3. Must a school district renting out school buildings to community groups also rent school facilities to a Christian organization for the purposes of conducting Sunday worship? What if the group that wanted to rent the buildings were members of a group that promoted Wicca?

# Zobrest et al. v. Catalina Foothills School District
# 509 U.S. 1, 113 S. Ct. 2462 (1993)

**GENERAL RULE OF LAW:** Government programs that neutrally provide benefits to a broad class of citizens, without reference to religious classification, are not readily subject to an establishment clause challenge simply because sectarian institutions may also receive an attenuated financial benefit.

**PROCEDURE SUMMARY:**

**Plaintiffs:** James Zobrest (P), a deaf child, and his parents

**Defendant:** Catalina Foothills School District (School District) (D)

**U.S. District Court Decision:** Granted defendant summary judgment on the ground that the interpreter would act as a conduit for the child's religious inculcation, thereby promoting his religious development at government expense and in violation of the establishment clause

**U.S. Court of Appeals Decision:** Affirmed because the IDEA, if applied as plaintiffs' petitioners proposed, would have the primary effect of advancing religion and thus would run afoul of the establishment clause. By placing its employee in the sectarian school, the government would create the appearance that it was a "joint sponsor" of the school's activities

**FACTS:** James Zobrest (P), deaf since birth, asked defendant school district to provide a sign language interpreter to accompany him to classes at a Roman Catholic high school in Tucson, Arizona, pursuant to the Individuals With Disabilities Education Act (IDEA) and its Arizona statutory counterpart.

James Zobrest (P) attended grades one through five in a school for the deaf and grades six through eight in a public school operated by **respondent** Catalina Foothills School District. While Zobrest (P) attended public school, the School District (D) furnished him with a sign language interpreter. For religious reasons, Zobrest's parents enrolled him for the ninth grade in Salpointe Catholic High School, a sectarian institution. When Zobrest (P) requested that the School District (D) supply him with an interpreter at Salpointe, the School District (D) concluded that providing an interpreter on the school's premises would violate the Constitution. The Arizona Attorney General concurred in this decision, and the School District (D) accordingly declined to provide the requested interpreter.

**ISSUE:** Does the establishment clause bar a public employee from being placed in a sectarian school in order to provide a student with services related to the student's disability?

**HOLDING AND DECISION:** (O'Conner, J.) No. The establishment clause does not necessarily prevent the defendant school district from furnishing a disabled child enrolled in a sectarian school with a sign language interpreter in order to facilitate his education. Government programs that neutrally provide benefits to a broad class of citizens defined without reference to religion are not readily subject to an establishment clause challenge just because sectarian institutions may also receive an attenuated financial benefit.[41] Reasoning similar to that employed in *Mueller* and *Witters* applies here. The service in this case is part of a general government program that distributes benefits neutrally to any child qualifying as disabled under the IDEA, without regard to the sectarian-nonsectarian or public-nonpublic nature of the school the child attends. By affording parents the freedom to select a school of their choice, the statute ensures that a government-paid interpreter will be present in a sectarian school only as a result of individual parents' private decisions. Since the IDEA creates no financial incentive for parents to choose a sectarian school, an interpreter's presence there cannot be attributed to state decision making. A public employee's physical presence in a sectarian school does not, by itself, make this the same type of aid that was disapproved in *Meek v. Pittenger* (1975) and *School Dist. of the City of Grand Rapids v. Ball* (1985).[42] In those cases, the challenged programs gave sectarian schools direct grants of government aid, instructional equipment and materials, teachers, and guidance counselors, thereby relieving these schools of costs they otherwise would have been forced to bear in order to educate their students. Here, the child is the primary beneficiary, and the school receives only an incidental benefit. In addition, an interpreter, unlike a teacher or guidance counselor, neither adds to nor subtracts from the sectarian school's environment. Rather, he merely interprets whatever material is presented to the class as a whole. Furthermore, there is no absolute bar to the placement of a public employee in a sectarian school.

**COMMENT:** In *Mueller,* the Court rejected an establishment clause challenge to a Minnesota law allowing taxpayers to deduct certain educational expenses from their state income tax, even though the vast majority of those deductions (perhaps over 90%) went to parents whose children attended sectarian schools. Two factors, aside from the states' traditionally broad taxing authority, influenced that decision: The law permits all parents, whether their children attend public school or private, to deduct their children's educational expenses; also, under Minnesota's scheme, public funds become available to sectarian schools only as a result of numerous private choices of parents of school-age children. This distinguished *Mueller* from other cases involving the direct transmission of assistance from the state to the schools themselves.

*Witters* was premised on virtually identical reasoning. The Court upheld an establishment clause challenge to the State of Washington's extension of vocational assistance, as part of a general state program, to a blind person studying to become a pastor at a private Christian college. Looking at the statute as a whole, the Court said that "any aid provided under Washington's program that ultimately flows to religious institutions does so only as a result of the genuinely independent and private choices of aid recipients. The program creates no financial incentive for students to undertake sectarian education." Like the law at issue in *Mueller*, Washington's program is made available generally and without regard to the sectarian-nonsectarian or public-nonpublic benefits. In light of these factors, Washington's program, even as applied to a student who sought state assistance so that he could become a pastor, would not advance religion in a manner inconsistent with the establishment clause.

The Court found that the same reasoning applied with equal force here. This actually may have been easier to decide than *Mueller* and *Witters*—here, no government funds ever found their way into the coffers of a sectarian school.

The school district countered that this case differed from *Mueller* and *Witters* because here, a public employee was required to be physically present in a sectarian school. The school district therefore argued that this case more closely resembles *Meek v. Pittenger* (1975) and *School Dist. of the City of Grand Rapids v. Ball* (1985). In *Meek,* the Court struck down a statute that provided massive aid to private schools, more than 75% of which were church-related, by way of a direct loan of teaching material and equipment. The material and equipment covered by the statute included maps, charts, and tape recorders. According to the respondent school district, if the government could not place a tape recorder in a sectarian school in *Meek,* then it surely could not place an interpreter in Salpointe. The statute in *Meek* also authorized state-paid personnel to furnish auxiliary services, including remedial and accelerated instruction and guidance counseling, on the premises of religious schools. That part of the statute also offended the First Amendment. *Ball* similarly involved two public programs that provided services on private school premises: Public employees taught classes to students in private school classrooms. Relying on *Meek,* the Court also found that those programs violated the Constitution. Seemingly, if the government could not provide educational services on the premises of sectarian schools in *Meek* and *Ball,* then surely it could not provide Zobrest with an interpreter on the premises of Salpointe.

Here, the Court held that the reliance on *Meek* and *Ball* was misplaced for two reasons. First, the programs in those cases, through direct grants of government aid, relieved sectarian schools of costs they otherwise would have borne in educating their students—the equivalent of a direct subsidy to religious schools from the state. The program challenged in *Ball,* which provided teachers in addition to instructional equipment and material, in effect "subsidized the religious functions of the parochial schools by taking over a substantial portion of their responsibility for teaching secular subjects. This kind of direct aid is indistinguishable from the provision of a direct cash subsidy to the religious school."

The extension of aid to James Zobrest, however, does not amount to an impermissible direct subsidy of Salpointe because Salpointe is not relieved of an expense that it otherwise would have assumed in educating its students. Also, any attenuated financial benefit that Salpointe ultimately received was directly attributable to the private choices of individual parents. Handicapped children, not sectarian schools, were the primary beneficiaries of the IDEA interpreter program. Any benefit to the sectarian school in this case was incidental at most.

Second, the task of a sign language interpreter is quite different from that of a teacher or guidance counselor. The establishment clause lays down no absolute bar to placing a public employee in a sectarian school. The Court felt that such a flat rule, smacking of antiquated notions of taint, would indeed exalt form over substance. Nothing in the record suggested that a sign language interpreter would do more than accurately interpret whatever material is presented to the class as a whole. In fact, ethical guidelines require interpreters to transmit everything that is said in exactly the same way it was intended. Zobrest's parents chose, of their own free will, to place him in a pervasively sectarian environment. The sign language interpreter they requested would neither add to nor subtract from that environment, and hence the provision of such assistance was not barred by the establishment clause.

## Discussion Questions

1. Compare the results of *Zobrest* with the decision made by the Supreme Court in *McCollum*.

2. The Supreme Court referred to special education students as a "broad class of citizens defined without reference to religion" and allowed the interpreter into the Catholic school. Do you think the Court would also consider low-income students a "broad class of citizens defined without reference to religion" and allow special tutoring to low-income students who attend a religious school? Why or why not?

3. What is the "clear secular purpose" of the IDEA, now IDEIA?

4. May public school employees whose work is done at a religious school spend all of their time inside the school building?

# Good News Club v. Milford Central School
# 533 U.S. 98, 121 S. Ct. 2093 (2001)

**GENERAL RULE OF LAW:** A school district violates an organization's free speech rights when it excludes it from meeting after hours at the school.

**PROCEDURE SUMMARY:**

**Plaintiff:** Good News Club (P)

**Defendant:** Milford Central School (Milford) (D)

**U.S. District Court Decision:** Granted summary judgment in favor of Milford (D)

**U.S. Court of Appeals Decision:** Affirmed

**U.S. Supreme Court Decision:** Reversed

**FACTS:** Under New York law, respondent Milford (D) enacted a policy authorizing district residents to use its building after school for, among other things, (1) instruction in education, learning, or the arts and (2) social, civic, recreational, and entertainment uses pertaining to the community welfare. Stephen and Darleen Fournier, district residents eligible to use the school's facilities upon approval of their proposed use, are sponsors of the Good News Club (P), a private Christian organization for children aged 6 to 12. Pursuant to Milford's (D) policy, they submitted a request to hold the Club's weekly afterschool meetings in the school. Milford (D) denied the request on the ground that the proposed use—to sing songs, hear Bible lessons, memorize scripture, and pray—was the equivalent of religious worship prohibited by the community use policy. The Good News Club (P) filed suit. It alleged that the denial of the Club's application violated its free speech rights under the First and Fourteenth Amendments. The District Court ultimately granted Milford (D) summary judgment in finding the Club's subject matter to be religious in nature, not merely a discussion of secular matters from a religious perspective otherwise permitted by Milford (D). Because Milford (D) had not allowed other groups providing religious instruction to use its limited public forum, the court held that Milford (D) could deny the Club (P) access without engaging in unconstitutional viewpoint discrimination.

**ISSUE:** May a school district deny a religious group after-hours access to its buildings in order to engage in religious instruction?

**HOLDING AND DECISION:** (Thomas, J.) No. When the state establishes a limited public forum, the state is not required to allow persons to engage in every type of speech. The state may be justified in reserving its forum for certain groups or for the discussion of certain topics. The state's power to restrict speech, however, is not without limits. The restriction must not discriminate against speech on the basis of viewpoint, and the restriction must be reasonable in light of the purpose served by the forum. Speech discussing otherwise permissible subjects cannot be excluded from a limited public forum on the ground that the subject is discussed from a religious viewpoint. The guarantee of neutrality is respected, not offended, when the government, following neutral criteria and evenhanded policies, extends benefits to recipients whose ideologies and viewpoints (including religious ones) are broad and diverse.

**COMMENT:** The problem discussed in this case is a common one for school districts. Many allow outside organizations to utilize school facilities after school hours. Here, the school district did not want to allow a religious group to utilize the facility because the district believed that doing so would violate the establishment clause. The decision set the precedent that a school district may not deny a religious group after-hours access to its buildings in order to engage in religious instruction. Restriction would violate the group's free speech rights. Because the school district established a limited public forum, it must not discriminate against speech on the basis of viewpoint. Here the restricted viewpoint was a religious one. Furthermore, any restrictions that the school board established must be reasonable. Limiting religious speech, a subject matter distinction, was not permissible. The principle being upheld was the guarantee of neutrality, a revered First Amendment principle.

## Discussion Questions

1. If a school district denies a nontraditional religious group access to its buildings after school, is it violating that group's free speech rights?

2. What groups may a school deny access to its buildings?

3. Will a school violate the establishment clause by offering financial incentives to certain organizations that hold meetings at the school?

# Susan Tave Zelman, Superintendent of Public Instruction of Ohio, v. Simmons-Harris 536 U.S. 639, 122 S. Ct. 2460 (2002)

**GENERAL RULE OF LAW:** A program involving true private choice to aid poor schoolchildren, with no evidence that the state deliberately skewed incentives toward religious schools, is sufficient for the program to survive establishment clause scrutiny.

**PROCEDURE SUMMARY:**

**Plaintiff:** Doris Simmons-Harris (P), on behalf of Ohio taxpayers

**Defendant:** Susan Tave Zellman (D), superintendent of public instruction of Ohio

**U.S. District Court Decision:** Summary judgment in favor of Simmons-Harris (P)

**U.S. Court of Appeals Decision:** Affirmed

**U.S. Supreme Court Decision:** Reversed

**FACTS:** The State of Ohio established a pilot program to provide educational choices to families with children who reside in the Cleveland City School District. Cleveland's public schools had been among the worst-performing public schools in the nation. The program provided tuition aid for students to attend a participating public or private school of their parents' choosing and tutorial aid for students who chose to remain enrolled in public school. Doris Simmons-Harris (P), on behalf of Ohio taxpayers, sought to enjoin the program on the ground that it violated the establishment clause. The Federal District Court granted Simmons-Harris (P) summary judgment, and the Sixth Circuit affirmed. The Supreme Court reversed, holding that the program was entirely neutral with respect to religion. It provided benefits directly to a wide spectrum of individuals, defined only by financial need and residence in a particular school district. It permitted such individuals to exercise genuine choice among options—public and private, secular and religious. The program was, therefore, a program of true private choice. In keeping with an unbroken line of decisions rejecting challenges to similar programs, the Court held that the program did not offend the establishment clause.

**ISSUE:** Does a program enacted for the valid secular purpose of providing educational assistance to poor children in a demonstrably failing public school system have the forbidden effect of advancing religion?

**HOLDING AND DECISION:** (Rehnquist, C.J.) No. The establishment clause of the First Amendment, applied to the states through the Fourteenth Amendment, prevents a state from enacting laws that have the "purpose" or "effect" of advancing or inhibiting religion. That a program is one of true private choice, with no evidence that the state deliberately skewed incentives toward religious schools, is sufficient for the program to survive scrutiny under the establishment clause. The amount of government aid channeled to religious institutions by individual aid recipients is not relevant to the constitutional inquiry of whether a government program violates the establishment clause. Government programs that neutrally provide benefits to a broad class of citizens defined without reference to religion are not readily subject to an establishment clause challenge. No reasonable observer would think a neutral program of private choice, in which state aid reaches religious schools solely as a result of the numerous independent decisions of private individuals, carries with it the imprimatur of government endorsement. The constitutionality of a neutral educational aid program does not turn on whether students primarily chose to attend, and therefore have state funds used at, sectarian rather than secular schools.

**COMMENT:** This case has already become almost infamous in school circles because it allowed vouchers to go to private (and public) schools. School districts that are under pressure across the country believe that this decision will encourage the expansion of voucher programs and accordingly further weaken underfunded school systems subject to charter/community school competition.

The Ohio legislature established this pilot program to provide educational choices to families with children who resided in the poor-performing Cleveland Municipal School District. Tuition aid was provided for students to attend a participating public or private school of their parents' choosing. Opponents believed that this violated the establishment clause. Even though more than 90% of the participating schools were religious, the Supreme Court held that the program was entirely neutral with respect to religion. It provided benefits to individuals based only on financial need and residence, providing genuine choice among public and private, secular and religious. The program was, therefore, a program of true private choice. In keeping with an unbroken line of decisions rejecting challenges to similar programs, the Court held that the program did not offend the establishment clause because it did not advance religion. Whether large amounts of money eventually went to religious institutions was not relevant because the issue was whether the programs neutrally provided benefits without reference to religion. Some persuasively argue that this private choice program carries the imprimatur of government endorsement. The Court, however, believed that constitutionality—of neutral educational aid—simply does not turn on whether and why, in a particular area at a particular time, most private schools are run by religious organizations or most recipients choose to use the aid at a religious school.

## Discussion Questions

1. What is the real fear of school professionals if voucher programs continue to expand?

2. If almost all participating schools are religious in nature, how can the public see this as anything but government support of religion?

3. Does this case settle the question of whether voucher programs are constitutional?

Additional case briefs can be found on the SAGE Web site at the following address:
http://www.sagepub.com/aquilacasebriefs

# NOTES

1. Everson v. Board of Education of the Township of Ewing, 330 U.S. 1, 67 S. Ct. 504 (1947).
2. Reynolds v. United States, 98 U.S. 145 (1879).
3. Lemon v. Kurtzman, 403 U.S. 602, 91 S. Ct. 2105 (1971).
4. Lee v. Weisman, 505 U.S. 577 (1992).
5. Wisconsin v. Yoder, 406 U.S. 205 (1972).
6. Zobrest et al. v. Catalina Foothills School District, 113 S. Ct. 2462 (1993).
7. Zelman v. Simmons-Harris, 536 U.S. 639, 122 S. Ct. 2460 (2002).
8. See Everson v. Board of Education of the Township of Ewing, 330 U.S. 1, 67 S. Ct. 504 (1947).
9. See Lemon v. Kurtzman, 403 U.S. 602, 91 S. Ct. 2105 (1971).
10. See School Dist. of the City of Grand Rapids v. Ball, 473 U.S. 373 (1985).
11. See People of State of Illinois ex rel. McCollum v. Board of Ed. of School Dist. No. 71, Champaign County, 333 U.S. 203, 68 S. Ct. 461 (1948) and Zorach v. Clauson, 343 U.S. 306 (1952).
12. Wolman v. Walter, 444 U.S. 801 (1977).
13. See Cochran v. Louisiana State Bd. of Ed., 281 U.S. 370, 50 S. Ct. 335 (1930).
14. See Mallory v. Barrera, 544 S. W. 2d 556 (1976).
15. See Rosenberger v. Rector of University of Virginia, 515 U.S. 819 (1995).
16. School Dist. of the City of Grand Rapids v. Ball, 473 U.S. 373 (1985).
17. See Mitchell v. Helms, 530 U.S. 1296 (2000).
18. See Board of Ed. of Central School Dist. No.1 v. Allen, 392 U.S. 236, 88 S. Ct. 1923 (1968).
19. See Everson v. Board of Education of the Township of Ewing, 330 U.S. 1, 67 S. Ct. 504 (1947).
20. See Aguilar v. Felton, 473 U.S. 402, 105 S. Ct. 3232 (1985).
21. See Agostini v. Felton, 117 S. Ct. (1997).
22. See Lemon v. Kurtzman, 403 U.S. 602, 91 S. Ct. 2105 (1971), in which the Supreme Court enunciated a three-part test for determining whether a particular government action will withstand an establishment clause challenge. See Aguilar v. Felton, 473 U.S. 402 105 S. Ct. 3232 (1985), in which the Supreme Court held that a New York City program that used federal funds received under Title I violated the establishment clause.
23. See Wolman v. Walter, 433 U.S. 229 (1977).
24. Board of Education of Kiryas Joel Village School District v. Louis Grumet, 114 S. Ct. 2481 (1994).
25. Jackson v. Benson, 578 N. W. 2d 602 (Wis.1998); Bush v. Holmes, 767 So.2d 668 (Fla. Dist. Ct. App. 2000).
26. Zelman v. Simmons-Harris, 536 U.S. 639, 122 S. Ct. 2460 (2002); Committee for Public Education v. Nyquist, 413 U.S. 756, 93 S. Ct. 2814 (1973).
27. See Mueller v. Allen, 463 U.S. 388, 103 S. Ct. 3062 (1983).
28. See Santa Fe Independent School District v. Doe, 530 U.S. 290 (2000).
29. See People of State of Illinois ex rel. McCollum v. Board of Ed. of School Dist. No. 71, Champaign County, 333 U.S. 203, 68 S. Ct. 461 (1948).
30. See Zorach v. Clauson, 343 U.S. 306, 72 S. Ct. 679 (1952).
31. See School Dist. of Abington Township, Pennsylvania v. Schempp, 374 U.S. 203, 83 S. Ct. 1560 (1963).
32. See County of Allegheny v. ACLU, Greater Pittsburgh Chapter, 492 U.S. 573, 109 S. Ct. 3086 (1989).
33. See Lee v. Weisman, 112 S. Ct. 2649 (1992).
34. West Virginia v. Barnette, 319 U.S. 624 (1943).
35. Wisconsin v. Yoder, 406 U.S. 205 (1972).

36.  See Mitchell v. Helms, 530 U.S. 1296 (2000).

37.  Trietley v. Board of Ed. of Buffalo, 409 N.Y. S. 2d 912, 915 (App. Div. 1978).

38.  Deeper Life Christian Fellowship, Inc. v. Sobol, 948 F. 2d 79, 83–94 (1991).

39.  Cornelius v. NAACP Legal Defense and Education Fund, 473 U. S. 788 (1985).

40.  Widmar v. Vincent, 454 U.S. 263, 102 S. Ct. 269 (1981).

41.  See Mueller v. Allen, 463 U.S. 388, 103 S. Ct. 3062 (1983); Witters v. Washington Dept. of Services for Blind, 474 U.S. 481 (1986).

42.  Meek v. Pittenger, 421 U. S. 349 (1975); School Dist. of the City of Grand Rapids v. Ball, 473 U.S. 373 (1985).

# 3

## No Child Left Behind Act

*I talk about No Child Left Behind like Ivory soap: It's 99.9 percent pure or something. . . . There's not much needed in the way of change.*

—Margaret Spellings, Secretary of Education

## OVERVIEW · · · · · · · · · · · · · · · · · · · · · · · · · · · · · · · · · · · · · · · · · · ·

The results of the No Child Left Behind Act (NCLB) have been mixed, at best. Initially, many school people were skeptical, but the guarantee that this was not another "unfunded mandate" held great promise. Further, the underlying guarantee that all children would be able to read by school year 2012–2013 (a guarantee later seemingly expanded to include mathematics) was a compelling promise. However, as 2012 nears, NCLB's implementation has been disappointing, with concerns developing almost weekly. Some argue that high-stakes assessment, with its potentially dire consequences, has forced many classrooms into becoming nothing more than "test-prep centers."

The No Child Left Behind Act was enacted January 8, 2002, expanding choices for parents and focusing resources on proven educational methods while providing accountability for results. The NCLB law is widely considered the most significant federal education act since Congress approved its original version, the Elementary and Secondary Education Act (ESEA), in 1965. As an education reform **bill**, NCLB has dramatically increased the role of the federal government in K–12 education. It encompasses 45 programs while continuing ESEA's focus on increasing student achievement, improving accountability, and making sure that fully qualified teachers teach all children. Additionally, parents have the right to request information about the qualifications of their child's teacher and any paraprofessionals who work with their child.

Whether Education Secretary Margaret Spellings is correct or not in her assertion that the NCLB is close to perfect (like Ivory soap) and needs little change is certainly open to

63

question. Of course, it is not surprising that Spellings strongly supports the law. As President George W. Bush's domestic policy chief, she helped craft the NCLB and now enforces it as his top education official. Nevertheless, her view that the law needs little change is notable because it differs so sharply from other stakeholders, including many teachers, school administrators, and lawmakers. Further, more than 80 organizations have signed a statement urging fundamental changes, in areas such as how student progress is measured and how schools are penalized when they fall short.

NCLB is roughly 1,100 pages and includes thousands of pages of additional rules and expensive regulations. NCLB's reauthorizing legislation will probably even surpass these massive numbers in paperwork and complexity. The first major federal court challenge to NCLB is *Pontiac v. Spellings,* in which a diverse group of school districts and education associations is asking the court to declare that the law means what it says and prevent the U.S. Department of Education from denying federal funds to states and school districts that refuse to spend their own money on complying with the law's regulations.[1] These regulations, according to the plaintiffs, form a bureaucratic maze, often to the point of costly absurdity.

The basic components of NCLB deal with accountability in the form of adequate yearly progress and school improvement and teacher and paraprofessional quality. The new law requires all students, not only those eligible for Title I services, to make adequate yearly progress (AYP) on a series of standardized tests. AYP will be the measure of student improvement against which schools will be judged for purposes of meeting federal standards. The AYP requirements are proving to be too difficult to achieve, especially for those schools serving low-income students, because school districts must meet AYP in many subject areas for each minority group as well as for all students. These standards are extremely difficult for diverse school districts to attain and to retain. Even normally high-performing districts are running afoul of AYP in subgroups of children with disabilities, resulting in the district sometimes being designated as a district needing "school improvement," a negative designation not acceptable to normally high-performing school districts. A school's failure to make AYP over a number of years could lead to a series of corrective actions that may ultimately result in restructuring, closure, or takeover of the school by the state or a private management company.

In reference to teacher quality, NCLB stresses the important role that teacher quality plays in promoting student achievement. It required that all teachers be "highly qualified" in the subjects they teach by the end of the 2005–2006 school year. "Highly qualified" means that public elementary and secondary school teachers must have obtained full state certification or passed the state teacher licensing examination; hold a license to teach in the state in which they are teaching; and not have had a certificate or license requirement waived on an emergency, temporary, or provisional basis. There are special concerns regarding "highly qualified" status for special education teachers who are designated as teachers of record who teach children with disabilities and general education students in the same classroom.

The premise is that parents and teachers will know how well their schools are doing because since the 2002–2003 school year, states and local school districts have had to publish annual report cards in an easy-to-understand format to inform parents and the community. These report cards must provide information about students' achievement on state assessments compared to other students in the state and district, graduation rates, and teacher qualifications/credentials.

NCLB, through the most recent Title I authorization, emphasizes the same high standards and accountability for paraprofessionals as it does for teachers and students. NCLB contains some significant changes involving the paraprofessionals' qualifications and duties. Like teachers, paraprofessionals must meet new educational requirements in order to continue as or to become a Title I paraprofessional. In addition, the new law specifically lists the duties that paraprofessionals should perform. A newly hired paraprofessional must have completed two years of postsecondary education or be a high school graduate who can demonstrate on a "formal state or local academic assessment" the skills necessary to assist in the classroom instruction of reading, writing, and mathematics.

## Case Study

### Another Unfunded Mandate

You are superintendent of a small urban district. Your student population is entirely minority, with no white students and only a few non-English-speaking students. The property value of the homes in your school district is extremely low compared to suburban districts and even the large urban district that abuts your district. Historically, the performance of your students has been poor on all state tests. The new performance mandates required by NCLB seem almost impossible to meet. Each of your schools is failing the new national standards. You have provided as much funding as you can afford, but nothing seems to help. The cost to implement the highly qualified teacher provisions has also caused you to spend money that the district does not have. When NCLB was enacted, the government guaranteed that there would be no unfunded mandates and specifically stated that it shall be construed not to "mandate a State or any subdivision thereof to spend any funds or incur any costs not paid for under this Act." This does not seem to be the case because you must provide more and more funds that you do not have. You have decided to join a group that plans to sue the federal government for failing to live up to its promise of not requiring mandates without funding them (unfunded mandates).

### Discussion Questions

1. Will you be supported in your argument that "if it's not funded, it's not required" relieves you of the obligation to meet these federal mandates?

2. Do you think that school districts are overreacting to the requirements of NCLB? Why?

3. Does NCLB provide support for private schools? School choice programs?

# IMPORTANT CONCEPTS

- **The No Child Left Behind Act:** The No Child Left Behind Act was enacted January 8, 2002, to expand choices for parents, to focus resources on proven educational methods, and to provide accountability for results.

- **Implementation has been criticized:** High-stakes assessment, with its potentially dire consequences, has forced many classrooms to become test-prep centers.

- **AYP is too difficult to achieve:** The adequate yearly progress (AYP) provisions of NCLB will cause many schools to fail, especially those serving low-income students.

- **Consequences of failure to make AYP:** A school's failure to make AYP over a number of years will lead to a series of corrective actions that may ultimately result in restructuring, closure, or takeover of the school by the state or a private management company. In addition, failing schools may also be denied some funding.

- **Teachers must be certified:** Being highly qualified means that public elementary and secondary school teachers must have obtained full state certification or have passed the state teacher licensing examination; hold a license to teach in the state; and not have had a certificate or license requirement waived on an emergency, temporary, or provisional basis.

- **Teachers must be highly qualified:** A teacher is deemed highly qualified if she has three things: (1) a bachelor's degree; (2) full state certification or licensure; and (3) the ability to prove that she knows all the subjects she teaches.

- **Paraprofessionals must be highly qualified:** To become a paraprofessional in a program that receives Title I funds, a newly hired paraprofessional must have completed two years of postsecondary education or be a high school graduate who can demonstrate on a "formal state or local academic assessment" the skills necessary to assist in the classroom instruction of reading, writing, and mathematics.

- **Annual report cards:** Parents and teachers know how well their schools are doing because since the 2002–2003 school year, states and school districts have had to publish annual report cards in an easy-to-understand format for parents and the community. These report cards provide information about student achievement on state assessments vis-à-vis other students in the state and district, graduation rates, schools needing improvement, and teacher qualifications/credentials.

- ***Pontiac v. Spellings:*** The first major federal court challenge to NCLB was *Pontiac v. Spellings*. A diverse group of school districts and education associations asked the court to effectuate the plain meaning of the law and prevent the U.S. Department of Education from denying federal funds to states and school districts that refuse to spend their own money on the law's regulations.

- **Drill and kill:** "Drill and kill" has become the standard protocol for many school districts because schools must improve to avoid NCLB punishment.

# NO CHILD LEFT BEHIND ACT

The reauthorization of the Elementary and Secondary Education Act (ESEA)—which has been renamed the No Child Left Behind Act (NCLB)—was enacted January 8, 2002, to expand choices for parents, to focus resources on proven educational methods, and to provide results-based accountability. NCLB is an education reform bill that has dramatically increased the role of the federal government in K–12 education. It encompasses 45 programs while continuing ESEA's focus on increasing student achievement, improving accountability, and making sure that fully qualified teachers teach all children. Further, parents have the right to request information about the qualifications of their child's teacher and any paraprofessionals who work with their child.

When NCLB was enacted, the promise was real. The offer included widespread achievement gains among students, with significant increases in federal funding to support those gains. The results have been mixed, at best. Many educational professionals were skeptical, but the guarantee that this was not another "unfunded mandate" held great promise. However, NCLB's implementation has been disappointing, and recently concerns have developed almost weekly. High-stakes assessment, with its potentially dire consequences, has forced many classrooms to become test-prep centers. Many schools will fail to meet AYP, especially those serving low-income students. Supposedly, 19 blue ribbon schools have already been identified as "low achieving." Is this a validation of those who argue that further refinement is needed?

# COMPONENTS OF THE NCLB ACT

## Accountability

*Adequate Yearly Progress (AYP).* The new law requires all students to meet AYP, not just those eligible for Title I services. AYP has become the measure of student improvement against which schools will be judged for purposes of meeting federal standards. A school's failure to make AYP over a number of years will lead to a series of corrective actions that may ultimately result in restructuring, closure, or takeover of the school by the state or a private management company. Each state must set measurable goals for student achievement on state tests in order to ensure that students are "proficient" (as defined by the state) in reading and math within 12 years. Using the 2001–2002 school year as the baseline set of scores, states are required to set numerical targets (in each subject and grade) for the percentage of students who will be proficient over the next 12 years. The NCLB requires that all students in Grades 3 to 8 undertake annual reading and math assessments.

States select and administer their own tests, and they had until the 2005–2006 school year to develop and implement these assessments. The law authorizes federal funding for the development of these tests. States were also required to develop science content standards by 2005–2006 and to begin administering state science assessments in the 2007–2008 school year. Science assessments are required at least once in Grades 3–5, 6–8, and 10–12.

Finally, states will be required to participate in the National Assessment of Educational Progress (NAEP) every other year, provided that federal funding is sufficient to cover the cost of test administration. However, the results of NAEP cannot serve as the basis for sanctioning states, school districts, schools, or students. All students must take these tests. Results of these tests will be broken down within each state by school district and school, as well as by gender, each major racial and ethnic group, disabled status, limited English proficient (LEP) status, economically disadvantaged status, and migrant status. Each subgroup must make AYP. Additionally, the law requires that students with disabilities, English language learners, and all others be tested; however, appropriate modifications and accommodations (consistent with IDEIA) are permitted, where needed, for students with special needs.

*School Improvement.* The new law imposes sanctions based primarily on students' performance on state assessments. Sanctions are grouped into three categories: school improvement, corrective action, and school restructuring.

A school that fails two years in a row (e.g., Years 1 and 2, or 2002–2003 and 2003–2004) to meet AYP—or the numerical goal set by the state for that academic year—for all subgroups of students will be placed in school improvement status (Year 3). In the first year of school improvement, a school will be required to

1. prepare a two-year improvement plan;

2. use at least 10% of its Title I funds for professional development;

3. provide public school choice (if allowable by state law), with 5% to 15% of Title I funds used to pay for transportation costs to implement school choice;

4. notify parents of the school's status;

5. receive technical assistance from the school district; and

6. receive federal school improvement funds.

If a school fails to meet AYP three years in a row, it is placed in a second year of school improvement (Year 4). Such schools will be required to continue the activities from the first year of school improvement and provide supplemental services. These include before school and after school tutoring for low-achieving, disadvantaged students within that school, among other requirements. Parents will choose providers of supplemental services from a list of state-approved providers, which may include the district or outside groups. These outside groups include community-based organizations or for-profit companies, such as the Sylvan Learning systems. An additional 10% of the school district's Title I funds may be used for either these services or transportation to implement public school choice.

If a school again fails to meet AYP for the fourth year in a row, it is placed in "corrective action" (Year 5). Such schools must continue to provide public school choice and supplemental services and do at least one of the following:

1. Implement a new curriculum.

2. Decrease local decision making.

3. Appoint an outside expert.

4. Extend the school day or year.

5. Replace staff relevant to failure.

6. Restructure internal organization.

If a school again fails to meet AYP (fifth year in a row), it is placed in a second year of "corrective action" (Year 6). Such schools must continue to provide public school choice and supplemental services, and a plan must be prepared and arrangements made for restructuring, including at least one of the following:

1. Reopen as a charter school.

2. Replace the principal and other staff deemed relevant to failure.

3. Turn the school over to a private management company.

4. Turn the school over to the state.

5. Make other major reforms.

## Teacher Quality

It is important to note that NCLB stresses the essential role that teacher quality plays in promoting student achievement. NCLB requires that all teachers hired and teaching in a program supported with funds under Title I must be "highly qualified." It also requires that all teachers must be highly qualified in the subjects they teach by the end of the 2005–2006 school year. To be highly qualified, public elementary and secondary school teachers must have obtained full state certification or passed the state teacher licensing examination; hold a license to teach in the state; and not have had a certificate or license requirement waived on an emergency, temporary, or provisional basis. Elementary teachers who are new to the profession must hold at least a bachelor's degree and must demonstrate, by passing a rigorous state test, subject knowledge and teaching skill in reading, writing, mathematics, and other areas of the basic elementary school curriculum. Similarly, secondary school teachers who are new to the profession must hold at least a bachelor's degree and must demonstrate a high level of competence in each of the academic subjects they teach. This may be accomplished by passing a rigorous state subject matter test. Alternatively, teachers may complete an undergraduate major in the subject, a graduate degree, or coursework equivalent to an undergraduate academic major. Current elementary, middle, and secondary teachers who are not new to the profession must hold at least a bachelor's degree and must have met similar standards. Teachers who do not meet the above qualifications may undergo a high objective state evaluation to demonstrate competence in all academic subjects.

## Parental Notice

Parental notice is ensured because since the 2002–2003 school year, states and school districts have been required to publish annual report cards. These report cards must be published in an easy-to-understand format to help parents and the community understand how well their schools are doing. These report cards will provide information about student achievement on state assessments vis-à-vis other students in the state and district, graduation rates, schools that are in need of improvement, and teacher qualifications/credentials. Regardless of the criticism of NCLB, the provisions and implementation of the parental notice practices have been widely applauded.

## Paraprofessionals

Because paraprofessionals work alongside teachers and play a key role in most Title I programs, they often help provide the extra academic support that students need to meet the new high standards of achievement. With this in mind, NCLB, through the last Title I authorization, emphasizes the same high standards and accountability for paraprofessionals as it does for teachers and students. Previously, Title I–funded paraprofessionals were required to have a high school diploma, and there were no limits on their duties. Under NCLB, the law contains some significant changes involving the paraprofessionals' qualifications and duties; the new reauthorization seems to retain these new standards. Like the requirements for teachers, the law lists new educational requirements that paraprofessionals must meet (discussed above) in order to continue as or become Title I paraprofessionals. In addition, the new law specifically lists the duties that paraprofessionals should perform.

Under NCLB, paraprofessionals in Title I programs hired after January 8, 2002 had will have to meet new standards. As an example, to become a paraprofessional in a program that receives Title I funds, a newly hired paraprofessional must have completed two years of postsecondary education or be a high school graduate who can demonstrate on a "formal state or local academic assessment" the skills necessary to assist in the classroom instruction of reading, writing, and mathematics.

## CONCERNS AND RELATED ISSUES

### Political Concerns

Although there is resounding debate about the effectiveness of NCLB, few would argue about its critical importance in this period of educational change. No matter how good NCLB may be, it will suffer from the idiosyncrasies of our political system. While elementary and secondary education is almost universally (and possibly unfairly) acknowledged as inadequate, NCLB may fail because of the low success rate of public policy initiatives. This is partially due to inadequate technical knowledge to deliver policy outcomes, but more often because of the combative nature of the political structure, which must seemingly create winners and losers and conflicting views of success and failure. This politicizing is now causing NCLB to be tossed about like the political football that it has become.

### Flawed and Underfunded

Many argue that this law is seriously flawed as well as underfunded. But the importance of NCLB's goals has led most to work to "fix and fund" the law. At the same time, others have already filed legal challenges. Some state, as well as some individual, causes of action have already surfaced, with other individualized issues certain to develop. In addition to the court suit included in the Case Briefs below, there are other pending issues, for example, other developing state lawsuits as well as recently enacted Utah legislation favoring state legislation over

NCLB. The Utah legislature passed House Bill 1001, directing state education officials to comply with state education goals before they consider the provisions of the federal NCLB. Nevertheless, the first major federal court challenge to NCLB is *Pontiac v. Spellings*. A diverse group of school districts and education associations is asking the court to declare that the law means what it says and prevent the U.S. Department of Education from denying federal funds to states and school districts that refuse to spend their own money on the law's regulations. NCLB is roughly 1,100 pages and includes thousands of pages of additional rules and expensive regulations. These regulations, according to the plaintiffs, form a bureaucratic maze, often to the point of costly absurdity. For example, they cite regulations that exempt newly arrived immigrant students from standardized reading tests, but not the math tests. Some correctly argue that the absence of just two students in a low-incidence student category on testing day can give an entire school a federal failing label in that subgroup. The reason for this is that every school must meet AYP in all subgroups (potentially 37 subgroups), and there is no difference in the result for a school that for several consecutive years meets AYP in 36 of 37 subgroups versus a school that only meets AYP in 1 subgroup. This creates a confusing and seemingly unfair situation. In theory, students can transfer from a "failing" school to a neighboring school, even if the neighboring school is severely overcrowded; additionally, the failing school district has to pay the transfer costs. An especially galling point is that the cost to meet the law's regulations is expensive; for example, Texas spends $1.2 billion annually, diverting roughly 300 tax dollars per student from classrooms to meet federal rules and regulations.

## School Choice and Other Traditional Concerns

Many opponents argue that NCLB, with its high-stakes assessment, has created a climate of desperation. The potentially dire consequences of low student performance scores has forced many classrooms to alter traditional educational instruction to focus on test preparation so that their individual classroom scores—as well as the school and school district's scores—do not reflect negatively on their performance. This phenomenon has been called "drill and kill," and it is unquestionable that it has become the standard protocol for many school districts that have schools that must improve or face internal and external negative consequences. This does not mean that there are not many positive aspects of NCLB, but opponents believe that the AYP provisions of NCLB will cause many schools to fail, especially those serving low-income students. Furthermore, many fear that there will continue to be a reduced emphasis on social studies, art, music, and other programs because of the focus on high-stakes standardized testing. This uncomfortable situation has developed at the same time as the expansion of educational alternatives in the form of school choice. As schools experience difficulties with external performance measures, there has been a radical increase in the number of students attending charter and voucher schools. In some cases, these schools have been relieved (at least initially) from NCLB requirements.

## Problems With "Highly Qualified" Provisions

When President George W. Bush and the U.S. Department of Education signed NCLB into law, the stated goal was to improve school performance. A teacher is deemed highly qualified if he or she has three things: (1) a bachelor's degree; (2) full state certification or licensure; and (3) proof that he or she knows all the subjects he or she teaches. Most realize that teachers make the most difference in student achievement. Therefore, to improve student performance, the adherents of NCLB have imposed the "highly qualified teacher" requirement. NCLB mandated that every teacher of a core academic subject be "highly qualified" by the end of the 2005–2006 school year. Unfortunately, there is little agreement on what constitutes "teacher quality" or what needs to be done to ensure that every student has access to high-quality teachers (HQT). Confounding the highly qualified teacher discussion is the concern about funding and politics. Clearly, the costs are going to be, and have already been, significant. More important is that NCLB's attempt to professionalize the teaching force threatens public education's traditional authority structure. Further, HQT has resulted in thousands of teachers having to complete additional coursework and professional development. It is not only costly but takes time to complete this additional work. An interesting anomaly is that a teacher may take classes to be highly qualified, and then if a teaching assignment needs to be changed (common in smaller districts), the result may be that she is no longer highly qualified in the new assignment.

## Highly Qualified Special Education Teachers

The more difficult problem will be with highly qualified special education teachers at the secondary level. The problem is complicated by specific classroom discipline issues, especially when the special education teacher must work in conjunction with the regular teacher. Essentially, every special education teacher who teaches a traditional subject must be highly qualified in that specific discipline. Figure 3.1 describes what constitutes a highly qualified teacher under IDEIA.

# PRO AND CON

## Pro: NCLB is Holding Educators' Feet to the Fire

While you may call NCLB unwieldy, underfunded, arbitrary, or stigmatizing, it is undeniably providing a healthy focus on poorly performing students—especially minorities and the poor. Just because large urban schools look bad on the NCLB report cards, it should not be assumed that a specific school or district has incompetent staff and teachers. The numbers in the headlines look bad, but these numbers are driven by demographics; many of the worst-performing schools are courageously struggling to educate an unusually high number of disadvantaged children. While exasperating, it is also true that an urban poor school can be doing very well in many or most respects, yet end up on the "failing" side of the complex matrix that is used to classify schools. With as many as 37 categories and with scores cross-tracked by subject, ethnicity, poverty, and related factors, otherwise fine schools may be "in need of improvement." For example, if not enough special education students do well enough in reading, the school may fall into an improvement category. Nevertheless, this is also a strength of NCLB because averages can no longer be used to hide the difficulties of specific groups within the much higher scores of the majority. While the results seem to document that Hispanics and African Americans do not do as well, and while math is the chief culprit placing schools on the low-performing lists, NCLB is rightly focusing attention on education's failures. Teachers, boards, and administrators must remain conscious of the "achievement gaps" and do something about them. This type of public accountability has never happened before, and many would argue that it is a good thing.

**Figure 3.1**    What Constitutes a Highly Qualified Special Education Teacher Under The Individuals With Disabilities Education Improvement Act of 2004

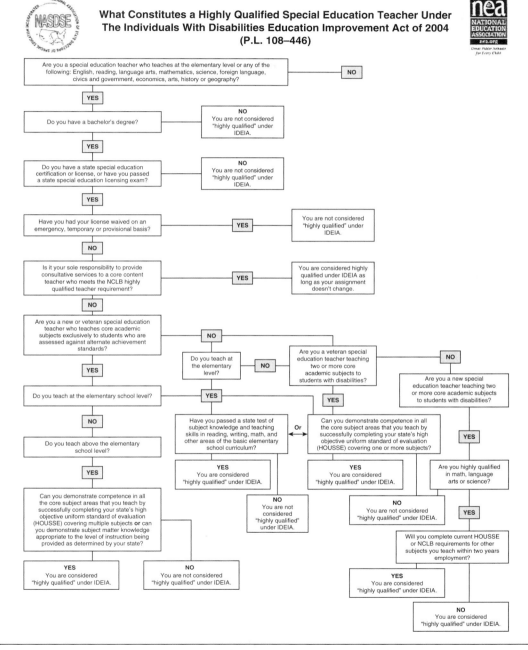

SOURCE: From "IDEA and NCLB: Intersection of Access and Outcomes" by Relabate, P. and Foley, B. Retrieved from http://www.nea.org. Reprinted with permission from Patti Relabate and the National Education Association.

Thus, NCLB is an inevitable result of poor instruction in basic skills as well as miserable performance by poor children of color. NCLB is the result of this frustration as federal and many state policymakers responded to the seeming wall of denial from the education community by assuming responsibility for their students' poor performance as well as by trying to redress the massive failure of African American, Latino, and poor students generally. Further, while critics of NCLB argue that it focuses on issues of proficiency in reading and math with achievement gaps determined through massive testing, supporters argue that the cause is not NCLB but rather inadequate school district management practices.

## Con: Federalism Is Not the Answer to Fixing Our Schools

Several recent secretaries of education have argued that the federal government should develop and adopt a national test to measure the progress of American students. This limiting of local control and supplanting by the federal government is not new. Actually, this approach was rejected by our founding fathers: The Constitution grants no authority to the federal government to regulate education, reserving it to the states through the Tenth Amendment. The issue underlying a federal testing program is whether it would lead to a federal curriculum to ensure that students are fairly evaluated on the subject matter they are taught. Yet, many would argue that centralizing education is not a sound policy in a global era in which innovation and flexibility are required. Of course, students must learn basic skills, but who is best to ensure this? Further, would federal control make it even more difficult for parents to have any direct effect on the education of their children?

Local and state control would seem to allow the local school community more access and input, but a federalist position has held sway for many years. The result is that there is more federal and less state and local control. The rallying cry was announced by President George W. Bush with his warm acceptance of test-based accountability: He called for an end to the "soft bigotry of low expectations" and put America's schools "on a new path of reform, and a new path of results." Nor should it be forgotten that liberals such as Senator Ted Kennedy added to this inauguration, holding that NCLB was a truly important victory for poor and minority children.

## Impact of NCLB

After five years, the results of NCLB are mixed, at best. As its reauthorization is now being debated, there have been numerous opinions and reports arguing for reauthorization and as many demanding modification and elimination. What follows is a summary of the report by Jack Jennings and Diane Stark Rentner of the Center on Education Policy.[2] In response to the reauthorization of NCLB, the summary is a fairly accurate presentation of the impact of NCLB after five years of its influence on public schools.

- State and district officials believe that student achievement on state tests is rising. This is an optimistic position. Nevertheless, it is not as clear whether students are really gaining as much as rising percentages of proficiency test scores would suggest.

- Although schools are spending more time on reading and math, it may be at the expense of subjects not tested.

- More attention is being paid to the alignment of curriculum and instruction, and schools are analyzing test score data much more closely.

- Low-performing schools are undertaking modest makeovers rather than radical kinds of restructuring.

- Although many educators are skeptical that this will really improve the quality of teaching, schools and teachers have made considerable progress in demonstrating that teachers meet the law's academic qualifications.

- NCLB has required that students take far more tests. This continues the pattern of 15 years of standards-based reform.

- Schools are focusing attention on achievement gaps and the learning needs of traditionally underperforming groups of students, specifically low-income ethnic and racial minorities as well as limited-English speakers and students with disabilities.

- The percentage of schools on state "needs improvement" lists has been steady but is not growing. Schools designated as "needs improvement" are subject to NCLB sanctions, such as being required to offer students public school choice or tutoring services.

- The role of the federal government in education is continuing to expand.

- While NCLB requirements have also required expanded local government and school district roles, there has been inadequate federal funding to carry out these expanded duties.

## Case Study

### Why Does a Special Education Teacher Have to Be Highly Qualified?

The "highly qualified" provisions of NCLB require that all special education teachers who teach a traditional class must meet the "highly qualified" requirements for each discipline that they teach where they are the teacher of record. This means that a special education teacher trained to assist a child with a disability (e.g., special learning disability, emotionally disturbed) must become highly qualified in the specific subject (math, English, etc.) that teacher wishes to teach. This is required in every state and in every school district that is trying to meet AYP. The result is that if a teacher is teaching social studies to her group of students with disabilities, she must meet the "highly qualified" standards for a social studies teacher. Although special inservice programs have been developed to assist these teachers in meeting the various "highly qualified" subject matter standards, many special education teachers object. They claim that this is unfair treatment. Some threaten to leave education or teach in another area.

### Discussion Questions

1. Are these "highly qualified" provisions fair to teachers of the disabled?

2. Are there any reasonable alternatives?

3. Do these teachers have an equal protection argument to claim that they are not being treated equally to regular education teachers?

# CONCLUSION . . . . . . . . . . . . . . . . . . . . . . . . . . . . . . .

This chapter explores how the Elementary and Secondary Education Act, renamed No Child Left Behind, has affected education law and the education system. The statute has dramatically increased the role of the federal government in school operation. In a variety of ways, the statute aims to require accountability, as measured quantitatively through student performance, and to ensure the quality of teachers, as measured through achievement of particular certifications.

Specifically, NCLB requires that all students in a school make Adequate Yearly Progress (AYP). States select and administer the tests that determine whether a student has made AYP. The law authorizes federal funding for these tests. The statute mandates that student progress, as well as teacher qualifications/credentials, are published to allow parents and others to review and analyze it.

Every other year, the states will participate in the National Assessment of Educational Progress (NAEP), in which all students take national tests. The results of these tests will be broken down by student demographic and distinguished on student characteristics such as race, wealth status, special needs status, and so on. Each student demographic must make AYP on these tests. Some students, according to special needs and other relevant statuses, may be appropriately accommodated in a manner consistent with federal law. Schools are placed in categories based on their students' performance, and they are sanctioned or rewarded for their ability or failure to make AYP. This system is intended to improve quality and accountability. However, some have argued that a system that reduces funding to inadequate schools and increases funding to flourishing schools does nothing more than perpetuate disparity in educational quality.

In an effort to ensure teacher quality, NCLB requires that all teachers be "highly qualified." This requires teachers to have a minimum amount of education in their field of instruction and to pass various certification standards.

Some have contended that the law is flawed and underfunded. They argue that the law sets standards for student performance at a level difficult—or even impossible—for low-income districts to achieve. In addition, the 1,100-page statute arguably creates a bureaucratic and inefficient maze of regulations, many of which do not adequately address the problems that the statute was devised to remedy. According to some, because funds are directly linked to performance on standardized tests, the statute has turned schools into "test-prep centers" rather than educational institutions.

Although the case coverage in this area is still scant, read the following cases to gain a sense of the intense debate about this legislation. Notice who may assert rights against the legislation, as well. You will no doubt encounter this Act in the future. The cases are meant to give the reader a sense of the various facets of education that are affected. Refer to these cases as you read the textbook. As you become more familiar with how the law affects school boards, educators, students, and local governments, you may be able to more fully appreciate the heated controversy over the effects of legislation of this kind.

# CASE BRIEFS · · · · · · · · · · · · · · · · · · · · · · · ·

## ASSOCIATION OF COMMUNITY ORGANIZATIONS FOR REFORM NOW V. NEW YORK CITY DEPARTMENT OF EDUCATION 269 F. SUPP. 2D 338 (S.D.N.Y., 2003)

**GENERAL RULE OF LAW:** NCLB contains no procedure for parents or students to seek judicial, administrative, or any other remedies for alleged noncompliance with the dictates of the Act. NCLB does not reflect the clear and unambiguous intent of Congress to create individually enforceable rights.

**PROCEDURE SUMMARY:**

**Plaintiff:** Association of Community Organizations for Reform Now (P), a community association, et al.

**Defendant:** New York City Department of Education (D), et al.

**U.S. District Court Decision:** Association's (P) motion to dismiss NCLB claim was granted. Motion for preliminary injunction was denied as **moot**.

**FACTS:** The schoolchildren all attended public schools that were identified as failing schools by the state education department (D). To the extent that parents did receive information regarding their rights to transfer their children pursuant to the NCLB, the information was allegedly inaccurate and incorrectly informed parents that their transfer requests would be rejected. In addition, in violation of the NCLB, the city department of education rejected outright the vast majority of transfer requests. The court held that Congress did not intend to create individually enforceable rights with respect to the notice, transfer, or supplemental educational services (SES) provisions contained in the NCLB. First, the NCLB was drafted to focus on the regulation of states and local educational agencies and not on conferring any direct benefit, entitlement, or rights upon individuals, such as parents and students. Second, the NCLB's transfer and SES provisions had an aggregate focus and were not concerned with a particular individual student's ability to receive a benefit under the statute. Finally, the statutory scheme contained no procedures for individuals to seek remedies for violations of the statute.

**ISSUE:** Do the parents of schoolchildren subject to the NCLB have individually enforceable rights when incorrectly informed about transfer requests?

**HOLDING AND DECISION:** No. Congress has authorized, pursuant to its federal spending powers, states as well as local educational agencies to receive federal funds in order to carry out the purposes of the NCLB, provided that they abide by various conditions and requirements imposed by the Act. States receiving NCLB funds must have the state educational agency submit to the secretary of education a plan that demonstrates that the state has adopted challenging academic content standards. Local educational agencies that receive NCLB funds must abide by the requirements in § 6316 of the Act. In connection with the supplemental educational services (SES) and transfer provisions, the NCLB contains a parental notification provision that requires, among other things, that the local educational agency provide notice to parents if a school in which their child is enrolled is designated for school improvement, corrective action, or restructuring and notice to parents if transfer is an option or if their child is eligible to receive SES.

**COMMENT:** The result of this decision, unless reversed above, is that parents will have little opportunity to protect their child's rights (as well as their own) should school districts fail to treat them properly. Absent some malicious action, there is little chance of recovery or judicial correction. The "penalties" section of NCLB outlines the procedures available in the event of noncompliance by states with NCLB provisions. This section of the statute contains no procedure for parents or students to seek judicial, administrative, or any other remedies for alleged noncompliance with the dictates of the Act. The NCLB simply does not reflect the clear and unambiguous intent of Congress to create individually enforceable rights. The statute lacks the necessary rights-creating language. Because it is focused on the regulation of states and local educational agencies and on improving the condition of children collectively, it therefore lacks the individual focus suggestive of congressional intent to create personal rights. The seeming final nail in the coffin is that the enforcement scheme of the statute indicates a congressional intent to centralize enforcement and thereby to avoid the possibility of individual lawsuits and multiple interpretations of provisions of the Act. Consequently, plaintiffs cannot maintain an action under 42 U.S.C.S. § 1983 to enforce provisions of NCLB. Of course, this issue will be a major arena of concern with the upcoming first reauthorization of NCLB.

## Discussion Questions

1. Where does this leave parents if they wish to protect their children from what they consider to be unfair or incorrect NCLB actions by school districts?

2. If this issue is appealed, what arguments would the plaintiffs propose?

3. If a child was injured due to the failure to carry out some required action under NCLB, could the parents sue in state court to enforce their child's rights?

# FRESH START ACADEMY V. TOLEDO BOARD OF EDUCATION 2005 U.S. DIST. LEXIS 5336 (N.D. OHIO, 2005)

**GENERAL RULE OF LAW:** Providers of supplemental educational services may not bring an action under 42 U.S.C.S. § 1983 or under an implied private right of action to enforce any provisions of the No Child Left Behind Act, as it does not evince an unambiguous congressional intent to create rights enforceable by such individuals.

**PROCEDURE SUMMARY:**

**Plaintiff:** Fresh Start Academy (P), a private provider of tutoring services

**Defendant:** Toledo Board of Education (D)

**U.S. District Court Decision:** Defendant's Motion to Dismiss was granted

**FACTS:** A private provider of tutoring services (P) sued the Toledo Board of Education (D), alleging that the Board (D) misappropriated funds it received under the NCLB, blocked the plaintiff from obtaining funds and qualified students for supplemental educational services (SES), and engaged in preferential treatment by allowing certain SES providers access to school facilities. Fresh Start Academy (P) would like to provide tutoring services to Toledo public school students in exchange for funds made available to the Board (D) under NCLB. As part of the NCLB, Congress has appropriated and allocated to the states funds to enable local education agencies (LEA) and a state educational agency (SEA) to carry out the Act's requirements. The Act instructs LEAs, like the Board (D), to make a specified amount of the LEA's federal allocation available for SES. It also allows an SEA, again like the state board of education, to use a portion of its federal allocation to help an LEA pay for supplemental educational services. The Board moved to dismiss Fresh Start's (P) **complaint**, arguing that all of Fresh Start's (P) claims depend upon rights NCLB never conferred upon Fresh Start (P).

**ISSUE:** Does an SES provider have a cause of action against a school district for not allowing it access to funds allocated through NCLB?

**HOLDING AND DECISION:** No. NCLB deals with a local educational agency, such as a public board of education (or a state education agency), which takes certain actions when an elementary school that it serves fails to make AYP. NCLB provides no procedure for individual entities (in this case a private provider of services) to enforce its requirements. NCLB's "penalties" provision only allows the secretary of education to withhold funds from states that do not meet the Act's requirements. If Congress wanted to create new rights enforceable under 42 U.S.C.S. § 1983, it must do so in clear and unambiguous terms—no less and no more than what is required for Congress to create new rights enforceable under an implied private right of action. Where the text and structure of a statute provide no indication that Congress intends to create new individual rights, there is no basis for a private suit, whether under 42 U.S.C.S. § 1983 or under an implied right of action. The typical remedy for state noncompliance with federally imposed conditions is not a private cause of action for noncompliance. Rather, it is an action by the federal government to terminate funds to the state. Providers of supplemental educational services may not bring an action under 42 U.S.C.S. § 1983 or under an implied private right of action to enforce any provisions of the NCLB because the Act does not evince an unambiguous congressional intent to create rights enforceable by such individuals. NCLB sets out minimum requirements for qualified "providers" of supplemental educational services and states that a "provider" may be a nonprofit or for-profit entity and may even be the local educational agency itself.

## Discussion Questions

1. How does this decision square with the court's decision in *Association of Community Organizations for Reform Now v. New York City Department of Education* (2003), in which neither the parent nor child had standing to initiate a law suit under NCLB?

2.  If this case had "gone the other way," what types of future litigation under NCLB might have been generated?

3.  Do the plaintiffs have a better, as good, or worse possibility for success upon appeal than do the parents and children in the New York case?

# SCHOOL DISTRICT OF THE CITY OF PONTIAC, ET AL. V. SPELLINGS, FILED APRIL 20, 2005

**GENERAL RULE OF LAW:** Too early for any rule of law to develop.

**PROCEDURE SUMMARY:**

**Plaintiffs:** School District of the City of Pontiac, various school districts from MI, TX, VT, DC, CT, IL, IN, NH, OH, PA, and UT (School Districts) (P)

**Defendant:** Margaret Spellings, Secretary of U.S. Department of Education (Secretary of Education) (D)

**U.S. District Court Decision:** Filed April 20, 2005, no decision rendered

**FACTS:** The nation's largest teachers' union joined school districts in several states (P) filing a federal lawsuit charging the Department of Education with failing to provide adequate funding for the No Child Left Behind initiative. On January 8, 2002, President George W. Bush signed into law the 2001 reauthorization of the Elementary and Secondary Education Act of 1965 (ESEA), the principal federal statute relating to primary and secondary education at the state and local levels. The reauthorization is titled the No Child Left Behind Act (NCLB). This Act was enacted by Congress pursuant to its power under the spending clause of the United States Constitution. The spending clause permits Congress to condition the receipt of federal funds on the recipients' compliance with certain obligations, if the conditions under which the federal funds will be made available are unambiguously set forth in the statute. The NCLB initiative provides as follows: "Nothing in this Act shall be construed to . . . mandate a State or any subdivision thereof to spend any funds or incur any costs not paid for under this Act." The former secretary of education made a statement on December 2, 2003, restating this provision, saying, "If it is not funded, it's not required. There is language in the bill that prohibits requiring anything that is not paid for." The School Districts (P) claim that the Secretary of Education (D) is violating this provision by requiring states and school districts to comply fully with all the provisions of the NCLB mandates even though they (P) have not been provided with sufficient funds to pay for such compliance. The School Districts (P) assert that by forcing the compliance without providing the funding, the Secretary of Education (D) is violating the spending clause of the United States Constitution. The complaint alleges many instances when requests for waivers from the mandates of NCLB due to lack of funding were denied. The complaint also alleges that these denied requests make clear that the Secretary of Education (D) will not grant waivers from NCLB based on lack of funding.

**ISSUE:** Whether the extensive mandates of NCLB have been properly funded. If not, has compliance with those underfunded mandates been waived?

**HOLDING AND DECISION:** Complaint filed. Decision pending.

**COMMENT:** The School Districts (P) want the court to issue an order stating they (P) are not required to spend non-NCLB funds on compliance with NCLB mandates. Furthermore, the Secretary of Education (D) cannot use a school district's noncompliance as a basis for withholding future NCLB funds. Since its creation, NCLB has been the subject of much debate. As early as 2003, the Vermont Teachers' Union vowed to take legal action against the Education Department because union members believe this is a power struggle with the federal government. The new federal law provides states with unprecedented levels of funding. In exchange, states must meet numerous requirements aimed at increasing school accountability to ensure that every child—regardless of socioeconomic factors—receives the education he or she deserves. Meeting the deadlines laid out in NCLB was expected to be a tough and challenging task, but one that needed to be done. The President signed this bill in an attempt to require schools to be more accountable and in an attempt to provide them with the resources to do so. It is becoming apparent that the attempts at funding may be failing, and the states are seeking legal action remedies. The day before this suit was filed, Utah passed House Bill 1001, directing state education officials to comply with state education goals before they consider the provisions of the federal NCLB. Utah is the first of many states unhappy with the federal education law to pass a legislative challenge to it. In February, a bipartisan statement through the National Conference of State Legislatures was issued, stating that all 50 state legislatures opposed NCLB. The statement attacked the education program's unconstitutional extension of federal power in an area traditionally left to state control and accused the government of coercing states into compliance. It also recommended essential changes in the measurement of student progress, the punishment for underachieving schools, and guidelines for allowing waivers for struggling school districts. The statement also expressed concern that the education reform would further segregate schools and provide incentives for good teachers to leave needy schools.

## Discussion Questions

1. With the cost of complying with NCLB escalating dramatically, has the federal government put itself in an impossible situation when by originally stating that it would pay for the entire cost of implementing NCLB?

2. How valid is the claim of states that believe that NCLB is an education power "grab" by the federal government? Why or why not?

3. When P.L. 94-142 was first enacted, the federal government said that it would provide 40% of the cost of implementing its requirements. States have never received 40% of the funding for special education services. How might this impact the NCLB situation?

Additional case briefs can be found on the SAGE Web site at the following address:
http://www.sagepub.com/aquilacasebriefs

## NOTES

1. School District of the City of Pontiac, et al. v. Spellings, filed April 20, 2005.
2. Jennings, J., & Stark Rentner, D. (2006, October). Ten big effects of the No Child Left Behind Act on public schools. *Phi Delta Kappan, 88*(02), 110–113.

# Part II

# Students' Rights

# 4

# School Attendance

*But it is far from clear that there is any justification for the compulsory attendance laws themselves. . . . Like most laws, compulsory attendance laws have costs as well as benefits. We no longer believe the benefits justify the results.*

—Milton and Rose Friedman,
*Free to Choose: A Personal Statement*

## OVERVIEW

Every state requires school-age children to obtain some form of education. The argument against compulsory education espoused by Milton Friedman's quote that begins this chapter is not new. The last great attack on compulsory education occurred in the nineteenth century. Compulsory education was seen as an unnecessary governmental tactic that denied parental authority and weakened private schools.

While attending school, students are subject to a variety of rules and regulations regarding their conduct and academic pursuits. Of course, students are not without certain constitutional and statutory rights; however, the tensions between such rights and the regulations that impact them frequently lead to litigation. With this in mind, the thrust of this chapter is to review and consider those regulatory laws, as well as policies and practices that involve students' attendance and residency. Related student rights issues will be considered in subsequent chapters.

Because improved education of youth benefits everyone, the state has the right, if not the responsibility, to require education. Thus, the laws of each state contain a compulsory school attendance statute. The general basis for compulsory education is the common law doctrine of **parens patriae**, which permits government, as guardian of the people, to enact laws for the common good. To ensure that compulsory education included private as well as public education, the U.S. Supreme Court held in 1925 that no state could limit its compulsory education requirement to attendance at public schools.

America has a long history of accepting private schools so long as the private program of instruction meets minimum state standards.[1] Interestingly, private schools operate under the law of contract because the parents have entered into a contract with the private school to educate their children. Therefore, to recover against a private school, parents must prove that there was a violation of their contractual rights or, alternatively, establish a clear abuse of discretion on the part of the private school.

Students may be permitted to receive instruction in the home, so long as a parent or other instructor is competent to teach and the program of instruction is roughly equivalent to that offered in public schools.[2] Home schooling has recently grown and expanded significantly. Further, with the expansion of choice and the improvement of and greater ease of access to curricula through the Internet, it would appear that home schooling will continue to increase in popularity.

There are some exceptions to state compulsory education laws. For example, in some states, married students are exempt from compulsory school attendance. Also, in many states, those who have reached a certain minimum age and are certified to work in specific jobs are exempt. Religious exceptions also exist, with the most famous being the Amish exception. Amish children who have completed the eighth grade are exempt from further compulsory education.[3] However, courts have denied religious conviction exemptions in most other situations in which parents sought to remove their children from school. Even with these exceptions, courts have generally denied exemptions from state compulsory education laws, especially those based on allegedly unsafe school conditions or school curricula that failed to instruct students in the tenets of a specific religious faith. The consequences of noncompliance with compulsory attendance statutes may vary from state to state, but it is clear that there are consequences. The most common "penalties" include prosecution of parents, expulsion of students, violators being held in contempt of court, and the child being made a ward of the state.

Marriage tends to emancipate a youth. Thus, compulsory attendance laws do not apply to youth under the age of 16 (unless otherwise required to attend school) who are married. Marriage, effectively, releases both a parent and the state's control over the underaged youth.

All states have residency requirements that oblige a public school district to educate school-age children who reside within district boundaries and intend to remain there. Parents of students who want to attend a district in which they do not reside are required to pay tuition to the neighboring district. Also, most courts have refused to permit the establishment of limited guardianships in neighboring districts so that student athletes can attend school tuition-free in those districts.

State legislatures have enacted statutes that allow local agencies to pass regulations that are designed to protect the public health. This is important for schools because unhealthy students could endanger the health and well-being of other students. States may authorize local school districts to condition a student's attendance at public or private schools on her receipt of vaccinations against communicable diseases. Regardless, unhealthy students' presence in school must not endanger the health of others.

## Case Study

### Schooling at Home or a Real Education

A private Christian school operates in your school district. The Peacefuls have a daughter, Ima Peaceful, aged 5, who is enrolled as a student in the school. As part of the enrollment process, the Peacefuls were provided with a copy of the school's admission policies, which stated,

> The school reserves the right to refuse admittance, suspend, or expel any student who does not cooperate with policies established in this book. The high standard and biblical principles that our school holds apply to afterschool hours as well. If any parent or student refuses to follow those standards, then they place the student's privilege of attending our Christian school in jeopardy.

After a series of events involving Ima Peaceful, a disagreement arose between the Peacefuls and the administration. In a letter dated November 27, the Peacefuls were asked to withdraw Ima from the school. If they failed to do so, Ima would be dismissed on December 3.

That September, Ima had informed her mother (P) that while she was playing on the playground at school, two male kindergarten students accosted her. The next day, Mrs. Peaceful telephoned the school principal and informed him of the incident. The principal indicated that he would speak to the children concerning this matter and that if the incident occurred again, he would punish the children according to the school's corporal punishment policy. In October, Ima told her mother (P) that one of the boys involved in the first incident accosted her again in a similar fashion. The Peacefuls went to the school to meet with the principal and suggested that the boy be physically punished. The principal telephoned the boy's parents and arranged a meeting with them. With their consent, the principal paddled the boy.

Mrs. Peaceful demanded to know the outcome. The principal assured her that everything was handled according to school policy. Unsatisfied with this response, the Peacefuls decided to meet with the Reverend even though he had no day-to-day school responsibilities. Ima told her mother of another incident when a classmate spit on her as they were leaving the school. Mrs. Peaceful then confronted the teacher in charge of the classroom. According to the teacher, the spitting was an accident caused by a boy with a dental malformation. Mrs. Peaceful, again unsatisfied with the response, demanded to speak with the principal. She called him "unchristian" and accused him of "working with the devil."

The principal then contacted the Reverend and explained that no agreement was in sight on matters involving Ima. The Reverend, the titular head of the school, decided that a working relationship between the school administration and the Peacefuls was not possible, and ultimately he asked the Peacefuls to withdraw their daughter from the school and refused to refund their tuition.

### Discussion Questions

1. Can this school act in such an arbitrary and capricious manner?
2. Did this Christian academy unconstitutionally expel Ima Peaceful?
3. Other than seeking readmission, what other civil recourses do the Peacefuls have?
4. Why can this private school's discipline actions differ from those of a public school?
5. Should the Peacefuls receive a refund of their tuition?

# IMPORTANT CONCEPTS

- **Attendance mandated by law:** Each state has enacted a compulsory school attendance statute with penalties for noncompliance.

- **Alternatives to public schooling:** Private schooling and home instruction are acceptable alternatives to public education.[4]

- **Few exceptions to mandatory attendance:** Exceptions to compulsory school attendance are sometimes granted to married students, working students, and those with certain religious convictions who are opposed to schooling.[5]

- **Home schooling is an acceptable alternative to public schooling:** Home schooling is equivalent as long as the subject matter is roughly equivalent to that taught in the public school and the home instructor can adequately teach.[6]

- **Penalties in the face of noncompliance:** In response to noncompliance with compulsory attendance statutes, the state may prosecute parents and students may be held in contempt, expelled from school, or made wards of the state.

- **Obligation to educate resident students:** School districts are obliged to educate school-age children so long as they reside within district boundaries.

- **Out-of-district school attendance:** A student who resides in one district has no right to attend school in another but may do so if she obtains the permission of both districts.

- **Reasonable health regulations permissible:** Local school boards may be empowered by statute to pass regulations, such as those requiring vaccinations, which are designed to protect the public health.

- **Textbook fees permissible:** No federal laws or constitutional provisions prohibit the states from assessing textbook usage fees.

- **Private schools operate under contract law:** Private schools operate under the law of contract because the parents and children voluntarily enter into a contract with the school board. While constitutional rights cannot be violated, the basic law of contract applies regarding issues controlled by the contract.

- **Undocumented children residing in the United States are entitled to public education:** To find otherwise would be to punish children for the actions of their parents who brought them to the U.S.[7]

# SCHOOL ATTENDANCE

## Compulsory Attendance

The laws of each state contain a compulsory school attendance statute. Although the famed economist Milton Friedman disagrees with the need for compulsory attendance laws (see the quote that opens this chapter), each school attendance statute includes penalties for noncompliance. The legal basis for compulsory education is the common law doctrine of parens patriae, which permits the government, as guardian of the people, to enact laws for the common good. Education fosters the enlightenment of the citizenry and thus contributes to the well-being of the state. In 1925, the U.S. Supreme Court declared that no state could limit compulsory education to attendance at public schools. An Oregon statute would have limited compulsory education to only public education, effectively disfranchising private schools.[8] In *Pierce v. Society of the Sisters* (1925), the Court, in "balancing the equities," had to balance the right of parents to supervise the upbringing of their children with the right of the state to establish educational standards, and the Court supported the parents' liberty interest.

Accordingly, a series of alternatives to public education have developed. Recently, "choice" options, such as vouchers, have also been developed (see Chapter 15). The following alternatives to public school education may be permissible in specific circumstances.

## Private Schools

Students may attend private schools, so long as the private program of instruction meets minimum state standards.[9] Private schools operate under the law of contract because the parents entered into a contract with the private school to educate their children. Absent a violation of constitutional rights, the law of contract will cover disputes. In the case of *Allen v. Casper* (1993), the court held that contract law, not the law of due process, governs expulsion from a private school.[10] To state a noncontractual claim against a private school, the complainant must show a clear abuse of discretion on the part of the private school.

## Home Schooling

Students may be permitted to receive instruction in the home, so long as a parent or other instructor is competent to teach and the program of instruction is roughly equivalent to that offered in public schools.[11] In the mid-fifties, only two states allowed home schooling. Today, however, all states allow some form of home schooling. With the increased options and the improvement of and greater ease of access to curricula through the Internet, it would appear that home schooling options will continue to increase. Furthermore, the stringent curriculum and testing requirements established in many states during the 1970s and 1980s have been attacked and reduced or eliminated in state court actions. In some cases, students have been exempted from compulsory attendance requirements—while in others, requests for exemptions have been denied.

## Statutory Exceptions

In a few states, those who have reached a certain minimum age and are certified to work in specific jobs are exempt from mandatory school attendance. Additionally, there is a marriage exception, which is based on the notion that marriage tends to emancipate a youth. Compulsory attendance laws usually do not apply to youth under the age of 16 (unless otherwise required to attend school) who are married, even if state law prohibits the marriage of a girl under the age of 16. Marriage, effectively, releases both parents' and the state's control of the underaged youth.

For example, *State v. Priest* (1946) concerned a 14-year-old girl who was regularly truant as well as neglected. The state of Louisiana had a truancy officer take her into custody and commit her to a state girls' school based on the parens patriae doctrine. During this time, the girl was married. While sympathetic to the state and lower court's concern for the girl's welfare, the state supreme court overturned the decision based on the fact that the girl had married and was assuming the responsibilities of a married woman.[12]

## Religious Convictions Exception

Although a state has the right to establish reasonable regulations, this right must be balanced against an individual's fundamental rights and interests. This balancing of equities is especially dramatic when religion is at odds with compulsory attendance laws. Amish children who have completed the eighth grade have been exempted from further compulsory education.[13] However, most other religious conviction exemption claims are denied. The Amish exception is very unusual. It is based on the Amish's history of providing for the vocational needs of their youth. It is also based on the Amish's concern over the negative influence that education at a public high school could have on their youth. It should be remembered that *Wisconsin v. Yoder* (1972) is a limited decision based on the fact that the Amish have a long religious history; in addition, illiteracy is not a consideration because Amish children must attend at least eight years of school.

## No Exceptions Granted

Apart from the exceptions noted above, courts have denied exemptions from state compulsory education laws based on allegedly unsafe school conditions or school curricula that failed to instruct students in the tenets of a specific religious faith. Although the consequences of noncompliance with compulsory attendance statutes may vary from state to state, it is clear that there are consequences. The following "penalties" have been most commonly identified:

1. *Prosecution of parents:* The parents of noncompliant students may be prosecuted in criminal or civil court.

2. *Expulsion of students:* Students who are excessively truant may be expelled.

3. *Held in contempt:* Students who are excessively truant may be held in contempt of court if they disobey a court order to return to school.

4. *Made wards of the state:* In extreme cases, truant students may be made wards of local juvenile courts and supervised by probation officers.

## Residency Requirements

A public school district is obliged to educate school-age children who reside within district boundaries and intend to remain there. Tuition-free admission to public schools may be denied to minors if their primary reason for maintaining a presence in a particular district is to attend public school; in *Martinez v. Bynum* (1983), a bona fide residence requirement was upheld.[14] As a rule, a student who resides in one district has no right to attend school in another. However, he may do so if he obtains both districts' permission. In most such cases, the student's parents are required to pay tuition to the neighboring district. However, most courts have refused to permit the establishment of limited guardianships in neighboring districts so that student athletes can attend school tuition-free in those districts. In a surprising and upsetting case (to states with many undocumented migrant workers), the U.S. Supreme Court overturned a Texas statute that denied a public school education to undocumented school-age children.[15] The rationale was that undocumented children of alien parents cannot be denied a public education because of the actions of their parents, especially when the parents were enticed into the country—and often allowed to remain—to provide a service.

## Public Health Requirements

Local agencies may be empowered by their respective state legislatures to pass regulations designed to protect public health. Such regulations are important in schools because unhealthy students could endanger the health and well-being of other students. States may authorize local school districts to condition a student's attendance in public or private school on her receipt of vaccinations against communicable diseases. Most courts refuse to uphold challenges to mandatory vaccination requirements, including those that are based on religious grounds, and parents can be subject to arrest or fine for failure to vaccinate their children. However, a few states, by statute, exempt students from such requirements if they practice a religion whose tenets specifically prohibit such procedures. Regardless, these exempted students' presence in school must not endanger the health of others.

## Fees

The U.S. Supreme Court has not ruled on whether the assessment of textbook fees violates the equal protection clause (or any other provision) of the U.S. Constitution. Thus, disputes concerning such fees are resolved by state courts in accordance with each state's constitution and statutes. When the assessment of textbook fees is permitted by law and upheld by state courts, fees are usually waived for those who can demonstrate that they are unable to pay. Assessments of fees for school courses and school supplies have frequently been challenged in court. Fees for academic courses have sometimes been found to violate a student's right to a fair education. In other cases, such fees have been struck down while fees for elective courses have been permitted.

## Case Study

### Is Schooling at Home Equivalent Instruction?

As superintendent of the Happy Hearts School District, you have a problem. Your school board is unhappy with the fact that the Simpsons, Homer and Marge, have decided to home school their child, Bart. While your state allows home schooling as long as there is "equivalent instruction," your school board feels that more stringent control and management would be appropriate. They demand that you declare this home schooling to be not equivalent. Homer Simpson taught Bart art, which Homer taught in an area private school, and Marge prepared special texts that covered all the traditional subjects taught to children of Bart's age in the Happy Hearts schools. Marge Simpson supplemented her own prepared texts with numerous maps, textbooks, charts, and outlines. She also tested Bart regularly. However, neither Simpson was a certified teacher. On standardized tests taken after home instruction, Bart scored higher than the national median, except in science. The violation of the statute requiring equivalent instruction constitutes a misdemeanor punishable by a fine.

### Discussion Questions

1. Does the home instruction provided by the Simpsons meet the standards of "equivalent instruction?"

2. Can a state require that the parents be certified teachers?

3. Are children educated at home deprived of social companionship and peer companionship that leaves them ill-equipped to deal with society at large?

4. In balancing the equities, what are the arguments on both sides?

5. What is your guess as to how No Child Left Behind impacts home-schooled students? Why?

## CONCLUSION . . . . . . . . . . . . . . . . . . . . . . . . . . . . .

The state has the right, if not the responsibility, to require education. Each state, therefore, has a compulsory school attendance statute. However, the Supreme Court has ruled that no state may compel students to attend only public schools. Private schools and home schooling are acceptable, so long as they meet state standards and the program of instruction is roughly equivalent to that offered in public schools.

However, in some states, those who have reached a certain age and are certified to work in specific jobs may be exempt from mandatory school attendance. In addition, some states grant an exception to married students. When religion is at odds with compulsory attendance, few religious exceptions are granted, though a notable exception is Amish children. Exceptions are generally not granted when students claim that their school is unsafe or does not instruct them in their religious beliefs. While the consequences of noncompliance with compulsory attendance statutes may vary from state to state, they generally include prosecution of the parents, student expulsion, the student being held in contempt, or the student being made a ward of the state.

A public school district is obliged to educate school-age children who reside within district boundaries and intend to remain there. A student who resides in one district has no right to attend public school in another, though generally he may do so if the district agrees and a special tuition is paid. Further, most states have refused to permit the establishment of limited guardianships in neighboring districts so that student athletes can attend school tuition-free in those districts.

Local school districts may condition a student's attendance at a school upon his receipt of vaccinations against communicable diseases. Religious reasons for nonvaccination are generally not accepted, and parents can be subject to arrest or fine if their children do not attend school because they did not comply with the vaccination requirement. However, a small minority of states do grant a religious exemption.

Because the Supreme Court has not yet ruled on whether textbook fees violate the equal protection clause, state courts generally resolve these disputes. Academic fees are sometimes found to violate a student's right to education. Also, these fees are generally waived for those who demonstrate significant financial need.

The cases that follow illustrate the extent of student rights and the continuous court battles that have defined them.

# CASE BRIEFS . . . . . . . . . . . . . . . . . . . .

## PIERCE V. SOCIETY OF THE SISTERS OF THE HOLY NAMES OF JESUS AND MARY 68 U.S. 510, 45 S. CT. 57 (1925)

**GENERAL RULE OF LAW:** A law requiring children to attend public schools unreasonably interferes with parents' liberty interest in directing the upbringing and education of their children.

**PROCEDURE SUMMARY:**

> **Plaintiff:** Society of Sisters (Sisters) (P), a corporation empowered to establish and maintain private schools

> **Defendant:** Pierce (D), the Governor of Oregon

> **U.S. District Court Decision:** Held for Sisters (P), granting a preliminary order restraining Pierce (D) from enforcing the compulsory education law

> **U.S. Supreme Court Decision:** Affirmed

**FACTS:** Oregon enacted the Compulsory Education Act of 1922, which, effective 1926, required every parent, guardian, or other custodian of a child between 8 and 16 to send the child to public school. Failure to comply was a misdemeanor. Sisters (P), a corporation empowered to establish and maintain private schools, filed suit, alleging that the law impermissibly infringed its property interests and the parents' right to choose where their children attended school. The district court agreed, finding that the parents' right to select where their children attended school was a liberty interest protected by the Fourteenth Amendment. The court issued a preliminary order restraining Pierce (D), the governor of Oregon, from enforcing the law. Pierce (D) appealed.

**ISSUE:** May a state require parents to send children between the ages of 8 and 16 to public school?

**HOLDING AND DECISION:** (McReynolds, J.) No. A law requiring children between the ages of 8 and 16 to attend public schools impermissibly interferes with parents' liberty interest in directing the education of their children. Rights guaranteed by the Constitution may not be abridged by legislation that has no reasonable relation to some legitimate purpose. Compelling attendance at public schools is not a legitimate purpose. The state may lawfully regulate all schools and require that all children of a certain age attend some school meeting certain standards. However, the state may not standardize children by forcing them to attend only public schools. Thus, the district court did not err in ordering Pierce (D) to stop enforcing the compulsory education law. Affirmed.

**COMMENT:** There was a major standing problem (a party's *interest in* and therefore *right to* bring suit) in *Pierce* because the plaintiff was a corporation, which ordinarily could not claim Fourteenth Amendment liberty protections. The Court, however, overcame this problem by recognizing the threat, posed by the law, to the plaintiff's business and property interests. Obviously, the parents and/or guardians of private school students would have been the plaintiffs of choice (i.e., the parties with the most direct interest in the issues under consideration). Although the corporation also had a clear interest in the outcome, the Court may have been less stringent in applying standing requirements because the constitutional issue before the Court was so substantial.

## Discussion Questions

1.  Does the Fourteenth Amendment permit parents to direct the education of their child?

2.  Can the state compel attendance at public schools?

3.  Can a corporation, such as the Society of the Sisters, claim liberty protections under the Fourteenth Amendment?

# NEW JERSEY V. MASSA 95 N.J. SUPER. 382, 231 A.2D 252 (1967)

**GENERAL RULE OF LAW:** Home schooling of children in subject matter equivalent to that provided in public schools meets the requirements of a state's compulsory education law.

**PROCEDURE SUMMARY:**

**Plaintiff:** New Jersey (P)

**Defendants:** Mr. and Mrs. Massa (D), parents of a child they taught at home

**State Municipal Court Decision:** Held for New Jersey (P)

**State Superior Court Decision:** Reversed

**FACTS:** The Massas (D) taught their 12-year-old daughter, Barbara, at home rather than sending her to public elementary school or junior high. Mr. Massa (D) taught Barbara art, which he taught at local schools, and Mrs. Massa (D) prepared special texts that covered all the subjects traditionally taught to children of Barbara's age in the public schools. Mrs. Massa (D) supplemented her own prepared texts with numerous maps, textbooks, charts, and outlines, and she tested Barbara regularly. Neither Mr. nor Mrs. Massa (D) was a certified teacher. Barbara scored higher than the national median on standardized tests, except in math. The Massas (D) lived in New Jersey (P), which had a compulsory education law requiring parents to send their children to New Jersey (P) public schools or to provide their children with "equivalent instruction elsewhere." Violation of the statute constituted a misdemeanor and subjected the violators to a fine. Mr. and Mrs. Massa (D) were prosecuted in a New Jersey municipal court and convicted. They appealed to the New Jersey Superior Court.

**ISSUE:** Does home schooling of children in subject matter equivalent to that provided in public schools meet the requirements of state compulsory education laws?

**HOLDING AND DECISION:** (Collins, J.) Yes. Home schooling of children in subject matter equivalent to that provided in public schools meets the requirements of a state's compulsory education law. Here, Barbara Massa was taught all subjects covered in local public schools; was tested regularly; and was subject to circumscribed periods of instruction, study, and recreation. New Jersey's (P) requirement that she receive "equivalent" instruction does not require formal enrollment in a private school or group instruction. Reversed.

**COMMENT:** Some states, such as California, would not necessarily have prohibited home schooling of Barbara by her parents, but they would have required that the parents be certified teachers.[16] Here, the New Jersey court did not require credentials because the New Jersey legislature had not inserted this requirement in the compulsory education statute. The court reasoned that if the legislature had intended to require credentials, it would have explicitly referred to them in the language of the statute. The other principal concern in cases such as this is whether children at home, who are deprived of the social companionship and peer comparison found in the typical school setting, grow up ill-equipped to deal with society at large. In other parts of its opinion, the court discounted this concern despite the fact that a teacher in Barbara's new school testified that Barbara was having some difficulty adapting to the group instructional environment.

## Discussion Questions

1.  Does a student who is home schooled qualify for special services?

2.  Can a home-schooled child be expected to meet the same standards if her "teachers" are not certified educators?

3.  How do you think No Child Left Behind impacts these students?

4.  Why must a teacher attend four years of school in order to become certified to teach when a parent can teach without certification? Should there be a minimum requirement of education for the parents who teach their children?

# WISCONSIN V. YODER 406 U.S. 205, 92 S. CT. 1526 (1972)

**GENERAL RULE OF LAW:** The First Amendment right to free exercise of religion protects a religious way of life that requires children older than 13 to devote themselves to a vocation. This overrides a state's compulsory education requirement that all children attend public high school.

**PROCEDURE SUMMARY:**

**Plaintiffs:** The State of Wisconsin (P) and the school district administrator for the public school system in Green County, Wisconsin

**Defendant:** Yoder (D), an Amish parent

**State Trial Court Decision:** Held for Wisconsin (P)

**State Supreme Court Decision:** Reversed

**U.S. Supreme Court Decision:** Affirmed

**FACTS:** The Amish religion and way of life stresses independence and separateness from society and freedom from the competitiveness that defines much of American life. It is characterized by self-sufficiency and requires that children past the age of 13 devote themselves to a vocation such as farming, building, and so on. Many Amish communities build their own schools for children under the age of 13, but some send their children to public schools through the eighth grade. However, all keep their children in the Amish community and away from public high schools. Wisconsin's (P) compulsory education law required that children up to the age of 16 attend public school or an "equivalent" private school. The Amish parents in Green County, Wisconsin, including Yoder (D), were prosecuted under this law for refusing to send their children to a traditional school. Yoder (D) was convicted and appealed to the Wisconsin Supreme Court, which held that Yoder (D) and the other Amish parents were merely asserting their First Amendment right to free exercise of their religion. Yoder (D) claimed that the Amish way of life was inseparable from the Amish religion, and therefore the First Amendment likewise protected this way of life. The state supreme court reversed Yoder's (D) conviction, and Wisconsin (P) appealed to the U.S. Supreme Court.

**ISSUE:** Does the First Amendment right to free exercise of religion protect a religious way of life that, contrary to a state's compulsory education law, requires children older than 13 to devote themselves to developing practical skills and a vocation in lieu of further education?

**HOLDING AND DECISION:** (Burger, C.J.)Yes. The First Amendment right to free exercise of religion protects a religious way of life that requires children older than 13 to devote themselves to a vocation and overrides a state's compulsory education requirement that all children attend public high school. A state's interest in universal education, however important in developing civic integration and political awareness, cannot justify the severe intrusion into the basic religious tenets and practices of a sincerely held religious belief. Here, the Amish religion and culture is based on three centuries of tradition in this country, and the Amish religion and mode of life are inseparable and interdependent. Wisconsin (P) has not made the particularized showing necessary to justify the substantial intrusion into the Amish faith that its compulsory education law requires. Further, the purpose of Wisconsin's (P) law, to inculcate civic virtues in its young citizens, is largely met through Amish culture, which emphasizes self-sufficiency, community, and practical vocations. Affirmed.

**COMMENT:** Although the Supreme Court here appears very respectful of Amish religion, this respect almost certainly arises from the Amish's long tradition of self-sufficiency and simple values held up as the American ideal. Indeed, in one part of the opinion, the Court explicitly refers to the Amish as models of Jefferson's "sturdy yeoman" who forms the backbone of American democracy. In another part, it noted that there was, in fact, only "a minimal difference between what the state would require [in its compulsory education law] and what the Amish already accept." The Court, given this tradition, was ready to accept that the Amish were sincere in their beliefs and were not "creating" a religion in order to evade Wisconsin's laudable aim of universal education. However, the Court in future cases can be expected to give close scrutiny to "ways of life" also claiming to be "religions." Elsewhere, the Court commented on this, noting that "[it] cannot be overemphasized that we are not dealing with a way of life and mode of education by a group claiming to have recently discovered some 'progressive' or more enlightened process of rearing children for modern life."

## Discussion Questions

1. Does the First Amendment protect the Amish's religious principle that children past the age of 13 no longer attend school and instead begin a vocation of farming or an apprenticeship in a trade such as building or furniture making?

2. How is a distinction made between a religious tenet and a cultural tenet of a group that does not want their children educated in a public school?

3. How does this ruling impact state laws that interfere with religious practices that violate dress codes (such as religions that require face coverings)?

# PLYLER V. DOE 457 U.S. 202, 102 S. CT. 2382 (1982)

**GENERAL RULE OF LAW:** A statute violates the equal protection clause when it withholds from local school districts state funds used to educate children not "legally admitted" into the United States and when it authorizes districts to deny enrollment to these children.

**PROCEDURE SUMMARY:**

**Plaintiff:** Undocumented school-age children (i.e., illegal immigrant children) (P)

**Defendant:** Texas Public School Districts (D)

**U.S. Fifth Circuit Court of Appeals Decision:** State revisions of education law violate the equal protection clause of the Fourteenth Amendment

**U.S. Supreme Court Decision:** Affirmed

**FACTS:** The Texas legislature revised its education law, Tex. Educ. **Code** Ann. § 21.031, to authorize local school districts (D) to deny public school enrollment to children not legally admitted to the U.S. Plaintiffs, undocumented school-aged children, challenged the revision on equal protection grounds.

**ISSUE:** Does a statute violate the equal protection clause when it denies illegal immigrant children access to free public education and when it withholds public school funding to districts that admit illegal immigrants?

**HOLDING AND DECISION:** (Brennan, J.) Yes. The Court affirmed the decision of the Fifth Circuit, noting that if the state wished to deny undocumented school-aged children (P) the free public education that it offered to other children residing within its borders, the state must show that denial furthered some substantial state interest. The illegal aliens challenging the statute may claim the benefit of the equal protection clause, which provides that no state shall "deny to *any person within its jurisdiction* the equal protection of the laws." Thus, the aliens were granted this protection despite their lack of full U.S. citizenship. Whatever his status under the immigration laws, an alien is a "person" in any ordinary sense of that term. The discrimination contained in the Texas statute cannot be considered rational unless it furthers some substantial state goal. Although undocumented, resident aliens cannot be treated as a "suspect class," and although education is not a "fundamental right" (either of which would require the state to justify the statutory classification by showing that it serves a compelling governmental interest), nevertheless the Texas statute imposes a lifetime hardship on a discrete class of children not accountable for their disabling status. These alien children should not be penalized for the actions of their parents. These children (P) neither affect their parents' conduct nor their own undocumented status.

Texas' statutory classification cannot be sustained by the argument that it furthers its interest in the "preservation of the state's limited resources for the education of its lawful residents." Even assuming that the influx of illegal aliens has a negative economic impact, charging tuition to undocumented children would likely not decrease illegal immigration. Nor is there any merit to the suggestion that excluding undocumented children eliminates any burdens. The record did not show that exclusion of undocumented children is likely to improve the overall quality of education in the state. In addition, there is no merit to the claim that undocumented children should be excluded because their unlawful presence renders them less likely than others to remain within the state's boundaries and to put their education to productive social or political use.

**COMMENT:** The Court points out that because education is not a fundamental right and undocumented aliens are not a suspect class (a class in need of heightened constitutional scrutiny), the Supreme Court applied the rational relationship test to the revisions. The Supreme Court held that Texas did not have a state interest substantial enough to deny illegal immigrant children free public education. Therefore, discrimination here was not rational and violated the equal protection clause.

## Discussion Questions

1. What were some of the reasons the court gave for allowing illegal immigrant children access to free public education?

2. When the court looked at the constitutionality of the Texas revisions, what did it say would withstand a constitutional challenge?

3. Do you think the Court would decide differently if the influx of illegal immigrants impeded the state's ability to educate children legally residing in Texas?

# STATE OF WISCONSIN V. POPANZ
# 112 WIS.2D 166, 332 N.W.2D 750 (1983)

**GENERAL RULE OF LAW:** Compulsory education laws that require guardians to ensure that their children attend public or private school on a regular basis must specifically define "private school" in order to meet constitutional standards of procedural due process.

**PROCEDURE SUMMARY:**

**Plaintiff:** Wisconsin state superintendent of the Department of Public Instruction (P)

**Defendant:** Popanz (D), father of three school-age daughters

**State Court Decision:** Held for Wisconsin (P)

**State Supreme Court Decision:** Reversed

**FACTS:** Popanz (D), whose daughters had previously been enrolled in Wisconsin's public schools, joined the Church of the Free Thinker, a not-for-profit corporation organized under Wisconsin law. Popanz (D) attempted to send his girls to a private "school" administered by this church. In order to ensure that he was complying with Wisconsin's compulsory education law, Popanz (D) requested that his daughters' prior schools forward to the Free Thinker school their transcripts and recommendations on curriculum. Under Wisconsin law, parents with children between the ages of 6 and 18 were required to ensure that their children attended public or private school regularly. The administrator at the public school who processed Popanz's (D) requests refused to send the transcripts because he believed that the Free Thinker school was not a "private school." The administrator believed the Free Thinker school did not comply with the compulsory education act because the school was not listed in a state directory of nonpublic schools. However, the compulsory education act did not define a "private school" as one that had to be listed in this publication. Popanz (D) was convicted of violating the act and sentenced to two 90-day jail terms. He appealed to the Wisconsin Supreme Court, arguing that Wisconsin's failure to define "private school" violated his constitutional due process rights.

**ISSUE:** Must compulsory education laws specifically define "private school" in order to meet constitutional standards of procedural due process?

**HOLDING AND DECISION:** (Abrahamson, J.) Yes. Compulsory education laws that require guardians to ensure that their children attend public or private school on a regular basis must specifically define "private school" in order to meet constitutional standards of procedural due process. Procedural due process requires that laws set forth fair notice of prohibited or required conduct and proper standards for law enforcement. Here, no definition of "private school" was provided in the statute or in any regulations that construed the statute. It was left to administrators to improvise, on an ad hoc basis, which institutions met the state requirement. This lack of notice left parents such as Popanz (D) to act at their peril. States such as Wisconsin must provide objective standards defining which institutions are appropriate; subjective interpretations of which institutions are appropriate are not permissible. Reversed.

**COMMENT:** Typically, private schools are defined in comparison with public schools, that is, as offering academic grades comparable to those established in the public system. Therefore, in this case, the administrator's decision not to provide Popanz (D) with records of his daughters' attendance may have been based as much on inability to confirm a requisite parallel curriculum as on a prejudice against "unorthodox" churches. However, in reaching its decision, the court expressly noted that the administrator did not visit the Free Thinker school or ask any questions about its curricula, educational backgrounds of the teachers, types of instructional materials or facilities, or time schedules. This failure highlighted the "subjective" nature of the administrator's decision and the failure of the Wisconsin statute to define "private school."

Additionally, violating a compulsory education statute is a criminal offense. To be convicted of a criminal offense, the defendant must be proven guilty "beyond a reasonable doubt," which usually means that all jurors must concur in the verdict (less serious criminal offenses might use the "clear and convincing" standard). Civil liability, however, need only be proven "by a preponderance of the evidence," which usually means that only a majority of jurors must concur in the verdict. Criminal liability carries a higher burden of proof because incarceration, a restriction on someone's free will and liberty, is possible. Civil liability, alternatively, threatens only monetary damages (and on rare occasions, injunctive relief). The higher standard in *Popanz* is needed because there is a possibility of incarceration.

## Discussion Questions

1. What does procedural due process require?

2. If you were faced with an education law that failed to define a key term, what would you do? Why?

3. What was the relevance of the "standard of proof" to this case?

---

Additional case briefs can be found on the SAGE Web site at the following address:
http://www.sagepub.com/aquilacasebriefs

---

# NOTES

1. See State of Wisconsin v. Popanz, 112 Wis.2d 166, 332 N.W.2d 750 (1983).
2. See New Jersey v. Massa, 95 N.J. Super. 382 (1967).
3. See Wisconsin v. Yoder, 406 U.S. 205, 92 S. Ct. 1526 (1972).
4. See Pierce v. Society of the Sisters of the Holy Names of Jesus and Mary, 268 U.S. 510 (1925).
5. See Wisconsin v. Yoder, 406 U.S. 205, 92 S. Ct. 1526 (1972).
6. See New Jersey v. Massa, 95 N.J. Super. 382 (1967).
7. See Plyler v. Doe, 457 U.S. 202, 102 S. Ct. 2382 (1982).
8. See Pierce v. Society of the Sisters of the Holy Names of Jesus and Mary, 268 U.S. 510, 45 S. Ct. 571 (1925).
9. See State of Wisconsin v. Popanz, 112 Wis.2d 166, 332 N.W.2d 750 (1983).
10. Allen v. Casper, 622 N.E.2d 367 (Ohio App. 8th Dist. 1993).
11. See New Jersey v. Massa, 95 N.J. Super. 382 (1967).
12. State v. Priest, 210 La. 389, 27 So. 2d 173 (1946).
13. See Wisconsin v. Yoder, 406 U.S. 205, 92 S. Ct. 1526 (1972).
14. Martinez v. Bynum, 461 U.S. 321, 103 S. Ct. 1838 (1983).
15. See Plyler v. Doe, 457 U.S. 202, 102 S. Ct. 2382 (1982).
16. See People v. Turner, 121 Cal. App. Supp.2d 861, 263 P.2d 685 (Cal. Super. Ct. 1953), which held that instruction by a private tutor is "equivalent" if the tutor possesses a valid state credential for the grade taught.

# 5

---

# Student Conduct and Discipline

*I know a man who is firm—he's firm in his pants, he's firm in his shirt, his character is firm—but most . . . of all, his belief in you, the students of Bethel, is firm. Jeff Kuhlman is a man who takes his point and pounds it in. If necessary, he'll take an issue and nail it to the wall. He doesn't attack things in spurts—he drives hard, pushing and pushing until finally he succeeds. Jeff is a man who will go to the very end—even the climax—for each and every one of you. So vote for Jeff for A.S.B. vice president—he'll never come between you and the best our high school can be.*

—*Bethel School Dist. No. 403 v. Fraser* (1986)

## OVERVIEW . . . . . . . . . . . . . . . . . . . . . . . . . . . . . . . . . . . . . . . .

When educational equality issues are discussed, the case that automatically comes to mind is the 1954 case of *Brown v. Board of Education*.[1] Similarly, *Tinker v. Des Moines Independent Community School District* (1969) is the hallmark case that dealt with the issue of student rights.[2] In *Tinker,* the Supreme Court recognized that public school students have the First Amendment right of free speech in the classroom. Prior to this decision, students did not enjoy free speech and other rights while in school. Essentially, *Tinker* initiated the argument whether the rights of students and the rights of adults were coterminous. Previously, school authorities could do essentially whatever they deemed appropriate and reasonable in school because education was considered a privilege. *Tinker* opened the door to an extensive exploration of student rights, including free speech, discipline, compulsory attendance, residency, sexual harassment, and search and seizure. These rights are still being examined and clarified. Some, including this writer, believe that due to social and educational conditions, the Supreme Court has limited the extent of *Tinker* rights. Regardless, *Tinker* remains a focus for litigation and the determination of the proper treatment of students in our schools.

The common law position was that schools and students shared a mutual relationship. Teachers needed to have wide latitude in exercising control over students in order to accomplish the results that society expects of its schools. Whether this was an inherent or statutory power was not worthy of debate as long as the schools were given the necessary latitude and discretion to deal with students. The common law understanding was that schools acted **in loco parentis**, "in place of the parent." This concept remains in place today and is used in school cases to justify the actions of school authorities. Thus, school boards are vested with sufficient authority to regulate conduct that affects the welfare of the school system and its students and personnel.

Although public school students are generally entitled to freedom of speech and expression, their rights are not coextensive with those of adults and may be more regulated under certain circumstances. Generally, obscene statements and conduct are not afforded First Amendment protection. The Court has held that the prohibition of "vulgar and offensive" language in schools is an appropriate function of the public educational system.[3] Similarly, expression that might reasonably be expected to lead to a "substantial disruption of or material interference with school activities" will not be afforded First Amendment protection.[4] Protected First Amendment speech or conduct expresses a political or ideological viewpoint in a nondisruptive manner. In *Tinker,* the expressive rights of students who wore arm bands to protest the Vietnam War were upheld. Noting that the students' conduct had not led to a disturbance of any kind, the Court warned school officials that "a mere desire to avoid [the] discomfort and unpleasantness that always accompany an unpopular viewpoint was insufficient to justify the regulation of free expression rights."

*Tinker* was quickly distinguished, however. Now, a school may constitutionally adopt a policy that prohibits students from wearing items expressing messages unrelated to school activities. However, these policies must uniformly apply to all types of noneducation speech, without singling out any particular message. In addition, the school must establish a history of disruption caused by the wearing of such items.[5]

Freedom of the press, like freedom of speech and expression, is guaranteed by the First Amendment. In the schools, free press issues usually arise in connection with student publications. A recent Supreme Court decision has established that school officials' control over the contents of a school-sponsored student newspaper does not violate the First Amendment, so long as the control is reasonably related to legitimate pedagogical concerns.[6] It would appear that the basic tenets of *Tinker* are now open to question. At best, after *Hazelwood,* school-sponsored student publications have fewer First Amendment protections than before. However, most courts are still wary of prior administrative reviews of student publications because of the potential for curtailment of free press rights.

The Fourth Amendment to the U.S. Constitution prohibits the government from conducting *unreasonable* searches and seizures of people and their belongings. The Fourth Amendment has been interpreted to require that state authorities have "probable cause" to believe that contraband exists before they may conduct a warrantless search. However, in the context of schools, this standard has been lowered. School authorities need only have a "reasonable suspicion" that contraband exists before a warrantless search is justified.[7] When considering whether a search is justified, a two-part analysis is used. First, authorities must initially have a reasonable motivation to search a purse or locker (i.e., something reasonably incited their suspicion). Second, the search itself must be reasonable (i.e., it must not be more intrusive than is reasonably justified). Obviously, such a subjective standard requires that the more intrusive the search, the higher degree of suspicion and more extensive evidence school officials must have.

As schools continue to be at the forefront of the battle against drugs, the Court has expanded the power of the schools to conduct warrantless searches. First, there was *New Jersey v. T.L.O.* (1985), which expanded the school's authority to search students. Then, in *Vernonia School District 471 v. Acton* (1995), the Supreme Court reacted to the pervasive drug and safety problem in schools by allowing random searches of students in athletic activities without specific suspicion.[8] This further limited students' expectation of privacy. Further, the Court upheld an even more invasive form of drug testing: mandatory urinalysis. In *Board of Education Independent School District No. 92 of Pottawatomie County v. Earls* (2002), random drug testing was imposed on all students taking part in extracurricular activities, not just those participating in sports programs.[9]

School boards establish codes of conduct, and students who are guilty of serious misconduct are subject to disciplinary action. Disciplinary actions must be accompanied by some form of procedure designed to ensure that the disciplinary process is fundamentally fair.[10] In light of *Goss v. Lopez* (1975), courts have been as concerned with procedural due process guarantees as they have been with the substantive nature of the policy or procedure itself. Substantive due process, which occurs when a policy or statute "insults the "conscience," is a relatively new idea. Traditional procedural due process, on the other hand, has a long history. This concept, also called "natural justice," can be traced back to the Magna Carta in 1215 and has since then been part of our common law. To ensure procedural due process, school officials must make sure that there is "fundamental fairness," which requires, among other things, that both sides have an opportunity to present their positions.

The courts have responded to litigation about gangs, violence, and unrest in today's schools by informally developing a reasonableness standard. When applying a reasonableness standard, the court is making a ruling based on a standard of what appears just, fair, and reasonable when analyzing school situations to determine the appropriateness of the student behavior in question. Looking at recent cases provides a clear justification for this re-emersion of the common law doctrine of reasonableness. In *T.L.O.,* the Court used a reasonableness analysis to justify lowering the adult standard for warrantless student searches from "probable cause" to "reasonable suspicion."[11] When the reasonableness standard was applied to free speech, the Supreme Court in *Bethel* adopted a lower standard when looking at protecting students from speech activity at a school assembly, "especially in a captive audience from exposure to sexually explicit, indecent, or lewd speech."[12] The reasonableness doctrine is enunciated even more explicitly in *Hazelwood.* In that case, the school principal's excising of two articles from the school newspaper was upheld even though similar prior censorship of an adult newspaper is impermissible.[13]

It appears that the continuing qualification of a student's expressive rights has obfuscated the basic tenets of *Tinker.* A final example of the more recent application of the reasonableness standard in support of school officials can be seen in *Pottawatomie,* in which invasive, suspicionless drug testing was allowed.[14] This allowance partially accommodates school officials who face escalating threats of violence and drug use in schools.

## Case Study

### Art or Violence: Where Do You Draw the Line?

You are the Happy Hearts School District's hearing officer responsible for all students who are involved in suspension and expulsion hearings. Happy Hearts is a suburban school district abutting a major urban area. The principal of the middle school has suspended—and recommended for expulsion—a student because he drew violent cartoons. These cartoons depict stick figures being shot, stabbed, and blown up. Problems arose when it was discovered that two of the figures were named after current middle school teachers.

   The school board has adopted a zero tolerance policy regarding violent images, statements, and actions. The record shows that the drawings were part of a hand-drawn comic book taken from the student by a teacher at the school. The student is currently serving a 10-day suspension pending the upcoming expulsion hearing. The student's statement includes his honest belief that he was simply completing a class project for art class. He appears to be sincerely surprised at the problems that his "comic" book has caused. Furthermore, he claims that he didn't know that there was a zero tolerance policy for "violent images, statements and actions."

### Discussion Questions

1. Based on the information provided, how would you decide this case?

2. What general rule(s) of law apply here?

3. What are the arguments on both sides?

4. Do any practical considerations enter into your decision?

# IMPORTANT CONCEPTS

- **Broad authority to regulate conduct:** School boards are given broad powers to regulate conduct that affects the welfare of the school system.

- **Compelling justification must exist:** When a regulation impacts a student's constitutional rights, school officials must demonstrate a compelling need to regulate student conduct as adopted and stated in the regulation.

- **First Amendment rights may be regulated:** While public school students are generally entitled to freedom of speech and freedom of the press, these rights may be regulated under certain circumstances.

- **No right to certain speech:** Defamatory statements, obscenities, and inflammatory statements are among the forms of speech that are not protected by the First Amendment to the U.S. Constitution.

- **Prior restraint unacceptable:** Prior administrative reviews of student publications are legally suspect because of the potential for infringing students' rights to freedom of the press. This means that the court could apply a higher standard when there is a prior restraint issue.

- **Freedom of association may be limited:** Public school officials may deny access to student groups whose purposes for meeting are not in line with existing curriculum.

- **Establishment of religion prohibited:** Courts frequently invalidate decisions by school officials to provide access to student religious groups on the grounds that such assistance amounts to state sponsorship of religion.

- **Common forms of punishment:** When authorized by law and imposed fairly, corporal punishment, suspension from school, expulsion from school, and academic sanctions are all acceptable forms of punishment.

- **Political or ideological viewpoint:** Speech or conduct that expresses a political or ideological viewpoint in a nondisruptive manner is protected by the First Amendment.

- **Recognition of secret societies:** Courts consistently uphold school officials' decisions to deny recognition to so-called secret societies, such as fraternities and sororities.

- **First Amendment protections:** Since *Hazelwood,* school-sponsored student publications have fewer First Amendment protections than in the past.

- **Dress and grooming requirements:** The courts of appeals are split in regard to dress and grooming requirements for students. Half support schools in an effort to regulate student conduct, while the others support students' right to free expression.

- **Search of students:** The Fourth Amendment standard of "probable cause," which applies to adults, has been lowered to "reasonable suspicion" when determining whether a search of a student is constitutional.

- **Student discipline:** Disciplinary actions must be accompanied by some form of procedure designed to ensure that the discipline process is fundamentally fair.[15]

- **Due process:** Strict due process guarantees are usually provided to students who face suspension or expulsion actions.

- **Testing for drugs:** The power of schools to conduct random, suspicionless searches of non-athletes has been condoned because schools are in a "special needs" category with expanded search latitudes and because of the students' lower expectation of privacy.

- **Reasonableness standard:** Looking at recent cases provides a clear justification for this re-emersion of the common law doctrine of reasonableness.

# STUDENT CONDUCT

## Authority to Regulate Student Conduct

School boards are vested with sufficient authority to regulate conduct that affects the welfare of the school system and its students and personnel. In most cases, the burden of proving that a particular rule or regulation is unreasonable falls on the party challenging it. In those cases in which a rule or regulation impacts a constitutional right, the burden shifts to school officials to demonstrate a compelling need to regulate the conduct in the manner proscribed. For instance, preventing married high school students from participating in extracurricular activities implicates a fundamental constitutional right, the equal protection clause of the U.S. Constitution.[16] In general, a rule or regulation may not be so vague as to permit arbitrary application. In particular, a rule or regulation must provide affected students with adequate information, usually called notice, about what is expected of them. Under normal circumstances, you cannot punish people for conduct that they did not know was improper.

## Freedom of Speech and Expression

The First Amendment to the U.S. Constitution, applied to the states through the Fourteenth Amendment, limits the government's authority to interfere with citizens' free speech and expression rights. "Expression" is usually defined as conduct that communicates an idea. While public school students are generally entitled to freedom of speech and expression, their rights are not coextensive with those of adults in other settings and may be regulated under certain circumstances. The following forms of speech and conduct are not protected by the First Amendment in the school setting.

*Defamatory Statements.* Statements that are false, that are communicated to someone other than the defamed party, and that expose the defamed party to shame or ridicule are defamatory and, as such, are not protected by the First Amendment. They must contain assertions of fact, not opinion. A public official, such as a school board member, who believes she has been defamed must prove, in addition to the foregoing, that the defaming party acted recklessly and with malice.

*Obscenities.* Generally, obscene statements and conduct are not afforded First Amendment protection. The U.S. Supreme Court has specifically held that the prohibition of "vulgar and offensive" language in the schools is an appropriate function of the public educational system.[17]

*Inflammatory Expression.* Forms of expression that might reasonably be expected to lead to a "substantial disruption of or material interference with school activities" will not be afforded First Amendment protection.[18]

*Political or Ideological Viewpoint.* Speech or conduct that expresses a political or ideological viewpoint in a manner that is not disruptive is protected by the First Amendment.

*Landmark Opinion.* In *Tinker v. Des Moines Indep. Comm. School Dist.* (1969), the Supreme Court upheld the rights of students who had been suspended from school for wearing arm bands to protest the war in Vietnam. Noting that the students' conduct had not led to a disturbance of any kind, the Court warned school officials that "a mere desire to avoid [the] discomfort and unpleasantness that always accompany an unpopular viewpoint" was insufficient to justify the regulation of free expression rights.

*Tinker Distinguished.* A school may constitutionally adopt a policy that prohibits students from wearing items that bear a message unrelated to school activities, but only if that policy applies to all types of noneducational speech without singling out any particular message. Also, the school must show a history of disruption caused by the wearing of such items.[19]

## Freedom of Press

Freedom of the press, like freedom of speech and expression, is guaranteed by the First Amendment. In the schools, free press issues usually arise in connection with student publications. A recent Supreme Court decision has established that official control over the contents of a school-sponsored student newspaper does not violate the First Amendment, so long as the control is reasonably related to legitimate pedagogical concerns.[20] It would appear that the basic tenets of *Tinker* are now open to question. The traditional analysis of *Tinker* is that a student publication is not any less deserving of First Amendment protections than a nonschool publication. Moreover, removal of sponsorship may be construed in certain circumstances as an attempt to stifle or curtail free press rights (i.e., censorship). Nevertheless, after *Hazelwood,* school-sponsored student publications have fewer First Amendment protections than before. Notwithstanding, most courts are wary of prior administrative reviews of student publications because of the potential for curtailment of free press rights. Prior restraint policies must be narrowly tailored to the achievement of clearly stated goals, must set forth unambiguous restraint criteria, and must provide students with an opportunity to challenge unfavorable decisions.[21]

## Dress and Appearance

Approximately half of the federal circuit courts of appeals have declared that grooming restrictions curtail constitutionally protected expression, while the other half have upheld such restrictions as not affecting constitutional rights or as permissibly infringing on them in order to prevent disruptions in the school setting.[22] Regulations of student attire have been invalidated by some courts based on what has been termed the constitutional right to wear clothes of one's own choosing (grounded in the Fourteenth Amendment). However, regulations that merely restrict immodest dress have generally been upheld.

## Fourth Amendment Searches

The Fourth Amendment to the U.S. Constitution prohibits the government from conducting *unreasonable* searches and seizures of people and their belongings. The Fourth Amendment standard of "probable cause," which applies to adults, has been lowered to "reasonable suspicion" when determining whether a search of a student is appropriate.[23] The lowered standard is rational when you consider that the items found in the search will not be used for prosecution; as well, the standard is a reflection of the Court's understanding of the multiple problems of drugs, gangs, and violence that face today's educators. When considering a search, a two-part analysis is used. First, authorities must have a reasonable motivation to search a purse or locker (i.e., something reasonably incited their suspicion). Second, the search itself must be reasonable (i.e., it must not be more intrusive than is reasonably justified). Further, the standard requires that principals have a heightened degree of suspicion, and the more intrusive the search the more extensive the necessary evidence must be.

For example, in *People v. William G.* (1985), a principal noticed a student holding a calculator case that had an odd bulge. The principal confiscated the case, searched it, and found marijuana. The court felt that, absent evidence other than the bulge in the calculator case, the principal did not have "reasonable suspicion" of contraband that would justify a search. Some prior knowledge of this student's involvement in the school's drug culture or some "tip" from an informant was necessary to meet the standard of reasonableness.[24]

## Drug Testing

As schools continued to be at the forefront of the battle against drugs, the Court expanded the power of the schools to conduct warrantless searches. Ten years after *T.L.O.,* the Supreme Court again expanded the authority of schools to search students. In *Vernonia School District 471 v. Acton* (1995), in reaction to the problem of drugs and safety, schools were allowed to conduct random searches of students without specific suspicion. The *T.L.O.* standard of suspicion at the inception of the search was further reduced, providing students with an even more limited expectation of privacy. Precedents have developed to deal with some search situations in schools. For example, with canine searches, there must be a greater individualized suspicion for person searches than for locker searches (of course, at the beginning of the year, schools must provide notice in student codes of conduct and formal announcements that locker searches will be conducted). The most invasive drug testing, using urinalysis, was allowed in *Board of Education of Independent School District No. 92 of Pottawatomie County v. Earls* (2002).

In *Acton,* a urinalysis was required for participation in sporting events. The rationale was that these events included students with a greater likelihood of involvement in the drug culture and, further, there was a safety issue. Then in *Pottawatomie,* the random drug testing was imposed on all students taking part in all extracurricular activities, not just sports programs. The power of schools to conduct random, suspicionless searches of nonathletes was condoned because schools were in a "special needs" category that expanded search latitudes (similar to random drug testing of airline pilots) and because of students' lower expectation of privacy.

## Student Organizations

The freedom of individuals to associate with others is not specifically enumerated in the First Amendment to the U.S. Constitution, but it is implied. Courts recognize that individuals express their views more effectively when they do so through associations with others. Education-related clubs and societies provide an opportunity for students to associate with fellow students. In the higher education setting, school officials are prohibited from denying recognition to or restricting the activities of student organizations based on the content of their organizational philosophies.[25] At the high school level and below, school officials have more latitude in dealing with student organizations; they can deny access to groups that are not extensions of the existing curriculum.

*Effect of Providing Access to Extracurricular Groups.* If, however, noncurriculum-related student organizations are provided access, the school's policy must not discriminate based on the philosophies of the various organizations (see exception, below).[26]

*Problems Arising From Providing Access to Student Religious Organizations.* Attempts to regulate religious groups often pit students' free speech and association rights against the Constitution's proscription of the establishment of religion. In the context of the public schools, courts often invalidate decisions by school officials to provide access to student religious groups on the grounds that such assistance amounts to state sponsorship of religion.

*Recognition of Secret Societies.* Courts consistently uphold school officials' decisions to deny recognition to so-called secret societies, such as fraternities and sororities.

## STUDENT DISCIPLINE

### Regulation of Student Conduct

Most states, through their subordinate agencies (usually county and local school districts), establish codes of conduct within the public schools. Students who are guilty of serious misconduct are subject to disciplinary action. School officials are not only authorized to establish and enforce disciplinary regulations, they also are *required* to do so. The question is usually not whether teachers have the right to impose physical punishment, but rather to what degree and how reasonable is the punishment. Disciplinary actions must be accompanied by some form of procedure designed to ensure that the disciplinary process is fundamentally fair.[27] Historically, courts have been as concerned with the due process guarantees afforded disciplined students as they have been with the validity of disciplinary regulations and the severity of punishments imposed.[28] The concept of procedural due process, also called natural justice, can be traced as far back as 1215 in the Magna Carta and has continued through common law. In applying procedural due process to principals in schools, the key is that there must be "fundamental fairness" and that both sides must have the opportunity to present their positions.

### Forms of Punishment

In most states, school officials are authorized to inflict reasonable physical punishment on a student's body with the intention of modifying unacceptable behavior. The U.S. Supreme Court has declared that corporal punishment does not violate the Eighth Amendment's proscription of "cruel and unusual punishment" and the Fourteenth Amendment's guarantee of procedural due process.[29] The permanent or temporary removal of students from school is a common form of punishment for serious disciplinary infractions. Strict due process guarantees are usually provided to students who face suspension or expulsion actions.[30] Note, however, that expulsion from privately operated schools is generally governed by contract law and does not implicate due process. Absent a clear abuse of discretion on the part of the private operator, courts will not interfere in matters of contract.[31]

Additionally, a suspension without immediate hearing based on an out-of-school offense that resulted in a pending juvenile court **proceeding** was held to comply with due process, though the state court declined to provide the student with heightened due process protections associated with criminal proceedings.[32]

School officials are authorized to give students failing grades, place them on probation, and remove them from academic programs in response to substandard academic performance. However, the courts are at odds over whether it is permissible to impose such sanctions as punishment for misconduct that is unrelated to academics.

## REASONABLENESS STANDARD

A reasonableness standard has informally been developed by the courts in response to the problems and concerns that schools and teachers face in today's increasingly violent schools characterized by gangs and unrest as well as a significant increase in litigation. While the reasonableness doctrine has long been the standard in **tort** law, the reasonableness standard has developed in the student rights area as courts attempt to balance the rights of students with the need for schools to preserve control and regulate behavior (a balancing of the equities). Prior to the recent *Tinker* expansion of student rights, the common law determinant of appropriate teacher-student behavior was a variation of reasonableness; that is, teachers were allowed to impose discipline deemed reasonable. Obviously, determining what is "reasonable" is difficult. Because all eventualities cannot be detailed in rules, sometimes the courts must determine whether a school action or policy is reasonable.

Looking at recent cases provides a clear justification for this re-emersion of the common law doctrine of reasonableness. In *T.L.O.,* the Court used a reasonableness analysis to justify lowering the standard for warrantless student searches from "probable cause" to "reasonable suspicion." When reasonableness was applied to free speech in a school setting, the Supreme Court in *Bethel* used a lower standard when trying to protect students from "sexually loaded" speech activity at a school assembly. This was a special concern because these students were a "captive audience" unable to escape from "exposure to sexually explicit, indecent, or lewd speech." The quote beginning this chapter is an example of this inappropriate speech. Allowing school administrators to censor such "explosive" speech, if such censorship is deemed reasonable and appropriate, allows school authorities to avoid chaos while providing reasonable protection to the free speech rights of students. The reasonableness doctrine is enunciated even more explicitly in *Hazelwood.* In that case, the school principal's excising of two articles from the school newspaper was upheld even though this prior censorship would never be supported when dealing with adults and a regular newspaper. Qualifications on students' free speech rights may have obfuscated the *Tinker* ruling, certainly making its application unclear. Even though many believe that a school-sponsored/affiliated student publication should have First Amendment protections, this is clearly not the case. Courts have supported schools that deny First Amendment protections to student publications—which are part of the school curriculum—if the school deemed the denial "reasonable." This is true even though such action clearly would have violated the First Amendment if applied to an independent newspaper. Thus, in order to provide support to beleaguered school officials, the Court has limited the rights of students even though *Hazelwood* may be construed as stifling or curtailing free press rights. The application of the reasonableness standard favoring schools and school officials is clearly demonstrated in

*Pottawatomie*. In that case, invasive, suspicionless drug testing was allowed because of safety concerns in increasingly violent schools. Therefore, in the context of safety and administrative regulations, a search unsupported by probable cause may be reasonable when special needs, beyond the normal need for law enforcement, make the **warrant** and probable cause requirement impracticable. Thus, it now appears that while schoolchildren do not shed their constitutional rights when they enter the schoolhouse, their Fourth Amendment rights are different in public schools than elsewhere. The "reasonableness" inquiry cannot disregard the schools' custodial and tutelary responsibility for children.

## Case Study

### Drugs in Her Brassiere

Happy Hearts High School, like so many other American secondary schools, has been experiencing an increase in drug-related activity. The school security force has been instructed to be especially vigilant in regard to behavior that relates to drug use and drug trafficking. An outside security guard was patrolling the student parking lot when she noticed a girl acting strangely. The girl was moving furtively between cars and seemingly looking for someone or something in and around the cars. When the security guard asked her to stop, she ducked down and tried to evade detection. Upon securing her, the security guard asked her name. The security guard was able to determine that the girl had given the guard the wrong name. The security guard, with a female teacher, took the young girl into a restroom and searched her pockets and purse. The search failed to locate anything unusual. The security guard then asked the girl to remove her jeans. When she again found nothing, the security guard made a visual inspection of the girl's brassiere. This last search located a small quantity of illegal drugs.

### Discussion Questions

1. In light of *T.L.O.*, was this search legal? Why or why not?
2. What was the reason for believing the girl was hiding drugs?
3. Who "pays" if the search is found unconstitutional?

## CONCLUSION

School boards are vested with sufficient authority to regulate conduct that affects the welfare of the school system and its students and personnel. If a student challenges this regulation, he must show that it was unreasonable. The board may then rebut this assertion by showing a compelling need for the regulation.

First Amendment protections of freedom of expression do not extend as far to students in the classroom as they do to adults. Students who utter certain ideological statements in class may be reprimanded. Also, a school may constitutionally adopt a policy that prohibits students from expressions that convey a message unrelated to school activities, so long as a single unrelated message is not singled out for exclusion.

The Supreme Court has held that official control of student publications (notably student newspapers) does not violate the First Amendment. Nevertheless, this control must be related to legitimate pedagogical concerns. However, courts are still generally wary of prior review of student publications. Prior restraint policies must be narrowly tailored to the achievement of appropriate pedagogical goals.

The federal appellate circuit courts are equally divided regarding grooming restrictions. Half declare that grooming restrictions at schools curtail constitutionally protected expression while the other half generally finds these restrictions permissible. Regarding student dress and attire, the courts usually permit restrictions on immodest dress.

School officials need only a "reasonable suspicion" of contraband to search a student's possession (as opposed to the "probable cause" standard required by the police when searching adults). The standard is lowered for student searches because the search is not aimed at eliciting prosecutorial evidence and because of the heightened security threats in schools. As schools continued to be at the forefront of the war on drug culture, the Court expanded the power of the schools to conduct warrantless searches. Schools have been allowed to conduct random searches without specific suspicion.

In the higher education setting, school officials are prohibited from denying recognition to or restricting the activities of student organizations based on the content of their organizational philosophies. However, at the high school level and below, schools officials have more latitude in denying student access to organizations that are not extensions of the existing curriculum.

School officials are not only authorized to establish and enforce disciplinary regulations, they also are required to do so. Teachers are authorized to use physical forms of punishment, but only to a certain degree. Disciplinary actions must be accompanied by some form of procedure defined to ensure that the disciplinary process is fundamentally fair. The permanent or temporary removal of students from school is a common form of punishment for serious disciplinary infractions.

Although the reasonableness doctrine has long been the standard in tort law, it has developed in the student rights, area as courts attempt to balance the rights of students with the need for schools to preserve control and regulate behavior. Teachers are allowed to impose "reasonable" discipline. Of course, determining what is "reasonable" is difficult and always open to question.

As you proceed through the Case Briefs, see if you agree with this writer, who believes that *Tinker* is being confined. Look at the reasons courts use to allow or censor student speech and press, or their reasoning in allowing warrantless searches. Then, compare this examination with your understanding of *Tinker;* try to list just what conduct teachers and administrators may or may not regulate.

# CASE BRIEFS ...............................

## BOARD OF EDUCATION OF INDEPENDENT SCHOOL DISTRICT NO. 92 OF POTTAWATOMIE COUNTY V. EARLS 122 S. CT. 2559 (2002)

**GENERAL RULE OF LAW:** A demonstrated problem of drug abuse is not, in all cases, necessary to the validity of a testing regime, but some showing does shore up an assertion of special need for a suspicionless general search program.

**PROCEDURE SUMMARY:**

**Plaintiff:** Earls (P), on behalf of students of Pottawatomie County

**Defendant:** Board of Education of Pottawatomie County (D)

**U.S. District Court Decision:** Granted the School District (D) summary judgment

**U.S. Court of Appeals Decision:** Reversed

**U.S. Supreme Court Decision:** Reversed

**FACTS:** The Student Activities Drug Testing Policy (Policy) adopted by the Tecumseh, Oklahoma School District (D) requires all middle and high school students to consent to urinalysis testing for drugs in order to participate in any extracurricular activity. In practice, the Policy has been applied only to competitive extracurricular activities sanctioned by the Oklahoma Secondary Schools Activities Association (OSSAA). Respondent high school students and their parents brought this 42 U.S.C. § 1983 action for equitable relief, alleging that the Policy violates the Fourth Amendment. The District Court granted the School District (D) summary judgment. The Tenth Circuit reversed, holding that the Policy violated the Fourth Amendment. It concluded that before imposing a suspicionless drug testing program, a school must demonstrate some identifiable drug abuse problem among a sufficient number of those tested, such that testing that group will actually redress its drug problem. The court then held that the School District (D) had failed to demonstrate such a problem among Tecumseh students participating in competitive extracurricular activities. The Supreme Court reversed.

**ISSUE:** Before imposing a suspicionless drug testing program, must a school district demonstrate some identifiable drug abuse problem among a sufficient number of those tested, such that testing that group will actually redress its drug problem?

**HOLDING AND DECISION:** (Thomas, J.) No. The Fourth Amendment to the United States Constitution protects the right of the people to be secure in their persons, houses, papers, and effects against unreasonable searches and seizures. Searches by public school officials, such as the collection of urine samples for drug testing, implicate Fourth Amendment interests. The court must, therefore, review a school district's drug testing policy for "reasonableness," which is the touchstone of the constitutionality of a governmental search. Therefore, in the context of safety and administrative regulations, a search unsupported by probable cause may be reasonable when special needs, beyond the normal need for law enforcement, make the warrant and probable cause requirements impracticable. "Special needs" inhere in the public school context. Although schoolchildren do not shed their constitutional rights when they enter the schoolhouse, Fourth Amendment rights are different in public schools than elsewhere; the "reasonableness" inquiry cannot disregard the schools' custodial and tutelary responsibility for children. In particular, a finding of individualized suspicion may not be necessary when a school conducts drug testing. A demonstrated problem of drug abuse is not, in all cases, necessary to the validity of a testing regime, but some showing does shore up an assertion of special need for a suspicionless general search program. The need to prevent and deter the substantial harm of childhood drug use provides the necessary immediacy for a school testing policy. Testing students who participate in extracurricular activities is a reasonably effective means of addressing a school district's legitimate concerns in preventing, deterring, and detecting drug use.

**COMMENT:** This case has caused a great deal of consternation with many school people. The suspicionless drug testing program has moved from extracurricular football programs where there was a suspicion of inappropriate drug use by football players to all students participating in an extracurricular program. This expansion has caused a serious chill on liberals who oppose such arbitrary application. The fear is that it is far too intrusive an approach to accomplish the legitimate school interest in preventing, deterring, and detecting drug use.

## Discussion Questions

1. May a school district drug-test any student?

2. Does this rule apply only to urinalysis drug tests?

3. How far do you think suspicionless drug testing might be extended?

---

# HAZELWOOD SCHOOL DISTRICT V. KUHLMEIER
## 484 U.S. 260, 108 S. CT. 562 (1988)

**GENERAL RULE OF LAW:** Official editorial control over the contents of a school-sponsored student newspaper does not violate the First Amendment when the control is reasonably related to legitimate pedagogical concerns.

### PROCEDURE SUMMARY:

**Plaintiff:** Kuhlmeier (P), former student and student newspaper staff member

**Defendant:** Hazelwood School District (Hazelwood) (D)

**U.S. District Court Decision:** Held for Hazelwood (D), finding no First Amendment violation

**U.S. Court of Appeals Decision:** Reversed

**U.S. Supreme Court Decision:** Reversed

**FACTS:** A high school journalism class wrote and edited a newspaper as part of the school's curriculum. Each issue was reviewed by the school principal before publication. In one issue, the principal deleted two articles. The first article discussed the pregnancy experiences of three of the school's students, and the principal feared that the students could be identified from the article. He believed that this violated their privacy rights. He also believed that the article's references to sexual activity and birth control were inappropriate reading for the school's younger students. The second article discussed divorce and quoted a student complaining about her father's conduct. The principal believed that the article should not be published without first giving the father a chance to respond or consent to publication. Kuhlmeier (P), a student on the paper's staff, filed suit. He alleged that the deletions violated his First Amendment rights, requested an injunction against further school interference, and also requested monetary damages. The district court found in favor of Hazelwood (D), holding that no First Amendment violation occurred and that the principal's actions were reasonable. The court of appeals reversed, and the U.S. Supreme Court granted Hazelwood's (D) request for review.

**ISSUE:** May school officials exercise editorial control over the contents of a school-sponsored student newspaper when such control is reasonably related to legitimate pedagogical concerns?

**HOLDING AND DECISION:** (White, J.) Yes. School officials may exercise editorial control over the contents of a school-sponsored student newspaper for legitimate pedagogical concerns without violating students' First Amendment rights. The First Amendment rights of students are not necessarily the same as those of adults in other settings. The school environment is special, and a school is not required to tolerate student speech inconsistent with the school's educational mission. The school paper at issue was not a public forum but merely a part of the school curriculum under the teacher and school's control. There was no intent to "open" the pages of the newspaper to the indiscriminate ideas of student reporters or editors. Therefore, Hazelwood (D) was entitled to regulate the paper's contents in a reasonable manner, as the district court correctly found. Reversed.

**COMMENT:** *Hazelwood* gives great latitude to school officials in censoring student expression in school-sponsored activities and events. School assemblies, theatrical events, and sporting events all likely constitute school-sponsored activities within the rule of *Hazelwood*. The dissent, however, argued unsuccessfully that the stricter standard of review applied in *Tinker*, where the Court struck down a school ban on the wearing of arm bands, should be applied here regardless of whether the student speech or expression at issue occurred in a school-sponsored event. Clearly, the viability of *Tinker* needs to be addressed in a future case. It can be argued that *Hazelwood* is a limited distinguishing of *Tinker*, which would apply in only a specific fact situation. A more accurate position is that *Hazelwood* (in light *of T.L.O.* and *Bethel*) has drastically modified student protections that *Tinker* guaranteed children in the school setting. A "reasonableness" standard has been applied when analyzing student freedoms. Clearly, when considering both *Bethel* and *Hazelwood,* it is clear that the dissent's position, that the rights of students are coextensive with those of adults, is no longer accurate. School newspapers are no longer "public forums" that are immune from content regulation. Although *Tinker* has not been overturned, its doctrine—that a school should be a marketplace of ideas and that the proper socialization for a free people is the early exercise of freedom—has been greatly limited. As the dissent feared, school personnel have been less prone to hesitate before prohibiting student expressions that *Tinker* seemingly protected. Of course, when a school creates a "public forum" within the school, it still relinquishes its discretion to censor student expression. In order to preserve their discretion, school personnel must clearly distinguish curricular activities from activities intended to allow students to express their views. For example, one reason that school authorities prevailed in *Hazelwood* was that the school newspaper was part of the school-controlled curriculum.

## Discussion Questions

1. Can school officials control the contents of a school-sponsored student newspaper?

2. In your opinion, is the *Hazelwood* decision a limitation of the previous *Tinker* decision, or does the *Hazelwood* decision relate only to school-sponsored events and activities?

3. Would the Supreme Court have ruled differently if the student newspaper was produced by an extracurricular group meeting after school hours?

# BETHEL SCHOOL DISTRICT NO. 403 V. FRASER
# 478 U.S. 675, 106 S. CT. 3159 (1986)

**GENERAL RULE OF LAW:** A society's interest in teaching students socially acceptable behavior and in protecting minors from exposure to vulgar and offensive language outweighs a student's First Amendment free speech rights.

**PROCEDURE SUMMARY:**

**Plaintiff:** Fraser (P), a high school student

**Defendant:** Bethel School District No. 403, Washington (D)

**U.S. District Court Decision:** Held for Fraser (P)

**U.S. Court of Appeals Decision:** Affirmed

**U.S. Supreme Court Decision:** Reversed

**FACTS:** Fraser (P) made a speech during a student assembly in which he nominated a fellow student for student government. During the speech, he made sexually suggestive comments that induced students in the crowd to mimic the implied sexual acts and to laugh, as well as confused the younger students who did not understand the creative references. Fraser (P) had been warned by teachers who reviewed the speech that it was inappropriate in a high school setting. After five teachers submitted letters to the principal substantiating the event, Fraser (P) was suspended by Bethel School District (D) for three days for giving the speech. He was also removed from the list of candidates for graduation speaker. Despite these punishments, Fraser (P) in fact attended school on the third day of his "suspension" and actually spoke at graduation. Nonetheless, he sued Bethel (D) in federal court, alleging that his suspension violated his free speech rights. Both the district court and the Ninth Circuit Court of Appeals agreed with him, and Bethel (D) appealed to the U.S. Supreme Court.

**ISSUE:** Does a society's interest in teaching students socially acceptable behavior and in protecting minors from exposure to vulgar and offensive language outweigh a student's First Amendment free speech rights?

**HOLDING AND DECISION:** (Burger, C. J.) Yes. A society's interest in teaching students socially acceptable behavior and in protecting minors from exposure to vulgar and offensive language outweighs a student's First Amendment free speech rights. The content of Fraser's (P) speech here was not political. Unlike the students in *Tinker* who wore black arm bands to protest the Vietnam War, Fraser (P) here merely made a lewd and indecent speech that offended some fellow students and confused many others too young to understand the implications. Further, Fraser (P) was not deprived of due process because the Bethel School District (D) had issued, prior to his speech, disciplinary rules governing obscene language and behavior. In addition, teachers had specifically warned Fraser (P) against giving the speech in its present form, which was replete with sexual innuendo. Reversed.

**COMMENT:** Consistent with the "original intent" trend in constitutional interpretation, Chief Justice Burger in his majority opinion explicitly relied on historical evidence that the founding fathers did not intend free speech protection for language such as that used by Fraser (P). Burger cited, for example, *The Manual of Parliamentary Practice,* drafted by Thomas Jefferson, which prohibits the use of "impertinent language." Burger, however, blithely ignored the patent irrelevance of such a reference, given that specialized and orderly rules of speaking in parliamentary debate necessitate much more restriction than those needed in general speech. Justice Marshall issued a stinging dissent, noting that he would have required Bethel School District (D) to actually demonstrate that Fraser's (P) speech disrupted the student assembly. Justice Brennan, in a concurrence (he sided with the majority because he found Fraser's (P) conduct to be actually disruptive), quoted Fraser's (P) brief address, which was actually much tamer than the majority (which omitted any quotation from it) implied. It has already been determined that the constitutional rights of students in public schools are not automatically coextensive with the rights of adults in other settings. It is important to realize that what may be a First Amendment violation in one case would not be in another. The time, place, and manner of the speech must also be considered. Note that the Court's decision in *Bethel* turned on the nature of Fraser's (P) speech. Here, the speech was nonpolitical and, thus, not afforded the protections designed to protect political expression in a free society. When viewed in light of previous school cases, such as *T.L.O.,* and later cases, such as *Hazelwood,* it is clear that the Court is establishing a "reasonableness" standard when dealing with public education. It seems clear that the lowering of this standard was due to the concern for the difficult task that schools face in today's educational environment of violence, family instability, gangs, and drugs. *Bethel* is merely continuing to apply the reasonableness standard.

## Discussion Questions

1. Does this case bother you? What are the arguments in support of the Fraser speech?

2. How important was it that Fraser was warned by two teachers that his speech was inappropriate?

3. If this speech were given in your school today, would it still be considered inappropriate? Why or why not?

4. If the Court had supported Fraser, what do you think school principals would have done regarding similar assemblies in the future?

# NEW JERSEY V. T.L.O. 469 U.S. 325, 105 S. CT. 733 (1985)

**GENERAL RULES OF LAW:** (1) When a school official conducts a search of a student's belongings, the Fourth Amendment requires only "reasonable suspicion," not the higher standard of "probable cause" required for police searches. (2) Evidence found by a school official conducting a search of a student's belongings based on reasonable suspicion cannot be suppressed under the exclusionary rule.

## PROCEDURE SUMMARY:

**Plaintiff:** State of New Jersey (P)

**Defendant:** T.L.O. (D), a high school student

**State Juvenile Court Decision:** Held for New Jersey (P), denying T.L.O.'s (D) motion to suppress evidence

**State Appellate Court Decision:** Affirmed

**State Supreme Court Decision:** Reversed, sustaining T.L.O.'s (D) motion and ordering evidence suppressed

**U.S. Supreme Court Decision:** Reversed, denying T.L.O.'s (D) motion and admitting evidence

**FACTS:** A teacher at a New Jersey (P) high school found two girls smoking in the bathroom. She brought them to the assistant vice principal's office, where one of the girls admitted to smoking. The other girl, T.L.O. (D), denied she had smoked, claiming that she was not a smoker. The assistant vice principal then asked her to come into his private office, where he opened her purse and found a pack of cigarettes. While reaching for the cigarettes, he noticed a package of rolling papers commonly associated with marijuana usage. He decided to search the entire purse thoroughly. His search uncovered marijuana, a pipe, plastic bags, a large number of dollar bills, and a list of people who owed T.L.O. (D) money. The matter was turned over to police. A juvenile court hearing adjudged T.L.O. (D) delinquent. T.L.O. (D) appealed on the grounds that the search was unconstitutional. Specifically, T.L.O. (D) contended that the vice principal lacked probable cause under the Fourth Amendment to conduct the search of her purse, and the allegedly illegally seized evidence should be suppressed under the exclusionary rule. The juvenile court denied T.L.O.'s (D) motion, and the appellate division affirmed. The New Jersey Supreme Court, however, reversed and ordered the evidence suppressed. New Jersey (P) appealed, and the U.S. Supreme Court granted review.

**ISSUES:** (1) Is the standard for Fourth Amendment searches of students the same "probable cause" standard required for police searches? (2) Can evidence found by a school official during a search of a student's belongings based on reasonable suspicion be suppressed?

**HOLDING AND DECISION:** (White, J.) (1) No. When a school official conducts a search of a student's belongings, the Fourth Amendment requires only "reasonable suspicion," not the higher standard of "probable cause" that is required for police searches. The search in this case did not violate the Fourth Amendment. The warrant and probable cause requirements of the Fourth Amendment for police searches would only serve to "unduly interfere with the swift and informal disciplinary procedures needed in schools." As such, a school official's search of a student depends on whether the circumstances dictating the search aroused reasonable suspicion. Reasonable suspicion for such a search can be drawn from the two-pronged inquiry presented in *Terry v. Ohio* (1968).[33] First, reasonable grounds for the search must exist at the time of the search's inception. Here, a suspicion that the search might produce evidence that T.L.O. (D) violated the law or rules of the school was reasonable under the circumstances in which she was found in the bathroom. Second, the scope of the search should be limited to reasonable objectives. Here, reasonable suspicion supported searching the purse for cigarettes. Then, seeing the rolling papers raised reasonable suspicion, which supported searching further for marijuana. Thus, the evidence acquired from the search was properly obtained. (2) No. Evidence found by a school official conducting a search of a student's belongings based on reasonable suspicion cannot be suppressed under the exclusionary rule. Reversed.

**COMMENT:** The concurring and dissenting justices were correct when they forecasted that this decision would create an extremely broad reasonableness standard for school officials under the Fourth Amendment. Clearly, the "rolling" search (i.e., one in which reasonable suspicion arises each time new evidence is found, even if the subsequent suspicion is unrelated to the reason for the initial search) is authorized in this case. It is now constitutional so long as there is reasonable suspicion for the initial search. Some liberals question whether the Fourth Amendment now provides a student with any protection from an unreasonable search and seizure. One question left unresolved is whether a student who is sent to the office for a minor offense can be subjected to an extensive and invasive search based on a reasonableness analysis.

## Discussion Questions

1. Explain the difference between probable cause and reasonable suspicion related to student searches in a school facility.

2. Under the exclusionary rule, why could the drugs have been excluded in the juvenile court action if the Court had ruled that the search was unconstitutional?

3. What are the difficulties in deciding that a proposed search is reasonable? What can an administrator base his or her suspicions on before conducting a search?

4. Would it be reasonable for a principal to search a student for drugs based on a report from a first-time "snitch"? What if this snitch had correctly identified drug users twice before?

# TINKER V. DES MOINES INDEPENDENT COMMUNITY SCHOOL DISTRICT
# 393 U.S. 503, 89 S. CT. 733 (1969)

**GENERAL RULE OF LAW:** If students engage in silent, passive, symbolic acts of pure speech and do not threaten substantial or material interference with school order, their activities are protected by the First Amendment right of free speech.

## PROCEDURE SUMMARY:

**Plaintiffs:** Tinker (P) and other public school students in Des Moines, Iowa

**Defendant:** Des Moines Independent Community School District (School District) (D)

**U.S. District Court Decision:** Held for School District (D)

**U.S. Court of Appeals Decision:** Affirmed **en banc**

**U.S. Supreme Court Decision:** Reversed

**FACTS:** Tinker (P), a high school student in Des Moines, Iowa, and two other students protested the Vietnam War by wearing black arm bands to school. The Des Moines principal, forewarned of this silent protest, adopted a rule banning the wearing of black arm bands under penalty of suspension. Tinker (P) and the others were asked to remove the arm bands or leave school. Tinker (P) and the others decided to continue their protest and did not return to school until after the winter holiday. Tinker (P), through his father, sued the School District (D) in federal district court, alleging that the school's ban on wearing arm bands violated his First Amendment free speech rights. The federal court ruled against Tinker (P) on the grounds that the school rule was a reasonable way to prevent disturbance of school discipline. The Eighth Circuit Court of Appeals affirmed, and Tinker (P) appealed to the United States Supreme Court.

**ISSUE:** Are the activities of students who engage in silent, passive, symbolic acts of pure speech, such as wearing arm bands, protected by the First Amendment if they do not pose a threat of substantial or material interference with school order?

**HOLDING AND DECISION:** (Fortas, J.) Yes. The rights of students to speak freely are protected by the First Amendment. Speech that is largely symbolic, silent, and passive, such as the wearing of black arm bands to protest a foreign war, constitute pure speech, which is entitled to the greatest form of protection under the Constitution. This speech may only be regulated if it threatens to materially and substantially interfere with school order or discipline. Here, only a few of thousands of students wore the arm bands, and the School District (D) had only an undifferentiated fear or apprehension of disturbance—not enough to outweigh the students' freedom of speech. A mere desire to avoid discomfort and unpleasantness associated with the expression of unpopular views does not warrant suppression of this fundamental right. Reversed.

**COMMENT:** The Court was also swayed by the fact that the school had previously allowed other "symbols" constituting pure speech, such as iron crosses (associated with Nazism) and buttons of particular political candidates. The School District (D) had singled out Vietnam War protestors for this one prohibition. However, not all courts have been so protective of symbolic speech when the danger of disruption was greater than it was here. For example, the Fifth Circuit Court of Appeals has held that symbols indicating a desire to perpetuate segregation, such as the Confederate flag, must be removed from school premises.[34] In a closer case, the federal district court in California has held that "vulgar retouchings" of photographs of President Nixon in a school newspaper warranted suspension of high school student editors for 10 days.[35] Furthermore, *Tinker* has been distinguished by two more recent cases, *Bethel* and *Hazelwood*.

## Discussion Questions

1. Is a student's right of free speech protected when he or she engages in silent, passive, and symbolic acts of pure speech?

2. Would the Supreme Court have ruled differently if there were a greater percentage of students protesting during school hours?

3. In the *Tinker* case, the students protested with black arm bands. To what extent are other "symbols" protected by a student's right to free speech (political, religious, etc.)?

# GOSS V. LOPEZ 419 U.S. 565, 95 S. CT. 729 (1975)

**GENERAL RULE OF LAW:** The Fourteenth Amendment requirement of procedural due process mandates that students threatened with suspension from school for 10 days be given a prior opportunity to contest their suspension.

**PROCEDURE SUMMARY:**

   **Plaintiffs:** Lopez (P) and eight other public school students in Columbus, Ohio

   **Defendant:** Goss (D), superintendent of Columbus, Ohio, Public School System

   **U.S. District Court Decision:** Held for Lopez (D)

   **U.S. Supreme Court Decision:** Affirmed

**FACTS:** Nine high school students in Columbus, Ohio, including Lopez (P), were involved in demonstrations or lunchroom disturbances that resulted in their suspension from school for 10 days. Lopez (P) and the others were given no opportunity prior to their suspension to challenge the reasons for their discipline. Under Ohio law, public school principals were required to give 24-hours' notice to the parents of a student suspended for 10 days. Only in the case of expulsion was a student given an opportunity to appeal a principal's decision to the board of education. Here, the parents of Lopez (P) were orally informed the day after the suspensions that their child had been disciplined. Lopez (P) sued Goss (D) and other administrators of the Columbus Public School System in federal court. Plaintiffs alleged that the students' constitutional rights to due process were violated because they were denied an opportunity to refute the charges against them prior to their suspensions. The district court found for Lopez (P), and Goss (D) appealed to the U.S. Supreme Court.

**ISSUE:** Does the Fourteenth Amendment requirement of procedural due process mandate that students threatened with suspension from school for 10 days be given a prior opportunity to informally contest their suspension?

**HOLDING AND DECISION:** (White, J.) Yes. The Fourteenth Amendment requirement of procedural due process mandates that students threatened with suspension from school for 10 days be given a prior opportunity to informally contest their suspension. Students have a property interest in their education and a liberty interest in their reputation, which may not be taken away without a prior hearing. Ten days is not an insubstantial or trivial period of time to be deprived of an education, and the effect on a suspended student's reputation and chances for future education or employment should not be underestimated. However, in the case of a 10-day suspension, the student need only be given oral or written notice of the charges against him as well as an opportunity to present his side of the story. An informal hearing or give-and-take between student and disciplinarian should precede the suspension, although if a student's presence poses an immediate danger to persons or property or disrupts the academic process, no informal hearing need be held. Further, if the suspension is to exceed 10 days, or if expulsion is threatened, more formal hearings may be required. Here, Lopez (P) and the other plaintiffs were given no opportunity to rebut the charges against them before being suspended. Therefore, they are ordered reinstated, their suspensions reversed, and records of their suspensions expunged. Affirmed.

**COMMENT:** Education, considered one of the chief obligations a state owes its citizens, cannot be withdrawn without procedural due process. As this case demonstrates, a student need not be threatened with permanent deprivation of education before he is assured the right to a hearing; however, the type of hearing and its degree of formality will depend on the length of time the student is required to be absent from school. It is important to note that the Supreme Court here established a "bright line" rule that applies only to 10-day suspensions; suspensions of shorter duration may not require a face-to-face meeting, although it would be prudent for a principal or administrator to discuss potential disciplinary actions as short as one day, and some would argue that suspensions of any length deserve the same protection. Each case, with its varying potential impairment, would determine "what process is due." Regardless, some procedural protection would be required unless the state action is **de minimis**. Many states have overreacted to the *Goss* decision. The Court merely requires an informal notice and hearing to satisfy due process in a short-term suspension. Some school districts have provided far more protection. Of course, as the length of the suspension increases, the more formal protections attach. With an extended suspension or expulsion, more formal legal protections should be provided, including counsel and the right to present and confront witnesses. For student suspensions of up to 10 days, the following should be provided: (1) written or oral notice of the charges; (2) if the student denies the charges, an explanation of the evidentiary basis; and (3) an opportunity for the student to present his or her side of the situation. These procedures should come before the suspension, unless the student's ongoing presence in the school poses a threat. Should the student's removal be required, a notice and hearing must follow in a reasonable time.

## Discussion Questions

1. The type of hearing and its degree of formality will be based on the length of a student's suspension. Which party involved decides on the type of hearing and its degree of formality?

2. If a student's removal from a school is required, a notice and hearing must follow in a reasonable time. What amount of time is considered to be reasonable?

3. Explain the "bright line" rule and when it should be applied by an administrator.

Additional case briefs can be found on the SAGE Web site at the following address:
http://www.sagepub.com/aquilacasebriefs

# NOTES

1. Brown v. Board of Education, 531 U.S. 958 (1954).
2. Tinker v. Des Moines Independent Community School District, 393 U.S. 503, 89 S. Ct. 733 (1969).
3. See Bethel School Dist. No. 403 v. Fraser, 478 U.S. 675, 106 S. Ct. 3159 (1986).
4. See Tinker v. Des Moines Independent Community School District, 393 U.S. 503, 89 S. Ct. 733 (1969).
5. See Guzick v. Drebus, 431 F.2d 594 (6th Cir. 1970). See also Tate v. Bd. of Ed. of Jonesboro, Ark. Special Education District, 453 F.2d 975 (8th Cir. 1972).

6. See Hazelwood School District v. Kuhlmeier, 484 U.S. 260 (1988).

7. See New Jersey v. T.L.O., 469 U.S. 325 (1985).

8. Vernonia School District 471 v. Acton, 515 U.S. 646 (1995).

9. Board of Education Independent School District No. 92 of Pottawatomie County v. Earls, 536 U.S. 822 (2002).

10. See Goss v. Lopez, 419 U.S. 565 (1975).

11. New Jersey v. T.L.O., 469 U.S. 325 (1985).

12. Bethel School Dist. No. 403 v. Fraser, 478 U.S. 675, 106 S. Ct. 3159 (1986).

13. Hazelwood School District v. Kuhlmeier, 484 U.S. 260 (1988).

14. Board of Education of Independent School District No. 92 of Pottawatomie County v. Earls, 536 U.S. 822 (2002).

15. See Goss v. Lopez, 419 U.S. 565 (1975).

16. See Beeson v. Kiowa County School District, 567 P.2d 801 (Colo. App. 1977).

17. See Bethel School Dist. No. 403 v. Fraser, 478 U.S. 675, 106 S. Ct. 3159 (1986).

18. See Tinker v. Des Moines Indep. Comm. School Dist., 393 U.S. 503, 89 S. Ct. 733 (1969).

19. See Guzick v. Drebus, 431 F.2d 594 (6th Cir. 1970); see also Tate v. Bd. of Ed. of Jonesboro, Ark. Special Education District, 453 F.2d 975 (8th Cir. 1972).

20. See Hazelwood School District v. Kuhlmeier, 484 U.S. 260 (1988).

21. See Eisner v. Stamford Board of Education, 440 F.2d 803 (2d Cir. 1971).

22. See Massie v. Henry, 455 F.2d 779 (4th Cir. 1972); see also Davenport v. Randolph County Board of Education, 730 F.2d 1395 (1984), and Bishop v. Colaw, 450 F. 2d 1069 (8th Cir. 1971).

23. See New Jersey v. T.L.O., 469 U.S. 325 (1985).

24. People v. William G., 709 P.2d 1287 (S. Ct. Calif. 1985).

25. Widmar v. Vincent, 454 U.S. 263, 102 S. Ct. 269 (1981).

26. See Board of Education of the Westside Community Schools v. Mergens, 496 U.S. 226 (1990).

27. See Goss v. Lopez, 419 U.S. 565 (1975).

28. See also Warren v. National Association of Secondary School Principals, 375 F. Supp. 1043 (1974), in which a student's removal from an honor society without adequate pre-dismissal safeguards violated due process. See also Palmer v. Merluzzi, 868 F.2d 90 (3rd Cir. 1989), in which a student's suspension from extracurricular activities did not require any more due process than he had been provided earlier, when he had received 10-day academic suspension.

29. See Ingraham v. Wright, 430 U.S. 651, 97 S. Ct. 1401 (1977).

30. See C. J. v. School Board of Broward County, 438 So.2d 87 (1983), and Tibbs v. Board of Education of Township of Franklin, 276 A.2d 165 (NJ Super. Ct. 1971).

31. See Allen v. Casper, 622 N.E.2d 367 (Ohio App. 8 Dist 1993).

32. See S. v. Board of Education of S.F. Unif. Sch. Dist., 97 Cal. Rptr. 422 (1971).

33. Terry v. Ohio, 392 U.S. 1 (1968).

34. Smith v. St. Tammany Parish School Board, 448 F.2d 414 (5th Cir. 1971).

35. Baker v. Downey City Board of Education, 307 F. Supp. 517 (D.Cal. 1969).

# 6

# Student Records

*The Family Educational Rights and Privacy Act is a federal law that protects the privacy of student education records. The law applies to all schools that receive funds under an applicable program of the U.S. Department of Education*

— Family Educational Rights and Privacy Act[1]

## OVERVIEW · · · · · · · · · · · · · · · · · · · · · · · · · · · · · · · · · · · · · · · · · · · · · ·

The Family Educational Rights and Privacy Act (FERPA), also identified as the Buckley Amendment, was enacted in 1974. Its major purpose was to establish who could and could not view student records. Essentially, this law ensures that parents can access their children's school records and prohibits the release of those records without parents' permission, except to those who have a "right to know." Initially, school people believed that FERPA would be harmful. For example, teachers would put nothing critical in student records because they feared a **libel** court action by disgruntled parents. Also, counselors feared that nonconfidential recommendations would not benefit students because recipients of these nonconfidential recommendations would tend to discount them because of their favorable nature. The enactment of FERPA was triggered by the many abuses of school records, such as the extensive sharing of information with outsiders while still limiting parental access.

FERPA considers education records to be any records, files, documents, or other materials that contain information directly related to a student and that are maintained by the school or by a person acting on behalf of the school. This definition encompasses even those documents that may be in a teacher's or principal's desk, as well as those in an official student file (including computer files). Disciplinary and academic files are protected. Nevertheless, any information contained in a student's record is, with few exceptions, considered confidential and cannot be released without written agreement by the parent or guardian (or student, upon reaching 18 years of age). Of course, FERPA excludes instructional and internal personnel records that are for school use and not shared with anyone (other than a substitute teacher, for the purpose of instruction). Furthermore, any teacher's personal notes or personal memory aids are not education records under FERPA.

Federal law provides that a school district may disclose "directory information" without prior written parental consent. "Directory information" includes the student's name, address, telephone listing, date and place of birth, major field of study, dates of attendance, participation in officially recognized activities and sports, weight and height of members of athletic teams, date of graduation, and awards received. In two major court cases, the Supreme Court ruled on the issue of whether student-graded papers fell into the category of protected educational records. In *Owasso Indep. School Dist. No 1–11 v. Falvo* (2002), the Court held that since peer grading did not turn the student papers into FERPA-protected educational records, the school board may permit teachers to use peer grading over a parental objection.[2]

Other issues regarding FERPA have been a point of interest for school professionals. For example, FERPA does not prohibit the transmission of confidential information that is not recorded. Surprisingly, some teachers incorrectly believe that they should not disclose information about neglect and abuse. FERPA cannot be used as a defense, and the failure to disclose will almost certainly violate a state law regarding notification of abuse and neglect. Of course, schools need to be very careful not to disclose confidential information to a newspaper or similar agency. Absent a court order, school principals should provide both parents with school grades and general information about their child. Additionally, FERPA allows school officials to share information about a student with others in the school who might need this information to protect the health and safety of other students or teachers. FERPA does not preclude the destruction of student records. In fact, one result of FERPA has been the massive destruction of student records.

School districts are required by the Health Insurance Portability and Accountability Act (HIPAA) to inform students and their families of the school district's legal duties and privacy practices with respect to student health information. All schools must protect students' health information while complying with the HIPAA requirements, as well as follow all laws regarding the use of health information. Essentially, all student health information is private. This means that all information that a school district collects about students and their health is confidential. To comply with HIPAA, the school district must maintain procedures that ensure that health information is collected and stored in a protective manner. The information must be protected from release to anyone other than necessary school personnel, usually defined as those having a "need to know" in order to keep students safe. Another feature is that parents may request a copy of the health information that the school district has collected regarding a student in order to ensure the information is accurate.

## Case Study

### Peer-Graded Papers or Educational Records?

Sometimes teachers ask students to score each other's tests, papers, and assignments while explaining the correct answers to the entire class. A parent of one of your students tells you that this peer-grading practice violates FERPA. She argues that peer grading embarrasses her children, who do not do as well as their classmates. She asks you, as superintendent, to ask the school board to adopt a policy banning peer grading. Her attorney argues that under FERPA, schools and educational agencies receiving federal financial assistance must comply with certain conditions. One condition is that sensitive information about students may not be released without parental consent. She argues that her children's grades are "education records" as defined under the Act because they contain information directly related to students.

## Discussion Questions

1. Should peer-graded papers be considered education records?

2. What are the arguments on both sides?

3. How would you rule? Why?

4. If the parent's position is upheld, what impact might it have on how a teacher teaches?

# IMPORTANT CONCEPTS

- **Purpose of FERPA:** FERPA is designed to protect the privacy of students and assure fairness in the storage and use of school records.

- **Students' records are confidential:** The information contained in a student's record is, with few exceptions, considered confidential and cannot be released without written agreement by the parent or guardian or an 18-year-old student.

- **Some information can be released:** Information about a student that can be released includes the following directory information: (the student's name, address, telephone listing, date and place of birth), major field of study, dates of attendance, participation in officially recognized activities and sports, weight and height of members of athletic teams, date of graduation, and awards received.

- **Student can correct inaccurate information:** An eligible student, as well as the parent or guardian of a student under 18, is entitled to a hearing to challenge the contents of the records and to have corrected or deleted any inaccurate or misleading information.

- **Student can disagree with the record:** An eligible student or parent or guardian who disagrees with something in the student's record may insert into the student file a written statement that indicates the concern.

- **Peer-graded papers are not education records:** The Supreme Court held that peer grading does not turn student papers into FERPA-protected education records, and teachers may use peer grading over parental objection.[3]

*(Continued)*

(Continued)

- **Student health information:** The Health Insurance Portability and Accountability Act (HIPAA) requires school districts to inform students and their families of the school district's legal duties and privacy practices with respect to student health information.

- **Privacy standards under HIPAA:** HIPAA requires school districts to have procedures and practices in place that ensure that health information is collected and stored in a manner protected from all except necessary school personnel.

- **Disciplinary and academic information included:** FERPA-protected records include information that may be in a teacher's or principal's desk, as well as in an official student file (including computer files). This includes disciplinary and academic information.

- **Unrecorded information:** FERPA does not prohibit the transmission of unrecorded confidential information.

- **Abuse and neglect:** FERPA does not prohibit disclosure of personal information related to abuse and neglect.

- **Health and safety of others:** FERPA does not preclude school officials from sharing information about students with others in the school who might need this information to protect the health and safety of students or teachers.

- **Destruction of records not precluded:** FERPA does not preclude the destruction of student records. School districts should review state law because it often details how long student records must be retained.

- **Parent may not challenge grades:** FERPA does not allow a parent to challenge the fairness of a teacher's grade, although it does allow the parent to question the accuracy of the recording of the grade.

- **Universities must also comply:** Universities must also comply with FERPA and provide only "directory information." Unless the student denies the university the right to share, the following directory information may be provided: student's name; local and permanent addresses; telephone numbers; e-mail addresses; date and place of birth; major field of study; dates of attendance; classification; degrees, honors, and awards received; most recent educational institution attended; participation in officially recognized activities and sports; weight and height of members of athletic teams; and a photograph.

## PRIVACY AND ACCESS TO STUDENT RECORDS

Parents and guardians and students 18 years and older have the right to review and question the contents of official school records. School districts usually insist that requests to review a school record be made in writing to a specific official or office (e.g., law department). Parents and guardians, and students 18 years or older, are entitled to a hearing to challenge the contents of the records. They are also entitled to have corrected or deleted any inaccurate or misleading information. Additionally, they may insert into the student file a written statement disputing the records. FERPA applies to all educational institutions, public and private, that receive financial assistance from the federal Department of Education, funds which have become of increasing importance during these times of financial exigency. FERPA is designed to protect the privacy of students and assure fairness in the storage and use of school records. FERPA was passed by Congress over the objection of school professionals, who feared that its impact would be detrimental. Its enactment was triggered by many abuses of school records, especially the sharing of information with outsiders while parents' access was limited. There were other abuses, such as when a mother was told that she could not see the records that triggered her son's transfer to a class for the mentally handicapped. In another case, a father had to get a court order to see his son's school records after teachers informed him that his son needed psychological treatment.[4] These abuses occurred in the 1960s, at the same time that the CIA and FBI had almost complete access to student records in more than half of our school districts.

Pursuant to FERPA, education records are "records, files, documents and other materials that contain information directly related to a student and . . . are maintained by an educational . . . institution or by a person acting for such . . . institution."[5] This includes information that may be in a teacher's or principal's desk, as well as in an official student file (including computer files). Disciplinary and academic information is protected. However, FERPA does not protect instructional and internal personnel records that are for school use and not shared with anyone (other than a substitute teacher for the purpose of instruction). Additionally, a teacher's personal notes and personal memory aids are not considered education records. Nevertheless, a student's record is, with few exceptions, confidential and cannot be released without written agreement by the parent or guardian or an 18-year-old student. However, a school may show or turn over records without permission (1) to other officials of the same school system; (2) to officials of other schools in which the student seeks or intends to enroll; (3) to certain federal, state, and local authorities performing functions authorized by law; (4) to the juvenile justice system, but usually only when under **subpoena** or court order; (5) to accrediting agencies; and (6) in emergencies, to protect a student's health or safety. Federal law does stipulate that a school district may disclose "directory information" without prior written parental consent. Upon request, pursuant to the No Child Left Behind Act, military recruiters may have access to directory information, including the student's name, address, and telephone number. Directory information will not be disclosed for any profit-making purpose. Parents and guardians and students 18 years and older have the right (upon written request) to refuse to allow the district to designate any or all of the information as directory information. Finally, FERPA allows a parent to see the education records that the school gives to an individual providing service to the school or records maintained by someone acting for the school (see Chapter 16, Case Study: Are School Lawyers' Records Protected in a Juvenile Court Proceeding?).

## Case Law

It is interesting that the U.S. Supreme Court heard no cases dealing with FERPA for more than a quarter of a century. These were considered minor issues for the lower courts.

Students and parents who attempted to file a lawsuit against school districts found that FERPA did not provide a private cause of action.[6] In *Fay v. South Colonie Central School District* (1986), a court held that FERPA may be the basis for a damage suit against a school.[7] FERPA also protects material in student files that has been received from outsiders. For example, a parent's critical letter to a teacher about her son was considered a protected FERPA record.[8] Then, in 2002, two cases were issued by the U.S. Supreme Court regarding FERPA. The examples below deal with the issues involved in those cases.

1. A mother in Oklahoma challenged a school board's practice of allowing teachers to use peer grading (children grade each others' papers and call the scores out to the teacher). She believed that this practice embarrassed her children and violated their privacy rights. The Court had to deal with the issue of whether student-graded papers constituted FERPA-protected records. The Court held that because peer grading did not turn the student papers into education records covered by FERPA, the school board may permit teachers to use peer grading over the mother's objection.[9]

2. A male undergraduate student claimed that university administrators violated his rights when they released his records to state officials without his knowledge or consent. This was done when the student was accused, at that time with unsubstantiated accusations, of sexual misconduct involving a female student. The Supreme Court held that although this student's records were disclosed impermissibly, the plaintiff did not have a private cause of action under Section 1983. Section 1983 of the Civil Rights Act of 1871 is the most used means for plaintiffs to get into federal court when they believe a state actor has injured them. Otherwise, they would have to secure redress in a state court. *Gonzaga Univ. v. Doe* (2002) held that a plaintiff did not have a private right of action to allow access to a federal court using Section 1983. Rather, the available remedy was to file a complaint with the U.S. Department of Education. In light of the fact that the student was clearly injured by a denial of certification as a public school teacher, this case has limited the use of FERPA as a means to redress claims.[10]

## Other Records Issues

- FERPA does not prohibit the transmission of unreported confidential information. Nevertheless, the transmission of some information by a teacher would be considered unprofessional, possibly unethical, and might violate some state privacy provisions.

- Some teachers have argued that they do not have to disclose information about neglect and abuse because FERPA precludes disclosure of all personal information. This is not true. Failure to disclose information related to neglect and abuse will almost certainly violate state law.

- Schools need to be very careful not to disclose confidential information to a newspaper or similar agency. A local school board was successfully sued for disclosing a child's medical condition (severe emotional and behavioral problems) to a news reporter.[11]

- School principals need to follow the directive of the juvenile court and/or the domestic relations court when dealing with parental issues. Courts are now very careful to specify which parent in a divorce has major family responsibility for the child. However, FERPA does not preclude the noncustodial parent from receiving information about his or her child. Thus, a school district should provide both parents with school grades and general information about their child.

- The noncustodial parent also has the right to review the records of his or her child, unless this is prohibited by a court order.

- FERPA does not preclude school officials from sharing information about students with others in the school who might need this information to protect the health and safety of students or teachers. This includes disciplinary information that might be necessary to protect the health and safety of another member of the school community.

- FERPA does not preclude the destruction of student records. School districts do need to review state law because it often details how long student records must be kept. The only federal limitation on destruction of student records is when there is a request to inspect those records. One practical result of FERPA has been the massive destruction of student records.

- FERPA does not allow a parent to challenge the fairness of a teacher's grade, although it does allow the parent to question whether a grade was recorded accurately.

## HEALTH INSURANCE PORTABILITY AND ACCOUNTABILITY ACT

### Duty

School districts are required by HIPAA to inform students and their families of the school district's legal duties and privacy practices with respect to student health information. All schools must protect students' health information while complying with HIPAA requirements, as well as follow all laws regarding the use of health information. A school district should designate a specific individual as the HIPAA compliance officer responsible for carrying out the mandates specified in the statute.

### Issues

Essentially, all student health information is private. This means that all information that a school district collects about students and their health must be kept confidential. To comply with HIPAA, the school district's procedures and practices must ensure that health information is collected and stored in a manner calculated to prevent the release of information to anyone other than school personnel who need to know in order to keep students safe. In addition, a student's family may request a copy of the health information that the school district has collected so they may review it for accuracy.

## Rationale

HIPAA was created in 1996 to make health insurance more affordable and accessible. Provisions in HIPAA require Health and Human Services to adopt national standards for certain electronic health care transactions, codes, identifiers, and security. These rules have already had a major effect on health care organizations. Clearly, in a day and age when Americans change jobs as often as their clothes, HIPAA allows people to carry health insurance throughout their job transitions, thus the "portability" in the title of the Act.

---

### Case Study

#### Noncustodial Parent Wants to Attend School Conferences

You are principal of an elementary school in a suburban school district that has a reputation for working closely with parents. At the upcoming parent-teacher night, parents visit their child's teacher to learn about the curriculum and to discuss their child's progress. At the end of the school day, as you are preparing for parent-teacher night, you get a call from the mother of one of your fourth graders. You have a court order declaring her the custodial parent while the father has visitation on alternate weekends. The mother informs you that the father wants to come to the parent-teacher night in order to obtain damaging information about her son to use in court the following week. She is afraid that the teacher's comments about her son's learning difficulties will be used to change her parental rights. She pleads with you to not allow the father to participate this year.

#### Discussion Questions

1. Should the principal contact the father to discuss this?

2. What are the issues in this situation?

3. What should the principal do? Why?

4. In a separate but related situation, should the noncustodial parent have access to grade reports and other general information about his child?

---

## CONCLUSION . . . . . . . . . . . . . . . . . . . . . . . . . . . . . . . . . . . .

The Family Educational Rights and Privacy Act (FERPA) guaranteed that adult students and parents of minor students have access to the student's records. In addition, a school must obtain written consent from the adult student or minor student's parents before disclosing student records. Some school officials first opposed FERPA because they feared that negative indications in these records might give rise to unfair lawsuits.

FERPA protects written and computer files and can also apply to information located in a teacher's or principal's desk. Disciplinary and academic files are protected. FERPA does not protect instructional and internal personnel records that are for school use and not shared with anyone. Additionally, the Act does not apply to a teacher's personal notes and personal memory aids. However, there are some exceptions to FERPA's confidentiality requirements, such as disclosure to schools in which the student seeks to enroll.

Directory information, which includes a student's name, address, telephone number, and so on, may be disclosed without the student's consent, although it may not be disclosed for a profit-making purpose. Also, although FERPA does not necessarily prohibit the transmission of unrecorded confidential material, such transmission may still be unethical and violate state privacy legislation. FERPA also does not prohibit the transmission of information related to child abuse or neglect. In fact, failure to disclose this information usually violates state law. Moreover, FERPA does not preclude a noncustodial parent from requesting confidential records about his or her child.

FERPA also does not preclude the destruction of records, though other state laws may do so. The only federal limitation on destruction of student records is when there is a request to inspect those records.

School districts are also required by the Health Insurance Portability and Accountability Act (HIPAA) to inform students and their families of the school district's legal duties and privacy practices with respect to student health information. Essentially, all student health information is private, and school districts are charged with the duty to maintain the confidential nature of this information.

The cases that follow give examples of the various types of records that fall within and outside the scope of FERPA. This area of law results in a tug-of-war (what has been called a "balancing of the equities") between students' rights and the rights of various others. You will also notice the conflicts that arise between FERPA and other legislation. Read the following cases and apply the courts' reasoning to other documents you may encounter.

# CASE BRIEFS . . . . . . . . . . . . . . . . . . . . . . .

## OWASSO INDEPENDENT SCHOOL DISTRICT NO. 1–11 V. FALVO 122 S. CT. 934 (2002)

**GENERAL RULE OF LAW:** Papers are records under the Family Educational Rights and Privacy Act of 1974 only when and if they are maintained by an educational agency or institution or by a person acting for such agency or institution. Peer-graded assignment student papers are not, as soon as they are graded by another student, "maintained" within the meaning of FERPA.

**PROCEDURE SUMMARY:**

**Plaintiff:** Kristja Falvo (P), mother of schoolchildren

**Defendant:** Owasso School District (D)

**U.S. District Court Decision:** Summary judgment granted to School District (D)

**U.S. Court of Appeals Decision:** Reversed

**U.S. Supreme Court Decision:** Reversed the judgment of the U.S. Court of Appeals and the case was remanded.

**FACTS:** Teachers sometimes ask students to score each other's tests, papers, and assignments as the teacher explains the correct answers to the entire class. After grading, the student returns the graded paper to the student who prepared it. Kristja Falvo (P) contends that this practice, which the parties refer to as "peer grading," violates the Family Educational Rights and Privacy Act of 1974 (FERPA). Kristja Falvo (P) claimed that the peer grading embarrassed her children. She asked the School District (D) to adopt a uniform policy banning peer grading and requiring teachers either to grade assignments themselves or at least to forbid students from grading papers other than their own. Under FERPA, schools and educational agencies receiving federal financial assistance must comply with certain conditions. One condition specified in the Act is that sensitive information about students may not be released without parental consent. "Education records" is defined, under the Act, as "records, files, documents, and other materials" containing information directly related to a student.

**ISSUE:** Are peer-graded classroom work and assignments education records?

**HOLDING AND DECISION:** (Kennedy, J.) No. Papers are records under the Family Educational Rights and Privacy Act of 1974 only when and if they are maintained by an educational agency or institution or by a person acting for such agency or institution. Peer-graded assignment student papers are not, as soon as they are graded by another student, "maintained" within the meaning of FERPA. The score on a student-graded assignment is not "contained therein," until the teacher records it. The teacher does not maintain the grade while students correct their peers' assignments or call out their own marks, nor do the student graders maintain the grades within the meaning of FERPA. The word "maintain" suggests that FERPA records will be kept in a filing cabinet in a records room at the school or in a permanent secure database, perhaps even after the student is no longer enrolled. The phrase "by a person acting for an educational institution," as used in the law, modifies "maintain." Even if one were to agree that students are acting for the teacher when they correct another student's assignment, that is different from saying they are acting for the educational institution in maintaining it. FERPA requires "a record" of access for each pupil. This single record must be kept "with the education records." This suggests Congress contemplated that education records would be kept in one place with a single record of access. By describing a "school official" and "his assistants" as the personnel responsible for the custody of the records, FERPA implies that education records are institutional records kept by a single central custodian, such as a registrar, not individual assignments handled by many student graders in their separate classrooms.

**COMMENTS:** This seemingly innocent case caused school teachers a great deal of consternation. Not only is the practice of "peer grading"—students grading each other's classroom work and assignments—very common, but also the case was considered an invasion of standard teaching practices. In reaction, the Court understood this concern. It stated that if homework or class work were considered to be FERPA-protected education records, then "this would impose substantial burdens on the teachers across the country." This would also force teachers to correct daily student assignments and "would make it much more difficult for teachers to give students immediate guidance." However, most agree that once the teacher collects these papers and records the scores in the grade book, they become education records under FERPA.

## Discussion Questions

1. May a school allow a student to work in the office where grades are recorded?

2. Does allowing a student to help the teacher grade papers violate a student's right to privacy?

3. If students were to submit papers anonymously, would students be allowed to grade all papers?

# GONZAGA UNIV. V. DOE 536 U.S. 273 (2002)

**GENERAL RULE OF LAW:** The Family Educational Rights and Privacy Act (FERPA) does not create any personal rights under Section 1983.

**PROCEDURE SUMMARY:**

**Plaintiff:** Doe (Student) (P)

**Defendant:** Gonzaga University (University) (D)

**Spokane County Trial Court Decision:** Held in favor of Student

**Washington Court of Appeals Decision:** Reversed FERPA portion of decision in favor of University

**Washington Supreme Court Decision:** Held in favor of University on **negligence** claim, but held against University on FERPA claim, finding that it creates a federal (not individual) enforceable right

**U.S. Supreme Court Decision:** Held in favor of University on FERPA claim

**FACTS:** Student (P) attended Gonzaga University (D) to pursue teaching credentials and become a Washington elementary school teacher. Washington required all new teachers to obtain an **affidavit** of good moral character from a dean of their university. The "teacher certification specialist" at University (D) overheard students discuss Student's (P) acts of sexual misconduct against a female undergraduate student. In response, the specialist launched an investigation and eventually informed Student (P) that he would not receive the affidavit. Student (P) brought suit against University (D), asserting violations of various laws, including a violation of the Family Educational Rights and Privacy Act (FERPA) that allegedly arose from the release of personal information to unauthorized persons during the investigation.

**ISSUE:** May a student bring suit under Section 1983 against a private university for damages to enforce FERPA, which prohibits federal funding of educational institutions with a policy or practice of releasing education records to unauthorized persons?

**HOLDING AND DECISION:** (Rehnquist, C. J.) No. FERPA does not create enforceable rights under Section 1983. Section 1983 is available when an individual is deprived of rights secured by the U.S. Constitution or federal laws. The language of FERPA makes it clear that Congress did not intend to create private rights when it created FERPA. In order for a federal law to create private rights, the text of the law must "unambiguously" demonstrate intent to create such rights. The text of FERPA does not contain the "rights-creating" language necessary to unambiguously create enforceable rights, so the Student's (P) FERPA claim fails.

**COMMENTS:** This case dealt with the issue of whether a plaintiff could get into federal court using FERPA as the cause of action through Section 1983. At issue was whether FERPA violations would allow a plaintiff to sue a private university for an alleged violation of the plaintiff's privacy right. The Supreme Court's unwillingness to support such a claim put a limit on an individual's right to secure redress in a private university setting. While far from earthshaking, if this decision had gone the other way, it would have opened the door for more extensive application of FERPA in private and other settings.

## Discussion Questions

1. Was the important concern in this case whether Gonzaga University properly or improperly refused the plaintiff an affidavit of good moral character?

2. If the decision had supported the plaintiff, what would have been the impact?

3. Why do some plaintiffs want to get their case decided in federal court rather than a state court?

# PRICE V. YOUNG 580 F. SUPP. 1 (E.D. ARK. 1983)

**GENERAL RULE OF LAW:** A student who is refused membership in an honor society has no private right of action under the Family Educational Rights and Privacy Act of 1974, and claims of equal protection, due process, and constitutional infirmity due to vagueness are not supported.

**PROCEDURE SUMMARY:**

**Plaintiff:** Bobby Smith (Father) (P)

**Defendants:** Harvey Young (superintendent), members of the school board of the Russellville School District, and Shirley Dodd (National Honor Society sponsor) (School Officials) (D)

**U.S. District Court Decision:** Held in favor of School Officials, dismissing Price's complaint as a matter of law

**FACTS:** Father's (P) children attended schools in the Russellville School District. One of the children, Kevin Smith, qualified academically for National Honor Society membership. Teachers anonymously submitted evaluations of National Honor Society applicants. As a result of the evaluations, Kevin Smith was not invited to become a member of the National Honor Society. Father (P) brought suit against the School Officials (D) individually and on behalf of Kevin Smith.

**ISSUE:** Does a student have a claim against a school or school officials based on denial of membership in the National Honor Society as a result of teacher evaluations, which are a uniform part of the selection procedure in addition to satisfaction of academic criteria?

**HOLDING AND DECISION:** (Woods, J.) No. The Family Educational Rights and Privacy Act of 1974 does not create a private right of action. Kevin Smith was not entitled to due process of law because no property interest arises out of membership in the National Honor Society, so no violation of due process occurred. The same selection criteria applied to all applicants, so Kevin Smith was not denied equal protection. The selection criteria for candidates for the National Honor Society were clear, so the claim of constitutional infirmity due to vagueness is not supported. Father (P) brought no valid claim against School Officials (D), so the complaint is dismissed as a matter of law.

**COMMENTS:** The 1974 enactment and application of the FERPA protections soon led to the establishment of extensive and unprecedented privacy rights for students in our public schools. Nevertheless, there were no FERPA cases that reached the Supreme Court for almost 25 years. Issues involving student privacy rights were found to be minor in nature and handled at lower-court levels. In this case, the issue was whether a plaintiff could use FERPA as a cause of action to get his case into federal court. A lower court held that FERPA did not provide an avenue to go into court to argue a privacy right regarding the failure to obtain membership in a student honor society because a teacher "blackballed" the student. While seemingly unfair, this case was important because it did not allow a child the opportunity to use FERPA as a means to secure National Honor Society membership even though the student met the basic requirements.

## Discussion Questions

1. How important is securing membership in the National Honor Society?

2. Could the student and parent secure redress in any other manner after losing the opportunity to use FERPA as the basis for their claim?

3. If FERPA could have been used to argue that the student had been treated unfairly, what other school claims might have been generated?

# DOE V. KNOX COUNTY BOARD OF EDUCATION
# 918 F. SUPP. 181 (E.D. KY. 1996)

**GENERAL RULE OF LAW:** Although the Family Educational Rights and Privacy Act (FERPA) does not create a private right of action, an action may still arise under Section 1983 against a school district for violations of FERPA, and Eleventh Amendment immunity will not protect a local school district from liability.

**PROCEDURE SUMMARY:**

**Plaintiff:** Jane Doe (Student) (P)

**Defendant:** Knox County Board of Education (School Board) (D)

**Trial Court Decision:** Held for (P), finding that Eleventh Amendment immunity did not apply to School Board (D) and that violation of FERPA may allow a Section 1983 civil rights claim

**FACTS:** Student (P), a 13-year-old hermaphrodite, brought suit under Section 1983 asserting the School Board (D) violated her civil rights by allegedly discussing her educational placement, medical condition, and disability with a newspaper reporter after a protective order barring such disclosure was issued by a hearing officer at a due process hearing regarding the educational plan for Student (P). References to Student's (P) medical condition, behavioral and emotional problems, and educational plan appeared in the newspaper and the board of education's meeting agenda.

**ISSUE:** Is a school board **liable** for discussions with the media in violation of a protective order issued under the provisions of FERPA?

**HOLDING AND DECISION:** (Coffman, J.) Yes. The Eleventh Amendment does not extend immunity to local school boards. Further, while FERPA does not create a private right of action itself, a violation of FERPA may be vindicated in a Section 1983 action. However, the School Board (D) will only be liable if the information disclosed was "personally identifiable." The trial court found the "personally identifiable" issue to be a question for the jury.

**COMMENTS:** In this case, the trial court would determine if the School Board (D) was liable for violating FERPA and releasing "personally identifiable" information. This case established that while FERPA did not create a private right of action, a plaintiff could still get into federal court using Section 1983 as the cause of action. Here, a state actor violated the rights of the plaintiff, thus allowing Section 1983 to be used in this FERPA scenario. The Eleventh Amendment requires state and federal branches of government to provide comity for the other level. The Eleventh Amendment provides an immunity to protect both levels of government. In essence, both the state and federal level must show respect for the other. This respect, or comity, was not at issue here to provide Eleventh Amendment immunity to the school board (state) in its application of a federal statute, FERPA. Because the information about the student's medical condition was confidential, the school district's disclosing this information to a newspaper reporter was a violation.

## Discussion Questions

1. May a school district disclose confidential medical information about a student, or does FERPA protect against such an action?

2. If FERPA does not provide a cause of action to get into federal court, why does Section 1983 apply? (Note: Remember that school personnel are state actors.)

3. What is this concern about Eleventh Amendment immunity?

# WARNER V. ST. BERNARD PARISH SCHOOL DISTRICT 99 F. SUPP. 2D 748 (E.D. LA. 2000)

**GENERAL RULE OF LAW:** A parent who experiences job loss and other negative consequences may bring a lawsuit for violation of privacy and rights under the Family and Educational Rights and Privacy Act against a school district that releases the parent's personal letter to her son's teacher to the media.

**PROCEDURE SUMMARY:**

**Plaintiffs:** Debra Warner (Parent) and her son Scott Warner (P)

**Defendants:** St. Bernard Parish School District, Sam Boyd, Dr. Daniel Daste, and Wayne Warner (School Officials) (D)

**Trial Court Decision:** Dismissed Parent's (P) First Amendment claim, but found privacy claim and procedural due process claim actionable

**FACTS:** Debra Warner (P) brought action against School Officials (D) for releasing to the media a letter she wrote to her son's teacher. The letter requested that the teacher not expose her son Scott to certain teachings. In making her point, Debra Warner (P) expressed her opinion on politically sensitive issues. The letter was released to the media because Debra Warner (P) was a candidate for St. Bernard Parish Council. Debra Warner asserted that she lost the election and her job as a result of an article in the local newspaper that contained portions of the controversial letter. Ms. Warner (P) also claimed she was forced to withdraw her son from the school district as a result. Debra Warner (P) brought suit against School Officials (D), claiming that the release of the letter without her permission violated her free speech under the First Amendment, the procedural due process rights of both Debra and Scott Warner, and rights under the Family and Educational Rights and Privacy Act (FERPA).

**ISSUE:** Does the law protect against media disclosure of a personal letter from a parent to a teacher?

**HOLDING AND DECISION:** (Mentz, J.) Yes. Parent's (P) First Amendment claim against the School Officials (D) must be dismissed because the actions of the School Officials (D) "amount[ed] to no more than publication of information which subjected the Warners to criticism, reproach, and scorn." Parent (P) has valid privacy claims against the School Officials (D) under the Fourteenth Amendment. Specifically, disclosure of personal information by the government violates an individual's right to privacy if the individual has a legitimate expectation of privacy that outweighs the public need for disclosure. Additionally, the Fourteenth Amendment protects the constitutional right "to direct the upbringing of one's children." The letter was a personal and private statement from a parent to a teacher. Further, FERPA protects education records, such as the letter Debra Warner sent to her son's teacher, from being disclosed without written parental consent.

**COMMENTS:** At issue in this case is whether FERPA protects a parent from having a personal letter to a teacher disclosed to the media. The parent in this case did not have a First Amendment protection against disclosure because the disclosure merely disclosed information that caused her criticism and discredit. But a parent does have a valid privacy claim against governmental disclosure of personal information. The parent in this case had a legitimate expectation of privacy that outweighed the public's need for disclosure. This case established that FERPA protects education records, such as the letter by Warner to her son's teacher. Such correspondence falls within the protection of the statute and may not be disclosed without parental consent.

## Discussion Questions

1. Did the plaintiff prevail on the First Amendment claim or the Fourteenth Amendment claim involving an expectation of privacy? Why?

2. What is the impact of the fact that FERPA protects this type of third-party transmission?

3. In a different situation, could the public's need for disclosure outweigh an individual's right to privacy? Under what circumstances?

Additional case briefs can be found on the SAGE Web site at the following address:
http://www.sagepub.com/aquilacasebriefs

## NOTES

1. Family Educational Rights and Privacy Act, 20 U.S.C. § 1232(g); 34 CFR Part 99 (1974).
2. Owasso Indep. School Dist. No 1–11 v. Falvo, 534 U.S. 426 (2002).
3. Owasso Indep. School Dist. No 1–11 v. Falvo, 534 U.S. 426 (2002).
4. See Van Allen v. McCleary, 211 N.Y.S.2d 501 (N.Y. Sup. Ct. 1961).
5. 20 U.S.C § 1232(g)(a)(4)(A).
6. See Price v. Young, 580 F.Supp. 1 (E.D. Ark. 1983).
7. Fay v. South Colonie Central School District, 802 F.2d 21 (2d Cir. 1986).
8. See Warner v. St. Bernard Parish School District, 99 F.Supp.2d 748 (E.D. La. 2000).
9. See Owasso Indep. School Dist. No 1–11 v. Falvo, 534 U.S. 426 (2002).
10. See Gonzaga Univ. v. Doe, 536 U.S. 273 (2002).
11. Doe v. Knox County Board of Education, 918 F.Supp. 181 (E.D. Ky.1996).

# 7

# English Language Learners

*There is no equality of treatment merely by providing students the same facilities, textbooks, teachers, and curriculum; for students who do not understand English are effectively foreclosed from any meaningful education.*

—*Lau v. Nichols* (1974)[1]

## OVERVIEW . . . . . . . . . . . . . . . . . . . . . . . . . . . . . . . . . . . . .

Unfortunately, the traditional attitude regarding today's non-English-speaking students has been to allow them to "sink or swim," just as it was for Irish, Jewish, Italian, Polish, German, and other non-English-speaking immigrants early in the twentieth century. Today, there is little doubt that non-English speakers are at a decided disadvantage in our schools. Furthermore, many non-English speakers not only want language support, but also a program that allows their children to appreciate their original cultural heritage as well. Overcoming this linguistic disadvantage is a challenge that can be addressed in many ways. Yet, there is nothing in statute or case law that mandates a bilingual or bicultural education.

*Lau v. Nichols* (1974) is the only bilingual education case to reach the Supreme Court. The San Francisco School Board only provided special English instructional support to 1,000 of the 2,800 Chinese students who needed instructional assistance. Similar to rulings in special education cases, in this case the defendants were unsuccessful in claiming that insufficient funding relieved them of their obligation to provide such services. The Court felt that not understanding English and receiving no support effectively prevented these students from receiving an education. The Court refused to make any statements regarding what specific educational programs or techniques were necessary for remediation, leaving specific remedies to educators, under the supervision of the lower court. Disagreements over the most appropriate remedy have generated other lawsuits as well as regulations and guidelines to assist school districts. In *Lau v. Nichols* (1974), the Court did not rule on the basis of the Fourteenth Amendment's equal protection clause. Rather, the Court applied Title VI of the Civil Rights Act of 1964, which bars discrimination under federally assisted programs on the grounds of "race, color, or national origin."[2]

Congress enacted the Bilingual Education Act in 1968, revising this enactment in 1974, 1988, and 1994, in response to the growing concern regarding the needs of non-English-speaking students. A basic principle has been that bilingual programs should be developed in consultation with parents of limited-English speakers. Following general parental preference, integration with all others students (rather than separate programs) has been preferred, with separate instruction when necessary for linguistic support. California and other states have laws related to bilingual education. Most of these state laws provide only for transitional bilingual education (language services limited to a specific number of years), but there is no requirement that limits them from providing more instruction in the student's native language. Additionally, some states have passed "English Only" laws, which require all classes to be conducted in English. These statutes, which impact far more than education, have resulted in controversy. Such an extreme position impacts all state official acts.

Some argue that "black English" is a distinct language spoken by some African Americans and that it is different from what can be viewed as "standard English." If accurate, this creates a language barrier denying these African American students an equal educational opportunity. In *Martin Luther King, Jr., Elementary School Children v. Michigan Board of Education* (1979), the plaintiffs claimed that teachers' lack of awareness of "black English" was a contributing factor in students' failure to learn and, thereby, a denial of their equal educational opportunities. The federal court, while not requiring bilingual education or even the teaching of black English, did require that teachers receive inservice education in black English.[3]

## Case Study

### Let's Treat These New Immigrants Like Our Grandparents Were Treated

Your school district has experienced a significant increase in foreign students as a result of a religious controversy on another continent that turned violent. As the controversy became more violent, more and more people who do not speak English moved into your urban school district. You have tried to provide English as a Second Language classes and related instructional support such as tutoring. Despite your best efforts, and mainly because of the limited number of qualified teachers, only a few hundred of these children are receiving even the most minimal of support—supplemental classes in English. Literally thousands of students are not even receiving supplemental language instruction, and those who are receiving instruction receive inferior instruction. A controversy is beginning to simmer as more and more of your limited resources are being expended to provide language support. Many parents believe that their grandparents came to America and learned English in the school or by immersion in the community, and these new immigrant children should do it the same way. The vast expenditure of limited resources on children who are likely to do poorly has resulted in parent complaints in the newspaper and at school board meetings.

You are unsure what to do. Parents of these non-English-speaking dominant minority group children want extensive upgrading of educational services or they will sue the school district. They claim that the district's practices provide unequal educational opportunities, in violation of the equal protection clause of the Fourteenth Amendment and § 601 of the Civil Rights Act of 1964. Both laws prohibit disbursing aid to racially discriminatory groups. While parents are asking for no specific remedy, teaching English to students of this minority group is one choice. Giving instructions to this group in their native language is another. There are others. The parents merely want your school district to apply its expertise to the problem and rectify the situation.

Although your state has not adopted an English-only statute, there is a great deal of support for it, especially in your community. You currently provide these students with equal facilities, textbooks, teachers, and curriculum. Yet, the parents of these minority children claim that requiring the children to speak English makes a mockery of public education—those who do not understand English are certain to find their classroom experiences wholly incomprehensible and in no way meaningful. What should you recommend at the next school board meeting?

## Discussion Questions

1. If your state has a law that requires that English shall be the basic language of instruction in all schools, does this change the situation?

2. Does not understanding English effectively preclude these children from any meaningful education?

3. Some argue that basic English skills are at the very core of what these public schools teach. What do you think?

# IMPORTANT CONCEPTS

- **Right to a bilingual and bicultural education:** There is no right to a bilingual or bicultural education in the Equal Educational Opportunities Act of 1974, Title VI. The education needs of the non-English-speaking student must be met.

- *Lau v. Nichols:* A lack of funds is no excuse for failing to provide a program for non-English-speaking students. The basic principle is that a child who cannot understand English is essentially precluded from an education unless there is a special program of instruction.

- **Nondiscrimination:** Courts have allowed limited ability grouping and classroom assignment systems that result in racially imbalanced classes. These have been considered nondiscriminatory and necessary in order to implement effective bilingual programs.

*(Continued)*

(Continued)

- *Lau v. Nichols* **educational programs:** Numerous educational programs might meet the *Lau v. Nichols* (1974) mandate. These include English as a Second Language, bilingual education, or a combination of both. Controversies over the most appropriate remedy have generated other lawsuits as well as regulations and guidelines to assist school districts.

- **Parental involvement:** A basic principle has been that bilingual programs should be developed in consultation with the parents of students with limited English.

- **"English Only" laws:** California and other states have passed "English Only" laws. These states require all classes to be conducted in English.

- **Black English:** The issue is whether "black English" is a distinct language different from standard English and, if so, whether this language barrier denies students an equal educational opportunity.

# BILINGUAL-BICULTURAL EDUCATION

There is little doubt that non-English speakers are at a decided disadvantage in our schools, but this challenge can be addressed in many ways. Many non-English speakers not only want language support, but they also want a program that allows their children to appreciate their cultural heritage. However, there is nothing in statute or case law that mandates a bilingual-bicultural education. What is necessary is a program to cure the language deficiencies of schools' non-English-speaking students. Of course, this does not preclude providing a remediation program that includes a bilingual and/or bicultural component, should a school district desire to do so. What is required is to provide for the language needs of non-English-speaking students.

*Matter of McMillan* (1976) concerned North Carolina parents of Indian descent who refused to send their children to school because the school board would not provide instruction about their culture and heritage.[4] They argued that their intense belief in their Indian culture and heritage was equivalent to the constitutional protection provided to those with religious convictions. This interesting legal theory equating a deeply held belief in one's heritage with a religious conviction was not supported by the court.

# LEGAL BASIS

The only bilingual education case to reach the U.S. Supreme Court was *Lau v. Nichols* (1974). In that case, the San Francisco School Board provided special English instructional support to only 1,000 of the 2,800 Chinese students needing instructional assistance. The board argued that it did not have sufficient funds to provide services to all students. The Court, however, did not agree with that argument. The Court held that not understanding English and receiving no support effectively denied a student an education. Interestingly, the Court refused to make any statements regarding what specific educational programs or techniques were necessary for remediation. This "hands-off" policy is not unusual because higher courts tend to avoid specifying remedies, thus leaving specific remedies to be decided by educators under the supervision of lower courts. Numerous educational programs might meet the court's mandate, including English as a Second Language, bilingual education, or a combination of both. Not surprisingly, disagreements over the most appropriate remedy have generated other lawsuits as well as regulations and guidelines to assist school districts.

In *Lau v. Nichols* (1974), the Court did not rule on this issue based on the Fourteenth Amendment's equal protection clause. Instead, the Court used Title VI of the Civil Rights Act of 1964, which bars discrimination under federally assisted programs on the ground of "race, color, or national origin." Courts often decide issues on non-Constitutional grounds when statutory requirements can settle the issue. In this situation, the Court found based its decision on § 601 of the Civil Rights Act of 1964, which bans discrimination based "on the ground of race, color, or national origin" in "any program or activity receiving Federal financial assistance."

In 1970, Health, Education, and Welfare (HEW), now the Department of Education, made the guidelines more specific, requiring federally funded school districts "to rectify the language deficiency in order to open" the instruction to students who had "linguistic deficiencies." Therefore, if state law permits a school district to determine "when and under what circumstances instruction may be given bilingually," it might require "the mastery of English by all pupils in the schools." In such an instance, bilingual instruction would be authorized only "to the extent that it does not interfere with the systematic, sequential, and regular instruction of all pupils in the English language."[5]

In 1974, Congress enacted the Equal Educational Opportunities Act (EEOA) which required that school systems develop appropriate programs for non-English-speaking students. In interpreting this statute, courts have required appropriate remedial programs to ensure educational opportunity, but have given individual school districts a "substantial amount of latitude" to meet these requirements.[6]

## CASTANEDA GUIDELINES

Many of the programs for non-English speaking students developed as a result of the EEOA were for native speakers of the Spanish language. With the ever-growing Hispanic population, this will continue to be a significant issue. In 1986, in *Castaneda II,* the court found that ability grouping and classroom assignment systems designed to implement effective programs were nondiscriminatory.[7] An ongoing problem is the shortage of bilingual teachers and, therefore, a greater need for inservice teacher training to improve teachers' bilingual skills. Eventually, guidelines developed to help determine whether remediation programs were appropriate. The three *Castaneda I* guidelines that eventually developed were (1) Is the school district's program based upon recognized sound educational theory or principles? (2) Is the school district's program or practice designed to implement the adopted theory? (3) Has the program produced satisfactory results?

## BILINGUAL EDUCATION ACTS

In response to the growing concern regarding the needs of non-English-speaking students, especially Spanish speakers, Congress enacted the Bilingual Education Act in 1968, later revising this enactment in 1974, 1988, and 1994. From the first statute that followed the *Lau* case to the most recent bilingual enactment, a basic principle has been that bilingual programs should be developed in consultation with parents of limited-English speakers. Following parental preference (although some argue that Hispanic parents are not being heard), integration with other students (rather than separate programs) has been preferred. Separate linguistic instruction, when necessary, has also been provided. Initially, funding was provided for low-income students with limited English proficiency. With the second bilingual enactment, this coverage was expanded to include all limited-English-speaking students in order for all to make effective progress.

## RELATED ISSUES

### "English Only" Statutes

Many states, including Massachusetts, Texas, and California, have laws related to bilingual education. Some even pre-date *Lau v. Nichols* (1974). Most state laws only provide for transitional bilingual education (i.e., language support for a specific period of time to enable students to become proficient in English), but there is no requirement that prevents schools from providing more instruction in the student's native language. California and other states have passed "English Only" laws, which require all classes to be conducted in English. Thus, bilingual education can only be provided through a waiver procedure specified in state law. Obviously, these statutes, which delve into far more than education, have been controversial. This extreme position impacts all state official acts (e.g., driver's license tests), which must be conducted in English only. Some have opined that English Only statutes smack of the post–World War I statute in Nebraska that prohibited teaching a foreign language to children under 14. This law was clearly a response to the fear that German immigrants would rear their children with something other than American democratic ideals. The *Meyer v. Nebraska* (1923) case features a rare situation in which a law or statute failed the Court's highly deferential "rational basis" test.[8] That case is interesting to consider in light of contemporary events that have given rise to a movement promoting English as the official language of individual states and the nation as a whole.

### "Black English"

The plaintiffs in *Martin Luther King, Jr., Elementary School Children v. Michigan Board of Education* (1979) argued that "black English" is a distinct language different from standard English and that African Americans' language barrier denies them an equal educational opportunity. As a result, teachers' lack of knowledge of "black English" was a contributing factor in the students' failure to learn and, thereby, a denial of equal educational opportunities. A district court supported this theory in regard to black students residing in low-income housing in an affluent section of the Ann Arbor, Michigan, school district. The federal district court did not require bilingual education or even the teaching of black English. However, it did require that teachers receive inservice education in black English. This issue resurfaced in the mid-1990s when the Oakland, California, School Board passed a resolution to treat "black English" as a second language, which it termed "ebonics." The board claimed that ebonics was genetically based and the primary language of many Oakland students. The Oakland School Board's action was taken voluntarily, not as a result of a court case; it generated a hailstorm of comments from all sides. This argument was highly controversial although supported by some; nevertheless the bilingual funds that Oakland requested were not provided by the federal government.

## Present Status

In the early years of the twenty-first century, bilingual education remains as controversial as ever. With the ever-growing Hispanic population, the underlying problems creating the issue will cause the unrest to escalate. One major problem is that there is no general agreement as to what is "best practice" in regard to meeting the needs of non-English-speaking students. This inability to identify effective programs leaves courts as well as school districts with little recourse when trying to provide equitable remedies for disenfranchised non-English-speaking students.

## Case Study

### It's My Heritage and You Should Recognize It

As superintendent of the Happy Hearts School District, you received a call from your middle school principal, who informed you that Mr. and Mrs. Standing Bull have not sent their two children to school for the past three days. They are upset because the school board refused to provide instruction about the Blackfoot Indian heritage and culture. The school board felt that if it acceded to the demands of this ethnic group, it would set a precedent for every other group in the school community. To compound the problem, the principal tells you that the Standing Bulls were offended by statements that their children's English teacher allegedly made about American Indians. They demand that curricula be instituted covering current problems American Indians are facing and that a steering committee be established to implement a policy against racism in any of its virulent forms. You have a meeting with the school board tomorrow afternoon to take action regarding the Standing Bull issue.

### Discussion Questions

1. What recommendation should you make to the school board?

2. What are the arguments on both sides?

3. Should it matter in this case that there were complaints about the racial intolerance of teachers in this school in past years?

# CONCLUSION . . . . . . . . . . . . . . . . . . . . . . . . . . . . . . . . .

Historically, students whose first language was not English were expected to learn English, and educational accommodations generally were not provided. However, recently some gains have been made, as the Supreme Court has held that not understanding English and receiving no support deprived a student of his education. The Court based its decision on the Civil Rights Act of 1964. However, the Court did not prescribe a remedy. Arguments have ensued over which remedy to institute, and school districts today are given a substantial amount of latitude in rectifying language deficiencies. The Supreme Court has found that ability grouping and classroom assignment systems designed to implement effective programs are nondiscriminatory and acceptable.

In response to the growing concern regarding the needs of non-English-speaking students, especially Spanish speakers, Congress enacted the Bilingual Education Act in 1968, which was later revised in 1974, 1988, and 1994. These Acts provided funding for low-income students with limited English proficiency. Most important, the Acts required that bilingual programs in schools be developed in consultation with the parents of limited-English-speaking students.

California and other states have passed "English Only" laws. These laws require all classes to be conducted in English. In these states, the statute mandates that bilingual education is administered only if school first receives a waiver. Some have opined that these requirements smack of the post–World War I statute that prohibited teaching a foreign language to children under the age of 14, which was instituted in response to a fear that German immigrants would rear their children with other than democratic ideals.

Some argue there is a "black English" spoken by African American students and that most teachers are not proficient in this dialect. If true, this would deny those students their right to be educated. One district court has supported this theory and accordingly required Ann Arbor, Michigan, teachers to attend inservice education in black English. Further, the Oakland School Board attempted to receive bilingual funds, arguing that black English was a dialect, but it was unsuccessful.

The cases that follow show the complexity of the issue concerning students whose first language is not English. A basic tenet underpinning the formation of the United States was to welcome immigrants. However, how can our school systems adopt this welcoming attitude when forced to teach students in English even though these students are not fluent in English? Nevertheless, in several states that have adopted English Only statutes, all business including education must be conducted in English. It is likely that more cases will force the courts to come to a reluctant decision regarding how best to address this growing concern of our non-English-speaking dominant minority group children.

# CASE BRIEFS ....................

# LAU V. NICHOLS 414 U.S. 563, 94 S. CT. 786 (1974)

**GENERAL RULE OF LAW:** Federally funded schools violate the Civil Rights Act of 1964 if they do not provide their non-English-speaking students with either English instruction or with classes in their native language.

**PROCEDURE SUMMARY:**

**Plaintiffs:** Lau (P) and other non-English-speaking Chinese students

**Defendant:** San Francisco Unified School District (D)

**U.S. District Court Decision:** Held for San Francisco Unified School District (D)

**U.S. Court of Appeals Decision:** Affirmed

**U.S. Supreme Court Decision:** Reversed

**FACTS:** California law required English to be the language of instruction in its schools and required graduating students to pass standard proficiency examinations given in English. However, the San Francisco Unified School District (D) did not provide its non-English-speaking students of Chinese descent with either course instruction in Chinese or separate classes on the English language. Lau (P) and other Chinese students filed a class action lawsuit against the school district in order to break down this language barrier, which effectively prevented them from getting an education equivalent to that received by English-speaking students. As federally funded institutions, the San Francisco schools were subject to the Civil Rights Act of 1964 as well as the Department of Health, Education, and Welfare (HEW) regulations. The HEW assured equal access to education for students of all races and mandated correction of language deficiencies that restricted student access to educational resources. The U.S. district court and the court of appeals both denied the students' (P) claim, in part on the ground that all students, regardless of race, enter school with unique disadvantages that the school itself had not caused and had no responsibility for correcting.

**ISSUE:** Do federally funded schools violate the Civil Rights Act of 1964 if they do not provide their non-English-speaking students with English instruction or with classes in their native language?

**HOLDING AND DECISION:** (Douglas, J.) Yes. Federally funded schools violate the Civil Rights Act of 1964 if they do not provide their non-English-speaking students with either English instruction or with classes in their native language. The Civil Rights Act bans discrimination based on race, color, or national origin in any program that receives federal financial assistance. The San Francisco Unified School District (D) is federally funded. Even though it provides its students of Chinese ancestry with the same facilities, textbooks, teachers, and curricula as its non-Chinese students, it has denied them meaningful access to education because these students cannot understand English, the language used in all classes. They are not provided instruction in the English language. This practice also violates HEW regulations, which require federally funded schools to correct language deficiencies that prevent non-English-speaking students from effectively obtaining the same education as English-speaking students. Reversed.

**COMMENT:** This case left many questions unanswered. First, the exact threshold number of non-English-speaking students of a particular ancestry that would trigger the need for special instruction was not specified. Justice Blackmun, in a concurring opinion, said that he had voted with the majority in this case principally because San Francisco had such a large number (2,800) of Chinese-speaking students, but his decision would have been different if only one or a few students had been involved. Although smaller school districts were given little guidance, an informal standard of 20 or more students with the same language difficulty (perhaps the size of the average classroom) appeared to develop soon after this decision was handed down. Second, because the Court based its decision on the Civil Rights Act and HEW regulations, it did not rule whether the failure to offer remedial English instruction violated the equal protection clause of the Fourteenth Amendment. Finally, no specific remedy was mandated by the Court, perhaps because the remedies were rather limited in number (e.g., English language classes or course instruction in the students' native language) and obvious. Also, the Court wished to leave the choice of remedy to the local school districts. Bilingual education was not required in order to correct such a language inequity. Any remedy that corrects the constitutional inequity will suffice.

## Discussion Questions

1. Under the Civil Rights Act of 1964, what would a school district be required to do if it had five high school students who spoke only the same non-English language?

2. How do you think this case would have been decided if the plaintiffs had used the Fourteenth Amendment as the basis of their complaint?

3. Why did the Supreme Court not suggest specific remedies to correct the problems identified in this case?

# MEYER V. NEBRASKA
# 262 U.S. 390, 43 S. CT. 625 (1923)

**GENERAL RULE OF LAW:** A law prohibiting the teaching of a foreign language to children before the eighth grade violates the Fourteenth Amendment.

**PROCEDURE SUMMARY:**

**Plaintiff:** Meyer (D), parochial school teacher convicted of violating the law

**Defendant:** The State of Nebraska (P)

**State Trial Court Decision:** Convicted Meyer (D)

**State Supreme Court Decision:** Affirmed

**U.S. Supreme Court Decision:** Reversed

**FACTS:** Nebraska (P) enacted a statute forbidding the teaching of a foreign language to children before the eighth grade. Meyer (D) taught German to a 10-year-old parochial school student and was convicted under the law. The state supreme court upheld the conviction and the law and stated that it was a valid exercise of the **police power**. Meyer (D) was granted review by the Supreme Court, where it was contended that the law violated the Fourteenth Amendment.

**ISSUE:** Does a law prohibiting the teaching of a foreign language to children before the eighth grade violate the Fourteenth Amendment?

**HOLDING AND DECISION:** (McReynolds, J.) Yes. A law prohibiting the teaching of a foreign language to children before the eighth grade violates the Fourteenth Amendment. The law unreasonably infringes upon the liberty rights guaranteed by the Fourteenth Amendment. Among these rights are the rights of teachers to teach and the rights of students to acquire knowledge. Though the state's goal of ensuring that students learn English and American ideals is worthy, the law at issue is an impermissible means of accomplishing it. There is no national emergency justifying the complete ban, and it has not been shown that mere knowledge of a foreign language is harmful. Further, there is no support for the suggestion that the law's purpose was to protect children's health by limiting their mental activities. Thus, there is no rational basis for the law. Reversed.

**COMMENT:** It is significant that the case arose shortly after World War I. The law was clearly a response to the fear that immigrants coming to the United States would rear their children with other than American democratic ideals. Also, the case is one of those rare situations when a law or statute failed the highly deferential "rational basis" test applied by the Court. This case has renewed relevance in light of contemporary events that have given rise to a movement promoting English as the official language of individual states and the nation.

## Discussion Questions

1. If the court would apply *Meyer* to a current law mandating teaching in only English, would the law be considered constitutional? Why or why not?

2. Name some controversial topics that a teacher should have the right to teach.

3. Is this type of problem going to escalate in importance, or can we simply wait out the current controversy?

# MARTIN LUTHER KING, JR., ELEMENTARY SCHOOL CHILDREN V. MICHIGAN BOARD OF EDUCATION 451 F.SUPP. 1324 (E.D. MICH. 1978)

**GENERAL RULE OF LAW:** Students in a public school with "black English" as their native language may bring a cause of action against their school system for the school system's failure to take appropriate action to help students overcome language barriers, but they may not bring a cause of action against a school system for denial of equal protection for failure to consider the students' cultural, social, and economic background to determine eligibility for special education services, or for the school system's failure to provide materials to the low-income students that are not used in the school, but that middle- and higher-income students may have available in their homes.

**PROCEDURE SUMMARY:**

**Plaintiffs:** Elementary school students of Martin Luther King, Jr., Elementary School (Students) (P)

**Defendants:** Michigan Board of Education (Board) and other school authorities (D)

**State Trial Court Decision:** Held for Board (D) on equal protection claim, and dismissed all of students' (P) claims except their claim alleging they were denied an equal educational opportunity

**FACTS:** Students (P) brought suit against Board (D), claiming that the Board (D) and various school authorities (1) failed to take appropriate action to help them overcome the language barriers they experienced as native speakers of "black English" rather than standard English; (2) failed to consider the cultural, social, and economic deprivations of the students in determining eligibility for special education services; and (3) violated their right to a free education by not providing them with the books and other materials available in the homes of middle- and higher-income students. The students (P) brought suit through their mothers and the Student Advocacy Center, a nonprofit corporation in Michigan, against the Board (D) along with the Ann Arbor School District Board, the Michigan Superintendent of Public Instruction, the Ann Arbor School Superintendent (Harry Howard), the Ann Arbor School Pupil Personnel Director (Hazel Turner), and the principal of Martin Luther King, Jr., Elementary School (Rachel Schreiber). The students asserted the first claim under §§ 1703 and 1706, alleging a violation of their right to an equal educational opportunity. The students asserted the second claim under § 1983, alleging a violation of equal protection guaranteed by the Fourteenth Amendment, and § 2000(d), alleging a violation of their right to benefits of federal financial assistance. The students asserted the third claim under Article 8, Section 2 of the Michigan Constitution and § 380.1147(1) of the Michigan Compiled Laws Annotated, alleging a violation of their right to a free education. The Board (D) filed a motion to dismiss the action for failure to state a claim and the district court must decide whether to grant or deny the motion.

**ISSUES:**

1. May students in a public school system with a "black English" background bring a cause of action under §§ 1703(f) and 1706 for failure of the school system to take appropriate action to overcome language barriers that hinder equal participation by students in instructional programs?

2. May students in a public school system who have experienced cultural, social, and economic deprivations bring a cause of action for failure of the school district to consider their background when determining eligibility for special education services?

3. Must a public school system provide its lower-income students with books and other materials that are not used in the school, but that nevertheless may be available in the homes of middle- and higher-income students?

**HOLDING AND DECISION:** (Joiner, J.)

1. Yes. Section 1703(f) requires school authorities to take appropriate action to overcome whatever language barriers might exist, in order to enable all students to participate equally in educational programs. "Language barriers" include those experienced by students with a foreign language as their native language as well as students with "black English" as their native language. In order to establish a cause of action under § 1703(f), the plaintiffs must show that an educational opportunity was denied "on account of race, color, sex, or national origin" and that the school system failed to take action to overcome language barriers severe enough to hinder the equal participation of the students in educational programs. The issue here is whether the students stated a valid cause of action sufficient to prevent the cause of action from being dismissed by the court. The district court found that the claim alleged by the students should not be dismissed because if the failure of the school system to act to overcome the "language barrier" experienced by students with a background in "black English" hindered the students' equal participation in educational programs and was tied to the students' race, a violation of § 1703(f) may be found.

2. No. There is no law or clause in the Constitution that specifically grants the right of students to special education services to overcome poor academic performance that arises from cultural, economic, or social deprivations. The equal protection clause of the Fourteenth Amendment allows creation of programs to remedy a problem without requiring the program to correct all programs at once. In other words, remedial programs are allowed to take care of problems only "one step at a time." The special education services program established by the school was meant to remedy a problem; the failure of the school to address the problem of poor performance arising from social, cultural, and economic deprivations at the same time does not provide the students with a cause of action. In addition, § 2000(d) prohibits any school system receiving federal financial assistance from denying benefits to anyone based on race, color, or national origin. The students failed to state that they were denied benefits *because of* their race, color, or national origin, instead asserting they were denied benefits because not enough students at the school experienced social, economic, and cultural deprivations for the school to create a program specifically designed to address these disadvantages. The district court granted the Board's (D) motion to dismiss.

3. No. A school system must provide students with books and other supplies and equipment used in school as part of its obligation to provide a free education. The district court, however, refused to extend this requirement to also mean that school systems must provide lower-income students with all books and other materials that might be useful and that middle- and higher-income students might have available in their homes. The district court granted the Board's (D) motion to dismiss.

**COMMENTS:** Although the issue of "black English" was the most discussed aspect of the case, there were two other very important concerns being litigated. If students could argue that their cultural, economic, or social deprivations qualified them for special education services, this would have created an extensive, new entitlement that would have opened the door (if supported by higher courts) to extensive costly services that school districts would have to provide. The other issue, providing poor students with the same background and home benefits that higher-income students had as a matter of course, was one that equal education theorists had long argued. This court's decision to not require school districts to provide support and services that would try to equalize for past deprivations has halted this line of legal equity efforts. The issue that was supported by this court, as well as the lower court upon remand, was to require teachers to complete professional development in black English to help them to understand the needs of these youth. While this court supported the language barrier issue, the Office of Bilingual Education refused to provide financial assistance for black English, limiting extensively its application elsewhere.

## Discussion Questions

1. Do you think that requiring predominately white teachers to understand "black English" will help them to teach students more effectively? Will it have an impact on the students?

2. If the special education issue in this case had "gone the other way," what would have been some of the ramifications for school districts?

3. Do you agree with this decision? Why or why not?

# CALIFORNIA TEACHERS ASSOCIATION V. STATE BOARD OF EDUCATION 271 F.3D 1141 (9TH CIR. 2001)

**GENERAL RULE OF LAW:** A California law that requires teachers to present instruction "overwhelmingly" in English or "nearly all" in English is not unconstitutionally vague and, while it may have a minimal chilling effect on the educator's speech, the state's interest in English language instruction outweighs any First Amendment concerns, so the law will be upheld.

**PROCEDURE SUMMARY:**

**Plaintiff:** California Teachers Association (Teachers) (P)

**Defendant:** State Board of Education (Board) (D)

**State Trial Court Decision:** Held for Board (D), granting summary judgment

**U.S. Court of Appeals Decision:** Affirmed

**FACTS:** The California Teachers Association (P) brought a Section 1983 action against the State Board of Education (D), alleging that § 320 of Proposition 227 was unconstitutionally vague and overbroad in violation of the First and Fourteenth Amendments of the U.S. Constitution. Section 320 of Proposition 227 gives parents the right to sue teachers, administrators, and other officials in California public schools who "willfully and repeatedly" refuse to provide an "English language educational option." The district court granted the Board (D) summary judgment. The California Teachers Association appealed to the Ninth Circuit Court of Appeals to challenge the issue of vagueness only. The court of appeals affirmed the decision of the district court.

**ISSUE:** Must a law be struck down as unconstitutionally vague if it imposes liability on teachers and other school officials who willfully and repeatedly refuse to provide an "English language instructional curriculum"?

**HOLDING AND DECISION:** (Boochever, J.) No. Proposition 227 is sufficiently clear to be upheld. Proposition 227 mandates that educators use English as the language for instruction regardless of the first language of the student. Specifically, it requires that educators teach "overwhelmingly" in English or using "nearly all" English. Proposition 227 does provide for "sheltered English immersion" programs for students learning English. In this situation, the instruction in the classroom must be in English but curriculum and presentation may be designed for the students who are learning the English language. Parents may seek to have the English-only instruction requirement waived for their child, but otherwise it applies. The rule of law expressed in *Hazelwood,* that regulations of speech violate the First Amendment unless reasonably related to legitimate pedagogical concerns, applies to Proposition 227's English language restriction on instructional speech. The court used a balancing test to determine that the state's interests in English language instruction outweighed the concern of the Teachers (P) that Proposition 227's vagueness might result in a small possibility of chilling speech in violation of the First Amendment. The court found it unlikely that an educator trying in good faith to follow Proposition 227 would become civilly liable because to be civilly liable an educator must violate a statute "willfully and repeatedly."

**COMMENTS:** This is one of the few cases that addresses the growing problem of non-English-speaking dominant minority group students. Not only is there an increase in the number of legal and illegal immigrant students, but these students also lack adequate ESL instruction. With more and more school districts having a majority of students who do not speak English as their first language, this problem will continue and escalate. This case does not address the needs of non-English-speaking students because it concerns the potential liability of teachers under Proposition 227. It would probably be correct to say that most teachers would support the "English only" aspects of the state statute. Hopefully, American education will not again fail to address a problem until it becomes a crisis situation. The true issue is how best to educate non-English speakers. Legislative options merely avoid the real problem. For example, desegregation did not become an issue outside of the South for many years because of a false sense that there was no racism outside the South, where formal segregation laws were adopted. A less direct parallel is the drug problem. Our society really avoided dealing with drugs when the belief was that this was a ghetto problem; only when there was a realization that drugs were crippling all segments of our society did a major national anti-drug initiative develop.

## Discussion Questions

1. Does the decision in this case provide protection for the teacher plaintiffs who initiated the court action?

2. How does this state statute address the needs of the non-English-speaking dominant minority group students who fall under the purview of the statute?

3. Has the American educational system dealt with immigrant student populations in the past? Is our situation today different from the past?

# CASTANEDA V. PICKARD
# 648 F.2D 989 (5TH CIR. 1981)

**GENERAL RULE OF LAW:** The history of racial discrimination by a school district, as well as whether it has remedied any such history for a sufficient time period, must be determined before a ruling on whether the school district engaged in racially discriminatory practices.

**PROCEDURE SUMMARY:**

**Plaintiffs:** Mexican American children and their parents (Students) (P)

**Defendant:** Raymondville, Texas, Independent School district (School District) (D)

**State Trial Court Decision:** Held for School District (D)

**U.S. Court of Appeals Decision:** Affirmed in part and reversed in part, and remanded

**FACTS:** Plaintiffs, who are Mexican American students and their parents in a community comprised of approximately 77% Mexican Americans and nearly all of the remaining 23% "Anglos," brought suit against the School District (D), asserting that (1) its ability grouping system for classroom assignments used criteria that unlawfully segregated and racially discriminated against them; (2) the School District (D) discriminated against Mexican American faculty and administrators when making hiring and promotion decisions; and (3) the School District (D) prevented Mexican American students from equal participation in educational programs by failing to implement adequate bilingual programs to help them to overcome language barriers. Plaintiffs argued that the actions of the School District (D) violated their Fourteenth Amendment rights, as well as Section 1983, the Equal Educational Opportunities Act of 1974, and the Civil Rights Act of 1964. The District Court held for the School District (D), finding that none of its policies or practices violated the rights of the Students (P) under the U.S. Constitution or other laws. Plaintiffs appealed to the Fifth Circuit Court of Appeals.

**ISSUE:** Do the School District's (D) policies and practices in ability grouping students, in hiring and promoting faculty, and in its alleged failure to provide adequate bilingual programs result in violation of any rights of the Students (P) under the U.S. Constitution or other laws?

**HOLDING AND DECISION:** (Randall, J.) The history of the School District (D) must be considered before a decision can be reached on these issues. Ability grouping, on its own, will not violate the Constitution even if it results in segregation, if the School District (D) has achieved unitary status and maintained a unitary school system for a sufficient period of time. On the other hand, if unitary status has not been achieved, then ability grouping practices that have a markedly disparate impact on students of different races and a significant racially segregative effect will be barred. The district court did not rule on whether the School District (D) had a history of discrimination against Mexican Americans or if it remedied any history sufficiently to achieve unitary status. This issue is remanded to the district court to reach a conclusion on the School District's (D) history of racial discrimination against Mexican Americans. The district court should also evaluate whether the School District's (D) grouping of the students by their language ability and labeling of groups by intelligence level demonstrates an intent to discriminate by degrading children based on their ethnic backgrounds. In determining whether the School District (D) engaged in racial discrimination in its hiring and promotion, the district court failed to compare the racial composition of the pool of applicants to the racial composition of the relevant labor market. The relevant labor market is the geographical area from which the School District (D) would be reasonably expected to draw its applicants and must be considered in making a determination on employment discrimination. Moreover, the Students (P) brought an employment discrimination claim against the School District (D) for its failure to hire and promote Mexican American teachers, but the district court only addressed whether the School District (D) discriminated in its hiring practices, without addressing whether the School District's (D) promotion practices were discriminatory. The district court's finding that the bilingual program did not violate the rights of Students (P) is affirmed, but all other issues on appeal are reversed and remanded to the district court.

**COMMENTS:** This decision (or non-decision, as some might view it) is included to generate discussion regarding the nature of future issues relating to discrimination. The issues faced by non-English-speaking dominant minority groups are similar to, but also different from, those faced by African Americans in the latter half of the last century. From this case, a series of guidelines developed to provide some direction to those trying to serve these students. Nevertheless, it is clear that there has been a radical change in the Court's perspective regarding discrimination and affirmative action issues. Upcoming Supreme Court cases may clarify the issues discussed in this case, but these issues remain critical to the direction that our nation will take. Further, these are issues that future teachers and administrators need to consider, discuss, and debate as the number of non-English-speaking dominant minority group students continues to increase.

## Discussion Questions

1. Why did the higher court defer to the trial court to review the major issues in this case?

2. Why is the question of whether there has been a "history of discrimination" against Mexican Americans an important consideration in rendering a decision?

3. What are the potential concerns if a school district were required to consider promotion practices?

Additional case briefs can be found on the SAGE Web site at the following address:
http://www.sagepub.com/aquilacasebriefs

# NOTES

1. Lau v. Nichols, 414 U.S. 563, 94 S. Ct. 786 (1974).
2. Civil Rights Act, 42 U.S.C § 2000 et seq. (1964).
3. Martin Luther King, Jr., Elementary School Children v. Michigan Board of Education, 473 F.Supp. 1371 (E.D. Mich. 1979).

4. Matter of McMillan, 226 S.E.2d 693 (N.C. Ct. App. 1976).

5. Memorandum, May 15, 1970. This internal memorandum became a statement of policy that HEW, as well as enforcement arms such as the Office for Civil Rights, used when dealing with issues related to students with "linguistic deficiencies."

6. Castaneda v. Pickard, 648 F.2d 989 (5th Cir. 1981).

7. Castaneda v. Pickard (Castaneda II), 781 F.2d 456 (5th Cir. 1986).

8. Meyer v. Nebraska, 262 U.S. 390 (1923).

# 8

# Education of Students
# With Disabilities

*No child who is mentally retarded or thought to be mentally retarded can be assigned initially (or re-assigned) to either a regular or special educational status or excluded from a public education without a prior recorded hearing before a special hearing officer.*

*—Pennsylvania Assn. for
Retarded Children v. Commonwealth* (1971)[1]

## OVERVIEW · · · · · · · · · · · · · · · · · · · · · · · · · · · · · · · · · · · · · · · · ·

The historical growth of programs and services for children with disabilities developed very slowly. In 1817, Thomas Hopkins Gallaudet established what has become the American School for the Deaf. A few years later, New York and Pennsylvania—along with a few other states—established similar schools. During the 1830s, Horace Mann initiated efforts for those with disabilities other than deafness. Notwithstanding these early efforts, it was the disabled veterans returning from World War I who raised national awareness regarding the lack of services for the disabled, especially rehabilitation services. One reason for the failure to provide any significant financial resources for children with disabilities may have been public apathy. Another reason was that students with severe disabilities had many problems meeting the requirements and conditions established in public schools. For instance, most state laws provided that children with certain disabilities could be expelled from public schools. This left the parents of these children to educate them at home, find a residential school, provide private tutoring, or—as was most often the case—do nothing at all to educate their child.

In the 30 years prior to the Education for All Handicapped Children Act, only a few states provided any categorical funds for schools to meet the needs of children with special needs.[2] But these state programs, even when available, were extremely limited and rarely, if ever, served those who were the most severely disabled. Using the *Brown* rationale for equal educational opportunities, it seemed natural for the federal government to step in and do what the states could not, or would not, do. In the early 1970s, *Mills v. Board of Education of District of Columbia* (1972) guaranteed due process rights and protections to children with disabilities, thus expanding the *Pennsylvania Assn. for Retarded Children v. Commonwealth* (1971) consent agreement, which established basic parameters and guarantees for all children with disabilities.[3] Much of the language and information from **amicus curiae** briefs from these two landmark cases was incorporated in the Education for All Handicapped Children Act.

Many significant cases that clarified the special education statutory enactments have helped provide the guideposts that assist school districts to provide legally correct services to children with disabilities. Although many cases are still explicating key aspects of the major cases, there are many conclusions that can be drawn. For example, a classic case dealing with the extent of service necessary to meet the needs of children with disabilities was *Hendrick Hudson Central School District v. Rowley* (1982).[4] In that case, the court found that the Individuals With Disabilities Education Act (IDEA) did not require special services that would put a handicapped child's education on a level commensurate with that of nonhandicapped children; thus, school districts did not have to maximize educational benefits.[5] If school districts had been required to maximize services as proposed, the costs would have been prohibitive.

Another significant case that provides a bright line for school districts is *Irving Independent School District v. Tatro* (1984).[6] This case dealt with whether schools needed to provide clean intermittent catheterization (CIC) to students requiring the procedure. IDEA mandated that states provide a public education to handicapped children. This included special education and related services necessary to achieve this goal. CIC was held to be a "related service" necessary to promote educational access. While school professionals felt that this was a medical procedure not required by the statute, the Court held that "medical service" referred to complicated procedures not within the competence of school personnel. Because CIC was a simple procedure a nurse or even a layman was capable of performing, the Court found that public schools must offer it to children needing that service.

In *Grube v. Bethlehem Area School District* (1982), the court applied § 504 of the Rehabilitation Act of 1973 and held that school officials cannot exclude students with disabilities from an extracurricular activity solely because of their disabilities.[7]

Three major federal statutes protect all individuals with disabilities from discrimination and offer them equal access and opportunity with regard to governmental benefits, facility utilization, and employment. In the school setting, these statutes require school agencies to (1) identify children with disabilities; (2) evaluate their respective educational needs; and (3) assign them specially designed instruction and related services, when appropriate. The statute that deals specifically with children with disabilities is the Individuals With Disabilities Education Improvement Act (IDEIA).[8] The two others are antidiscrimination statutes—section 504 of the Rehabilitation Act of 1973 and the Americans With Disabilities Act—which protect both children and adults.[9] These three federal disability statutes that impact America's schools are discussed below.

## Case Study

### It Wasn't So Long Ago (Adapted From an Anonymous Narrative)

In 1960, the Smiths had a baby girl, Kathy. The initial excitement about the successful pregnancy and delivery was soon erased by a dark cloud. They were informed by the doctor that their beautiful daughter was retarded. Mrs. Smith explained her feelings in this way:

We felt horrible when the doctor told us that our beautiful baby girl was retarded. I can still hear his words: "You probably don't want to keep her. The state institution is the best place for infants like her. She really won't be able to learn anything. The staff at the institution will be able to take care of her better than you." I immediately hated the doctor. How could he be saying this to me about my brand-new baby girl? 1 felt as if I was having a nightmare and that at any moment I would awake and find that everything was okay.

Initially, we were so angry and couldn't help thinking negative thoughts, like Why did this happen to us? We didn't do anything wrong; this is unfair! We looked for someone to blame. We blamed the doctors and the staff at the hospital. It must be their fault; it couldn't be ours! Then, gradually, we both felt so guilty. We racked our brains for things that we might have done incorrectly during pregnancy. Did I fail? Was I exposed to any harmful substances? Although we lived in an old apartment building, we had thought everything there was safe, but now we had second thoughts about everything. We no longer trusted our own judgment anymore—on anything. We didn't know who to turn to for help and felt overwhelmed and lost. The only individuals we knew we could speak with were the doctors and staff at the hospital, who had already expressed their opinions to us in no uncertain terms.

We loved our baby and decided to keep her. Kathy was very slow at developing. At first, I was embarrassed to take her out of the house. We were always searching for effective ways to help her. Everything was so hard. Each little thing we did seemed like an enormous journey. When Kathy reached kindergarten age, she had passed some important developmental milestones. We knew she wasn't developmentally the same as other children her age, but we hoped that she might begin to catch up once she was in school.

Unfortunately, however, within the first week of kindergarten, we were contacted by the school and asked to remove Kathy from the school. We were told that she wasn't ready for school and that she took too much time away from the other children in the class. If we wanted Kathy exposed to any educational program, the only solution available to us was to place her in the state institution's school.

We were again devastated by this horrible decision and felt we had no educational option. We went through the identical grieving process as we had when Kathy was born. We finally decided to send our daughter to the state school. We were angry and felt guilty for sending her away, but we sincerely believed we had no other options available to us. Although we made the best decision for us at the time, we still feel guilty.

*(Continued)*

(Continued)

---

**Discussion Questions**

1. Was this situation common in the 1960s? What did school districts in your state do prior to the enactment of IDEA?

2. What would happen if this situation occurred in our schools today?

3. On a different note, some have argued that there is a growing wall separating regular education and special education. What does this mean? Is it accurate?

---

# IMPORTANT CONCEPTS

- **Lack of funds not a proper excuse**: A school district may not argue that a lack of funds prevents it from providing for special needs students.

- **"Free" and "appropriate" education (FAPE):** The Individuals With Disabilities Education Improvement Act (IDEIA), the primary source of disabilities-oriented legislation for children, guarantees all special needs children the right to a free, appropriate public education (FAPE).

- **No benefit need be demonstrated:** Accordingly, special needs children are not required to demonstrate that they can or will benefit from special education as a condition precedent to receipt of appropriate services.

- **No special treatment beyond duty to ensure equal access:** The IDEIA places an affirmative obligation on each state to ensure that equal access to a public education is not an empty guarantee. Beyond this, the legislation requires no special treatment of students with disabilities.

- **Individual with severe special needs may receive priority services:** However, within the spectrum of disabilities, children with severe special needs are guaranteed the same rights as those whose special needs are less severe. In fact, the IDEIA requires that severe cases be given priority.

- **Multiple special needs require commensurate services:** The IDEIA requires that educational services be provided to a child with cognitive special needs as well as multiple other special needs. Such services will not be limited to traditional academic training but must also include training in basic functional living skills.

- **Classroom disruptions:** Under the IDEIA, a state may not remove special needs students from their placements in response to disruptive conduct arising out of their disabilities. It may, however, follow normal safety procedures with regard to nonspecial-needs-related, immediate dangers.

- **Legally sufficient "notice" required:** Under the IDEIA, a school district must provide the parents of a child with special needs with sufficient notice of changes it may be contemplating in the child's educational program. Such a notice must contain the following: a description of procedural actions that have been taken; a description of any action the district proposes, or refuses, to take; a listing of the options that will be or have been considered; the reasons for rejecting any of the options; and a description of each evaluation component included in the student's individualized education program.

- **"Special needs" defined under ADA:** Under the Americans With Disabilities Act, a special needs person is one who has a physical or mental impairment that substantially limits a major life activity, a person who has a past record of such impairment, or a person who is regarded by other people as having such an impairment.

- **Conditions for qualification for employment [?] under ADA:** An individual with special needs is qualified under the ADA if, with or without reasonable accommodations, she can perform the essential functions of the employment position that she holds or desires to hold.

- **Protection from needs-based discrimination:** Section 504 of the Rehabilitation Act of 1973 provides that no otherwise qualified special needs person shall, solely by reason of her special needs, be excluded from participation in any federal program.

- **Reaches beyond education:** Thus, § 504 reaches beyond the educational context to protect all special needs persons of all ages from discrimination in a variety of programs and activities that receive federal financial assistance.

- **No affirmative action required:** Section 504 does not require affirmative action on behalf of special needs persons. It merely precludes discrimination.

## FEDERAL DISABILITY STATUTES

### Individuals With Disabilities Education Improvement Act of 2004 (IDEIA)

IDEIA deals with children with disabilities in elementary and secondary schools. Therefore, the focus of the discussion and cases in this chapter will be the needs of schoolchildren with disabilities. IDEIA is the successor statutory enactment to the Education for All Handicapped Children Act of 1975, often referred to as "Public Law 94-142." IDEIA basically guarantees a student with special needs the right to a free, appropriate public education (FAPE). Essentially, IDEIA is limited to special needs children who seek a public education. As of this printing, there are approximately 7 million children with some form of special needs. Under IDEIA, the U.S. Congress specifically imposed an obligation on each state to ensure that equal access to a public education was not an empty guarantee. Hence, a school district may not argue that a lack of funds prevents it from providing for special needs students. There are six basic principles that underpin IDEIA and its application in America's schools:

- Free, appropriate public education (FAPE)
- Appropriate evaluation

- Individualized education plan (IEP)
- Least restrictive environment (LRE)
- Parent and student participation in decision making
- Procedural due process

## The Rehabilitation Act of 1973, Section 504

Section 504 of the Rehabilitation Act of 1973, which prohibits discrimination on the basis of disability, was enacted before the Education for All Handicapped Children Act. Under the Act, school officials may not exclude a student with a disability from an extracurricular activity solely because of his disability.[10] Of course, § 504 reaches beyond the educational context to protect persons of all ages with disabilities from discrimination in a variety of programs and activities that receive federal financial assistance. However, § 504 does not require affirmative action on behalf of persons with disabilities. Rather, it merely prohibits discrimination.[11] Therefore, while § 504 is concerned with discrimination against individuals with disabilities in work situations, it also addresses the problems encountered by children with disabilities who seek equal educational opportunities.

Thus, § 504 is an antidiscrimination law, a broad civil rights law. It essentially forbids state and local governments, as well as any private organizations that receive federal funds, from discriminating against an otherwise qualified person with a disability solely because of that disability. Note that § 504 prohibits discrimination against all persons with disabilities, including school-age children, even if they do not need educational services. IDEIA, on the other hand, only requires special services for children with disabilities who are of school age. Because § 504 prohibits discrimination against "otherwise qualified" individuals solely because of disability, this law is applied most often to adult employment. Interestingly, § 504 provides broader protection than IDEIA, which protects only 13 disabling conditions: Section 504 has a very broad definition for eligibility. A child is protected under it if he has— or has had—a physical or mental impairment that substantially limits a major life activity, or he is regarded as handicapped by others. Major life activities include such things as walking, seeing, hearing, and learning.

## Americans With Disabilities Act of 1990 (ADA)

The most recent legislation dealing with disabilities is the Americans With Disabilities Act, which was enacted by Congress in 1990 and is considered the most important legislation for persons with disabilities since the Education for All Handicapped Children Act in 1975. A critical difference between ADA and § 504—both of which are antidiscrimination, civil rights legislation—is that the ADA extends coverage and protections to individuals employed by or using services of nonfederally funded entities. Unfortunately, like § 504, the ADA does not provide funding to help entities enforce its requirements. The four major areas of protective coverage for those with disabilities are employment discrimination, public services from state and local governments, privately owned public accommodations and services, and telecommunications.

The ADA prohibits discrimination against any qualified individual with a disability in job applications, hiring, training, compensation, fringe benefits, advancement, or any other term or condition of work. The ADA also forbids "disparate impact" discrimination in accordance with the principles of Title VII of the Civil Rights Act of 1964. It also prohibits the utilization of any standard, criteria, or administrative method that has the effect of discriminating because of special needs or that perpetuates such discrimination. The ADA requires that a school district make reasonable accommodations for the known disabilities of job applicants and employees. Importantly, once necessary and reasonable accommodations have been provided, the ADA encourages treating the worker with a disability just like the nondisabled worker. Thus, affirmative action plans, preferential treatment of special needs applicants and employees, and expensive accommodations or modifications of current workplaces are not mandated.

Looking at these three statutes—IDEIA, the Rehabilitation Act of 1973, and the ADA—as they apply to schools, it is clear that they have a profound effect on the lives of children with disabilities. Only IDEIA provides funding for school districts to provide a free and appropriate education (FAPE) to all children with disabilities, yet the three complement each other. While IDEIA protects children ages 3 to 21 in one or more categories of disability, § 504 provides protections to a broader group of children and adults with disabilities whom the IDEIA might not cover. While IDEIA provides appropriate special education services in schools, when these children become adults, the ADA helps them to use skills learned in schools to become successful and integrated into the larger community.

# INDIVIDUALS WITH DISABILITIES EDUCATION IMPROVEMENT ACT OF 2004 (IDEIA)

The Individuals With Disabilities Education Act (IDEA) of 1997 was reauthorized in 2004 as the Individuals With Disabilities Education Improvement Act. IDEIA establishes both substantive and procedural rights. The substantive right is to a "free, appropriate public education." The law also guarantees certain procedural mechanisms with respect to the manner in which the rights are implemented.

To qualify for federal IDEIA funding for the education of the handicapped, a state must have in effect a policy that assures all special needs children certain specified substantive rights. An approved plan detailing the state's goals, timetables, facilities, personnel, and services for educating children with disabilities must be on file. Additionally, IDEIA requires that federal funds must be allocated first to handicapped children who are not receiving an education, then to children with the most severe handicaps within each handicapped category. Further, IDEIA requires that special needs children have access to and participate in the general education curriculum.

Prior to IDEA, the pertinent law in effect was the Education for All Handicapped Children Act, which codified the right of every child with special needs to a public school education. Many are surprised to find that the first references to special education services for special needs individuals can be found in the 1965 Elementary and Secondary Education Act (ESEA).[12] Interestingly, the first and later No Child Left Behind (NCLB) legislation (a reauthorization of ESEA) also focus heavily on education of special needs individuals.

Of nearly 50 million preschool and school-aged children in the United States, more than 7 million have disabilities, gifts, or talents and need educational services tailored to their needs. NCLB presents a snapshot—in charts, tables, and graphs—of children with special needs, their education, and the professionals who serve them. It is offered in the hope of contributing to a clearer and more comprehensive national perspective, thus serving as an aid in knowledge building and decision making. The statistics are the best available at the time of publication.

## Educating Students With Special Needs

The year 2000 marked the 25th anniversary of federal legislation mandating a free, appropriate public education for individuals with disabilities. Before 1975, 4 million children with disabilities did not receive the help they needed to succeed in school, while another 1 million were simply excluded from school. Few infants, toddlers, or preschoolers received services. Today, under IDEIA, more than 7 million children from birth through 21 years of age receive a broad range of special education and early intervention services. In the 1998–1999 school year, special education services benefited 188,926 infants and toddlers ages 0 to 2; 573,637 preschool children ages 3 to 5; and 5,541,166 students ages 6 to 21. Thus, almost 9% of students ages 6 to 21 received special education services in the 1998–1999 school year.

## Special Needs Areas

IDEIA delineates 13 special needs categories:

1. specific learning disabilities (SLD)

2. speech or language impairments (SI or LI)

3. mental retardation (MR)

4. emotional disturbance (ED)

5. other health impairments (OHI)

6. multiple disabilities (MD)

7. hearing impairments (HI)

8. orthopedic impairments (OI)

9. autism

10. visual impairments (VI)

11. traumatic brain injury (TBI)

12. child with a special need

13. deaf-blindness

The "other health impairment" category includes children with Attention Deficit Disorder and other acute health problems. The "child with a special need" category covers ages 3 through 9 and is used at the discretion of state and local education agencies.

One of the problems that school people face when there is any new authorization such as IDEIA is that it takes time to understand and implement the new provisions. It takes even more time for the new requirements to be understood and then applied uniformly in the field. Further complicating the problem is that each state has adopted its own local rules, which expand and qualify aspects of the original legislation. With this comes the additional problem of having the state make changes to its own "adaptations" to IDEA prior to uniformly adopting the new IDEIA provisions. To provide some clarity, especially for schools and school districts that must immediately deal with these issues, Table 8.1 outlines a number of the key differences between the 1997 IDEA statute and the newly authorized 2004 IDEIA provisions.

## IDEIA's Free, Appropriate Public Education (FAPE) Requirement

To qualify for federal funds that are disbursed under IDEIA, a state must adopt a policy "that assures all handicapped children the right to a free, appropriate public education." Essentially, IDEIA has a zero-reject philosophy—no special needs child may be excluded from receiving a free, appropriate public education. Furthermore, no special needs child is required to demonstrate that he or she will benefit from special education as a condition precedent to receipt of appropriate services.[13] A free, appropriate public education must be specifically designed to meet the unique needs of the special needs schoolchild. IDEIA does not mandate equality of results (i.e., that special needs students receive special services to the degree that their education levels are commensurate with those of nonspecial needs students). It merely requires that special needs students "benefit" from instruction.[14] However, within the spectrum of disabilities, special needs children with severe disabilities are guaranteed the same rights as those with less severe disabilities. In fact, IDEIA requires that severe cases be given priority. The development of specific educational approaches is the responsibility of the state (which, of course, the state may delegate to local school districts within the state). Courts are available to determine whether compliance with IDEIA has been achieved. The legal issues that may arise are limited to the following:

1. *Compliance:* Has the state complied with the procedures set forth in IDEIA?

2. *Well-tailored plan:* Is the special needs child's individualized educational program reasonably calculated to enable the child to receive educational benefits?[15]

## IDEIA's Individualized Educational Program (IEP) Requirement

To ensure the provision of a free, appropriate public education, the individual needs of each student with special needs are guaranteed through an "individualized educational program" (IEP), which is developed in concert with a district representative; the child's general education teacher; a special education teacher; the child's parents; and, if appropriate, the child. Each individualized educational program must include the following:

1. *Vision statement:* A statement of what the child and parent feel is their vision of the result of the special services;

2. *Performance assessment:* A statement of the child's present levels of academic achievement and functional performance;

**Table 8.1**   IDEA/IDEIA Key Provisions: Past and Present

|  | IDEA 1997 | IDEIA 2004 |
|---|---|---|
| Discipline | IDEA students can be removed for 10 consecutive days, as can regular ed students. Services provided in alternative setting beyond 10 days with a **manifestation determination** and a **functional behavior analysis** (FBA). Students receiving special ed services can only be removed to an Interium Alternative Education Setting (IAES) for 45 days if they bring drugs or weapons to school | 10-day rule for suspension still applies. 45 school day removal of student on IEP may be done regardless of whether or not behavior was manifestation of the child's special need for **drugs, weapons or serious bodily injury**. Student on IEP removed to IAES (as an ordered change in placement) remains in IAES as "stay put" during appeal process. |
| Paperwork Reduction | No paperwork reduction currently in place | Up to 15 states may participate in federal pilot program granting waivers of statutory requirements in an effort to reduce paperwork |
| IEP | Reviewed and developed annually. All IEP team members required to be present at meeting | Emphasis of IEP development based on academic achievement and functional performance. Exceptions may be allowed for attendance of an IEP team member |
| Early Support | Districts can use up to 20% of IDEA funds for "special services" for high-cost, at-risk special needs students. General ed funds support prereferral services | Schools may spend up to 15% IDEA funds for early intervening services (K–12 with emphasis on K–3) |
| Parental Choice | If parent does not dispute district's program, privately placed child has no individual right to receive special education or related services | Expenditure for services in private school placement chosen by parent must be equal to proportionate amount of federal funds made available to LEA |
| Conflict Resolution | Does not specify role of lawyer in mediation room, left to decision of states | Mediation is option before due process. Agreement is binding. Two-year limit on filing a complaint |
| Research/ Training | The Office of Special Education Programs (OSEP) houses the department overseeing special education research | Research assigned from OSEP to IES. National Center for Special Ed Research created |
| Teacher Quality | Qualification mandates determined by states | Aligned with NCLB. Teachers in core subjects must be highly qualified by 2006. Bachelor's degree, license or certificate, and demonstrated content area knowledge required |

3. *General education curriculum:* How the special need affects the child's involvement in the general education curriculum;

4. *Goals and objectives:* A statement of annual academic and functional goals and short-term instructional objectives;

5. *Services and participation:* A statement of specific educational services to be provided and the extent to which the child will be able to participate in regular educational programs;

6. *Transition services:* A statement of needed transition services, including, when appropriate, a statement of interagency responsibilities with regard to services to be rendered at and after the time the student leaves the school setting;

7. *Time-line for services:* A statement of the projected initiation and duration of such services and action;

8. *Criteria for measuring success:* A statement of appropriate criteria and procedures for determining, at least annually, whether instructional objectives are being or have been achieved; and

9. *Performance:* A description of how the child's progress toward annual goals will be measured.

Each IEP must be reviewed—and, if appropriate, revised—at least once a year. Procedural guarantees require that parents be notified of proposed changes in placement. Parents may object to proposed changes at an impartial due process hearing. Beyond that, discontented parents may appeal to the state agency and even to a court of law.

## IDEIA's Education-Related Services Requirement

A "related service" is a service or program that must be provided in order for a child with special needs to benefit from special education. Speech pathology and audiology, psychological services, physical and occupational therapy, recreational programs, and certain medical and counseling services qualify as education-related services. Litigation has arisen over the difference between medical and related services. The U.S. Supreme Court held that the periodic provision of a clean intermittent catheter was a related, as opposed to medical, service because the special needs party could not receive an education without it, and the procedure for its installation was simple.[16] Under IDEIA, children with disabilities are entitled to, and therefore must be provided with, education-related services.

## Least Restrictive Alternative Requirement

A student is to be considered for general education first; then the IEP team looks at supports and services, as needed. Further, IDEIA requires that children with disabilities receive services that have the least number of restrictions, whenever and to whatever extent appropriate. The "least restrictive alternative" provision, in effect, mandates that children with special needs be included in special needs-free environments. This statutory preference for mainstreaming creates a tension between the desire for a less restrictive environment and a free, appropriate education (which may call for a more restrictive environment). The problem has been exacerbated by the recent emphasis on inclusion (see below).

## Inclusion

Inclusion is an expansion of mainstreaming, whereby children with disabilities are placed in regular classrooms. There is a strong difference of opinion regarding inclusion. Some educators believe that inclusion provides special needs children with the best educational environment available; others believe that it places children who do not function well in an environment that is not supportive and that often detracts from the education process. Furthermore, there is a fear that some districts may use inclusion as a budget-cutting device. Children with special needs may suffer if the regular classroom teachers with whom they are placed are not trained to handle their special needs. The overly zealous use of inclusion could result in erroneous placements and subsequent litigation. Even more intriguing is the possibility of a lawsuit filed by a nonspecial needs child who alleges the denial of rights because he or she did not receive a fair share of the teacher's time and attention.

## Disciplining Children With Disabilities

Neither IDEIA nor § 504 of the Rehabilitation Act of 1973, discussed below, preclude school professionals from disciplining students with disabilities for misbehavior unrelated to their disabilities.[17] However, a state may not remove special needs students from their placements in response to dangerous or disruptive conduct related to their disabilities. The "stay put" provision requires that a special needs student remain in his educational placement pending completion of an IEP review proceeding.[18] Even when discipline is justified, sanctions that materially interrupt a child's education (e.g., transfers, suspension, or expulsion) may constitute a change of placement, thereby triggering IDEIA's "stay put" requirement and other due process provisions.[19] If a student poses an immediate threat to the safety of others, she or he may be temporarily suspended. Many states allow for up to 10 days of suspension before a student is considered to be expelled. This 10-day suspension practice also applies to special needs students. Such a procedure balances school officials' interest in maintaining a safe learning environment with IDEIA mandates. It should be noted that new provisions of IDEIA will allow a hearing officer to issue an immediate removal of up to 45 days for any child (including a child with special needs) who violates drug or weapons policies or causes serious bodily injury. It is likely that there will be several different constitutional challenges regarding this and related IDEIA provisions.

# AMERICANS WITH DISABILITIES ACT (ADA) OF 1990

## Special Needs Status

A person with special needs is one who has a physical or mental impairment that substantially limits a major life activity, a person who has a past record of such an impairment, or a person who is regarded by other people as having such an impairment.[20] This ADA definition corresponds to the definition of a special needs person under the Rehabilitation Act of 1973.

## "Qualification" of Individuals With Disabilities for Purposes of Employment

An individual with special needs is qualified under the ADA if, with or without reasonable accommodations, she can perform the essential functions of the employment position that she holds or desires to hold. The phrase "essential functions" refers to job tasks that are fundamental and not marginal. An individual with special needs may not be denied a job simply because she is unable to meet a physical or mental requirement that is not really necessary to effective performance of the basic tasks of the job. Employers must make reasonable accommodations to the known physical or mental limitations of an otherwise qualified individual with special needs. The only limitation on this requirement is that if an employer can show that reasonable accommodations impose an undue hardship, then he can consider the person with special needs to be "not qualified."

In *Wallace v. Veterans Admin.* (1988), a hospital refused to hire a registered nurse who was a recovering drug addict because nurses normally handle controlled drugs.[21] The federal district court found, however, that only a small percentage of a nurse's time was actually spent handling drugs. Therefore, the hospital could make a reasonable accommodation by transferring the special needs nurse's drug-handling responsibilities to other nurses, who in turn could transfer some of their nondrug-related job duties to the special needs nurse.

In *Clarke v. Shoreline School District No. 412* (1986), a teacher's loss of eyesight eventually impaired his ability to carry out his teaching duties.[22] The school district suggested that the teacher undergo rehabilitation and retraining in order to accommodate the condition, but the teacher engaged in only minimal rehabilitation and no retraining. After determining that the safety of the teacher's students was in jeopardy, the school district dismissed the teacher. The court affirmed the dismissal based on its finding that the teacher's handicap materially and substantially affected his performance.

These definitions closely follow similar concepts that are contained in the Rehabilitation Act of 1973 and various state disabilities laws.

# SECTION 504 OF THE REHABILITATION ACT OF 1973

## Focus on Discriminatory Acts and Practices

Section 504 of the Rehabilitation Act of 1973 is a civil rights law that delineates actions that *cannot* be taken with regard to the treatment of special needs individuals. Section 504 represents a national commitment to end discrimination in the administration of any program that receives federal funds. In practical terms, funds may be withheld if the section's provisions are not complied with. In contrast, IDEIA provides a guideline concerning what *can* be done to upgrade education opportunities for special needs children.

## Similarities to ADA Provision on Employment-Based Discrimination

Staff and teachers with disabilities in our public schools are protected by both § 504 and the ADA with regard to employment concerns. For instance, a school employee with a contagious disease, such as AIDS, may be considered to be a special needs person under § 504.

AIDS, therefore, will constitute a protected special need if the following are met: the person with AIDS has a physical impairment that substantially limits one or more major life activities; he has a record of such an impairment; and, he is regarded by others as having such an impairment.[23] Both § 504 and the ADA prohibit special needs-based discrimination against persons who are "otherwise qualified" for government positions or benefits. They allow individuals to bring private suits to secure relief from special needs discrimination that arises in any phase of employment. Both § 504 and the ADA exclude from their purview actions taken in response to current drug and alcohol use. However, both protect former addicts and alcoholics who have successfully completed rehabilitation programs.

# DUE PROCESS ISSUES AND CONCERNS

## School District Procedural Concerns

Often, there is a need for a school district to provide specific information to the parent or parents of a special needs student. In providing such information, the district meets its "notice" requirements under IDEIA. A legally sufficient notice must contain the following:

1. *Proper safeguards:* a complete description of procedural actions and safeguards that have been taken;

2. *Action to be taken:* a description and explanation of any action the district proposes, or refuses, to take;

3. *Various options:* a listing of the options that will be or have been considered;

4. *Rejection of options:* the reasons for rejecting any of the options; and

5. *Method of evaluation:* a description of each evaluation component included in the IEP.

## Code of Federal Regulations, Title 34 (34 CFR)

Consent is required in at least two circumstances: prior to conducting a multi-factored evaluation of a student suspected to have special needs, and prior to the initial placement of such a student into a special education program. Additionally, school districts have an obligation to provide special education to students who need such programs, even if parents refuse to give their consent.[24] A parent has a right to an independent educational evaluation, at public expense, if he or she disagrees with a school district's evaluation.[25] Each independent educational evaluation (IEE) must be complete and must address the unique needs of the student. The process of working with the parent whose child needs an IEE must include, at a minimum, (1) an evaluation by a qualified examiner not employed by the district; (2) notice of the right to an independent evaluation at public expense if the parent disagrees with the school's evaluation; and (3) the name of organizations and individuals who are available to complete an IEE should the parent wish to have an independent evaluation completed. Further, the evaluation must be timely, performed by qualified persons, and assess each area of suspected special needs.[26]

Annual (or more frequent) meetings held for purposes of determining a special needs child's individual educational program must be attended by the following "team": the special needs child's general and special education teachers, a representative of the school district who is empowered to commit district resources, and the child's parents.[27] Any significant change in a special needs student's program requires team approval. A change of placement, such as a suspension from school of 10 or more days, is significant.[28]

## Case Study

### Steep Steps

George has cerebral palsy, mental retardation, and spastic quadriplegia, and he uses a wheelchair. His school district provided services such as transportation. When George reached 160 pounds, he was no longer able to ride the bus to school because the bus driver was unable to carry him down the steep concrete stairs that led from his front door to the street. Thereafter, his mother and father began to drive him to school in their van. When he returned home from school, George was forced to wait in the van for several hours each day until his father arrived home from work and could lift George from the van and carry him up the steps. George frequently missed school when the weather was too hot or too cold for him to wait in the van. George's parents decided to stop transporting George when he began complaining of pains in his legs from sitting in the van for such long periods. As a result, George was no longer able to attend school.

### Discussion Questions:

1. What is the legal issue that needs to be addressed?

2. Do the parents have a viable court case? Why or why not? If so, against whom?

3. What would they request as restitution?

4. Who will win? Why?

## Case Study

### Do Special Education Services Follow the Child to a Private School Setting?

You are superintendent of a public school district. Larry is a deaf student who had previously received IDEIA services in your middle school. Larry's parents requested that a sign language interpreter again be provided to their son; the interpreter would accompany Larry to all his classes at

*(Continued)*

(Continued)

the local Roman Catholic high school he now attends. His parents alleged that IDEIA and the free exercise clause of the First Amendment require the public school district to provide the interpreter. You question whether the interpreter would act as a conduit for the child's religious inculcation, thereby promoting his religious development at government expense, in violation of the establishment clause. You are also concerned because you fear that having a public school employee physically present at the sectarian school provides a direct benefit to that school by relieving it of costs of a service it would otherwise have to provide. There is also a concern that providing a public school employee to a private school creates the appearance of a "joint sponsorship" between your school system and the private school. You remember reading that this "symbolic union of government and religion" was found impermissible in the School Dist. of the City of *Grand Rapids v. Ball* (1985).[29] The parents argue that the child is the primary beneficiary, and the private school receives only an incidental benefit. In addition, an interpreter, unlike a teacher or guidance counselor, neither adds to nor subtracts from the sectarian school's environment but merely interprets whatever material is presented to the class as a whole.

### Discussion Questions

1. If a government program neutrally provides benefits to all, should the benefit be provided at a sectarian institution even if an attenuated financial benefit might result?[30]

2. Does the fact that a public employee will be physically present in a sectarian school make this type of aid unconstitutional?[31]

3. Should all IDEIA services provided to an eligible handicapped student in a public school be provided to an eligible student who attends a private school?

4. What if the private school does not want to provide the special services for disabled students?

# CONCLUSION

The focus of the discussion and cases in this chapter has been on needs of schoolchildren with disabilities. IDEIA is the successor statutory enactment to the Education for All Handicapped Children Act of 1975, which guarantees a student with special needs the right to a free, appropriate public education (FAPE). IDEIA specifically imposed an affirmative obligation on each state to ensure that equal access to a public education was not an empty guarantee. Hence, a school district may not argue that a lack of funds prevents it from providing for special needs students. There are six basic principles that underpin IDEIA and its application in America's schools: free, appropriate public education, appropriate evaluation, individualized education plan, least restrictive environment, parent and student participation in decision making, and procedural due process.

In addition to IDEIA, § 504 of the Rehabilitation Act of 1973 prohibits discrimination because of a disability. This statute was enacted before the Education for All Handicapped

Children Act. Under the Rehabilitation Act, school officials may not exclude a student with a disability from an extracurricular activity solely because of his disability. The most recent legislation dealing with disabilities is the Americans With Disabilities Act, enacted in 1990 and considered the most important legislation for persons with disabilities since the Education for All Handicapped Children Act. The critical difference between ADA and § 504—both of which are antidiscrimination civil rights legislation—is that the ADA extends coverage and protections to individuals employed by or using services of nonfederally funded entities. IDEIA delineates 13 special needs categories, which public school must address: specific learning disabilities, speech or language impairments, mental retardation, emotional disturbance, other health impairments, multiple disabilities, hearing impairments, orthopedic impairments, autism, visual impairments, traumatic brain injury, child with a special need, and deaf-blindness.

Inclusion is an expansion of the mainstreaming concept whereby children with disabilities are placed in regular classrooms. There is a strong difference of opinion regarding inclusion. Some educators believe that inclusion provides special needs children with the best educational environment available; others believe that it places children who do not function well in an environment that is not supportive and that often detracts from the education process. Neither IDEIA nor § 504 precludes school professionals from disciplining students with disabilities for misbehavior unrelated to their disabilities. However, a state may not remove special needs students from their placements in response to dangerous or disruptive conduct related to their disabilities. The "stay put" provision requires that a special needs student remain in his educational placement pending completion of an IEP review proceeding. If a student poses an immediate threat to the safety of others, she or he may be temporarily suspended. Many states allow for up to 10 days of suspension before a student is considered to be expelled. Interestingly, the new provisions of IDEIA will allow a hearing officer to issue an immediate removal of up to 45 days for any child (including a child with special needs) who violates drug or weapons policies or causes serious bodily injury.

# CASE BRIEFS · · · · · · · · · · · · · · · · · · · · · · · · · · · · · ·

## MILLS V. BOARD OF EDUCATION OF THE DISTRICT OF COLUMBIA 348 F. SUPP. 866 (D.D.C. 1972)

**GENERAL RULE OF LAW:** A school district must provide facilities that allow behaviorally retarded children to attend school.

**PROCEDURE SUMMARY:**

**Plaintiff:** Mills (P), representing a class of behaviorally and developmentally retarded children

**Defendant:** Board of Education of the District of Columbia School District (Board) (D)

**U.S. District Court Decision:** Held for Mills (P)

**FACTS:** A **class action** involving approximately 22,000 handicapped students was brought in U.S. district court on behalf of a class of seven children, represented by Mills (P), who had been denied enrollment in public school. Each child had some sort of developmental disorder. The local Board of Education (D), which did not provide any special programs or facilities, considered Mills (P) not capable of attending classes. The Board (D) also argued that lack of funds was sufficient reason to exclude the handicapped students from school. Mills (P) brought suit to compel the Board (D) to admit the seven children.

**ISSUE:** Must a school district provide facilities that allow behaviorally retarded children to attend school?

**HOLDING AND DECISION:** (Waddy, J.) Yes. A school district must provide facilities that allow behaviorally retarded children to attend school. The district code mandates that children shall attend school and further mandates that if an exceptional child would benefit from special instruction, he shall receive that special instruction. To deny poor public schoolchildren educational opportunities that are available to more affluent public schoolchildren violates due process. Consequently, it is no excuse that the Board (D) has no funds to pay for programs for the poor students represented in this case; the funds will have to be taken from less essential programs that benefit the more affluent students. [The court then fashioned a lengthy order mandating the provision of special education programs.]

**COMMENT:** Courts generally dismiss arguments centered on the Board's lack of funds. In *Goldberg v. Kelly* (1970), the Supreme Court found that a state's interest in streamlining a public assistance program was outweighed by its interest in preserving due process.[32] It should be noted, however, that the Supreme Court never ruled on the issue involved in this case. One concern was the lack of a procedure to determine the placement of a handicapped child. Courts have held that any placement must follow a due process procedure, which includes writing an individualized educational plan. Additionally, parents must be allowed to participate as monitors in the placement decision.

## Discussion Questions

1. Would the decision have been different if more affluent districts (rather than the District of Columbia) had been involved?

2. Why should a lack of funds be an insufficient reason to exclude high-cost special needs students?

3. To what extent are today's parents able to participate in the placement decision of their child?

4. Why is this decision and the consent agreement in *Pennsylvania Assn. for Retarded Children v. Commonwealth* (1971) considered so instrumental in the development of the Education for All Handicapped Children Act?

# HENDRICK HUDSON CENTRAL SCHOOL DIST. BOARD OF EDUCATION V. ROWLEY 458 U.S. 176 (1982)

**GENERAL RULE OF LAW:** The Education for All Handicapped Children Act does not require special services sufficient to maximize a handicapped child's education to a level commensurate with nonhandicapped children.

**PROCEDURE SUMMARY:**

**Plaintiff:** Rowley (P), a handicapped student

**Defendant:** Hendrick Hudson Central School District Board of Education (Board) (D)

**U.S. District Court Decision:** Held for Rowley (P)

**U.S. Court of Appeals Decision:** Affirmed

**U.S. Supreme Court Decision:** Reversed

**FACTS:** The Education for All Handicapped Children Act provided that handicapped children attending public schools should be given special educational programs to meet their particular needs. Rowley (P), who was almost completely deaf, was admitted to kindergarten. She was given a hearing aid, with which she achieved a measure of academic success. However, the Board (D) turned down a request made on her behalf that a sign language interpreter be provided. A suit was brought in U.S. district court, contending that Rowley's (P) educational opportunities could not be maximized without the interpreter. The district court held that the Act mandated services that would maximize a handicapped child's educational opportunities and mandated a sign language interpreter. The court of appeals affirmed, and the Supreme Court granted review.

**ISSUE:** Does the Education for All Handicapped Children Act require special services sufficient to maximize a handicapped child's education to a level commensurate with nonhandicapped children?

**HOLDING AND DECISION:** (Rehnquist, J.) No. The Education for All Handicapped Children Act does not require special services sufficient to maximize a handicapped child's education to a level commensurate with nonhandicapped children. In deciding whether such a requirement exists, the first place a court must look is in the Act's language. The Act states that special services are to be provided as are necessary to permit the child "to benefit" from instruction. There is no language to the effect that the benefits are to be maximized to the greatest extent possible. While Rowley (P) may be correct in her argument that the Act was passed with a desire to promote equal educational opportunity, the position asserted on her behalf would tend to indicate an effort to achieve equality of result, an impossible goal not likely contemplated by the Act. In short, it appears that all the Act requires is that special services be provided to handicapped students that would allow them to benefit from education. In view of the relative success that Rowley (P) so far experienced, it would seem that the Board (D) discharged its duty under the Act. Reversed.

**COMMENT:** It is well recognized that education is a matter traditionally left to the states and their political subdivisions. The Act in question recognized this, leaving much of its execution to the states. The Court noted that it would be inconsistent with this approach for the federal judiciary to regulate from the bench how the Act would be enforced. Rowley (P) argued that to receive a "free, appropriate education," she should have the opportunity to achieve her full potential commensurate with the opportunity provided to other children. This issue of "maximizing" one's opportunities is a critical one. If this decision had not been reversed, the potential cost would have been extensive, even prohibitive.

## Discussion Questions

1. Do you think the Supreme Court ruled this way because it was constitutionally sound, or because it would have been cost-prohibitive to apply this decision to other conditions?

2. In this case, the school district provided a hearing aid. If a student is nearsighted, should a district be required to provide glasses?

# IRVING INDEPENDENT SCHOOL DISTRICT V. TATRO
## 468 U.S. 883, 104 S. CT. 3371 (1984)

**GENERAL RULE OF LAW:** The Education for All Handicapped Children Act mandates that school authorities provide clean intermittent catheterization to students requiring the procedure.

### PROCEDURE SUMMARY:

**Plaintiff:** Tatro (P), a student with a congenital bladder defect

**Defendant:** The Irving School Board (D), administering the school attended by Tatro (P)

**U.S. District Court Decision:** Held for Tatro (P)

**U.S. Court of Appeals Decision:** Affirmed

**U.S. Supreme Court Decision:** Affirmed

**FACTS:** Tatro (P) was born with spina bifida. Unable to urinate normally because of a defective bladder, she required clean intermittent catheterization (CIC) every three to four hours to evacuate her bladder. The process was relatively simple, requiring no special medical knowledge, apart from about one hour of training. When Tatro (P) reached school age, her parents requested that the school authorities perform the procedure upon her as needed during the day. The Irving School Board (D) refused. The School Board (D) argued that CIC was a "medical service" that could not qualify as a "related service" because it did not serve the purpose of diagnosis and evaluation. A suit was brought on Tatro's (P) behalf to compel the Board (D) to administer the procedure. The district court held that the Education for All Handicapped Children Act and the Rehabilitation Act required that such services be provided. The court of appeals affirmed, and the Supreme Court granted review.

**ISSUE:** Does the Education for All Handicapped Children Act mandate that school authorities provide clean intermittent catheterization to students requiring the procedure?

**HOLDING AND DECISION:** (Burger, C. J.) Yes. The Education for All Handicapped Children Act mandates that school authorities provide clean intermittent catheterization to students who require the procedure. The Act mandates that states supply programs providing a public education to disabled children. This includes special education and necessary services related to achieving this goal. There can be no question that CIC is a "related service" necessary to promote educational access. It is true that the Act specifically precludes a school from being required to provide "medical services." However, this phrase refers to complicated procedures not within the competence of school personnel. CIC is a simple procedure that can be performed by a nurse or even a layman. Thus, CIC is a "related service" necessary to promote a disabled child's access to the educational system, and the Board must therefore provide it. Affirmed.

**COMMENT:** The lower courts based their decision on both the Education for All Handicapped Children Act and the Rehabilitation Act. The Court held, in an opinion released the same day, that the latter Act did not apply when the former was available and partially reversed the lower courts. The main result of this was that Tatro (P) ended up bearing the costs of her attorney fees because the Education for All Handicapped Children Act, unlike the Rehabilitation Act, did *not* provide for attorney fees. Regarding the provision of related services such as CIC, school personnel were very concerned because of their fears and apprehensions. In the 10 years since this ruling, school personnel have handled far more extensive procedures without difficulty.

## Discussion Questions

1. What relevance does the *Irving* decision have for those who work with disabled students?

2. How does the interpretation of a "related service" differ from that of a "medical service" in this case? How did the interpretation of these terms affect the decision of the court? What factors could have changed the interpretation of the terms in relation to the services being provided to disabled students in this case?

3. How does this ruling affect other services offered in schools, such as dispensing prescription medications to students? How do the Education for All Handicapped Children Act and the Rehabilitation Act affect the services provided to students in situations where medical personnel (nurses and others) are no longer available due to cutbacks?

# HONIG, CALIFORNIA SUPERINTENDENT OF PUBLIC INSTRUCTION V. DOE
## 484 U.S. 305, 108 S. CT. 592 (1988)

**GENERAL RULE OF LAW:** The Education for All Handicapped Children Act prohibits states from removing special needs children from their placements for dangerous or disruptive conduct arising out of their disabilities.

**PROCEDURE SUMMARY:**

**Plaintiffs:** Doe and Smith (P), suspended special needs students

**Defendant:** Honig (D), California Superintendent of Public Instruction

**U.S. District Court Decision:** Held for Doe (P), granting summary judgment and issuing a permanent injunction against Doe's (P) suspension and proposed expulsion

**U.S. Court of Appeals Decision:** Affirmed, with the addition that a suspension exceeding 10 school days was not a prohibited change in placement

**U.S. Supreme Court Decision:** Affirmed, except as to the Court of Appeals' modification

**FACTS:** In 1975, Congress enacted the Education for All Handicapped Children Act to assure that states provided all special needs children a free, appropriate public education. Section 1415 of the Act, called the "stay put" provision, required that a special needs child remain in his educational placement pending completion of any review proceedings. Smith (P) and Doe (P), both emotionally disturbed students, were suspended indefinitely (pending the outcome of expulsion proceedings) for violent conduct related to their disabilities. Doe (P), who had a history of reacting aggressively to peer ridicule, responded to the taunts of a fellow student by choking him and leaving neck abrasions. Doe also kicked out a school window while being escorted to the principal's office. Doe (P) filed suit, seeking to enjoin his suspension and the expulsion proceedings. Smith (P) experienced academic and social difficulties as a result of hyperactivity and low self-esteem. Smith (P) had a propensity for verbal hostility, and his disruptive behavior consisted of stealing, extorting money from fellow students, and making sexual comments to female students. Smith (P) intervened, contending the suspension and proposed expulsion violated the "stay put" provision of the Act. The district court agreed and enjoined the action. The court of appeals affirmed. The U.S. Supreme Court granted review.

**ISSUE:** Does the "stay put" provision of the Act prohibit states from removing special needs children from classrooms for violent or disruptive conduct arising out of their special needs?

**HOLDING AND DECISION:** (Brennan, J.) Yes. States may not remove special needs children from classrooms for violent or disruptive conduct related to their special needs. The language of § 1415 unequivocally prohibits removing the child while any proceedings are pending. The Court cannot read a "dangerousness" exception into the provision, as Honig (D) suggested. Congress clearly intended to strip schools of the unilateral authority they traditionally had to exclude special needs students. However, schools may still use their normal procedures for dealing with children who endanger themselves or others. Students who pose an immediate threat to the safety of others may be temporarily suspended for up to 10 school days. This provides schools with an adequate means of ensuring the safety of others. Thus, the lower courts properly balanced the school's interest in maintaining a safe learning environment and the mandates of the Act. Affirmed, except as to the court of appeals' addition that a temporary suspension could exceed 10 days.

**COMMENT:** The Act was passed after Congress found that school systems across the country excluded one out of eight special needs children from the classroom. It was based on Congress's judgment that not enough was being done on state and local levels to find suitable or appropriate ways of dealing with the problem. The Act demonstrates that Congress will take significant action in the fields of public elementary and secondary education even though these areas traditionally are left to state and local government. This case has caused more consternation among school administrators than any other recent decision, and they often feel that their hands are tied when dealing with disruptive behavior by handicapped students. Of course, when disruptive behavior is serious, school authorities may contact local authorities to remove the disruptive student.

## Discussion Questions

1.  Does the "stay put" provision mean that a special education student may not ever be suspended?

2.  How did the Supreme Court reconcile the rights of special education students with the rights of students to be safe in school?

3.  If school authorities contact local authorities to remove a student whose behavior is seriously disruptive, is the school violating that student's rights?

4.  Why did the Supreme Court reject the defendant's argument that a dangerousness exception be read into the law, which would allow school officials to unilaterally exclude special needs students?

# TIMOTHY V. ROCHESTER, NEW HAMPSHIRE SCHOOL DISTRICT 875 F.2D 954 (1ST CIR. 1989)

**GENERAL RULE OF LAW:** A handicapped child is not required to show that he could benefit from special education in order to be eligible for such education.

**PROCEDURE SUMMARY:**

**Plaintiff:** Timothy (P), a handicapped child

**Defendant:** Rochester, New Hampshire School District (D) (Rochester)

**U.S. District Court Decision:** Held for Rochester (D), that it did not have to provide special education to a child who could not benefit from same

**U.S. Court of Appeals Decision:** Reversed

**FACTS:** In 1975, Congress passed the Education for All Handicapped Children Act to ensure that handicapped children received an education appropriate to their unique needs. In 1980, Rochester (D) commenced meetings to determine whether Timothy (P) was educationally handicapped for purposes of the Act and thereby entitled to special education. Timothy (P) had been born two months premature in 1975 and suffered from severe respiratory problems as a result. He later suffered hemorrhaging and seizures that rendered him multiply handicapped and profoundly mentally retarded. Upon the evidence presented at the meetings, Rochester (D) concluded that Timothy (P) did not fall within the Act because he could not benefit from special education. Subsequently, Timothy (P) filed suit, alleging that the denial of special education violated his rights under the Act. The district court disagreed, holding that Rochester's (D) basis for denial was proper. Timothy (P) appealed.

**ISSUE:** Must a handicapped child demonstrate that he can benefit from special education to be entitled to such education under the Act?

**HOLDING AND DECISION:** (Bownes, J.) No. The Act does not require a handicapped child to demonstrate that he can benefit from special education in order for him to be entitled to such education. The language of the Act clearly guarantees all handicapped children the right to a free appropriate education. There is no exception for severely handicapped children. In fact, the Act requires that the most severe cases be given priority; it does not make ability to benefit a prerequisite to receiving special education. There is no question that Timothy (P), being multiply handicapped and profoundly mentally retarded, qualified under the Act's definition of handicapped child. Reversed.

**COMMENT:** The opinion repudiates the views of some educators who wish to limit special education for handicapped children. It greatly confirms Congress' judgment as to the need to provide for such children through national legislation rather than relying on state or local initiative. Further, the Court makes clear that the Act is not limited to traditional academic training, but must be broadly read to include basic functional living skills as well.

## Discussion Questions

1. Does a handicapped child have to prove that he or she may benefit from special education?

2. Whose responsibility is it to determine whether a child will benefit from special education services, and whose responsibility is it to determine what services should be implemented?

3. Why does the Education for All Handicapped Children Act require that the most severe cases receive priority?

# WINKELMAN, A MINOR, BY AND THROUGH HIS PARENTS AND LEGAL GUARDIANS, WINKELMAN ET UX., ET AL. V. PARMA CITY SCHOOL DISTRICT NO. 05-983, U.S. SUPREME COURT (2007)

**GENERAL RULE OF LAW:** Parents of disabled children may sue public schools over their children's education without hiring a lawyer, in accordance with the provisions of IDEIA.

**PROCEDURE SUMMARY:**

**Plaintiffs:** Jeff and Sandee Winkelman, parents of Jacob Winkelman, a minor (P)

**Defendant:** Parma City School District (D)

**State of Ohio, IDEIA Administrative Review Process:** Affirmed (D), (P) unsuccessful due to the hearing officer's ruling that (P) must be represented by legal counsel in order to continue the IDEIA procedural process

**U.S. District Court Decision:** Held for Parma School District (D)

**U.S. Court of Appeals (6th District) Decision:** Affirmed

**U.S. Supreme Court Decision:** Reversed

**FACTS:** The parents of an autistic child, Jacob Winkelman (P), participated with the Parma (Ohio) City School District (D) in the development of an individualized educational plan (IEP) for their son. Ultimately, however, they felt that the program offered was not appropriate to meet his needs, and they enrolled him in a private school. In accordance with the procedural rights provided to them by IDEIA, they filed for an administrative hearing. They claimed that the program the public school offered to Jacob did not provide him with a "free, appropriate public education" (FAPE). They also complained of a number of procedural violations that deprived them of a real role in the formulation of Jacob's IEP and requested a tuition reimbursement and other costs. All conceded that Jacob's parents had a right to contribute to the IEP process and, when agreement could not be reached, to participate in an administrative proceeding, including what the Act refers to as an "impartial due process hearing." Unsuccessful in the administrative process, the Winkelmans appealed to federal district court, and when again unsuccessful, to the Sixth Circuit Court of Appeals. At times, they had the assistance of an attorney, but they filed the appeal in federal court without a lawyer. The appellate court refused to let the case go forward unless the Winkelmans hired counsel.

The appellate court affirmed that special education law does not spell out the right for parents to represent their children in federal court, referencing the idea that courts generally do not allow people who are not lawyers to represent other people—although they may represent themselves. The Supreme Court reversed the lower court's decision, agreeing with the Winkelmans and allowing them to represent their son. The Court ruled that IDEIA does grant parents the right to represent their children at every stage of the process in disputes with schools over their children's IEP and education.

**ISSUE:** Does IDEIA grant parents independent, enforceable rights (not limited to procedural and reimbursement-related matters) to represent their children in the courts regarding disputes over their child's special education services?

**HOLDING AND DECISION:** (Kennedy, J.) Yes. IDEIA does grant parents the right to represent their child at every stage of the process in disputes with schools over their child's IEP. Kennedy's ruling rejected an assertion by the Parma City Schools (D) that parents could act as lawyers only in initial administrative hearings but not in later battles in federal courts. The goals of IDEIA include "ensuring that all children with disabilities have available to them a free appropriate public education (FAPE)," and "ensuring that the rights of children with disabilities and parents of such children are protected." To this end, the Act includes provisions in four areas of particular relevance to the Winkelman's (P) claim: procedures to be followed when developing a child's IEP; criteria governing the sufficiency of an education provided to a child; mechanisms for review that must be made available when there are objections to the IEP or to other aspects of IDEIA proceedings; and the requirement, in certain circumstances, that states reimburse parents for various expenses. While the Court's discussion of these four areas does not identify all the illustrative provisions, it does take particular note of certain terms that mandate or otherwise describe parental involvement.

IDEIA requires school districts to develop an IEP for each child with a disability, with parents playing "a significant role in this process."[33] Parents are to serve as members of the team that develops the IEP, and they must sign off on it—as do all members of the IEP team—and have the right to reject any item with which they disagree. The "concerns" parents have "for enhancing the education of their child" must be considered by the team. In addition, IDEIA accords parents additional protections that apply throughout the IEP process. This requires the IEP team to revise the IEP, when appropriate, to address certain information provided by the parents. The statute also sets up general procedural safeguards that protect the informed involvement of parents in the development of an education for their child.

**COMMENT: With this decision, the Supreme Court allows parents to represent themselves in claims under IDEIA.** The Court has opened the courthouse door to the parents of children with disabilities by holding that they have a personal right to have their children appropriately educated. This means they can proceed in federal court without a lawyer when bringing claims under this federal law, which provides that children with disabilities are entitled to a free, appropriate public education (FAPE).

Interestingly, Kennedy wrote that "it would be inconsistent" to allow parents to act as lawyers in administrative hearings but "bar them from continuing to assert these rights in federal court." Justice Scalia, in a separate opinion joined by Justice Thomas, agreed in part with the Court's majority but took a narrower view of when parents can go to court without lawyers. He felt that parents should be able to proceed pro se only when seeking reimbursement for private school expenses or redress for violations of their procedural rights, but not when seeking a judicial determination that the child's services were inadequate.

The case should now return to the appellate court in Cincinnati, which will consider the merits of the Winkelman's (P) claim that Parma (D) failed to provide an adequate plan (IEP) for educating their son in 2003–2004, his kindergarten year.

A major impact of this decision will be on cases in which parents have insufficient funds but strong evidence that schools have not complied with the federal law that mandates a FAPE. Some fear that this decision will open the floodgates, as parents of children with disabilities could legally go far beyond the school district without paying expensive legal fees, which many feel are outrageous. On the other hand, advocates for the disabled believe that the ruling will liberate parents nationwide who can not afford lawyers—or find one to represent them for free—by allowing them to go to court on their own to fight for their child's rights.

## Discussion Questions

1. Does this ruling go too far? Consider your school district. Will it bring additional lawsuits, increasing legal fees for school districts?

2. Will this ruling encourage parents to litigate rather than collaborate with school districts over their child's IEP?

3. As a school administrator, what new concerns must you consider prior to IEP team meetings, in order to prevent your district from ending up in court litigating the IEP team's decisions?

Additional case briefs can be found on the SAGE Web site at the following address:
http://www.sagepub.com/aquilacasebriefs

# NOTES

1.  Pennsylvania Assn. for Retarded Children v. Commonwealth, 334 F. Supp. 1257 (E.D. Pa. 1971).
2.  Education for All Handicapped Children Act, Pub. L. 94-142, 89 Stat. 773 (1975).
3.  Mills v. Board of Education of District of Columbia, 348 F.Supp. 866 (D.D.C. 1972).
4.  Hendrick Hudson Central School District v. Rowley, 485 U.S. 176 (1982).
5.  Individuals With Disabilities Education Act, Pub. L. 101-476, 104 Stat. 1142 (1990).
6.  Irving Independent School District v. Tatro, 468 U.S. 883 (1984).
7.  Grube v. Bethlehem Area School District, 550 F. Supp. 418 (1982).
8.  Individuals With Disabilities Education Improvement Act of 2004, Pub. L. 108-446, 118 Stat. 2647 (2004).
9.  Rehabilitation Act of 1973, Pub. L. 93-112, 87 Stat. 394 (1973); Americans With Disabilities Act, Pub. L. 101-336, 104 Stat. 327 (1990).
10.  See Grube v. Bethlehem Area School District, 550 F. Supp. 418 (1982).
11.  See Southeastern Community College v. Davis, 442 U.S. 397 (1979).
12.  Elementary and Secondary Education Act, Pub. L. 89-10, 79 Stat. 77 (1965).
13.  See Timothy v. Rochester, New Hampshire School District, 875 F.2d 954 (1st Cir. 1989).
14.  See, e.g., Hendrick Hudson Central School Dist. Bd. of Education v. Rowley, 458 U.S. 176 (1982).
15.  See Hendrick Hudson Central School Dist. Bd. of Education v. Rowley, 458 U.S. 176 (1982).
16.  See Irving Independent School District v. Tatro, 468 U.S. 883 (1984).
17.  See Goss v. Lopez, 419 U.S. 565 (1975).
18.  See Honig, California Superintendent of Public Instruction v. Doe, 484 U.S. 305 (1988).
19.  See Honig, California Superintendent of Public Instruction v. Doe, 484 U.S. 305 (1988).
20.  Americans With Disabilities Act, 42 U.S.C. § 12101.
21.  Wallace v. Veterans Admin., 683 F.Supp. 758 (D. Kan., 1988).
22.  Clarke v. Shoreline School District No. 412, King County, 729 P.2d 793 (Wash. 1986).
23.  See School Board of Nassau County, Florida v. Arline, 480 U.S. 273 (1987).
24.  See Code of Federal Regulations, Title 34 § 300.505b.
25.  See Code of Federal Regulations, Title 34 § 300.503c.
26.  See Code of Federal Regulations, Title 34 §§ 300.530–300.534.
27.  See Code of Federal Regulations, Title 34 § 300.344.
28.  See Code of Federal Regulations, Title 34 § 300.504.
29.  School Dist.of the City of Grand Rapids v. Ball, 473 U.S. 373 (1985).
30.  See Mueller v. Allen, 463 U.S. 388 (1983). See also Witters v. Washington Dept. of Services for Blind, 474 U.S. 481 (1986).
31.  See Meek v. Pittenger, 421 U.S. 349 (1975) and School Dist. of the City of Grand Rapids v. Ball, 473 U.S. 373 (1985), in which the challenged programs gave direct grants of government aid—instructional equipment and material, teachers, and guidance counselors—that relieved sectarian schools of costs they otherwise would have borne in educating their students.
32.  Goldberg v. Kelly, 397 U.S. 254, 90 S. Ct. 1011 (1970).
33.  See Schaffer v. Weast, 546 U.S. 49, 53 (2005).

# Part III

# Teachers' Rights

# 9

# Teachers' Rights and Concerns

*At present, courts seek to balance a teacher's private interests with that of the integrity of the educational system. Because the integrity of the system is reflected in its teaching staff, school boards have been permitted to regulate the conduct of teachers to a reasonable extent. Nevertheless, speech of a personal nature, rather than of public concern, may not be entitled to First Amendment protection.*

*—Connick v. Meyers* (1983)[1]

## OVERVIEW . . . . . . . . . . . . . . . . . . . . . . . . . . . . . . . . . . . . . . . . .

Common law provides school boards with the power from the state to hire, fire, and establish the basic conditions of employment of teachers. The authority to set teachers' salaries is implied by the local board's **express authority** to employ teachers, most often using specific salary schedules. These schedules must be reasonable in design and uniformly applied. In recent years, setting salaries has been part of a joint effort incorporated in the collective bargaining process. A school board may reduce salaries or even reduce staff, based on financial exigency.

Within the limits of state law, teacher assignments are at the discretion of local school boards. Realistically, teachers must accept assignments that they are competent to undertake. Because most state statutes are silent as to transfer rights, local school boards may adopt their own regulations in this area. Involuntary transfers are generally subjected to judicial scrutiny when the transfer is based, all or in part, on an action that is a violation of a teacher's constitutional rights. Teachers do not have a right to leave, but usually it is a benefit negotiated through the collective bargaining process. In addition to providing standard leave for sickness, maternity, and so on, school boards must also make reasonable leave accommodations for religious reasons. More recently, teachers have been granted federally guaranteed leave rights to handle family medical concerns.

During the post–World War II era, America faced many challenges regarding patriotism and loyalty. Education was not immune to this vicious period of anti-Communist hostility and attack. Ostensibly, loyalty oaths were seen as a means of safeguarding public service from disloyal conduct and prohibiting certain types of statements and conduct outside the school setting. Loyalty measures, defined by the Supreme Court, must objectively delineate the differences between loyal and disloyal conduct. Therefore, a teacher's loyalty cannot be questioned simply because he is a member of a group that was organized to further unlawful purposes. Rather, it must be shown that he joined the group with the *specific intent* of furthering an unlawful purpose or that he actually participated in unlawful activities.

Teachers, as public employees, do not give up their free speech rights as private citizens simply by signing a teaching contract. The classic free speech case for teachers was *Pickering v. Board of Education of Township High School District* (1968).[2] The Court supported Pickering even though his letter to the local newspaper was replete with error and resulted in a levy failure. The Court recognized that a teacher, as a private citizen, had the right to speak out on legitimate issues of public concern. This position was soon qualified by *Mt. Healthy v. Doyle* (1977), which held that the school board was required to show that it would have made the same decision—to not renew Doyle's employment contract—even if Doyle had not engaged in protected speech activity.[3] Courts tend to consider a teacher's private interests while trying to retain the integrity of the educational system. This allows school boards to regulate the conduct of teachers to a reasonable extent. Further, speech of a personal nature—rather than of public concern—may not be entitled to First Amendment protection.[4] The standard of analysis for freedom of speech and other constitutional rights merits strict scrutiny: The government must demonstrate a *compelling* reason for abridging a right subject to a strict scrutiny analysis. In order to prevail in a case against a teacher, a school board must demonstrate that the outside activity or conduct has a detrimental impact on the teacher's fitness to teach. Past practice had demonstrated that this is a high standard to meet.

Cases involving a teacher's right to academic freedom have caused difficulty over the years. While children in schools must be protected from harm, teachers have the right to academic freedom as long as they do not violate constitutionally valid regulations. As long as there is a valid educational purpose, a teacher's classroom actions will be protected. In *Keefe v. Geanokos* (1969), a teacher's use of a "dirty" word was held to be protected because the *Atlantic Monthly* article with the dirty word was used for a valid pedagogical purpose.[5] However, the court supported the school board, holding that a public school teacher does not have a First Amendment right to participate in the choice of the school curriculum.

Other teachers' rights issues vary greatly. A teacher may be disciplined if his immoral private conduct poses a substantial risk of coming to the attention of schoolchildren. Yet, civil rights legislation requires school districts to reasonably accommodate the religious practices of their employees. In order to test employees for drug and alcohol abuse, a warrant and reasonable suspicion are not necessarily required when there is a compelling public interest served by such tests and those interests outweigh the employees' privacy interests.[6] In comparison, in *In re Patchogue-Medford Congress of Teachers v. Bd. of Ed.* (1987), New York's highest court held that compulsory drug testing of probationary teachers is unlawful absent reasonable suspicion of drug use.[7] The ability of a school to test teachers for drugs, without suspicion, remains unclear; the issue is whether there was "reasonable suspicion" and whether the decision to test was based on individualized suspicion.

## Case Study

### The Teacher in Red

You are the superintendent of the Happy Hearts School District, a rural district with an agricultural focus. A nontenured, middle-aged divorcée, Ms. Lola Afair, has been employed for several years as a high school English teacher. Her classroom teaching performance has been better than satisfactory. Ms. Afair lives in the school community, and her now-grown son lives in an even smaller neighboring town. In the past, her son's friends, young ladies and men as well as married couples, visited him. Many still return to visit him, often staying in Ms. Afair's apartment because hotel and motel accommodations are generally unavailable in this smaller community. One young man, whom Ms. Afair considered her second son, visited often. In the spring, he visited for a week and even sat in on classes, which your office had approved. After private discussions, the school board notified her that her teaching contract would not be renewed for the next year. At a hearing, the school board stated that the reason for the dismissal was that Ms. Afair's allowing young men to stay in her home was conduct unbecoming a teacher. In the board's view, her social behavior suggested a strong potential for sexual misconduct. Ms. Afair filed suit under 42 U.S.C. § 1983; she contended that this reason was constitutionally impermissible.

### Discussion Questions

1. May an untenured teacher be dismissed for reasons unrelated either to the education process or working relationships within the school board and wholly without factual support?

2. Could the school board have dismissed Ms. Afair without stating a reason?

3. Regardless of whether the allegations against Ms. Afair were supported or not, do you think that school teachers should consider local community opinions of their personal life?

## IMPORTANT CONCEPTS

- **Salary schedules collectively bargained:** In recent years, the collective bargaining process has established employee salary schedules.

- **Reduction in force:** In times of financial exigency, a school board may reduce the salaries of all teachers, including tenured teachers, as long as the reduction is uniformly implemented.

- **Right to establish salaries:** A school board's authority to establish teachers' salaries is implied from the board's express authority to employ teachers. The only requirement is that the schedule is reasonably designed and uniformly applied.

- **Involuntary transfers:** Involuntary transfers are subjected to judicial scrutiny if transfers may be based on a teacher's prior exercise of a constitutional right.

*(Continued)*

(Continued)

- **Family medical concerns:** The federal government has recently provided guaranteed leave rights to handle family medical concerns. The Family and Medical Leave Act provides school employees with the right to take time off to look after their medical needs and the needs of their family.

- **Loyalty oaths:** To be constitutional, loyalty measures must objectively define the differences between loyal and disloyal conduct without being vague, overbroad, or otherwise unfocused.

- **Public sector employee rights:** Public employees do not give up all of their rights upon accepting positions in the public sector.

- **Teachers' private rights:** Courts seek to balance a teacher's private interests with retaining the integrity of the educational system. School boards have been permitted to regulate the conduct of teachers to a reasonable extent.

- **Personal speech:** Notwithstanding, speech of a personal nature—rather than of public concern—may not be entitled to First Amendment protection.

- **Fitness to teach:** To prevail in a case against a teacher, a school board must demonstrate that the outside activity or conduct has a detrimental impact on the teacher's fitness to teach.

- **Academic freedom:** When considering academic freedom, the balancing of equities compares teachers' right to teach a class in a manner they believe appropriate against the need to protect young people from inappropriate words and actions in a classroom.

- **Fourth Amendment searches:** A warrant and reasonable suspicion are not necessarily required to test employees for drug and alcohol use when the compelling public interests served by such tests outweigh the employees' privacy interests.[8]

## SELECTED TERMS AND CONDITIONS OF TEACHER EMPLOYMENT

### Teacher Salaries

The authority to set teachers' salaries is implied from the local board's express authority to employ teachers. Most school boards set and raise teachers' salaries according to specific salary schedules. The use of such schedules is not contrary to the law, so long as they are reasonably designed and uniformly applied.

In recent years, salary schedules have been negotiated between the school board and the representative school teacher group through the collective bargaining process. Nevertheless, a school board may reduce employee salaries for all teachers, including tenured teachers. When such an unusual situation develops, the only requirements are that the reduction must be uniformly applied and based on financial exigency.[9]

Even though *Phelps* allows a school board to make a reduction based on specific criteria and based on financial exigency, the ability of a governmental body to make such changes at will limits and weakens a teacher's rights. Thus, such provisions and actions that would limit the rights of teachers are rarely implemented, and then only after a court reviews the damaging action to ensure that there was a compelling need.

## Teacher Assignments, Transfers, and Leaves

Assignments within the purview of a teacher's teaching license are made at the discretion of local school boards. If the state has a specific statute or regulation regarding assignment or transfer, that statute must be followed. Nevertheless, practically speaking, teachers must accept assignments that they are competent to undertake. Very few state statutes speak to transfer rights; local school boards generally adopt their own regulations in this area.

Involuntary transfers—particularly those that involve changes in status—will be subjected to judicial scrutiny if it appears that a transfer is based, all or in part, on a teacher's prior exercise of his First Amendment (or other constitutional) rights. One exception to the state and local power to assign and transfer occurs when a school district is under constitutional scrutiny, such as when there is a federal court finding of de jure segregation.[10] A federal court may even abrogate the state law and collective bargaining agreements to ensure that injured plaintiffs' rights are restored.

Teachers are not entitled to leaves as a right, but rather as a benefit negotiated through the collective bargaining process. In addition to providing standard leaves for sickness, maternity, and so on, school boards must also make reasonable leave accommodations for religious reasons. The Family and Medical Leave Act provides guaranteed leave rights to handle family medical concerns.

## Oaths of Loyalty

Viewed in a favorable light, loyalty oaths are a means of safeguarding public service from disloyal conduct. These oaths were common following World War II. Practically speaking, loyalty oaths prohibit certain types of statements and conduct outside the school setting. In the past, such oaths also required that teachers swear that they had not engaged in certain prohibited activities prior to employment.

The U.S. Supreme Court has stated that loyalty measures must objectively define the differences between loyal and disloyal conduct. In a series of opinions spanning the 1950s and 1960s, the U.S. Supreme Court struck down as unconstitutional a series of loyalty oaths that were vague, overbroad, or otherwise unfocused. A teacher's loyalty cannot be questioned simply by reason of his membership in a group that may have been organized to further unlawful purposes, unless it can be shown that he joined the group with the *specific intent* of furthering an unlawful purpose or that he actually participated in unlawful activities. The Court has also upheld the constitutionality of an oath that requires that the speaker swear to uphold federal and state constitutions and faithfully discharge his position to the best of his ability.[11]

During the post-war hysteria over Communist infiltration, New York passed the Feinberg Law, which required reporting on the loyalty of teachers. While ostensibly constitutional, the law's complexity and extent were held to be unconstitutional. Citing the Fifth Amendment's protection against self-incrimination when refusing to answer congressional questions under oath has resulted in mixed holdings. Using a due process rationale, in 1956 the Court upheld a teacher's right to refuse to answer.[12] Yet, shortly thereafter, the Court upheld a teacher's dismissal for a wide range of reasons, including his refusal to answer questions.[13]

## Freedom of Speech and Expression

Public employees do not give up all of their rights upon accepting positions in the public sector. The First Amendment rights of teachers to freedom of speech as private citizens were discussed in the classic case of *Pickering v. Board of Education of Township High School District* (1968).[14] Even though Pickering's letter to the local newspaper was replete with error and resulted in a levy failure, the Court found in favor of the teacher, recognizing that a teacher had the right to speak out on legitimate issues of public concern as a private citizen, if this did not impact his teaching. The Court soon qualified that holding in *Mt. Healthy v. Doyle* (1977), by ruling that the school board did not have to rehire Doyle if it could show that it would have made the same decision—to not renew Doyle's employment contract— even if Doyle had not engaged in protected speech activity.[15] More recently, a similar position was taken in *Stroman v. Colleton County School District* (1993).[16] In applying the *Connick* precedent, the court found that free speech was not injured by the teacher's dismissal for his letter advocating that other teachers participate in a sick-out.

At present, courts seek to balance a teacher's private interests with that of the integrity of the educational system. Because the integrity of the system is reflected in its teaching staff, school boards have been permitted to regulate the conduct of teachers to a reasonable extent. Nevertheless, speech of a personal nature, rather than of public concern, may not be entitled to First Amendment protection.[17]

Freedom of speech, like other constitutional rights, merits so high a degree of protection that state representatives, such as local school boards, must demonstrate a compelling reason for abridging that right. For instance, a school board may impose reasonable regulations, such as requiring that male teachers wear a necktie, and the court is reluctant to impose its judgment even when these decisions may seem unwise, foolish, or uncompassionate.[18] The court will step in, however, when important constitutional rights are at stake, such as issues involving morality and fitness to teach (e.g., engaging in homosexual activities, various sexual activities, and the use of drugs). In order to prevail in a case against a teacher, a school board must demonstrate that the outside activity or conduct has a detrimental impact on the teacher's fitness to teach. Teachers have the right to comment on matters of public interest about the operation of the schools in which they work. A union teacher speaking out at a school board meeting is not a "negotiation" in violation of the collective bargaining agreement.[19]

## Academic Freedom

Issues related to academic freedom have long caused difficulty. Some describe a court's responsibility as the balancing of equities, judging one's rights against those of another. Academic freedom equities are a teacher's right to teach a class in a manner he or she believes appropriate, balanced against the need to protect young people from inappropriate words and actions in a classroom. Thus, while children in schools must be protected from harm, teachers have the right to academic freedom, as long as they do not violate constitutionally valid regulations.

The standard that has developed regarding academic freedom is to prove that there has been a "flagrant abuse of discretion" on the part of the school person.[20] Thus, as long as there is a valid educational purpose, a teacher's classroom actions will be protected. In *Keefe v. Geanokos* (1969), a teacher's use of a "dirty" word was held to be protected because the *Atlantic Monthly* article with the dirty word had a valid pedagogical purpose.[21]

A different result was reached when a teacher attempted to modify the curriculum, which is generally governed by the school board. In *Boring v. Buncombe County Board of Education* (1998), Boring selected an inappropriate play for her advanced acting students to perform in a state competition.[22] Later, the principal alleged that Boring failed to follow the school's "controversial materials" policy and transferred Boring to a new school. Boring argued that the policy did not cover dramatic presentations and sued on First Amendment grounds. She claimed that her transfer was a retaliatory action in response to the play's content. The court supported the school board's holding that a public school teacher does not have a First Amendment right to participate in choosing the school curriculum.

## Other Related Concerns

A school district may fire a teacher whose illegal or immoral public conduct poses a substantial risk of coming to the attention of schoolchildren.[23] Title VII of the Civil Rights Act of 1964 requires school districts to reasonably accommodate the religious practices of their employees.[24]

A warrant and reasonable suspicion are not necessarily required to test employees for drug and alcohol use when the compelling public interests served by such tests outweigh the employees' privacy interests.[25] New York's highest court has held, however, that compulsory drug testing of probationary teachers is unlawful absent reasonable suspicion of drug use.[26] Yet, the ability of a school to test teachers for drugs differs in some jurisdictions. In a 1998 case, *Knox County Education Association v. Knox County Board of Education,* the court upheld drug testing of teachers as long as there was "reasonable suspicion" and the decision was based on individualized suspicion.[27]

Breast-feeding is a fundamental right, like other Fourteenth Amendment–based rights, that cannot be restricted unless there is a compelling state interest and the restriction is narrowly tailored to restrict only the offending conduct.[28] A school district's refusal to accommodate a male teacher's request for a one-year child-rearing leave was held to be prima facie evidence of gender-based discrimination that amounted to an unlawful constructive discharge.[29]

There is no case law specifically addressing an administration's right to search a teacher's desk. The issue is whether such a search would violate the teacher's Fourteenth Amendment rights and whether the teacher has an expectation of privacy. In a nonschool case, the Supreme Court held that a government employer had to meet a standard of reasonableness when searching an employee's office.[30] It would appear that a teacher has no expectation of privacy regarding items that are not locked away from the general public. For example, a principal could look on a teacher's desk or even in an unlocked drawer as part of the normal and proper daily business of operating a school. However, a teacher would have an expectation of privacy with respect to a locked drawer or file cabinet, even if owned by the school board.

## Case Study

### This Pink Floyd Wasn't a Student

Marty Cool has been a tenured teacher in the Happy Hearts School District for many years. Mr. Cool showed his class an "R"-rated movie titled *Pink Floyd: The Wall* as a reward for their excellent classroom performance. Although Marty Cool was aware that the film contained some nudity, he did not preview the movie, instead asking a student who had seen the film to show the movie and edit out any parts unsuitable for class viewing. Cool had to leave the classroom several times during the film and, by **admission**, knew that some nudity remained. Upon hearing of the showing, the school principal asked for the videotape, which was subsequently viewed by the superintendent and the board of education. The board initiated action to terminate Marty Cool's teaching contract. Cool came to the hearing with an attorney to contest the charges, claiming that the film had educational value. The board voted for termination. Marty Cool then initiated an action in district court, claiming violations of his First and Fourteenth Amendment rights.

### Discussion Questions

1. Is conduct protected by the First Amendment only if it is expressive or communicative in nature?

2. Was Marty Cool's conduct in the present case entitled to such protection?

3. Which will impact the court more, Marty Cool's failure to preview the film or his leaving the room?

# CONCLUSION . . . . . . . . . . . . . . . . . . . . . . . . . . . . . . . .

School boards retain the power to hire and to terminate teachers. Generally, teachers' salaries are set according to specific schedules. Nevertheless, a school board may reduce teachers' salaries so long as the reduction is uniform and there is an established financial exigency.

The local school board has discretion to give assignments to teachers, unless there is a specific statute indicating otherwise. Generally, teachers must accept assignments that they are competent to undertake. However, if a transfer results from a teacher's exercise of his constitutional rights (such as a transfer for exercising free speech rights), then this transfer may be subject to judicial scrutiny.

Teachers are not entitled to school leave as a right. However, this is often a benefit obtained from collective bargaining agreements. In addition to standard leaves for sickness, maternity, and so on, school boards must also make reasonable leave accommodations for religious reasons.

Some districts require that teachers swear a loyalty oath. These prohibit teachers from making certain types of statements or engaging in certain types of conduct. In the past, such oaths required teachers to swear that they had not engaged in certain prohibited conduct prior to employment. The U.S. Supreme Court has required that boards objectively define loyal and disloyal conduct.

When a person becomes a public school teacher, his right to freedom of speech is not abrogated. Additionally, a public school teacher has a right to speak out on legitimate issues of public concern if this speech does not impact negatively upon his teaching. However, school boards may reasonably regulate a teacher's activities. Boards must show a compelling reason to regulate outside-the-classroom activity; specifically, they must show that it had a detrimental impact on the ability to teach. Inside the classroom, boards have been allowed to regulate teacher's expression, such as by requiring that male teachers wear a necktie.

Teachers have the right to academic freedom in their teaching so long as they do not violate constitutionally valid regulations. Generally, if a teacher manifests an "abuse of discretion" in his teaching practices, then he may be reprimanded. However, if the teacher has a valid educational purpose, then he generally will not be found to have abused his discretion. Content, on the other hand, is generally governed by the school board, and a teacher does not have a First Amendment right to modify curricula if that change is against the board's wishes.

The following cases examine teachers' rights in relation to the rights of students and school boards. Even *Connick* and *Skinner*, while not education cases, have direct impact on teachers and school systems. You will notice that teachers are subject to greater invasions of privacy than employees in normal business situations because teachers influence students. Look for the court's reasoning in each case as it balances the interests of the state, the teachers, the students, and the community.

# CASE BRIEFS ............................

# CONNICK V. MEYERS 461 U.S. 138 (1983)

**GENERAL RULE OF LAW:** In determining whether a condition of employment infringes upon an employee's freedom of expression, the Court must balance the employee's interest in commenting on matters of public concern against the state's interest in the efficient performance of public services.

**PROCEDURE SUMMARY:**

   **Plaintiff:** Sheila Meyers (P), an assistant district attorney

   **Defendant:** Harry Connick (D), the District Attorney

   **U.S. District Court Decision:** Held for plaintiff

   **U.S. Court of Appeals Decision:** Affirmed

   **U.S. Supreme Court Decision:** Reversed

**FACTS:** Meyers (P) served as an assistant district attorney in New Orleans for five and a half years. Meyers (P) was informed that she would be transferred to a different section of the criminal court. She voiced her opposition to the transfer to several superiors, including Harry Connick (D), the district attorney for Orleans Parish. Connick (D) informed Meyers (P) that she would be transferred despite her objections. Meyers (P) then prepared a questionnaire regarding various office policies and distributed it to the office. Meyers (P) felt that she was fully authorized to distribute the 14-point questionnaire. Connick (D) felt that she was creating a "mini" insurrection. The questions included "From your experience, do you feel office procedures regarding transfers have been fair?" and "Do you ever feel pressured to work in political campaigns on behalf of office-supported candidates?" Connick (D) learned of the questionnaire and terminated Meyers (P). He stated that her refusal to accept the transfer was the basis for termination. He also informed her that the distribution of the questionnaire was considered an act of insubordination. Meyers (P) brought suit under 42 D.S.C. Section 1983, claiming she was terminated for exercising her constitutional right of free speech. The district court held in favor of Meyers (P) and awarded her reinstatement, back pay, attorney's fees, and damages. The court of appeals affirmed. Connick (D) appealed.

**ISSUE:** In determining whether a condition of employment infringes upon an employee's freedom of expression, must the Court balance the employee's interest in commenting on matters of public concern against the state's interest in the efficient performance of public services?

**HOLDING AND DECISION:** (White, J.) Yes. In determining whether a condition of employment infringes upon an employee's freedom of expression, the Court must balance the employee's interest in commenting on matters of public concern against the state's interest in the efficient performance of public services. The government may not impose an employment condition that infringes upon the employee's constitutional right of freedom of expression. Connick (D) contended that such balancing was not necessary here because Meyers's

(P) questionnaire was related to internal office matters and did not constitute a matter of public concern. Speech relating to public issues is the highest form of speech protected by the First Amendment. The framers' enacted the First Amendment to ensure free debate on social and political issues. If Meyers's questionnaire related to matters of public concern, then it constituted political speech protected by the First Amendment. If her questionnaire was unrelated to matters of public concern, however, then the government must be afforded wide latitude in managing its offices without judicial review. However, an employee's speech, even if unrelated to matters of public concern, is not totally without First Amendment protection. When an employee engages in speech of a personal nature, a federal court may not review personnel decisions made by a government agency, absent unusual circumstances. Whether the employee's speech is a matter of public concern requires the Court to consider the content, form, and context of the speech.

Here, the issues raised in Meyers's (P) questionnaire did not relate to matters of public concern, but rather to office discipline and morale. While such issues may be of public concern if related to the efficiency of the agency's performance of its duties, her inquiries were made instead as part of an internal office dispute. To hold that such comments constitute a matter of public concern would subject almost every comment made in a government office to constitutional challenge. One question in Meyers's (P) questionnaire, however, related to a matter of public concern. Question 11 asked the other assistant district attorneys whether they "ever felt pressured to work in political campaigns on behalf of office-supported candidates." The Court noted that such pressure violates a fundamental constitutional right. Since this question related to a matter of public concern, the Court must determine whether Meyers's (P) dismissal was justified. The state's burden in showing that the dismissal was justified depends on the nature of the employee's expression. That determination requires the Court to consider the state's interest in the efficient discharge of its duties to the public. The state, as an employer, is entitled to wide latitude in the management of its employees and internal affairs. Furthermore, the employee actually does not have to first disrupt the office before the employer takes action. Since Meyers's (P) questionnaire constituted an employee grievance regarding an internal office policy, Connick (D) was justified in taking action he deemed necessary to avoid the disruption of the efficient operation of his office. Reversed.

**DISSENT:** (Brennan, J.) Meyers's (P) questionnaire involved speech regarding the operation of a government agency and thus constituted speech relating to a matter of public concern. Therefore, this speech is entitled to First Amendment protection. Moreover, her distribution of the questionnaire did not disrupt the efficient operation of the district attorney's office, nor undermine her relationships with her coworkers.

**COMMENT:** Traditionally, a public employee had no right to object to his conditions of employment, even if they infringed upon his constitutional rights. During the 1950s and 1960s, however, the Supreme Court rejected that rule. In a number of cases, the Court invalidated statutes and procedures enacted to discourage public employees from participating in public affairs or from joining associations that the government considered subversive.

## Discussion Questions

1. Can a condition of employment infringe upon an employee's freedom of expression? If so, how does the Court address this issue?

2. Did Connick violate Meyers's constitutional right of free speech? If so, how?

3. Did the opinion in *Pickering v. Board of Education* (1968) influence the outcome of this case?

# NAT'L GAY TASK FORCE V. BD. OF EDUCATION OF OKLAHOMA CITY 729 F.2D 1270 (10TH CIR. 1984)

**GENERAL RULE OF LAW:** A board may constitutionally fire a public school teacher who engages in public homosexual conduct that poses a substantial risk of coming to the attention of schoolchildren or employees. However, a board may not fire a teacher who merely advocates homosexual behavior at some indefinite future time.

**PROCEDURE SUMMARY:**

**Plaintiff:** National Gay Task Force (NGTF) (P)

**Defendant:** Oklahoma City Board of Education (D)

**U.S. District Court Decision:** Held for Oklahoma City Board of Education (D)

**U.S. Court of Appeals Decision:** Reversed

**FACTS:** An Oklahoma statute provided that its public schools could fire teachers for engaging in public homosexual conduct or activity. Public homosexual *conduct* was defined as indiscreet same-sex relations not practiced in private. Public homosexual *activity* was defined as advocating, soliciting, or promoting public or private homosexual activity in a way that created a substantial risk that the conduct would come to the attention of schoolchildren or employees. The NGTF (P), a national organization promoting homosexual rights whose members included teachers in the Oklahoma public school system, challenged the statute on constitutional grounds. It claimed that the statute violated its members' rights of free speech, privacy, and equal protection. The federal district court held that although the statute did restrict protected speech, it was constitutionally valid in light of the United States Supreme Court's earlier holding that a teacher be dismissed for personal expression only if it resulted in a "material or substantial interference or disruption in the normal activities of the school."[31] The NGTF (P) appealed.

**ISSUE:** May a board constitutionally fire a public school teacher who engages in public homosexual conduct that poses a substantial risk of coming to the attention of schoolchildren or employees?

**HOLDING AND DECISION:** (Logan, C. J.) Yes. A board may constitutionally fire a public school teacher who engages in public homosexual activity such as a public act of oral or anal intercourse that poses a substantial risk of coming to the attention of schoolchildren or employees. The equal protection clause does not, at least as of this writing, view homosexuals as a suspect classification that would warrant strict scrutiny of laws that treat them differently from other groups. However, the Oklahoma statute does penalize free speech concerning homosexuality. Also, it does not limit the firing sanction to those who **advocate** or incite the *imminent* breaking of a law. The First Amendment does not permit someone to be punished for advocating illegal conduct that is to be performed at some indefinite future time. Thus, the part of the statute requiring dismissal or suspension for speech related to breaking the law at an indefinite future date is severed as unconstitutional, and the remainder of the law is allowed to stand. Reversed.

**COMMENT:** A state has interests in regulating the speech of teachers that differs from its interests in regulating the speech of the general population. The state's interests outweigh the teacher's interests when a teacher's speech materially or substantially disrupts normal school activities—a standard the United States Supreme Court enunciated in *Tinker v. Des Moines Independent Community School District* (1969). However, a state may regulate general public speech in much more limited circumstances: when speech incites imminent lawlessness.[32] The majority opinion in this case prompted a vigorous dissent by Circuit Judge Barrett, who noted that the Oklahoma Criminal Code equated homosexual conduct with "unnatural, perverse, detestable, and abominable . . . sodomy" and that as a "crime against nature," expression of homosexuality in any form deserved absolutely no constitutional protection. His argument, in effect, called for the creation of a unique category of forbidden speech, which would have been unlike any other constitutional limitation on speech.

## Discussion Questions

1. Can a board fire teachers for public homosexual conduct if there is no risk of it coming to the attention of schoolchildren?

2. How did *Tinker v. Des Moines Independent Community School District* (1969) influence the decision in this case?

3. In *Brandenburg v. Ohio* (1969), the courts allowed the state to limit public speech when it incites imminent lawlessness. Is the *Brandenburg* case relevant to this case?

# PINSKER V. JOINT DISTRICT NO. 28J OF ADAMS AND ARAPAHOE COUNTIES 735 F.2D 388 (10TH CIR. 1984)

**GENERAL RULE OF LAW:** Title VII of the Civil Rights Act requires school districts to reasonably accommodate the religious practices of their employees but does not require them to provide paid leave for all religious holidays.

**PROCEDURE SUMMARY:**

**Plaintiffs:** Pinsker (P), a Jewish teacher in Aurora, Colorado; Aurora Teacher's Association

**Defendant:** Aurora School District (District) (D)

**U.S. District Court Decision:** Held for Aurora School District (D)

**U.S. Court of Appeals Decision:** Affirmed

**FACTS:** Teachers in the Aurora School District (D) were allowed 12 paid personal leave days, all of which might be used for sick time and a certain number of which could be used for religious observance. The District (D) also provided two additional paid "special" personal leave days, which could be used for religious holidays.

Christmas and Good Friday, however, were schoolwide holidays. Pinsker (P), a Jewish teacher, challenged the District's (D) policy because he, on average, had to take one day of unpaid leave per year in order to observe Yom Kippur, Rosh Hashanah, and other Jewish holy days. Pinsker (P) alleged in federal court that the District's (D) policy was not a reasonable accommodation under Title VII of the Civil Rights Act of 1964, and this policy unconstitutionally burdened his First Amendment right to free exercise. The district court ruled that the District's (D) leave policy was reasonable and that the economic impact of one day's unpaid leave did not burden Pinsker's (P) right to practice his faith. Pinsker (P) appealed to the Tenth Circuit Court of Appeals.

**ISSUE:** Does Title VII of the Civil Rights Act require school districts to reasonably accommodate the religious practices of their employees by providing paid leave for all religious holidays?

**HOLDING AND DECISION:** (Logan, C. J.) No. Title VII of the Civil Rights Act does require school districts to reasonably accommodate the religious practices of their employees but does not require them to accommodate in ways that spare the employee any cost whatsoever. Teachers are likely to have not only different religions, but also different degrees of devotion to their religions. School districts cannot be expected to negotiate leave policies broad enough to suit perfectly every employee's religious needs. Further, under the First Amendment, an employee's freedom to exercise his or her religion would only be jeopardized if the economic impact of the school policy put substantial pressure on him to modify religious behavior. Here, Pinsker's (P) loss of one day's wages per year did not constitute "substantial pressure." Affirmed.

**COMMENT:** The court's opinion also discusses several other interesting facts that weakened Pinsker's (P) case considerably. Although Pinsker (P) did take one day of unpaid leave per year for religious holidays, the district had an informal policy of not actually docking him for the missed day. Further, the district also had a formal policy of allowing a maximum of 20 teachers to take "special leave" on any one day, but it made an informal exception for Pinsker (P). The court also noted, seemingly advising the school district, that other districts avoided this problem entirely by allowing paid leave for Yom Kippur and Rosh Hashanah when they fell on school days, by increasing the number of paid days for all employees for religious observance or, more innovatively, by allowing teachers to make up religious leave by doing extracurricular work.

## Discussion Questions

1. The Court comments that one day's unpaid leave did not burden Pinsker's right to practice his faith. How many days do you think would be unreasonable?

2. How would a school's policy violate a teacher's First Amendment right to exercise his religion?

3. What were some of the facts that seemed to weaken Pinsker's case? Why?

# SKINNER V. RAILWAY LABOR EXECUTIVES ASSN. 489 U.S. 602, 109 S. CT. 1402 (1989)

**GENERAL RULE OF LAW:** A warrant and reasonable suspicion are not necessarily required to test employees for drug and alcohol use when the compelling public interests outweigh the employees' privacy interest.

**PROCEDURE SUMMARY:**

**Plaintiff:** Railway Labor Executives Assn. (Association) (P), a labor union

**Defendant:** Skinner (D), U.S. Secretary of Transportation

**U.S. District Court Decision:** Granted summary judgment for Skinner (D)

**U.S. Court of Appeals Decision:** Reversed

**U.S. Supreme Court Decision:** Reversed

**FACTS:** Skinner (D) promulgated regulations mandating that blood and urine tests be performed on certain railroad employees after major train accidents. The regulations also permitted breath and urine testing of employees who violated certain safety rules. The Association (P), the railroad employees' union, brought suit to enjoin enforcement of the regulations. It contended that these regulations violated the Fourth Amendment by not requiring a warrant and reasonable suspicion before a search could be conducted. The district court disagreed and granted summary judgment for Skinner (D). The court of appeals found that a particularized suspicion was essential and must exist in order for this testing to be found reasonable under the Fourth Amendment. The court of appeals, therefore, reversed and enjoined enforcement of the regulations. The U.S. Supreme Court granted review.

**ISSUE:** May the Fourth Amendment's warrant and reasonable suspicion requirements be waived to test employees for drug and alcohol use when the compelling state interests served by the test outweigh the employees' privacy interests?

**HOLDING AND DECISION:** (Kennedy, J.) Yes. The Fourth Amendment's warrant and reasonable suspicion requirements may be waived when testing employees for drug and alcohol use when legitimate state interests served by the test outweigh the employees' Fourth Amendment privacy concerns. The Fourth Amendment only forbids those searches that are unreasonable, and what is unreasonable is relative and depends on the circumstances. Though the regulation's mandated tests do implicate the Fourth Amendment, which generally requires a warrant and individualized suspicion before searches may be conducted, the government's compelling interests in the safety of the traveling public and of the employees themselves present a "special need" that makes the tests reasonable without a warrant or probable cause. A warrant protects the public by imposing rules and structure on a search. Here, the regulations that govern the circumstances under which the drug and alcohol tests were conducted serve the same purpose. They limit the intrusion by narrowly and specifically defining when a test is permissible. Further, the concerned employees have notice of these circumstances and limits. Not only is the public adequately protected without a warrant, but also imposing a warrant requirement would significantly hinder the testing program's objectives. Individualized suspicion is not required because the regulations pose limited threats to the employees' justifiable privacy expectations. The railroad industry is already subject to heavy safety regulations, and employees already submit to significant restrictions on their freedom; the additional restrictions these regulations create are minimal. Reversed.

**COMMENT:** In a companion case, *National Treasury Employees Union v. Von Raab* (1989), the Court upheld the warrantless and suspicionless drug testing of government drug enforcement employees.[33] The common denominator of the Court's opinions in *Skinner* and *Von Raab* is the categorization of tested employees as being in sensitive positions, creating a special need that justified the waiver of stringent Fourth Amendment requirements. Whether this exception will be extended to the school context depends on whether teachers, principals, or other school officials are found to hold similarly sensitive positions. The Court has not yet had an opportunity to address the issue. An appropriate case for consideration might involve mandatory drug and alcohol testing of a teacher who is being considered for tenure. The issue would be whether the board's potential granting of tenure, with its lifelong employment guarantee and opportunity to impact thousands of children, creates a compelling public interest that would outweigh the teacher's Fourth Amendment privacy interest.

## Discussion Questions

1. What factors will allow for a waiver of Fourth Amendment warrant and reasonable search requirements?

2. Why do you think the public wouldn't be adequately served if the warrant requirement wasn't waived?

3. What state interests do you think would be served by mandatory drug and alcohol testing of teachers considered for tenure? Do you think that these state interests can likewise be advanced by mandatory testing of all teachers?

# IN RE PATCHOGUE-MEDFORD CONGRESS OF TEACHERS V. BD. OF ED. 70 N.Y.2D 57, 517 N.Y.S.2D 456 (1987)

**GENERAL RULE OF LAW:** Compulsory drug testing absent reasonable suspicion of employees constitutes an unreasonable search and seizure violating state and federal constitutions.

**PROCEDURE SUMMARY:**

**Plaintiff:** Patchogue-Medford Congress of Teachers (Teachers) (P), a teachers' union

**Defendant:** Patchogue-Medford School District (School District) (D)

**State Court Trial Division Decision:** Held for plaintiff

**State Court Appellate Division Decision:** Affirmed

**State Court of Appeals (New York's highest court) Decision:** Affirmed

**FACTS:** The Patchogue-Medford School District (D) entered into a collective bargaining agreement with the Patchogue-Medford Congress of Teachers (P). The agreement required that all probationary teachers undergo a full physical examination in their first year of employment and during the final year of their probationary term. In 1985, the School District (D) informed the Teachers (P) that they would be required to also submit to a urinalysis examination. The School District (D) conceded that the purpose of the examination was to ascertain illegal drug usage. The Teachers (P) commenced suit to prohibit the examination, contending that it was unconstitutional and constituted an unreasonable search and seizure. The Teachers (P) sought declaratory and injunctive relief. The court granted an interim stay of the examination. The trial court held that the examination violated state statute and the collective bargaining agreement and constituted an unconstitutional search and seizure. The appellate division affirmed. The School District (D) appealed.

**ISSUE:** Does compulsory drug testing absent reasonable suspicion of employees constitute an unreasonable search and seizure violating state and federal constitutions?

**HOLDING AND DECISION:** (Wachler, J.) Yes. Compulsory drug testing absent reasonable suspicion of employees constitutes an unreasonable search and seizure violating state and federal constitutions. Requiring employees to submit to a urinalysis examination infringes upon the individual's reasonable expectation of privacy and thus violates state and federal constitutions. The purpose of the prohibition on unreasonable searches and seizures is to protect an individual against unwarranted governmental intrusions. These include intrusions into the individual's person and bodily integrity. The School District (D) contended that the urinalysis examination did not constitute a search or seizure because urine is a waste product with respect to which the individual can have no reasonable expectation of privacy, and collecting a urine sample does not invade an individual's bodily integrity. On the contrary, requiring an individual to discharge urine for the purpose of analysis for drug abuse constitutes a search and seizure. In determining whether the government's action is reasonable, the court must balance the reasons for the search against the extent of the intrusion into the individual's privacy rights. Since the School District (D) has a legitimate interest in ensuring that its teachers are fit for the classroom, it is not unreasonable to require them to submit to additional testing if the School District (D) has reason to question the individual's fitness. Thus, if the School District (D) has reasonable suspicion that a teacher is utilizing illegal drugs, then it may require that teacher to submit to a urinalysis. Here, the School District (D) did not have reasonable suspicion to believe that any of its probationary teachers were engaging in drug abuse. Thus, the urinalysis examination violated the requirements of both state and federal constitutions. Affirmed.

**CONCURRENCE:** (Simons, J.) The majority is correct in concluding that requiring probationary teachers to submit to urinalysis examinations constitutes an unreasonable search and seizure in violation of the federal Constitution. The plaintiffs, however, did not assert a claim that their constitutional rights were being violated under either the federal or state constitutions. Moreover, the majority wrongly applies state constitutional requirements. The matter should have been resolved on federal constitutional grounds.

**COMMENT:** The School District (D) contended that urine constitutes a waste product and, therefore, the Teachers (P) did not possess a reasonable expectation of privacy in respect to their urine samples. The general rule is that individuals do not have a reasonable expectation of privacy over things they intentionally abandon or throw away. The government, however, has no right to such waste products prior to abandonment. Here, the court applied a more lenient standard than probable cause and warrant requirements before conducting the examination. Factors to be considered include the privacy interests involved, the substantiality of the state's interests, and safeguarding of the individual's reasonable expectation of privacy against unbridled discretion.

## Discussion Questions

1. Why did the school district believe that a urinalysis did not equal search and seizure?

2. What *two* issues must the court balance to determine whether a governmental action was reasonable?

3. Must a school district have probable cause, like the police, to conduct a search of property? If so, explain. If not, identify what a school district needs to conduct a search, and explain.

# PICKERING V. BOARD OF EDUCATION: 391 U.S. 563 (1968)

**GENERAL RULE OF LAW:** A teacher may not be dismissed for the exercise of a constitutional right such as First Amendment protected free speech.

**PROCEDURE SUMMARY:**

**Plaintiff:** Martin L. Pickering, a teacher in Township High School District 205 (P)

**Defendant:** Board of Education, Will County Illinois (Board) (D)

**State Supreme Court Decision:** Held for the Board (D), rejecting Pickering's (P) claim that he could not constitutionally be dismissed from his teaching position

**U. S. Supreme Court Decision:** Reversed and remanded

**FACTS:** Martin Pickering (P), a high school science teacher, wrote a letter to the editor of the local newspaper criticizing the Board (D) for its allocation of funds between athletics and academics. The Board terminated Pickering's (P) teaching contract. The Board (D) was required to hold a hearing on the dismissal. After a full hearing, the Board (D) determined that the publication of the letter was detrimental to the efficient operation and administration of the schools in the district. The Board (D) cited that Illinois state statutes required Pickering's (P) dismissal. The Board (D) dismissed Pickering for writing and publishing the letter on grounds that the letter contained several false statements that damaged the reputations of the Board (D) and the superintendent, thereby impugning the integrity of the school system and competence of the Board (D) and school administration. Further, the Board (D) charged that these statements were potentially disruptive of faculty discipline and could possibly provoke "controversy, conflict, and dissension" among teachers, administrators, the board of education, and school district residents. Pickering (P) then sued the Board (D) on the grounds that his First Amendment rights were violated when he was terminated for exercising his right to freedom of speech.

**ISSUE:** Do school officials violate the First Amendment by terminating a teacher for writing a letter to the editor of a local newspaper in which he discusses important matters of public concern?

**HOLDING AND DECISION:** Yes. The Court held (8–1) that school officials do violate the First Amendment when they terminate a teacher for speaking out as a citizen on matters of public concern. Public school teachers, as public employees, are entitled to some First Amendment protections. The employer must show that the employee's speech in some way disrupts official functions and/or interferes with the effective performance of the employee. "The problem in any case is to arrive at a balance between the interests of the teacher, as a citizen, in commenting upon matters of public concern and the interests of the state, as an employer, in promoting the efficiency of the public services it performs through its employees." Pickering's action did not disrupt or interfere with the general operations of the school system, nor was Pickering's performance of daily classroom duties impeded. Statements in the letter did not target any school official that Pickering interacted with on a daily basis. Reversed and remanded.

## Discussion Questions

1. Does a school violate the First Amendment if it disciplines a teacher for speech that touches on a matter of public concern?

2. An employee under your supervision (as a building principal or district superintendent) actively engages in a campaign against the district's proposed school levy by telephoning members of the community to encourage a defeat of the proposed levy. What factors should you consider in deciding what actions should be taken with this employee?

3. How will you, as an administrator, balance your First Amendment rights with the service you provide as a state employee when commenting upon matters of public concern with parents, news media, and community leaders?

# MT. HEALTHY CITY SCHOOL DISTRICT BOARD OF EDUCATION V. DOYLE
# 429 U.S. 274, 97 S. CT. 568 (1977)

**GENERAL RULE OF LAW:** The termination of a teacher following his exercise of a constitutional right will be voided only if such exercise was the principal factor in the termination.

**PROCEDURE SUMMARY:**

**Plaintiff:** Doyle, a teacher (P)

**Defendant:** Mt. Healthy (Ohio) City School District Board of Education (School Board) (D), Doyle's (P) employer

**U.S. District Court Decision:** Held for Doyle (P)

**U.S. Court of Appeals Decision:** Affirmed

**U.S. Supreme Court Decision:** Reversed

**FACTS:** Doyle (P) was a nontenured teacher at the Mt. Healthy City School District from 1966 to 1971. During this time, he proved to be somewhat difficult, having been involved in several incidents. During one incident, he made insulting comments to two students, while during another he made an obscene gesture to students. He was also involved in several arguments with other teachers that almost escalated into fistfights, and he had problems with the principal. In 1971, he forwarded a memorandum from the school administration to a local radio station, which ran it as a news item. The memo from the school administration was about teacher dress and appearance (it also referred to teacher professionalism as well as the upcoming bond issue). Doyle was the elected president of the Mt. Healthy Teachers' Association. His final probationary year was tension-filled. Later that year, the School Board (D) refused to rehire him. Doyle (P) requested, and the School Board (D) provided, the reasons for the dismissal. Among the reasons given was Doyle's (P) contact with the radio station. Doyle (P) sued for reinstatement, contending that he had been terminated for exercising a First Amendment right. The district court ordered him reinstated, and the court of appeals affirmed. The Supreme Court granted review.

**ISSUE:** Will the termination of a teacher following his exercise of a constitutional right be voided only if such exercise was the principal factor in his termination?

**HOLDING AND DECISION:** (Rehnquist, J.) Yes. The termination of a teacher following his exercise of a constitutional right will be voided only if such exercise was the principal factor in the termination. A public employee may not be fired for exercising a constitutional right. However, this does not mean that one so doing becomes immune from termination. If a public employer can demonstrate that such exercise was something less than the principal factor, such as only one of numerous factors, then the termination may be valid. Here, there were numerous acts that Doyle (P) had committed that might have influenced the decision to terminate him. However, neither court below appeared to have ruled on whether Doyle's (P) termination was largely due to these incidents, so the matter must be decided on remand. Reversed.

**COMMENT:** An untenured teacher, unlike a tenured teacher, has little right to procedural due process because he does not have a property interest in employment. At the end of his contract term of employment, he may be terminated for almost any cause or no cause at all. Nonetheless, one thing an untenured teacher may not be fired for is solely exercising a constitutional right. This case distinguishes *Pickering*, which held that teachers had a constitutional right to speak out freely on matters of public concern. Protected speech may not serve as the basis for the termination of employment. However, a school employee cannot simply cloak himself with the First Amendment by engaging in constitutionally protected conduct. Therefore, a teacher cannot be fired for speaking out on matters of public interest, but a teacher cannot prevent an employer from viewing the employee's total performance record when making a decision on rehiring. After *Doyle,* a school employee must establish that his statements were protected and that protected speech was a motivating, or substantial, factor in the board's termination or nonrenewal action. The school board must establish that it would have taken the termination or nonrenewal action regardless of the employee's protected conduct.

## Discussion Questions

1. Name some other ways Doyle could have handled receipt of the memo from school administration.

2. Since Doyle was a former president of the teachers' association, what relation, if any, do you think that had on the decision by the school board to terminate?

3. What lesson(s) does this case provide for nontenured/tenured teachers and boards of education?

---

Additional case briefs can be found on the SAGE Web site at the following address:
http://www.sagepub.com/aquilacasebriefs

---

# NOTES

1. Connick v. Meyers, 461 U.S. 138 (1983).
2. Pickering v. Board of Education of Township High School District, 391 U.S. 563 (1968). See also Chapter 12.
3. Mt. Healthy v. Doyle, 429 U.S. 274 (1977).
4. See Connick v. Meyers, 461 U.S. 138 (1983).
5. Keefe v. Geanokos, 418 F.2d 359 (1st Cir. 1969).
6. See Skinner v. Railway Labor Executives Assn., 489 U.S. 602 (1989).
7. In re Patchogue-Medford Congress of Teachers v. Bd. of Ed., 510 N.E.2d 325 (1987).
8. See Skinner v. Railway Labor Executives Assn., 489 U.S. 602 (1989).
9. See Phelps v. Bd. of Education of Town of West New York, 300 U.S. 319 (1937).
10. See, e.g., Jacobson v. Cincinnati Bd. of Educ., 961 F.2d 100 (6th Cir. 1992).
11. See Knight v. Board of Regents of University of State of New York, 269 F.Supp. 339 (1967); affd. 390 U.S. 36 (1968).
12. See Slochower v. Board of Higher Education of New York City, 350 U.S. 551 (1956).
13. Beilan v. Board of Education, School District of Philadelphia, 357 U.S. 399 (1958).
14. Pickering v. Board of Education of Township High School District, 391 U.S. 563 (1968). See also Chapter 12.
15. Mt. Healthy v. Doyle, 429 U.S. 274 (1977).
16. Stroman v. Colleton County School District, 981 F.2d 152 (4th Cir. 1993).
17. See Connick v. Meyers, 461 U.S. 138 (1983).
18. See East Hartford Ed. Assn. v. Bd. of Ed., 562 F.2d 838 (2nd Cir. 1977).
19. See City of Madison v. Wisconsin Employment Relations Commission, 429 U.S. 167 (1976). See also Chapter 11.
20. Zykan v. Warsaw Community School Corp., 631 F.2d 1300 (7th Cir. 1980).
21. Keefe v. Geanokos, 418 F.2d 359 (1st Cir. 1969).
22. Boring v. Buncombe County Board of Education, 136 F.3d 364 (4th Cir. 1998).
23. See Nat'l Gay Task Force v. Bd. of Education of Oklahoma City, 729 F.2d 1270 (10th Cir. 1984).
24. See Pinsker v. Joint District No. 28J of Adams and Arapahoe Counties, 735 F.2d 388 (10th Cir. 1984).
25. See Skinner v. Railway Labor Executives Assn., 489 U.S. 602 (1989).
26. See In re Patchogue-Medford Congress of Teachers v. Bd. of Ed., 510 N.E.2d 325 (1987).
27. Knox County Education Association v. Knox County Board of Education, 158 F.3d 361 (6th Cir. 1998).
28. See Dike v. School Board of Orange County, Florida, 650 F.2d 783 (5th Cir. 1981).
29. See Schafer v. Board of Public Ed., 903 F2d 243 (3d Cir. 1990).
30. See O'Connor v. Ortega, 480 U.S. 709 (1987).
31. Tinker v. Des Moines Independent Community School District, 393 U.S. 503, 89 S. Ct. 733 (1969).
32. Brandenburg v. Ohio, 395 U.S. 444, 89 S. Ct. 1827 (1969).
33. National Treasury Employees Union v. Von Raab, 109 S. Ct. 1384 (1989).

# 10

# Teacher Certification, Licensure, and Contracts for Employment

*A person has no constitutional right to be employed as a teacher in the public schools, as such employment is not an uninhabited privilege and he (or she) has no right to serve except on such terms as the state prescribes.*

—78 Corpus Juris Secundum, § 154

## OVERVIEW . . . . . . . . . . . . . . . . . . . . . . . . . . . . . . . . . . . . . . . .

For the most part, the law concerning the licensure and employment of teachers is the province of state legislatures. In past years, the term "certification" was more commonly used. Most states have now transitioned to a licensure model as the move toward professionalizing American education intensifies. Today, a license that must be renewed (compared to certification, which is permanent) is the preferred model as education strives to be seen in the same light as other professions (e.g., law and medicine). Unless otherwise noted, the term license will be used herein to include certification.

Because licensure requirements are a state responsibility, a variety of models have been created. Further, local school boards are required to follow state mandates, but they may impose certain additional requirements as they see fit. With this in mind, all states have laws that require potential public school teachers to secure a license that may be conditional on completing preparation programs, reaching a certain score on a specific examination, and passing criminal background checks. However, neither state laws nor agency regulations may unduly infringe on teachers' federal constitutional rights or rights created by federal civil rights laws, except in specific cases and situations.

In addition to setting competency standards, a local school board may require that certain conditions be met prior to extending an offer of employment to a certificate holder.

These conditions can vary greatly. For example, federal courts have held that a local board may require a teacher to live within the boundaries of the school district (residency requirement), so long as it can demonstrate a rational basis for the requirement. In addition, so long as its standards are not applied in an arbitrary manner, a school board may require that teachers meet reasonable health and fitness requirements, for the protection of students and other employees. In fact, school boards once required teachers who were pregnant to take maternity leave based, in part, on this health and fitness argument (however, this is now deemed a violation of constitutional rights).[1] Another condition might involve blindness. Blindness is generally not a proper ground for declining to employ a teacher who is "otherwise qualified" for a position because ADA protection would apply. However, in some limited situations even this might be upheld.[2] A school board may prohibit teachers from accepting outside employment during the school year, although this condition is controversial. Because of the teacher uproar that this would create, it has rarely, if ever, been imposed.

School boards must utilize employment standards that are job related.[3] Additionally, if a school board's hiring practices result in racial imbalance, or have a disparate impact on older, more experienced teachers, such practices may be legally challenged.[4] Last, a school may not require that a teacher be of a specific religion when adherence to that religion is not essential to the teacher's performance of the teaching position.[5] The overriding principle in many of these cases is that employment practices and procedures must be applied uniformly.

There are two basic types of employment contracts. One is the tenure contract and the other is a term contract. Tenure contracts are those that allow a teacher to be terminated only for cause (i.e., only if a good reason for terminating the contract is apparent after various procedures have been followed that were designed to ensure fairness).[6] The other type of teacher employment contract is a term contract. A term contract is one of limited duration that may (or may not) be renewed at the discretion of the school board. Such contracts are probationary in nature and usually precede tenure contracts.

Employment contracts between school boards and teachers must meet all the conditions for an enforceable contract, unless some specific qualification has been provided by state law. Further, school boards must exercise the contract right and not delegate contracting rights to school superintendents or individual board members. As with all legal contracts, a contract between a local school board and a teacher must contain the following critical elements: offer, acceptance, and consideration. In other words, one party, usually the board, must make an offer of employment. The other party, the teacher, must accept it. Consideration exists when one party suffers a detriment—gives something up—in exchange for the other party's promise to perform. In these situations, consideration exists when the board suffers a detriment (money payment) in exchange for the teacher's promise to perform (to teach). "Consideration" can otherwise be thought of as a bargained-for exchange.[7] In addition to the aforementioned formalities, both parties must be competent to enter into a contractual relationship, the subject of the contract must be within the bounds of the law, and the contract must be memorialized in a form prescribed by law (usually in writing).

## Case Study

### Minimal Conditions for Pregnancy Leave

A large urban school district has a serious problem locating and retaining competent teachers. Many of their new teacher hires are young, and many of these teachers become pregnant. This causes a disruption in services to children. The school board adopted a policy to deal with these continuity issues. The board requires that pregnancy leave be granted only under certain conditions. First, the pregnant teacher must take leave five months before her due date. Also, she may not return to her former position less than three months after childbirth, preferably at the end of a grading period.

The teachers' union has vigorously opposed this board action. It claims that the action violates the due process and equal protection rights of the teacher. You have been employed by the school district to analyze the impact of this action.

### Discussion Questions

1.  What are the arguments in support of the pregnant teachers?

2.  What arguments support the board's concern for continuity?

3.  What do you recommend? Why?

## IMPORTANT CONCEPTS

-   **License to teach:** A teaching certificate is a state-approved license to teach and is issued once an applicant has satisfied certain minimum requirements.

-   **State responsibility:** The responsibility for certification rests with the state. The state legislature often delegates this responsibility to a state agency, such as a state board of education.

-   **No guaranteed employment:** A certificate does not guarantee employment; it merely indicates that the holder is legally fit to teach.

-   **Not a contract:** A certificate is not a contract; new conditions may be imposed on the holder after the certificate is issued and prior to its renewal.

-   **Boards given discretionary authority:** Most states give local school boards the discretionary authority to enter into employment agreements with teachers.

*(Continued)*

(Continued)

- **Rights of teachers:** However, where state law provides teachers with certain rights, local school boards may not alter or deny those rights.

- **Professional standards:** Most local school boards set professional and academic standards higher than standards for state certification.

- **Additional requirements:** Local school boards may require that teachers live within school district boundaries, remain healthy and reasonably fit, and refrain from engaging in outside employment.

- **Contract law applies:** Basic rules of contract law are applicable to teachers' contracts.

- **Statutory provisions predominate:** When state statutory provisions are in conflict with the terms of a teacher's contract, the statutory provisions will predominate, and the contract terms may be held unenforceable.

- **Nonclassroom-related responsibilities:** Nonclassroom-related responsibilities may be implied in the terms of a teacher's contract if they are reasonably related to the teacher's field of expertise or inherent in the duties of teaching.

# TEACHER CERTIFICATION

Certification is the process by which a state licenses a person to teach. The holder of a teaching certificate is deemed to be legally competent to teach (i.e., he or she has fulfilled certain minimum criteria set by the state as a prerequisite to licensure).

## State Responsibility

The responsibility for the licensure of teachers rests with each of the 50 states. As a result, statutes governing teacher certification vary from state to state. Most state legislatures delegate portions of their functions to state boards of education or similar state agencies. Understandably, state legislators must rely on the discretion and expertise of state education officials when it comes to setting the minimum professional qualifications necessary for licensure. The state legislature may set minimum certification requirements, but they may also provide certificate-issuing agencies with discretionary authority to impose standards that are higher than the minimum state requirements.

## Effect of Meeting Certificate Requirements

As a rule, if an applicant satisfies all pertinent certification criteria, a certificate will issue as a matter of course. In other words, a certificate cannot be denied arbitrarily or for no reason at all. As noted above, state agencies that are responsible for issuing certificates may be vested with some discretionary (as opposed to the perfunctory or "ministerial") authority.

In such cases, courts will not question a decision to deny the issuance of a certificate unless it appears that absolutely no valid basis for doing so existed.

## "Certificate" and "Contract" Distinguished

A teacher's certificate is not a contract and thus is not governed by the law of contracts. New or modified conditions may be imposed on the certificate holder after the certificate has issued. Also, a certificate holder may be required to pursue additional academic or continuing education courses if she wishes to renew or upgrade her certificate. A certificate may be revoked or suspended by the issuer for "good cause" (i.e., for a well-recognized and well-supported reason). This reason must not be arbitrary and must withstand a reasonable challenge.[8] For example, evidence of immoral activities, breach of the teaching contract, and lack of teaching competence all have been found to constitute good cause. Note, however, that because the revocation or suspension of certification is an extreme measure that generally results in loss of employment, courts usually require certificate-revoking agencies to establish and follow certain fair procedures in making such decisions.

## "Certification" and "Employment" Distinguished

A certificate does not guarantee its holder a specific teaching position. As discussed below, state legislatures generally vest authority for the employment of teachers in local school boards.

*Certification/Licensure by Examination.* Although at one time disfavored, examinations are now required by most states for teacher certification. The most common is the National Teacher Examination (NTE).[9]

*Academic Prerequisites.* Academic prerequisites include a college degree or degrees and course work in specified areas of curricula.

*Good Moral Character.* An applicant must possess good moral character at the time she applies for a certificate (and generally must evidence such character throughout the term of the certificate).

*Signing of a Loyalty Oath.* An oath of loyalty is permissible so long as it does not contravene an applicant's federal constitutional right to associate with those of her choice. Some states require an applicant to pledge her loyalty to state and federal constitutions.

*Minimum Age.* An applicant may be required to be of a specified age for certification purposes.

*U.S. Citizenship.* States may require U.S. citizenship as a condition of certification. The U.S. Supreme Court has stated that because the function of teaching is so closely tied to the operation of state government, a state may properly exclude from certification those individuals who have not submitted themselves to our "process of self-government."[10]

*Temporary Certification.* A state may waive its basic certification requirement. This is unusual and usually only happens when there is a specific shortage in a particular teaching area.[11]

# EMPLOYMENT OF TEACHERS

Once an individual has obtained a license or certificate attesting to his qualifications for a particular type of public school teaching post, he must face a second (and sometimes formidable) hurdle: obtaining an actual teaching position in the state in which he is certified. Employment requirements differ from certification requirements, just as the agencies responsible for making employment decisions (local boards) differ from those responsible for certification (state boards).

## Discretion Vested in Local School Boards

Most states vest the discretionary authority to hire and fire certified teachers, and the rights and responsibilities attendant with that authority, in local or regional school boards. In such cases, the local board *as a whole*—as opposed to the superintendent or individual board members—is responsible for all employment decisions.

## Breadth of Authority

The authority delegated to local boards is broad. Courts generally will not review a particular hiring decision unless it appears that the decision was made in an arbitrary or capricious manner or in violation of an applicant's statutory or constitutional rights. As a general rule, hiring decisions must be neutral as to race, religion, gender, and national origin.

## Standard of Employment

Consonant with their broad hiring authority, local school boards are often vested with the discretion to set professional and academic standards at a higher level than that set by the state's minimum certification requirements. Aside from setting competence standards, the local school board may require that any of the following conditions be met prior to extending an offer of employment to a certificate holder.

*Residency.* Federal courts have held that a local board may require a teacher to live within the boundaries of the school district, so long as it can demonstrate a rational basis for the requirement. Note, however, that some states prohibit by statute the adoption of such requirements.

*Health and Physical Fitness.* So long as its standards are not applied in an arbitrary manner, a school board may require, for the protection of students and other employees, that teachers meet reasonable health and fitness requirements. Many school boards once required teachers who were pregnant to take maternity leave based, in part, on a paternalistic health and fitness requirement. Such policies have now been found to violate federal constitutional rights.[12]

*Blindness.* As a general rule, blindness is not a proper ground for declining to employ a teacher who is otherwise qualified for a position.

*Outside Employment.* A school board may prohibit a teacher from accepting outside employment during the school year.

*Employment Standards.* School boards may only utilize employment standards that are job related.[13] Additionally, if a school board's hiring practices result in racial imbalance or have a disparate impact on older, more experienced teachers, such practices may be challenged in court.[14] Finally, a school may not require that a teacher be of a specific religion when adherence to that religion is not essential to the teacher's performance of the teaching position.[15]

*General Rule Concerning Employment.* Employment practices and procedures must be applied uniformly.

# TEACHERS' CONTRACTS

Local school boards have been delegated the exclusive authority to enter into employment contracts with prospective teachers. A contract, by definition, creates various rights and responsibilities in each of its parties. Questions sometimes arise as to whether (1) a contract was properly created; (2) additional rights and responsibilities should be read into the contract in light of preexisting statutory language, collective bargaining agreements, and the like (none of which were specifically referred to in the contract); and (3) additional rights and responsibilities are "implied" by custom or by the terms of the contract themselves.

## Basic Principles of Contract Law Apply

As with all legal contracts, a contract between a local school board and a teacher must contain the following critical elements:

*Offer and Acceptance.* One party (almost always the board) must make an offer of employment, and the other party (the teacher) must accept it.

*Legal Capacity.* Both parties must be competent to enter into a contractual relationship.

*Consideration.* There must be value or a benefit conferred by one party in return for the other party's performance (a bargained-for exchange).

*Legality.* The subject of the contract must be within the bounds of the law.

*Form.* The contract must be memorialized in a form prescribed by law (usually in writing).

## Common Types of Employment Contracts

*Tenure Contracts.* Contracts that provide for a teacher's termination only upon the existence of "cause." In other words, termination is permissible only if good reason is apparent after various procedures designed to ensure fairness to the teacher have been followed.[16]

*Term Contracts.* Contracts of limited duration that may (or may not) be renewed at the discretion of the school board. Such contracts are probationary in nature and usually precede tenure contracts. "Cause" is not needed to justify a refusal to renew a term contract.

## Effect of State Statutory Provisions and Outside Agreements

Teacher employment may also be governed by various state education statutes. In such cases, statutory requirements will be deemed a part of the teacher's contract as if fully spelled out therein. For instance, tenure provisions mandated by state law may be viewed as if they are a part of the local employment contract.

*Preemptive Effect of State Law.* Wherever a statutory requirement conflicts with the terms of a contract, the contract terms will be held unenforceable. In other words, state statutory requirements will preempt local contract terms. The only qualifications to this would be in a state such as Ohio, where O.R.C. 4117—Ohio's Collective Bargaining Law—allows for a properly negotiated teachers' contract to prevail over state law (with the exception of selected civil rights protections, which cannot be preempted).

*Collective Bargaining Agreements.* As with rights created by statutory provisions, rights also accrue to teachers under collective bargaining agreements.

## Implied Terms of Employment

Some courts have determined that teachers have an implied obligation to assume various responsibilities outside of classroom instruction that are not specifically provided for in their contracts. For example, male teachers may be expected to supervise the conduct of students in boys' restrooms. English teachers may be required to coach student plays. All teachers may be required to supervise study halls. Generally speaking, an implied obligation may be seen to exist if the nonclassroom assignment relates in a significant way to the teacher's area of instructional expertise or is fundamental to the teaching role.

# HIGHLY QUALIFIED TEACHERS

Under the No Child Left Behind (NCLB) Act, a teacher is deemed highly qualified if he or she (1) has obtained a bachelor's degree, (2) has obtained full state certification or licensure, and (3) is able to prove that he or she knows all subjects that he or she teaches. Most realize that teachers make the most difference in student achievement. Therefore, to improve student performance, the NCLB has imposed the "highly qualified teacher" requirement. NCLB mandates that every teacher of a core academic subject must be "highly qualified" by the end of the 2005–2006 school year. Unfortunately, there is little agreement on what makes a teacher "highly qualified" or what needs to be done to ensure that every student has access to high-quality teachers.

Confounding the highly qualified teacher discussion is the concern about funding and politics. Clearly, the costs are going to be, and have already been, significant. More important, NCLB's attempt to professionalize the teaching force threatens public education's traditional top-down authority structure. The elements of a qualified teacher are well-documented: a bachelor's degree from a four-year institution, full state certification, and demonstrated competence in the subject area. However, the more difficult problem arises with "highly qualified" special education teachers at the secondary level. The difficulties created by the highly qualified provisions as they apply to special education teachers were discussed in Chapter 3 (see also Chapter 3, Figure 3.1).

## Case Study

### Hiring the Best and Brightest

Your school board has informed you that they want you to hire the best new teachers. As superintendent, you recommend that the school board adopt a hiring policy that requires all new hires to pass the National Teacher Examination (NTE), developed and conducted by the Education Testing Service. Furthermore, you intend to provide a higher starting salary to those who score in the top quartile on the NTE. You have informally polled the school board members and believe that all board members will support your proposal, with the exception of the newly elected African American member. You have heard a rumor that the local chapter of the NAACP will oppose your motion and has also threatened a lawsuit based on discrimination. The school board attorney has indicated that you will prevail in court. What should you do?

### Discussion Questions

1. Isn't the proposed action discriminatory?

2. Even if it is discriminatory, is it unconstitutional?

3. Will the higher salary for those who score higher on the NTE be upheld?

## CONCLUSION . . . . . . . . . . . . . . . . . . . . . . . . . . . . . .

State legislatures are responsible for setting the standards and requirements for teacher licensure. This duty is generally delegated to a state board of education, which is better suited to establish educational standards. Previously, the trend had been to grant teachers a permanent certification once they met selective minimum requirements. However, the recent trend has been to grant teachers licenses, which must be periodically renewed.

Achieving licensure is not a guarantee of receiving a contract for employment. In addition, new requirements to maintain a license may be imposed at any time. Although boards have discretion to enter into agreements with teachers, these agreements are subject to state law. Generally, licensure requires passing an examination, meeting academic prerequisites, having a good moral character, possibly signing a loyalty oath, and having U.S. citizenship, as well as meeting a minimum age requirement.

Broad discretion to hire and to terminate new teachers is vested with the local school board. Courts generally will not review a particular hiring decision unless it appears that the decision was made in an arbitrary or capricious manner or in violation of an applicant's statutory or constitutional rights. Typically, aside from competence standards, boards may impose residency, health, and other pre-employment requirements.

Contract law requirements govern teachers' employment agreements. Therefore, employment contracts must contain an offer and acceptance; the parties must have legal capacity to contract; there must be consideration; the subject of the contract must be legal; and, generally, the agreement must be memorialized in writing. Teaching contracts usually come in two forms: tenure contracts are ongoing and allow termination only for cause, while term contracts are for limited duration with a renewal option. The terms of these contracts are subject to state law.

The following cases, as well as those provided on the Sage Web site, illustrate the constitutional issues to be considered in contractual negotiations with school boards and teachers. Not only do school boards need to be aware of the constitutional issues when hiring and firing, but they also need to be aware of the constitutional rights that teachers retain as state employees. The cases provided examine issues of pregnancy, race, tenure, pay scales, and religion, and they show how these issues affect the employment of teachers. Think through the discussion questions provided to fully develop thoughts on the constitutional issues facing school boards and teachers alike.

# CASE BRIEFS ......................................

# CLEVELAND BOARD OF ED. V. LAFLEUR
## 414 U.S. 632, 94 S. CT. 791 (1974)

**GENERAL RULE OF LAW:** Mandatory leave rules that create a conclusive presumption that all pregnant teachers become physically incapable of performing their duties after a specific period of pregnancy violate due process.

**PROCEDURE SUMMARY:**

> **Plaintiff:** LaFleur (P), a pregnant school teacher

> **Defendant:** Cleveland Board of Education (Board) (D)

> **U.S. District Court Decision:** Held for the Board (D), finding mandatory leave requirement constitutional

> **U.S. Court of Appeals Decision:** Reversed, finding the requirement violated the equal protection clause of the Fourteenth Amendment

> **U.S. Supreme Court Decision:** Affirmed, finding the requirement unconstitutional under the due process clause of the Fourteenth Amendment

**FACTS:** The Board (D) enacted a rule requiring pregnant school teachers to take maternity leave without pay five months before their expected due date. LaFleur (P), a junior high school teacher, informed the Board (D) that she was pregnant. Pursuant to the mandatory leave requirement, she was forced to stop working, without pay. LaFleur (P) thereafter filed suit under 42 U.S.C. § 1983, arguing that the requirement was unconstitutional. The district court rejected LaFleur's (P) argument and upheld the requirement. The court of appeals reversed, holding that the requirement violated the equal protection clause of the Fourteenth Amendment. The Board (D) sought, and the U.S. Supreme Court granted, review.

**ISSUE:** Is a mandatory leave rule that creates a conclusive presumption that pregnant teachers become physically incapable of performing their duties after four or five months constitutional?

**HOLDING AND DECISION:** (Stewart, J.) No. A mandatory leave rule that creates a conclusive presumption that pregnant teachers become physically incapable of performing their duties after four or five months violates the due process clause. This clause protects an individual's freedom of choice in matters of marriage and family life from unwarranted governmental intrusion. Government may not needlessly, arbitrarily, or capriciously infringe upon this freedom. The Board's (D) mandatory leave rule does just this. As long as the teacher gives substantial advance notice that she is pregnant, the arbitrary cutoff date of the Board's (D) rule has no valid relationship to the state's interest in preserving continuity of instruction. Such advance notice is already required by the Board (D). Imposing the mandatory leave cutoff date, in addition to this notice, goes too far. Affirmed.

**COMMENT:** The Court decided *LaFleur* on substantive due process grounds, finding that the requirement was an excessive infringement of a fundamental right. It seems, however, that the Supreme Court could have easily affirmed under the equal protection analysis applied by the court of appeals because the requirement was clearly sex-based and subject to intermediate scrutiny. Generally, the equal protection clause guarantees that similarly situated people will be treated similarly. For example, the government must show greater justification for distinguishing between men and women because the sex of an individual is, more often than not, an irrational basis for distinction. Under substantive due process, the government must show greater justification for imposing burdens on fundamental rights such as interstate travel, procreation, and marriage. Under either analysis, the government would have had a difficult time showing the requisite greater justification. The Court's ruling still provides for the Board's (D) concern for continuity, which is guaranteed by allowing return from maternity leave at specified, prearranged dates (e.g., the beginning of a new grading period). Also, the requirement that a doctor assist the pregnant teacher in deciding maternity leave and return-to-work dates deals with the Board's (D) concern for the unborn child and the mother. These concerns seem to be entirely reasonable, to ensure the school's normal operation. However, the pregnant teacher must give the school board some notice of departure so the board can plan to ensure a continuous and adequate education for the children. Of course, notice provisions must be rationally related to the school board's needs.

## Discussion Questions

1. Why is mandatory leave unconstitutional?

2. What are the school's interests that were said to be advanced by the mandatory leave rule?

3. What would the school district have to show for the Court to find the policy permissible?

# UNITED STATES V. STATE OF SOUTH CAROLINA 445 F. SUPP. 1094, AFFD. 434 U.S. 1026 (1978)

**GENERAL RULE OF LAW:** A state does not violate the Fourteenth Amendment when it uses the National Teacher Examination for hiring and setting teachers' pay scales.

**PROCEDURE SUMMARY:**

**Plaintiffs:** The federal government (P) and certain individuals

**Defendants:** The state of South Carolina (D) and various political subdivisions thereof

**U.S. District Court Decision:** Held for South Carolina (D)

**FACTS:** The Education Testing Service, Inc. offered a national standardized examination called the National Teacher Examination. South Carolina's system took a teacher's score into account when hiring and determining pay scales. The federal government (P) and certain private persons brought a lawsuit, contending that this practice constituted racial discrimination under the equal protection clause of the Fourteenth Amendment because African Americans, as a group, scored lower than whites.

**ISSUE:** Does a state's use of the National Teacher Examination to hire and set the pay scale of teachers violate the Fourteenth Amendment?

**HOLDING AND DECISION:** (Haynsworth, J.) No. A state does not violate the Fourteenth Amendment when it uses the National Teacher Examination for hiring and setting teachers' pay scales. To make out a case of racial classification, a plaintiff must show an intent to create and use a racial classification. If a plaintiff cannot do this, the challenged practice will be upheld, so long as it is rationally related to its stated goal. Here, no evidence existed that South Carolina (D) intended to create a racial classification in adopting the National Teacher Examination. A review of the record indicated that South Carolina (D) used the test to ensure that qualified teachers would be hired. This appeared to be a rational use of the test, so no equal protection violation occurred. Judgment for South Carolina (D).

**COMMENT:** The various plaintiffs challenged South Carolina's (D) practice not only under the Fourteenth Amendment but also under the 1964 Civil Rights Act. The issues were largely the same, but proof regarding intent is somewhat easier to establish under the Act, which is more result oriented. Nevertheless, the Court rejected the Civil Rights Act claims on much the same grounds as the constitutional claims. Without question, this ruling, which has been supported in other jurisdictions, has caused a great deal of concern to practicing administrators and teachers. These educators believe that factors other than a score on a test should control or strongly influence hiring and salary increases. Nevertheless, the use of test scores has increased for teachers and for students. Statewide student proficiency testing for graduation is now a common practice in most states. These programs have always been upheld when it is shown that the test meets validity standards and is a reasonable exercise of state authority.

## Discussion Questions

1. What would the plaintiffs need to show in order to prove this violated the Fourteenth Amendment?

2. What do you think is the school's purpose in using such a test?

3. Why has this decision concerned practicing administrators and teachers?

4. Contrast the rationale for allowing the NTE with *Griggs v. Duke Power Co.* (1971), below.

# HARRAH INDEPENDENT SCHOOL DISTRICT V. MARTIN 440 U.S. 194, 99 S. CT. 1062 (1979)

**GENERAL RULE OF LAW:** A school board may refuse to renew the contract of a tenured teacher who refuses to comply with a continuing education requirement designed to promote a legitimate state interest, if nonrenewal follows a hearing.

**PROCEDURE SUMMARY:**

> **Plaintiff:** Martin (P), a tenured teacher
>
> **Defendant:** Harrah Independent School District (District) (D)
>
> **U.S. District Court Decision:** Dismissed Martin's (P) complaint
>
> **U.S. Court of Appeals Decision:** Reversed; held for Martin (P)
>
> **U.S. Supreme Court Decision:** Reversed; held for District (D)

**FACTS:** Martin (P) was a tenured teacher employed by the District (D) since 1969. Martin (P) constantly refused to comply with the District's (D) continuing education requirements, which caused her to forfeit salary increases for the 1972–1974 school years. Sometime after 1973, the state legislature enacted a law mandating certain salary raises for teachers regardless of compliance with the continuing education policy. The District (D), denied its standard means of compelling compliance, notified Martin (P) that her contract for the next school year would not be renewed unless she completed continuing education before the end of the current year. Martin (P), at a hearing on the matter, informed the District (D) that she did not intend to comply. The District (D), after finding her refusal to be a "willful neglect of duty," voted not to renew her contract. Martin (P) filed suit, claiming the District (D) action denied her due process of law and equal protection in violation of the Fourteenth Amendment. The district court dismissed the complaint, and the court of appeals reversed. The U.S. Supreme Court granted review.

**ISSUE:** May a school board refuse to renew the contract of a tenured teacher who refuses to comply with a continuing education requirement designed to promote a legitimate state interest, when nonrenewal follows a hearing?

**HOLDING AND DECISION:** (**Per curiam**) Yes. A school board may refuse to renew the contract of a tenured teacher who refuses to comply with a continuing education requirement designed to promote a legitimate state interest, when nonrenewal follows a hearing. Martin (P) was informed of the District's (D) decision not to renew her contract unless she complied. She was given an opportunity to appear before the District (D) to challenge the decision. Further, the District (D) only conditioned renewal of Martin's (P) contract on compliance, not continued employment under the contract already in force. Thus, the District (D) violated neither Martin's (P) procedural nor substantive due process rights. Finally, the prospect of nonrenewal applied uniformly to teachers who refused to comply with a requirement that bore a rational relationship to the District's (D) objective; therefore, there was no equal protection violation. Reversed.

**COMMENT:** *Harrah* was a **unanimous** decision that illustrates that even tenured teachers' rights are subject to regulations aimed at promoting a legitimate educational interest. The ruling finds support in earlier decisions allowing the dismissal of tenured teachers for insubordination (defined as "a willful disregard of express or implied directions of the employer and a refusal to obey reasonable orders"). The District (D) order in *Harrah* was reasonable because it clearly served the legitimate state interest in providing high-quality education. In applying an equal protection argument, the Court required only a reasonable relationship to a state interest because the continuing education requirement did not infringe a fundamental right and thus did not demand the higher strict scrutiny standard.

## Discussion Questions

1. After Martin's renewal has been denied, does she have any expectation of future employment?

2. Does this case contradict the general assumption that tenured teachers can never be denied renewal?

3. Can Martin comply with the requirement and return to her position with or without her tenure?

---

# WARDS COVE PACKING COMPANY, INC. V. ATONIO 490 U.S. 642, 109 S. CT. 2115 (1989)

**GENERAL RULE OF LAW:** In employment cases, a comparison of the racial composition of qualified persons in the labor market and persons holding the at-issue jobs is the proper inquiry under disparate impact analysis.

**PROCEDURE SUMMARY:**

**Plaintiff:** Atonio (P), a nonwhite former cannery worker

**Defendant:** Wards Cove Packing Company, Inc. (D), employer

**U.S. District Court Decision:** Held for Wards Cove (D), finding no racial discrimination

**U.S. Court of Appeals Decision:** Reversed, finding that Atonio (P) had made a prima facie case of disparate impact

**U.S. Supreme Court Decision:** Reversed

**FACTS:** Certain canneries generally had two job classifications: cannery jobs and noncannery jobs. The cannery jobs were filled primarily by nonwhite workers. The noncannery jobs were predominantly filled by white workers. Atonio (P), a nonwhite former cannery job worker, filed suit against Wards Cove (D), alleging that its racially discriminatory hiring and promotion practices had a disparate impact in violation of Title VII of the Civil Rights Act of 1964. (A disparate impact is "the adverse effect of a facially neutral practice . . . that nonetheless discriminates against persons because of their race, sex, national origin, age, or disability and that is not justified by a business necessity.")[17] The district court held for Wards Cove (D), finding that the overrepresentation of nonwhite workers in the cannery jobs was because most of the cannery jobs were filled through a contract with a predominantly nonwhite union. The court of appeals reversed, holding that the statistics showing a high percentage of nonwhite workers in cannery jobs and a low percentage of such workers in noncannery jobs made a prima facie case of disparate impact. The U.S. Supreme Court granted review.

**ISSUE:** Is a comparison of the racial composition of qualified persons in the labor market and persons holding the at-issue jobs the proper inquiry in disparate impact analysis?

**HOLDING AND DECISION:** (White, J.) Yes. The comparison of the racial composition of qualified persons in the labor market and persons holding the at-issue jobs is the proper inquiry in disparate impact analysis. The court of appeals erred in holding that a comparison of the percentage of nonwhite cannery workers and the percentage of nonwhite noncannery workers may make out a prima facie disparate impact case. Under the correct rule, Wards Cove's (D) hiring and promotional practices cannot be said to have had a disparate impact on nonwhites if there was not a sufficient population of nonwhites who were qualified to hold noncannery jobs. Essentially, whites are disparately hired for noncannery positions because there are more whites in the market who are qualified for these noncannery positions. Under the court of appeals' approach, an employer could be made to defend its hiring and promotion practices any time a segment of its workforce was racially imbalanced. Reversed.

**COMMENT:** *Wards Cove* clarifies what exactly must be shown to establish a disparate impact claim under Title VII. No longer is it sufficient to simply show that the percentage of minorities in a particular job is less than the percentage of minorities in the population of the locality; it must also be demonstrated that there was a sufficient population of qualified minority workers. The Court's definition of the relevant comparison inquiry more narrowly tailors remedial efforts to the actual discriminatory acts or actors causing the need for the remedial efforts. Portions of this decision, which modified *Griggs,* were reinstated by Congress. As a public policy position, Congress wanted the more traditional Title VII analysis upon which *Griggs* was based.

## Discussion Questions

1. Wards Cove (D) stated that it filled its cannery vacancies through contracts with a predominantly nonwhite union, thus ensuring the employment of workers who were also nonwhite. Would there have been more of a racial balance if the contracting workers were diverse?

2. What is the importance of using a comparison of the racial composition of qualified persons in the labor market and persons holding the positions?

3. What is meant by using a "disparate impact" analysis?

# E.E.O.C. V. KAMEHAMEHA SCHOOLS/BISHOP ESTATE 990 F.2D 458 (9TH CIR. 1993)

**GENERAL RULE OF LAW:** A school cannot require that a teacher be of a specific religious denomination unless adherence to that faith is essential to the performance of the job.

**PROCEDURE SUMMARY:**

**Plaintiff:** E.E.O.C. (P)

**Defendant:** Kamehameha Schools (D)

**State District Court Decision:** Held for Kamehameha Schools (D)

**U.S. Court of Appeals Decision:** Reversed and remanded

**FACTS:** In 1884, at the time of her death, Bernice Pauahi Bishop was a member of the Hawaiian royal family. She was the largest landowner in Hawaii. Her Will established two schools (D) on the Hawaiian Islands; while both were boarding and day schools, one was for boys and the other for girls. The Will also stated that "the teachers of said school shall forever be persons of the Protestant religion." More than 100 years later, Carole Edgerton applied to the school to be a substitute French teacher. She was informed of the Protestant-only requirement. Edgerton filed a charge of religious discrimination with the E.E.O.C. (P).

**ISSUE:** May a school require a teacher to be of a specific religion even though religion has no relationship to the teacher's ability to perform the job of teaching secular subjects?

**HOLDING AND DECISION:** No. The Title VII exemption for religious educational institutions did not apply, neither did the religious curriculum exemption, nor was the adherence to the Protestant faith a bona fide occupational qualification for teaching at the schools. Kamehameha Schools (D) were chartered not as a religious organization, but as a nonprofit organization. The Schools (D) shifted from their 1955 standard of "developing in students an attitude of worship and reverence" to their 1989 standard of "students will be expected to develop to the best of his ability; skills needed to relate positively to self and others, maintain health, continue learning, enrich existence, and participate in contemporary society for a rewarding life." This shift suggests a secular emphasis. The Schools (D) adhered to the Protestant-only requirement, but teachers in off-campus programs did not have that requirement. The student body, on and off campus, did not constitute a Protestant majority. In fact, less than a third of its boarding and day school students were Protestant. Further, the religious curriculum for grades K–6 provided an overall Christian emphasis, but not exclusively Protestant. In the upper grades, students took comparative religion classes. Thus, requiring that teachers be Protestant was unfounded when a Protestant requirement did not exist anywhere else.

**COMMENTS:** The court's reasoning was that except for the Schools' (D) religion teachers, who had a bona fide occupational qualification under Title VII, all other teachers at the Schools (D) provided instruction in the traditional secular manner. There was insufficient evidence that adherence to the Protestant faith was essential to the performance of the teaching position. Three sections of the Civil Rights Act of 1964 were analyzed in light of the facts of the case. Although there were comparative religious studies, scheduled prayers and services, Bible verses in the school publication, and a hiring preference for Protestant teachers, the court felt that these factors were insufficient to trigger the religious educational institution exception. The religious curriculum exemption was also not appropriate because courses about religion and a general effort to teach good values do not constitute a curriculum that propagates religion, especially when the schools formally disclaim any attempt to convert non-Protestant students. Finally, the bona fide occupational qualification (BFOQ) exception was not appropriate when both the E.E.O.C. (P) and the Schools (D) stipulated that there was nothing "specific about the subject matter of any given teacher position . . . that would make a teacher being Protestant a bona fide occupational qualification."

## Discussion Questions

1. Taking a moral position, explain the wishes of the deceased Bernice Pauahi Bishop and the legality of her Will. How would you explain to her family members that being Protestant can no longer be a requirement to teach at Kamehameha Schools?

2. The Kamehameha Schools were chartered not as a religious organization, but as a nonprofit organization. Compare the schools' 1955 standard to their updated 1989 standard.

3. After considering this case, suggest changes that could make being a Protestant essential for job performance at the Kamehameha Schools.

# GRIGGS V. DUKE POWER CO.
# 401 U.S. 424, 91 S. CT. 849 (1971)

**GENERAL RULE OF LAW:** Employment standards that do not significantly relate to job performance violate the Civil Rights Act if they tend to exclude minority applicants.

**PROCEDURE SUMMARY:**

**Plaintiffs:** Job applicants at Duke Power Co. (P)

**Defendant:** Duke Power Co. (D), employer

**U.S. District Court Decision:** Held for Duke Power Co. (D)

**U.S. Court of Appeals Decision:** Reversed, in part

**U.S. Supreme Court Decision:** Reversed, holding for (P)

**FACTS:** Duke Power Co. (D), as part of its hiring process, required a high school diploma and administered an intelligence test if an employee desired a transfer or promotion. No evidence existed that either criterion was indicative of job performance for the employment positions at issue. African American Black applicants statistically performed worse than whites in both categories. A group of African American black applicants (P) challenged the standards in district court as a violation of the 1964 Civil Rights Act. The court of appeals held the standard valid, and the Supreme Court granted review.

**ISSUE:** Do employment standards that do not significantly relate to job performance violate the Civil Rights Act if they tend to exclude minority applicants?

**HOLDING AND DECISION:** (Burger, C. J.) Yes. Employment standards that do not significantly relate to job performance violate the Civil Rights Act if they tend to exclude minority applicants. The Civil Rights Act proscribes employment practices that exclude minority groups that have been victims of employment discrimination. A practice need not have a discriminatory intent; a discriminatory result is sufficient. If a challenged practice does not have a discriminatory intent and bears a significant relation to job performance, then it will not violate the Act. Here, however, no such showing was made. Therefore, the discriminatory impact was sufficient to implicate the Civil Rights Act. Reversed.

**COMMENT:** The Civil Rights Act is broader than the Constitution in two significant ways. The Constitution only acts as a restraint on government; the Act regulates private conduct as well. Further, the Act, unlike the Constitution, is not limited to intentional discrimination. Both differences were relevant to this case, for without the protection of the Civil Rights Act, the Constitution alone would probably not have been enough for the job applicants to prevail in this case. The holding in this case was limited significantly by *Wards Cove Packing Company, Inc. v. Atonio* (1989), by shifting the burden of proof from employers to employees. Recent congressional action has reinstated the Title VII protection enunciated in *Griggs*. This case also has significance for the study of teacher and administrator employment practices. It was in *Griggs* that the Court stated that broad and general testing is inadequate and cannot be used as the controlling factor unless it is a reasonable measure of job performance. This finding was used in *United States v. State of South Carolina* (1978), where it was held that the state's use of test scores for certification and salary purposes did not violate Title VII of the Civil Rights Act of 1964. Care must be exercised to distinguish between a court's use of a Title VII Civil Rights Act analysis and a Fourteenth Amendment equal protection analysis. Title VII prohibits the use of tests and diploma requirements when they operate to disqualify a disproportionate number of members of minority groups—unless the test and diploma requirements are directly indicative of job performance. In *Griggs,* the requirements were not shown to be directly related to job performance and were, therefore, invalid. Thus, an employer must be able to establish a direct correlation between whatever skill is being tested and performance on the job.

## Discussion Questions

1. Explain the relationship between Title VII of the Civil Rights Act and the Fourteenth Amendment equal protection clause.

2. After reading this case, pretend you are a manager of a manufacturing plant. Consider your hiring practices and requirements as well as how you post your vacancies. As the manager, would you consider giving a written general test (including asking applicants to write two paragraphs explaining how their transfer and/or promotion would contribute to the manufacturing plant) and a hands-on job performance/skills test for each employee wanting a job change?

3. A passing score on a standardized test is required to teach in the state of Ohio. The format may consist of a two-part general education test; tests relating to specific grades; and/or tests relating to specific areas such as science, counseling, special education, and so on. Consider this requirement in light of both *Griggs* and *United States v. State of South Carolina*.

---

Additional case briefs can be found on the SAGE Web site at the following address:
http://www.sagepub.com/aquilacasebriefs

---

# NOTES

1. See Cleveland Board of Ed. v. LaFleur, 414 U.S. 632 (1974).
2. Clarke v. Shoreline School District No. 412, King County, 729 P.2d 793 (Wash. 1986).
3. See Griggs v. Duke Power Co., 401 U.S. 424 (1971).
4. See Wards Cove Packing Company, Inc. v. Atonio, 490 U.S. 642 (1989).

5.  See E.E.O.C. v. Kamehameha Schools/Bishop Estate, 990 F. 2d 458 (9th Cir. 1993).

6.  See Harrah Independent School District v. Martin, 440 U.S. 194 (1979).

7.  Restatement (Second) of Contracts, § 71 (1981).

8.  See Amador v. New Mexico State Board of Education, 80 N.M. 336 (1969).

9.  See United States v. State of South Carolina, 445 F.Supp. 1094 (1978).

10.  Ambach v. Norwick, 441 U.S. 68, 99 S. Ct. 1589 (1979).

11.  See Oklahoma ex rel. Thompson v. Ekberg, 613 P.2d 466 (1980).

12.  See Cleveland Board of Ed. v. LaFleur, 414 U.S. 632 (1974).

13.  See Griggs v. Duke Power Co., 401 U.S. 424 (1971).

14.  See Wards Cove Packing Company, Inc. v. Atonio, 490 U.S. 642 (1989) (racial imbalance); Marshall v. Kirkland, 602 F.2d 1282 (8th Cir. 1979) (racial discrimination); and Geller v. Markham, 635 F.2d 1027 (2d Cir. 1980), *cert. den.,* 451 U.S. 945 (1981) (age discrimination).

15.  See E.E.O.C. v. Kamehameha Schools/Bishop Estate, 990 F. 2d 458 (9th Cir. 1993).

16.  See Harrah Independent School District v. Martin, 440 U.S. 194 (1979).

17.  *Black's law dictionary* (2nd pocket ed.). (2001). Eagan, MN: West.

# 11

# Collective Bargaining

*Employees not only have a right to join labor unions, but also may file suit for damages and injunctive relief under the Civil Rights Act of 1871 if this freedom is denied.*

—*AFSCME v. Woodward* (1969)[1]

## OVERVIEW · · · · · · · · · · · · · · · · · · · · · · · · · · · · · · · · · · · · · · · · · · · · · · · · · ·

Aside from issues pertaining to certification, contractual relations, and cessation of employment through termination or retirement, teachers are also concerned with the primary manner in which their contractual rights and responsibilities are determined—a process known as collective bargaining—and with the manner in which their salaries, assignments, and leaves are determined. Labor law in education includes collective bargaining, strikes, wages, hours, and working conditions.

At the beginning of the twentieth century, industries needed the farm workers who had no history of unionization. Owners had great power and exploited workers had low salaries and little, if any, job protection. In the private sector, there was a history of violence resulting in strikes and conflict between labor and management. During the Depression, Congress, led by President Franklin Roosevelt, used the commerce clause power (Article 1, § 8 of the Constitution) to pass the National Labor Relations Act (Wagner Act). Prior to the Wagner Act, labor relations were governed by the common law. However, this Act revolutionized labor relations in America. In addition to giving private workers the right to organize and bargain, it created the National Labor Relations Board to oversee the process of union certification, meetings, and investigation of unfair labor practices. Union power continued to grow, engendering public concern with the coal miners strike in 1943 that shut down the steel mills for several weeks. After World War II, organized labor conducted a series of strikes against almost all major industries. In 1946, when John L. Lewis led the mineworkers to strike for a second time, President Truman declared a national emergency and broke the strike by taking over the mines. Public sentiment shifted away from labor protection, resulting in the passage of the Taft-Hartley Act, which leveled the labor-management playing field. As a result of concern regarding union activities in the private sector, many states passed laws making public employee strikes illegal.

The public sector lagged far behind the private sector in their unionizing efforts. Public service was initially seen as a calling with pay incidental to providing a public service. The general attitude was stated by then-Massachusetts Governor Calvin Coolidge, who said, "There is no right to strike against the public safety by anyone, at any time." For many years, the attitude about any public sector strike was that it was unthinkable and intolerable. Although unions were viewed unfavorably by the general public, teachers did organize and even strike as unrest amongst teachers continued to escalate. The critical year when everything seemed to change regarding public sector bargaining was 1961. Albert Shanker and the New York Federation of Teachers won the right to serve as exclusive representative of New York teachers soon after the mayor claimed that there were no funds for teacher raises. However, after the mayor claimed this lack of funds, the city spent $14 million in overtime wages digging itself out of a blizzard. In 1961, Shanker took the New York teachers out on strike, eventually being arrested and jailed until the strike was finally settled. Shanker's strike won significant gains for teachers. These successes led to a major attitude change within the largest teachers' group, the National Education Association, as the success of a teachers' union forced a more aggressive posture.

Strange things happened when state teacher associations that had been dominated by school administrators and school board members began to lead militant collective bargaining actions. As collective bargaining became militant and contentious, administrators and board members felt totally out of place with these aggressive tactics, so they eventually left the teacher groups and formed their own state school board and administrative associations. School board members and school administrators were often angry and bitter as their authority was threatened when teacher groups (unions and associations) gained power and demanded shared decision making with school boards. In 1962, President Kennedy's famous Executive Order 10988 gave federal employees the right to organize and negotiate—but not to strike—eventually leading to state governments granting the same right to state employees. That same year, Wisconsin passed the first collective bargaining Act for public employees (teachers and police officers, among others). Eventually, most states passed similar laws patterned after the National Labor Relations Act.

The intent of these state collective bargaining laws was to promote constructive and orderly relationships between public employers and their employees. Today, few states still retain the old model of "meet and confer" that gives school boards control over the collective bargaining process. In the last quarter of the twentieth century, while private sector union membership declined appreciably, there was a significant increase in public sector union membership, especially in education. More than 80% of all teachers are unionized, with more than 2 million teachers in the National Education Association and one-half million affiliated with the American Federation of Teachers.

## Case Study

### Free Rider

A new teacher was hired by a public school district. At the time this teacher was hired, the teacher indicated that she had strong religious convictions that precluded her from joining the teachers' union. She was especially opposed to the teacher union's advocacy activities that conflicted with her religious convictions. After she was hired, when she was asked to join the union, she refused to join or to participate and also refused to pay any union dues whatsoever. Because the union advocates and obtains benefits for all members, the union felt that the teacher must pay the entire dues amount that a regular member pays. Alternatively, the union argued, even if the full amount of union dues was not required, a fair share must be paid. The teacher countered that the full amount of union dues would be tithed to her church, and she should not be required to support a teachers' union's political or advocacy activities. You are hired to settle this matter.

### Discussion Questions

1. What are the arguments for both sides?

2. What questions need to be answered before proceeding?

3. Who will prevail? Why?

4. How would you determine a fair share?

# IMPORTANT CONCEPTS

- **Union membership is lawful:** Teachers may legally maintain memberships in associations that are organized with respect to occupational interests.

- **State law genesis:** Collective bargaining is a creature of the state legislature; a majority of the states have granted some form of collective bargaining rights to their public employees.

- **Promotion of better labor-management relations:** Congress first granted private sector employees the right to bargain collectively in order to promote better labor-management relations. Today, state statutes that provide for public sector bargaining reflect the experiences of the private sector.

(Continued)

(Continued)

- **Public and private sectors differ:** However, public sector practices differ from those of the private sector in several respects: Often, public employees have no right to strike and are subject to various public budget-related restrictions; on the other hand, they, unlike their private sector counterparts, have inherent (constitutional) rights to equal protection and due process in the face of arbitrary government action.

- **Most issues must be bargained:** A majority of collective bargaining statutes mandate mutual bargaining between school boards and employee organizations, with certain exceptions carved out for those matters that touch upon "exclusive management rights."

- **State law governs:** The scope of required bargaining is governed expressly by state legislation or is implied from that legislation.

- **Some bargaining is at the will of school board:** Some states permit local school boards to engage in permissive bargaining (i.e., selective bargaining by choice, not by mandate).

- **Some items cannot be bargained:** Certain matters are nonnegotiable (i.e., not proper subjects of collective bargaining) because they implicate public policy or are matters over which a local board must be available to exercise instant discretion.

- **A few states permit consultations only:** A minority of states restrict all negotiations to "meet and discuss" consultations only, with ultimate decision-making authority left to local school boards.

- **Hands-off approach of the courts:** Because the majority of courts view collective bargaining as a province of the state legislature, their role has been limited to interpreting state statutes and constitutional provisions.

- **No right to strike:** The constitutional right to form and join labor unions does not supersede the common law barrier to public employee strikes (now codified in state statutes).

- **Use of injunctions to suppress strikes:** Where teacher strikes are prohibited, local school boards may seek to enjoin teachers from striking when presented with a legitimate threat of strike.

- **May not interrupt school functions:** Job actions, such as picketing, collective submission of resignations, and collective absences, may be restrained when they impede school functions or cause others to breach their contracts with school officials.

- **Inability to compromise:** An impasse in negotiations arises when an agreement cannot be reached and neither party is willing to compromise.

- **Dispute resolution tools are available:** Mediation; fact finding; and, ultimately, binding arbitration are the dispute resolution options that are available to parties that have reached an impasse.

- **All covered employees must pay fees or dues:** All employees in a bargaining unit must, as a condition of employment, either pay union dues as union members or pay a nonmember "agency fee" for representation.

# THE COLLECTIVE BARGAINING PROCESS

Public employers, such as local school boards, engage in collective negotiations with teachers' representatives in order to reach agreement as to the various rights and responsibilities of the parties. Most state legislatures have enacted laws that govern what is commonly referred to as the "collective bargaining process."

## Historical Overview

Traditionally, local school boards maintained total control over public school operations, including the hiring of personnel. This was in keeping with the notion that government, as sovereign, was immune from or "above" the forces presented by competing interests. In the 1960s, teachers sought a greater voice in the management and operations of their school systems. They turned to collective group action as a means of asserting their interests. The New York City teachers' strike, led by Albert Shanker, triggered a more aggressive posture. Public employees, such as teachers, may legally maintain memberships in associations that are organized with respect to occupational interests. A majority of states have now granted some form of collective bargaining rights to their public employees.

## Public Versus Private Sector Bargaining

Prior to 1932, labor relations in all sectors were governed by the common law. Courts favored management and readily used their injunctive powers to suppress strikes and boycotts. In 1932, Congress passed the Norris-LaGuardia Act for the primary purpose of preventing federal courts from enjoining union activities that arose out of labor disputes. Three years later, Congress passed the National Labor Relations Act of 1935 (NLRA), commonly referred to as the Wagner Act. The NLRA specifically encouraged collective bargaining as a means of promoting good management-labor relations. The NLRA also established the National Labor Relations Board, whose purpose was to remedy unfair labor practices.

Finally, the NLRA also created a procedure for determining the nature and extent of employee representation and placed a duty on both parties to bargain in good faith. In 1947, the NLRA was amended by the Labor Management Relations Act, commonly referred to as the Taft-Hartley Act. The Taft-Hartley Act, in turn, was amended by the Labor Management Reporting and Disclosure Act of 1959 (LMRDA). Both sets of laws placed limitations on union practices and activities following the widespread union mismanagement and corruption of the 1950s. Additionally, the LMRDA expressly provided for various rights of employees in the face of union abuses, established union election procedures, and established penalties for misappropriation of union funds.

Today, state statutes governing public sector bargaining reflect the experiences of the private sector, as evidenced in widespread rules pertaining to the scope of bargaining and employee representation procedures. Despite their similarities, public sector practices differ from those of the private sector in several fundamental respects. With only a few exceptions, U.S. voters, through their legislatures, have rejected the right of public school teachers to strike. Such laws are in conflict with the standard labor maxim that a party cannot fully negotiate unless it has the ability to reject the terms it has been offered. The public sector bargaining process is also limited by state and local budgets and various tax code restrictions.

However, unlike their private sector counterparts, public sector employees have inherent (constitutional) rights to equal protection and due process in the face of arbitrary government action. Further, state statutes commonly provide other protections, such as from discriminatory practices.

## The Scope of Collective Bargaining

State legislatures set the ground rules concerning the scope of the public sector bargaining process. Look to state statutes for an understanding of these three key issues: (1) In what areas can (or must) a local board refuse to negotiate? (2) In what areas must bargaining continue until both sides reach agreement? and (3) In what areas will bargaining be prohibited (i.e., when will "discussions" of issues alone be permitted prior to unilateral board decisions)? Essentially, school boards are required to bargain in good faith with teacher unions on matters relating to teacher employment and the fulfillment of professional duties.[2] In most states, collective bargaining statutes mandate mutual bargaining by local boards, with certain exceptions being carved out for those matters that touch upon "exclusive management rights." The scope of required bargaining is governed expressly by legislation or is implied from that legislation. In some states, local boards may engage in permissive bargaining (i.e., selective bargaining by choice, not by mandate).

For example, as of this writing, class size is not identified as a mandatory bargaining item in any state's laws. In several states, it is a permitted subject of bargaining. In other states, class size must be "discussed" during negotiations, but there is no requirement that the parties reach a negotiated settlement on the issue. In at least one state, it is viewed as a nonnegotiable item due to its policy ramifications. The negotiation of significant aspects of teacher performance evaluations is generally a permissible subject of bargaining. However, when performance evaluations are viewed as a condition of teacher performance, they may be held to be a mandatory bargaining subject.

Such matters as determinations of the school calendar, reductions in teacher workforce, oversight of the teacher assignment and transfer process, and the granting of tenure are not proper collective bargaining subjects. They are viewed as nonnegotiable items because they implicate public education policy or touch upon matters with respect to which a local board must be available to exercise instant discretion. A minority of states restrict all negotiations to "meet and discuss" consultations only, with ultimate decision-making authority left to local school boards. Because the majority of courts view collective bargaining as completely within legislative authority, their role has been limited to interpreting state statutes and constitutional provisions. When a state chooses not to mandate collective bargaining, courts will not compel school boards to negotiate with employee representatives. However, once a school board has extended recognition to qualified bargaining agents and has begun the bargaining process, the board's (and bargaining agents') actions may be subjected to judicial scrutiny.

## Teacher Strikes, Job Actions, and Impasses in Negotiations

### Strikes

The constitutional right to form and join labor unions does not confer a right to strike. There has always been a common law barrier to teacher strikes, based upon the principle that teachers are government employees and that a strike against government cannot be tolerated. In many states, the common law prohibition against teacher strikes is codified in state statutes. Some states allow for a limited right to strike, so long as certain conditions have been met (such as completion of the mediation and fact-finding process, written notice of an intent to strike, and the proffering of evidence that a strike will not endanger public health or safety). Where teacher strikes are prohibited, local school boards may seek to enjoin teachers from striking when presented with a legitimate threat of strike. Punishments for violations of court orders include fines, imprisonment of labor leaders for contempt, and dismissal of striking teachers.

### Job Actions

Picketing, even when peaceful in nature, may be prohibited if it impedes school functions or causes others to breach their contracts with school officials. Concerted submissions of resignations may lead to sanctions if it is determined this action interrupts services and therefore prevents a local board from fulfilling its duty to the public. Teacher absences unrelated to teaching functions may constitute a strike and serve as grounds for teacher dismissal.

### Impasses in Negotiations

An impasse in negotiations arises when an agreement cannot be reached and neither party is willing to compromise. When the parties reach an impasse, the following dispute resolution options are frequently available:

1. *Mediation.* A neutral person assists the parties to reach an agreement. The mediator is chosen jointly by the negotiating parties.

2. *Fact-finding.* A neutral third party investigates the causes of the dispute and offers solutions. Proposed solutions are not binding on either party. Fact-finding is usually chosen only after mediation has failed.

3. *Binding arbitration.* Similar to fact-finding, with the exception that the decision of the neutral arbitrator is binding on both parties.

## The Perpetuation of Teacher Unions

### Dues and Mandatory Fees

Unions depend on membership dues and, additionally, on the mandatory financial support of those nonmembers who benefit from union negotiations to the same extent as union members. The practical effect is that *all* employees in the bargaining unit must, as a condition of employment, either pay union dues as union members or pay a nonmember "agency fee" for representation. In 1977, the U.S. Supreme Court upheld the payment of agency fees by nonmembers as a means of promoting labor peace and eliminating so-called "free riders."[3] Fees assessed to nonmembers must be used to cover the costs of providing representation services only. They may not be used to pay for the costs of promoting political causes that are unrelated to representation.[4]

### Exclusive Privileges

Unions also perpetuate themselves through privileges gained by virtue of being the sole or majority bargaining agents for a group or groups of employees. Such privileges include dues check off, exclusive access to school facilities, and exclusive use of the school mail system. The result is that majority unions are strengthened, and minority unions find it more difficult to survive.

---

## Case Study

### Is Tenure Worth a Urinalysis Exam?

As superintendent, you must implement the new policy of the school board, which has voted to require all probationary teachers who are up for tenure to submit to a urinalysis examination. The school board concedes that the purpose of the examination is to ascertain the use of illegal drugs. You fear that the teachers' union will sue to prohibit the examination, contending that it is unconstitutional and constitutes an unreasonable search and seizure. The issue is whether compulsory drug testing of employees constitutes an unreasonable search and seizure in violation of state and federal constitutions, in the absence of reasonable suspicion. Because of your doubts, you have some concerns which need to be addressed.

### Discussion Questions

1. Isn't urine simply a waste product in which an individual can have no reasonable expectation of privacy, and thus the collection of the urine sample does not involve invading an individual's bodily integrity?

2. Because a school board has a legitimate interest in ensuring that its teachers are fit for the classroom, is it not reasonable to require them to submit to an additional test to determine their fitness prior to making a decision on tenure, which is essentially a million-dollar commitment for the school district?

3. Who should succeed in this situation?

---

## CONCLUSION . . . . . . . . . . . . . . . . . . . . . . . . . . . . . . .

In the past, public employers, such as school boards, maintained total control over public school operations. In the 1960s, teachers began pushing for a right to collectively organize and bargain. A majority of states have now granted some form of collective bargaining rights to public employees. Nevertheless, in many states public school teachers are statutorily prohibited from striking. The public sector bargaining process is also limited by state and local budgets and various tax code restrictions.

Regardless of the state, state statutes set the ground rules for collective bargaining. School boards are required to bargain in good faith with teacher unions on matters relating to teacher employment and the fulfillment of professional duties. Picketing, even when peaceful in nature, may be enjoined if it impedes school functions or causes others to breach their contracts with school officials. Unless precluded by a state statute, if the parties reach an impasse in bargaining, they may proceed to mediation, to a fact-finding inquiry, or to binding arbitration.

Members of teachers' unions generally must pay a fee. Even nonmembers who benefit from union negotiations are required to pay an "agency fee." School boards are usually free to set teachers' salaries according to a tenure scale. Also, school boards generally have discretion to require a teacher to accept an assignment that he is competent to undertake. Although rarely required, limited loyalty oaths may be required by school boards, generally indicating that the teacher has not engaged in certain prohibited activities prior to employment. Further, teachers' speech in the classroom, when personal in nature, may not be entitled to First Amendment protection.

Because teacher employment issues implicate many constitutional issues, the cases that follow will address the basic employment rights of teachers. Since public school teachers are employed by the state government, a variety of constitutional issues are raised in relation to their employment.

# CASE BRIEFS . . . . . . . . . . . . . . . . . . . . . . . .

## ABOOD V. DETROIT BOARD OF EDUCATION
## 431 U.S. 209, 97 S. CT. 1782 (1977)·

**GENERAL RULE OF LAW:** A union's expenditures for ideological causes not germane to its duties as a collective bargaining representative must be financed from dues or assessments paid by employees who do not object to advancing such causes and who are not coerced into doing so.

**PROCEDURE SUMMARY:**

**Plaintiffs:** D. Louis Abood (P) and nonunion teachers

**Defendant:** Detroit Board of Education (Board) (D)

**State Trial Court Decision:** Granted Board's (D) motion for summary judgment

**State Court of Appeals Decision:** Reversed trial court's retroactive application of 1973 agency shop clause and remanded

**State Supreme Court Decision:** Denied review

**U.S. Supreme Court Decision:** Vacated and remanded for further review by the trial court

**FACTS:** In 1967, the Detroit Federation of Teachers (Union) became "the exclusive representative of teachers employed by the Detroit Board of Education." A collective bargaining agreement between the Board (D) and the Union, effective from July 1, 1969, to July 1, 1971, contained an "agency shop" provision. This provision required nonunion employees to pay the Union a service charge equal to a Union member's regular dues. While the agreement did not require teachers to join the Union, a nonunion employee who neglected to pay the service charge was subject to discharge. In an action filed in state court, Abood (P) challenged the constitutionality of the agency shop clause by contending that it violated her rights under the First and Fourteenth Amendments because the Union was engaging in various political and other ideological activities that Abood (P) did not approve of and that were not collective bargaining activities.

**ISSUE:** Do union expenditures not germane to the union's primary functions necessarily violate the constitutional First and Fourteenth Amendment rights of employees who have contributed to the union treasury and who object to such expenditures?

**HOLDING AND DECISION:** (Stewart, J.) Yes. In general, agency shop provisions are constitutionally valid. As stated in *Railway Employees' Department v. Hanson* (1956) and *Machinists v. Street* (1961), Congress determined that unions can require nonunion members to share the costs of benefits afforded to them by the collective bargaining agency.[5] These benefits justify any constitutional infringement on those employees. Even though public employees differ from their private counterparts in regard to "the special character of the employer," and different types of collective bargaining occur in the two spheres, those differences do not necessarily translate into differences in First Amendment rights. Public employees do not incur a greater infringement of their constitutional rights; they are still free to express their opposing viewpoints in public or private, to vote in accordance with their convictions, and to participate in a full range of political activities open to other citizens. In *Hanson* the court noted, however, that unions could not require payment by nonunion members for expenses outside the scope of collective bargaining because such expenditures were not recognized by Congress as justifying this type of constitutional infringement. The *Street* court also concluded that money collected by a union could not be used to support political ideologies because Congress did not state that this type of expenditure was justified by the union shop agreement. A union can use its money for purposes "not germane to its duties as collective bargaining representative" only if the union uses the dues of employees who do not object to expenditures for those ideological causes or who are not coerced into doing so. Thus, a cause of action under the First and Fourteenth Amendments exists in this case if allegations concerning misuse or extortion can be proven. If so, two possible remedies exist: an injunction preventing expenses from being financed by opposing parties, or restitution.

**COMMENT:** Although different types of collective bargaining take place in the public and private sectors, the difference does not result in a greater infringement on public employees' constitutional rights. The Court pointed out that the public sector's collective bargaining was inherently political. In a concurring opinion, Justice Rehnquist questioned whether a public employee, as protected here by the First and Fourteenth Amendments, could truly "believe as he will and act and associate according to [personal] beliefs" when affected by an agency shop provision. Justice Stevens pointed out that remedies in these situations were determined on a case-by-case basis. Later cases would seem to support this position. Justice Powell commented that the majority opinion overturned two legal principles. Prior to this decision, Justice Powell argued, the First Amendment protected union members by allowing them to withhold money from public unions if they opposed the ideological causes the money was to be spent on. With this decision, however, the ability to withhold funding depends on whether or not the expenditure is related to collective bargaining. Second, Justice Powell pointed out that, prior to this decision, the state had the burden of proving that overriding state interests justified its action. According to Justice Powell, the Court has now reversed this principle. As a result, an employee claiming infringement of his First Amendment rights by a union in its spending practices bears the burden of proof. In other words, the employee must prove the union has spent funds in ways not related to collective bargaining.

## Discussion Questions

1. Are agency shop (required membership) provisions generally constitutionally valid?
2. Why are public employees different from private employees?
3. What activities can a union permissibly spend its nonmember dues promoting? What activities aren't permissible for the use of nonmember dues?
4. Why is it still constitutionally permissible for unions to collect dues from nonmembers?

# KENAI PENIN. BOR. SCH. DIST. AND KENAI PENIN. BOR. V. KENAI PENIN. ED. ASSN.
## 572 P.2D 416 (1977)

**GENERAL RULE OF LAW:** School districts are required to bargain collectively in good faith with teachers' unions on matters pertaining to employment and professional duty.

**PROCEDURE SUMMARY:**

**Plaintiffs:** Kenai Peninsula Education Assn. (Union) (P); Anchorage Borough Education Assn. (Union) (P), both teachers' unions; Matanuska-Susitna School Dist. (Board) (P), a school board

**Defendants:** Kenai Peninsula Borough School Dist. (Board) (D); Anchorage Borough School Dist. (Board) (D), both school boards; Matanuska-Susitna Education Assn. (Union) (D), a teachers' union.

**State Trial Court Decision:** Held for the Union (P) in one action, for the Board in another, and split on various issues in the third

**State Supreme Court Decision:** Affirmed in part, reversed in part

**FACTS:** This decision comprises three separate cases involving the same or similar issues. In the first two cases, the Unions (P) sued the Boards (D) to compel collective bargaining in good faith. In the third case, the Board (P) sought a **declaratory judgment** that certain issues were not negotiable. In all three cases, the Boards contended that submitting educational policies to a good faith collective bargaining requirement would remove the final decisions on such matters from the Boards, contrary to legislative intent. They argued that delegating any decision-making power on educational policy to labor unions would be unconstitutional because a teachers' union is a private organization and thus unaccountable to the public. The Unions countered that such delegation is perfectly proper, as there is no delegation of decision-making power inherent in a labor negotiations requirement. Furthermore, they claimed to represent professional employees, whose participation in negotiations was sanctioned by the legislature as professional advice to the Boards. Finally, Alaskan statutes on collective bargaining should be interpreted broadly, the Unions argued, because they are more comprehensive than those found elsewhere. The trial courts ruled in the Union's favor in the Kenai case, in the Board's favor in the Anchorage case, and for the Board on some issues and for the Union on others in the Matanuska-Susitna case. The subsequent three appeals were consolidated.

**ISSUE:** Are school boards required to bargain collectively in good faith with teachers' unions on matters pertaining to their employment and the fulfillment of their professional duties?

**HOLDING AND DECISION:** (Connor, J.) Yes. School boards must bargain collectively in good faith with teachers' unions "on matters pertaining to their employment and the fulfillment of their professional duties." By statute, school boards, as public sector employers, must negotiate with unions; however, the boards need not accept any union proposal. Statutes did not delegate sole decision-making power to either the union or the board. Since the power to delegate depends on the interpretation of statutes, case law from other jurisdictions must be examined as an aid to interpretation. Future enactments by the Alaskan legislature must provide specific guidance by stating which items would and would not be negotiable. In the meantime, however, questions concerning salaries, fringe benefits, work hours, and the amount of leave time are so closely connected with the economic well-being of the individual teacher that they must be held negotiable under Alaskan law. On the other hand, permitting teachers' unions to bargain on matters of educational policy could severely erode the autonomy of the school boards. Consequently, the ability of elected officials to perform in the broad public interest would be threatened because teachers' unions might wield too much power over governmental decisions. Therefore, matters affecting educational policy such as planning time, teachers' aides, class size, pupil-teacher ratio, and selection of instructional materials are not negotiable. However, the school boards should continue to meet and confer with the unions regarding these nonnegotiable matters, in order to benefit from their expertise.

**COMMENTS:** In both the private and public sectors, negotiable issues are broad. When collective bargaining involves teachers in the public schools, important issues in labor law and constitutional law may be involved. The trend in collective bargaining, in both the private and public sector, has been to require employers to bargain in good faith. To avoid a finding of bad faith, the parties are required by statutory law to make a reasonable effort to resolve their differences.

## Discussion Questions

1. Although the court decided one way, which side's arguments did you find the most persuasive? Why?

2. What matters did the court find are nonnegotiable? How should both the union and the board address these matters?

3. What matters did the court consider to be negotiable?

4. What do you think might be the possible effects if a school board was forced to accept any union proposals?

# CHICAGO TEACHERS' UNION V. HUDSON 475 U.S. 292, 106 S. CT. 1066 (1986)

**GENERAL RULE OF LAW:** There must be a balance between a union's compulsory subsidization of objectionable ideologies and a union's ability to collect money from all employees for collective bargaining procedures. Thus, the court must balance First Amendment interests against justifiable state limitations while minimizing infringements.

**PROCEDURE SUMMARY:**

**Plaintiffs:** Annie Lee Hudson (P) and other nonunion employees

**Defendant:** Chicago Teachers' Union (Union) (D)

**U.S. District Court Decision:** Held for the Union (D). Any decision should await the findings of the union procedure already invoked by the plaintiffs

**U.S. Court of Appeals Decision:** Reversed. Held the Union's (D) objection procedure and escrow option were inadequate

**U.S. Supreme Court Decision:** Affirmed

**FACTS:** In an effort to solve a "free rider" problem, the Chicago Teachers' Union (D) and the Chicago Board of Education entered into an agreement in 1982. The board agreed to deduct a certain fee from nonunion employees' paychecks, while the Union (D) was authorized to determine the fee. The Union (D) calculated the percentage of expenditures unrelated to collective bargaining. It deducted this amount from the fee assessed to members to arrive at the fee for nonunion employees. The Union (D) also developed a procedure to respond to nonunion employees' objections to the fee deduction. Prior to the fee deduction, no objections could be raised. However, after the deduction was made, a nonmember could object by submitting a letter within 30 days to the Union (D) president. The matter objected to was first reviewed by the Union's (D) executive committee, which would then notify the objector of its decision within 30 days. An objector could appeal this decision to the Union's (D) executive board within another 30 days. If the objector wished to appeal the executive board's decision, he could contact the Union (D) president, who would appoint an arbitrator to handle the dispute at the Union's (D) expense. The only remedies in the event an objection was sustained were a rebate to the objector and immediate reductions in future fees for all nonunion employees. The board approved the above procedure developed by the Union (D) without analyzing it. In December, 1982, deductions from nonunion employee paychecks began. The Union (D) printed a description of the deduction and the grievance procedures in a Union (D) newspaper, but no explanation of the deduction or Union (D) procedures was provided to nonunion employees by the board. Hudson (P) and other nonunion employees wrote objection letters to the Union (D). The Union (D) responded by advising them to follow the Union (D) procedure for objection. Hudson (P) and other nonunion employees filed suit, contending that the Union (D) procedures violated their First and Fourteenth Amendment rights and permitted the Union (D) to use their money for "impermissible purposes." The district court rejected the challenges and upheld the procedure. On appeal, the Union (D) advised the court that it had voluntarily placed all of the dissenters' agency fees in escrow to avoid any danger that their constitutional rights would be violated. Nevertheless, the court of appeals reversed, holding that the procedure was constitutionally inadequate. The Union (D) appealed, and the Supreme Court granted certiorari.

**ISSUE:** (1) Does the Union's (D) original grievance procedure infringe on objectors' First and Fourteenth Amendment rights? (2) Does the Union's (D) self-imposed remedy (i.e., the escrow account) infringe on nonunion objectors' First and Fourteenth Amendment rights?

**HOLDING AND DECISION:** (Stevens, J.) (1) Yes. Under an agency shop agreement (whereby a union may charge nonunion members a fee for acting as their bargaining representative, despite the limited infringement on the nonmembers' constitutional rights), procedural safeguards are necessary to prevent dissenting nonunion employees from being forced to subsidize ideological activities they oppose. At the same time, unions must not be restricted in their ability to require any employee to contribute to the cost of collective bargaining activities. The government interest in labor peace is strong enough to support an "agency shop" arrangement. However, the fact that those rights are protected by the First Amendment requires that the procedure be carefully tailored to minimize First Amendment infringement. Furthermore, the nonunion employee must have a fair opportunity to identify the impact of the governmental action on his interests and to assert a meritorious First Amendment claim. Here, the Union's (D) original procedure was flawed in three ways: (a) the procedure failed to minimize the risk of the Union's (D) improper use of the dissenters' funds, even if only for a short time; (b) the procedure did not provide nonunion employees with an adequate explanation as to how their deductions were calculated; and (c) the procedure did not provide a "reasonably prompt decision by an impartial decision maker" if an objection were raised. The nonunion employee, who bears the burden of objecting, is entitled to have his objections addressed in an expeditious, fair, and objective manner. The Union's (D) procedure, which was controlled from start to finish by the Union (D), an interested party since it was the recipient of the agency fees, did not meet these requirements. Affirmed. (2) Yes. While the Union's (D) self-imposed remedy (the escrow) curtailed the first flaw found in the original procedure noted above, it still did not address flaws (b) and (c). As such, the escrow procedure provided insufficient protection for constitutionally protected rights. Affirmed.

**COMMENT:** According to two of the concurring justices, a nonunion employee in the situation presented by this case should exhaust union arbitration procedures before resorting to the courts. This is the only way to proceed, at least initially. For a procedure to be deemed adequate by a court, the three flaws listed under the first holding must be remedied. Nevertheless, it would appear that the court infers that there is a right to decide on additional criteria if a situation so requires. Future cases will explore this possibility as nonunion employees continue to challenge their unions regarding constitutional concerns and the very high percentage of expenditures directly related to collective bargaining.

## Discussion Questions

1. Can service fees collected from nonunion members be used for activities unrelated to collective bargaining to which these nonmembers object? Why or why not?

2. Did the union's original grievance procedure infringe on the objector's First and Fourteenth Amendment rights? If so, in what way(s)?

3. What legal argument could Hudson use from the *Abood v. Detroit Board of Education* (1977) case?

# LEHNERT V. FERRIS FACULTY ASSN.
# 111 S. CT. 1950 (1991)

**GENERAL RULE OF LAW:** A union may only charge nonmembers for services that are germane to collective bargaining activity and justified by the government's interest in labor peace and avoiding free riders, but not for services that place significant, additional burdens on free speech.

**PROCEDURE SUMMARY:**

**Plaintiff:** Lehnert (P), nonunion college faculty member

**Defendant:** Ferris Faculty Association (Association) (D)

**U.S. District Court Decision:** Held for the Association (D)

**U.S. Court of Appeals Decision:** Affirmed

**U.S. Supreme Court Decision:** Affirmed

**FACTS:** Under Michigan law, one union served as the exclusive collective bargaining representative of public employees in a particular bargaining unit. The law permitted the creation of an agency shop, in which nonmembers were compelled to pay a service fee to the union. The Association (D) was the exclusive union for the faculty at Ferris State College (Ferris) and charged nonmembers a service fee equivalent to the amount of dues required of members. Lehnert (P) was on faculty at Ferris, but was not a member of the Association (D). Lehnert (P), along with other nonunion faculty members, filed suit, alleging that certain Association (D) uses of the fees collected from nonmembers violated their rights under the First and Fourteenth Amendments. The district court, finding the Association's (D) use of the fees to be sufficiently related to collective bargaining, held that the Association (D) could constitutionally charge Lehnert (P) for lobbying and electoral politics; bargaining, litigation, and other services on behalf of persons not in his bargaining unit; public relations efforts; miscellaneous professional services; meetings and convention of the parent union; and preparations for a strike. The court of appeals affirmed. The U.S. Supreme Court granted review.

**ISSUE:** May a union charge nonmembers for services that add significant burdens on free speech and are not germane to collective bargaining activity or justified by the government's interest in labor peace and avoiding free riders?

**HOLDING AND DECISION:** (Blackmun, J.) No. A union may only charge nonmembers for services that are germane to collective bargaining activity and justified by the government's interest in labor peace and avoiding free riders, but not for services that place significant, additional burdens on free speech. This rule was established in *Abood v. Detroit Board of Education* (1977), where the Court upheld, as facially constitutional, the same Michigan law challenged in this action. Under this rule, the Association's (D) lobbying and electoral politics activities may not be charged to Lehnert (P) because it would compel him to engage in core political speech that significantly burdens his First Amendment rights. The challenged public relations activities also impermissibly burden Lehnert's (P) First Amendment rights. The bargaining, litigation, and other services on behalf of persons not in his bargaining unit may not be charged to Lehnert (P) because they are not germane to the Association's (D) duties as exclusive bargaining representative. The miscellaneous professional services and parent union convention expenditures are constitutional because they do not infringe First Amendment rights but benefit Lehnert's (P) particular bargaining unit and are germane to the Association's (D) bargaining activity. Affirmed in part; reversed in part.

**COMMENT:** The constitutional dimensions of union security provisions such as agency shop agreements were first addressed in *Railway Employees v. Hanson* (1956), where "union-shop" agreements were validated as applied to private employees, as authorized by the Railway Labor Act (RLA). Although *Hanson* did not address how union dues could be utilized, *Machinists v. Street* (1961) addressed that issue in light of the RLA. Seeking to protect the expressive freedom of dissenting employees while promoting collective representation, the Court decided to "deny unions the authority to expend dissenters' funds in support of political causes to which those employees objected." Two years later, the Court reaffirmed, noting the distinction between union political expenditures and those "germane to collective bargaining." Only the latter can be properly charged to the nonmember. It was not until *Abood* that the Court addressed these issues in the public employment context, determining that, as in the private sector, agency shop agreements must not burden dissenters' First Amendment rights through compulsory subsidy of certain ideological activities. The Court in *Abood* did not attempt to precisely differentiate between chargeable and nonchargeable activities. *Lehnert* illustrates the tension created by attempting to promote collective representation while protecting the expressive freedom of those employees who do not wish to take part in the particular representative process. *Lehnert* relied on the general rule established in *Abood,* where the Court held that public employees who chose not to join a union serving as the exclusive collective bargaining representative could be compelled to pay a service fee. However, these nonmembers had a right not to have the fees used for support of ideological causes they opposed. *Lehnert* is an attempt to more precisely differentiate between those uses that are allowed and those charges that are not.

## Discussion Questions

1. Why does charging a nonmember for lobbying and electoral activities violate the First Amendment?

2. What are other activities that cannot be charged to nonmembers because they would violate their First Amendment rights?

---

Additional case briefs can be found on the SAGE Web site at the following address:
http://www.sagepub.com/aquilacasebriefs

---

## NOTES

1. AFSCME v. Woodward, 406 R.2d 137 (8th Cir 1969).

2. See Kenai Penin. Bor. Sch. Dist. and Kenai Penin. Bor. v. Kenai Penin. Ed. Assn., 572 P.2d 416 (1977).

3. See Abood v. Detroit Board of Education, 431 U.S. 209 (1977).

4. See Lehnert v. Ferris Faculty Assn., 111 S. Ct. 1950 (1991). See also Chicago Teachers Union v. Hudson, 475 U.S. 292 (1986).

5. Railway Employees' Department v. Hanson, 351 U.S. 225 (1956); Machinists v. Street, 367 U.S. 740 (1961).

# 12

# Teacher Dismissal, Retirement, and Discrimination in Employment

*No person in the United States shall, on the ground of race, color, or national origin, be excluded from participation in, be denied the benefits of, or be subjected to discrimination under any program or activity receiving Federal financial assistance.*

—Civil Rights Act of 1964

## OVERVIEW . . . . . . . . . . . . . . . . . . . . . . . . . . . . . .

Obviously, a school board may dismiss a teacher. The question is under what circumstances and according to what procedures. A teacher is considered to have a property interest in a teaching position if the position is the subject of a permanent contract or a statutory tenure provision. The due process clause of the Fourteenth Amendment prevents the government from taking life, liberty, or property from someone without due process of law. Because a teaching position can be considered a property interest, it is therefore protected by the Fourteenth Amendment. Provided that appropriate procedures are followed, the teacher's "procedural" due process rights are protected.[1] Procedural due process protections include the guarantees of notice of a school board's intended termination action, information on the charges, and an opportunity to be heard.[2]

Teacher dismissal is different from nonrenewal of a teacher's contract. Dismissal involves termination of a teacher who is either tenured or probationary, but still under some contract.[3] In addition to providing a teacher with due process protections, a school board generally must also establish that it has a good or justifiable *cause* supporting its decision to dismiss. The most common statutory grounds for dismissal are insubordination (a conscious disregard of authority) and incompetence (a lack of ability to perform effectively). Nonrenewal, of course, usually occurs at the end of the term of a nontenured teacher's contract, when the school board elects not to renew that contract. A probationary teacher is not entitled to procedural due process protections (proper notification, etc.) from a school board's nonrenewal decision because no property interest attaches to a mere expectation of reemployment.[4] Usually, a teacher whose contract is about to expire may be terminated for no reason at all or for any reason whatsoever.

In this chapter, we will discuss the two principal forms of termination—voluntary termination and involuntary termination. Voluntary termination occurs when a teacher retires, or simply decides to leave her position. Involuntary termination occurs when the school board, and not the teacher, makes the decision to end the teacher's employment. The manner in which a teacher may terminate or be terminated is usually governed by the terms of his or her employment contract, especially when a local school board seeks to dismiss a teacher while his or her contract is pending.

This chapter also explores the issues surrounding discrimination in employment. It examines protective statutes and explores issues related to diversity and affirmative action. Essentially, public employees are shielded by the equal protection clause of the Fourteenth Amendment of the U.S. Constitution as well as by selected federal statutes designed to protect our civil rights. In providing protection against discrimination, the equal protection clause of the Fourteenth Amendment provides generalized protection against discrimination, while the federal civil rights statutes provide specific protection against specific types of discrimination. The federal statutes that protect the citizen against employment discrimination are Title VII of the Civil Rights Act of 1964, the Age Discrimination in Employment Act (ADEA) of 1987, and the Americans With Disabilities Act (ADA). Acting in concert, with Title VII as the centerpiece, these statutes protect Americans against invidious discrimination based on the traditional classifications: race, sex, color, national origin, religion, age, and disability. A state may, through its statutory power, heighten the protection provided by federal statute. For example, a state may enact a statute that provides more protection than does federal law for its citizens with disabilities. However, state statutes may not in any way provide *less* protection than federal law. These federal statutes provide the "floor" of protection—the bare minimum. While states may add to this protection, they may not detract from it.

Title VII did not initially protect against discriminatory employment in educational institutions. However, in 1972, the law was amended to include protection against discrimination in teacher and administrator employment. Two areas of Title VII employment discrimination analysis are disparate treatment and disparate impact. *Disparate impact* deals with employment discrimination against a *specific* plaintiff. *Disparate treatment* deals with employment discrimination against a *general* classification of people. *Griggs v. Duke Power Co.* (1971) is the classic case dealing with disparate treatment.[5] Title VII does not specifically address affirmative action, which, when applied to employment, is a voluntary plan whereby a school district tries to remediate past discrimination. Providing a preference, even to a protected classification, is not allowed under Title VII, which tries to make hiring procedures neutral (absent an affirmative action mandate). School districts, even those with a history of discriminatory practices, must take care in applying voluntary affirmative action remedies because white applicants may claim they are subject to "reverse discrimination." *Wygant v. Jackson Board of Education* (1986) provides guidance regarding affirmative action and reverse discrimination using an equal protection clause analysis.[6] The key appears to be that any plan must be carefully tailored and have a less intrusive method to accomplish remediation of past discrimination.

Sexually discriminatory practices may be challenged under the equal protection clause of the Fourteenth Amendment, the Equal Pay Act of 1964, and Title IX of the Educational Amendments of 1972. Each of these protective enactments prohibits gender discrimination. If a teacher establishes a prima facie case of sex discrimination, the burden in the case then shifts to the school board to show that its hiring decision was based on nondiscriminatory reasons. Initially, Title IX did not cover employees, but successor legislation included sex discrimination as grounds to withhold federal financial assistance from an entire university. Later, *Franklin v. Gwinnett County Public Schools* (1992) allowed both compensatory and **punitive damages** to be recovered against a school district if it discriminated on the basis of sex.[7]

An essential element of a sexual harassment charge—as opposed to a hostile work environment charge—is that there is a demand that a subordinate provide sexual favors to keep his or her job or to improve his or her position. Sexual harassment ranges from verbal suggestions to overt acts and demands. A plaintiff may sue under both Title IX and Title VII. Under Title VII, sexual harassment is classified under one of two legal theories: "**quid pro quo**" or "hostile environment." Quid pro quo sexual harassment results when an employer (or his agent, usually a man) uses his superior status and power to have a subordinate (usually a woman) provide sexual favors for some job enhancement (a favor for a favor.) This is often called "put out or get out" harassment. In contrast, "hostile environment" sexual harassment is unwelcome, hurtful conduct by employer and/or coworkers that creates a "hostile environment," which results in resentment and unpleasantness in the workplace.

Selected other issues and statutes are also included below: (1) employer retaliation against an employee who informs the employer that an unlawful employment practice under Title VII has occurred; (2) the Equal Pay Act, which is intended to eliminate wage differences based on sex when equal effort, skill, and work are involved; and (3) the Age Discrimination in Employment Act (ADEA), which protects those who are at least 40 years old from age discrimination.

When dealing with discrimination against persons with disabilities, both the Americans With Disabilities Act (ADA) and § 504 of the Rehabilitation Act of 1973 provide adults with more protection. In contrast, the Individuals With Disabilities Education Improvement Act (IDEIA) deals specifically with children with disabilities' educational concerns. Section 504 provides protection when the employer receives federal funds, while ADA covers all employees in both the public and private sectors, as long as the company has 15 or more workers. In a case with AIDS implications, a teacher with tuberculosis was held to have a physiological handicap covered by § 504.[8] The question then turned on whether she was "otherwise qualified" and, if so, whether she could be "reasonably accommodated." Interestingly, courts have held that the appropriate equal protection analysis is not strict scrutiny because a handicapping condition is not a suspect classification entitled to the heightened analysis.[9]

Using the *Arline* rationale, in *Chalk v. United States District Court Central District of California and Orange County Superintendent of Schools* (1988), the court held that a teacher with AIDS cannot be prevented from returning to the classroom solely because of the fear and apprehension of parents.[10] Today, all schools train staff to utilize universal precautions (e.g., use of rubber gloves) whenever any blood or similar potentially contagious fluid is present.

## Case Study

### Teacher Dismissal and Retirement

You are high school principal in a small local school district. Your town is an insular and close-knit community that is isolated from any urban area. Three sophomore girls tell the guidance counselor that a young probationary teacher is treating them in an inappropriate manner. The young ladies accuse this male teacher of ogling their "physical attributes" and making comments with sexual overtones. They claim to feel uncomfortable in his class. The teacher denies these allegations. He claims that these young women are "out to get him" because he caught them cheating and informed them that they were going to fail his course. The sophomore girls appear credible, but they do say that they are not doing well in his class. After interviewing the girls as well as other students, you are convinced that the teacher acted inappropriately.

### Discussion Questions

1. What should you do?

2. What are your concerns regarding your action?

3. How common do you think this problem really is?

# IMPORTANT CONCEPTS

- **Property interest:** For purposes of due process, a teacher has a property interest in a teaching position when it is created by contract or under the authority of a tenure statute.

- **Protections attach to property interests:** Certain protections automatically attach to property interests, and an owner may not be dispossessed of his property without first being provided such protections.

- **Two common protections:** A teacher is generally entitled to notice of a school board's intention to terminate her and a hearing on the matter.

- **Good cause:** A tenured teacher, or one who is on probation but under contract, may not be dismissed unless there is "good cause" for doing so.

- **Common grounds for cause:** Common reasons for dismissing a teacher for cause include incompetence, insubordination, unprofessional conduct, immoral conduct, and neglect of duty.

- **Invalidation of dismissal:** If required due process protections are not provided and good cause is not found to exist, a dismissal action may be invalidated.

- **Nonrenewal versus dismissal:** A school board may choose not to renew a nontenured teacher's contract without providing due process or good cause. Some states, such as Ohio, have provided nontenured teachers an additional right to be informed of the reason for nonrenewal and to be given timely notification of poor performance and the opportunity to improve.

- **No property interest:** A nontenured teacher has no property interest in his teaching position, but rather merely an expectation of reemployment.

- **Exceptions to the rule:** Despite the fact that no due process or good cause is required for dismissal of a nontenured teacher, dismissal will be unlawful if it (1) contravenes other constitutional rights, (2) occurs in a climate of "de facto" tenure, or (3) damages or impugns the teacher in certain respects.

- **Legislation:** Retirement systems are created through state legislation.

- **Main elements:** Most employee retirement plans provide for employee contributions (annuities) and employer contributions (pensions).

- **State law predominates:** Local boards may not supersede statutory retirement provisions with their own regulations.

# TERMINATION OF EMPLOYMENT THROUGH DISMISSAL

The key issue is under what circumstances, and according to what procedures, a local school board may dismiss a teacher.

## Due Process Safeguards

The due process rights embodied in the Fourteenth Amendment provide for certain protections against arbitrary government actions that threaten property interests such as employment. A teaching position is generally considered a property interest, so long as it is the subject of a permanent contract or a statutory tenure provision. Terminating a teacher may be considered arbitrary if not carried out according to a well-defined procedure aimed at ensuring fairness for the teacher. When the appropriate procedures are followed, the teacher's "procedural" due process rights will be protected.[11] The most common procedural due process protection requires that a teacher receive notice of a school board's intended termination action. This includes notification of the charges and the opportunity for a hearing.[12] Other protections that may be offered include (1) adequate time to prepare for the hearing; (2) an opportunity to review the employer's evidence; (3) disclosure of the employer's witnesses; (4) representation by counsel; (5) an impartial hearing officer; (6) an opportunity to present evidence and witnesses and to cross-examine adverse witnesses; (7) an official record (i.e., transcript) of the hearing; and (8) an opportunity to appeal an adverse decision.

# Dismissal Versus Nonrenewal of a Teaching Contract

## "Dismissal" Defined

Dismissal involves termination of a teacher who is either tenured or probationary (not yet tenured) but under contract.[13] The dismissal of a teacher requires observance of procedural due process, discussed above. Aside from affording a teacher the appropriate due process protections, a school board generally must be able to show good or justifiable cause supporting its decision to dismiss. In some states, the acceptable grounds for cause are identified by statute. Failure to list one of the statutory grounds may lead to the invalidation of a dismissal action. Common statutory grounds include the following:

1. Insubordination. A conscious disregard of authority.

2. Incompetence. Lack of ability to perform effectively. For example, a local school board suspended and attempted to terminate a high school teacher for incompetence after he assigned his senior English class an article that contained a particularly vulgar term. The court of appeals sidestepped the issue of the teacher's competence but essentially found in favor of the teacher because censoring the article would have had a chilling effect on his academic freedom.[14]

3. Unprofessional conduct. For example, a local school board failed to renew the contract of a nontenured teacher because she allowed young men (friends of her son, who was in college) to stay in her home with her. The board felt that this conduct was unbecoming a teacher. The court held for the teacher, stating that this type of dismissal must be based on conduct related either to the education process or to working relationships within the institution.[15]

4. Immoral conduct. For example, a state board of public instruction revoked the teaching certificate of a male teacher upon obtaining evidence of his affair with a female colleague. The board failed to make any findings of fact or conclusions of law. The state supreme court reversed the board's decision, finding that a teaching certificate cannot be revoked without findings of fact that would enable a reviewing court to ascertain with reasonable certainty the factual and legal basis of the decision.[16]

5. Neglect of duty.

## Principals Also Protected

Under certain conditions protected by state statute, principals and teachers have similar tenure and nondismissal protections and guarantees.[17] In some states, such as Ohio, a principal can never receive tenure in the administrative position but can receive or retain teacher tenure. This is a valuable protection should the principal not be rehired as a principal when the contract term ends.

## "Nonrenewal of a Contract" Defined

Nonrenewal occurs when the school board elects *not* to renew a nontenured teacher's contract at the end of the contract term. A probationary teacher is not entitled to procedural due process protections in connection with a school board's nonrenewal decision (although some state statutes require that a teacher be notified of a nonrenewal decision before his contract expires) because no property interest attaches to a mere expectation of reemployment.[18] A teacher whose contract is about to expire may be terminated for no reason at all or for any reason whatsoever. Notwithstanding the above, certain conditions or actions of the school board may entitle a nontenured teacher to the notice and hearing that is generally provided to a tenured teacher prior to dismissal. The standard situation is when a nonrenewal decision is based on factors that are constitutionally infirm, such as those tied to racial animus or a desire to quell free speech rights.

For example, a nontenured teacher's contract was not renewed after several parents complained about the methods she employed in teaching the history of race relations. The court reasoned that the teacher's methods related to a legitimate educational objective and thus could not serve as grounds for dismissal. She was protected by her constitutional rights of freedom of expression and activity in the classroom.[19]

However, a school board's nonrenewal of a probationary kindergarten teacher's contract was upheld by the court of appeals. The teacher refused to teach portions of the school curriculum pertaining to patriotism and the flag because of her belief that doing so would violate her religious principles. The students' right to a balanced education was held to predominate over the teacher's First Amendment right; to hold otherwise would be to permit the teacher to impose her personal beliefs on her students.[20]

When a teacher can demonstrate that various practices and procedures of the school district create a de facto tenure system, a nonrenewal will be overturned.[21] When a teacher can demonstrate that a nonrenewal decision will damage his reputation, impugn his integrity, or foreclose other employment opportunities, there is a possibility of an inappropriate action. Finally, when a teacher can demonstrate that a nonrenewal decision violates his or her right to equal protection of the law based on a school district's differential application of a nonrenewal policy, relief may be provided.[22]

## Nonrenewal of Tenured Teacher Contracts

Even a tenured teacher's employment contract may not be renewed, so long as the evidence relied upon to establish good cause for nonrenewal is not arbitrary, irrational, unreasonable, or irrelevant to a school board's objective of maintaining an efficient school system.[23]

## Constitutional Rights Are Protected

A teacher may not be dismissed for exercising a constitutional right such as First Amendment–protected free speech. For example, Pickering, a teacher, wrote and published a letter in the local paper criticizing the school administration and the allocation of tax funds raised by the school. Even though the letter contained numerous inaccuracies and contributed to the loss of the school levy, the court overturned Pickering's dismissal. A teacher may not be dismissed for making public statements without proof that the statements were false and knowingly or recklessly made.[24]

However, the termination of a nontenured teacher following his exercise of a constitutional right will not be voided if the exercise of the constitutional right was incidental to termination.[25] In *Mt. Healthy v. Doyle* (1977), the court distinguished *Pickering,* ensuring that unsatisfactory nontenured teachers cannot use the Constitution to protect them from nonrenewal. For example, a teacher who has been informed of poor performance might engage in divisive speech and/or union activity to create constitutional protection. However, this will not protect him if the nonrenewal animus was unsatisfactory work and *not* the teacher's expression. Furthermore, conduct is protected by the First Amendment only if it is expressive or communicative in nature.[26]

# TERMINATION OF EMPLOYMENT THROUGH RETIREMENT

The legislatures of the various states created the retirement systems that are in place today. There is no question that retirement plans are constitutional, despite opponents' arguments that retirement benefits are gifts of public funds and serve no public benefit.

There are at least two elements to most retirement plans:

1. *Employee contribution:* A portion of retirement benefits are derived from the contributions of the employee who is covered by the plan. This is sometimes referred to as an *annuity.*

2. *Employer contribution:* The remainder of the retirement benefits is derived from the contributions of the employer. This is sometimes referred to as a *pension.*

Employee contributions are provided through deductions from the employee's salary during the period of his employment; employer contributions come from state coffers.

Most plans contain provisions governing eligibility, the amount of benefits to be received upon retirement, and the distribution of benefits upon the death of the retiree. Local school boards may not supersede state statutory retirement provisions with regulations of their own. For example, if a compulsory retirement age is set by state statute, a local district may not lower the compulsory retirement age for its employees. Because retirement plans are governed by statute rather than by contract law, a state legislature may make changes to existing plans as it sees fit. Such changes, however, may not disadvantage those who are already receiving retirement benefits.

# DISCRIMINATION IN EMPLOYMENT

This chapter also explores the issues surrounding discrimination in employment. It examines relevant protective statutes and explores issues related to diversity and affirmative action. Essentially, public employees are shielded by the equal protection clause of the Fourteenth Amendment to the U.S. Constitution as well as select federal civil rights statutes.

## Equal Protection Clause

The equal protection clause of the Fourteenth Amendment provides broad, general protection against discrimination, while federal civil rights statutes provide specific protection against specific types of discrimination. The federal statutes that protect citizens against employment discrimination are Title VII of the Civil Rights Act of 1964, the Age Discrimination in Employment Act (ADEA) of 1987, and the Americans With Disabilities Act (ADA). These statutes act in concert, with Title VII as the centerpiece, to protect Americans against invidious discrimination based on the traditional classifications of race, sex, color, national origin, religion, age, and disability. A state may enact statutes that add to federal protection. For example, the state of Ohio may enact a statute that provides more protection (it may not provide less) to persons with special needs than does federal law. Thus, Ohio citizens with special needs would have more protection than required by federal law. Ohio statutes, however, may not in any way detract from federal protection.

Title VII did not initially protect against discriminatory employment in educational institutions. However, in 1972, the law was amended to protect against discrimination in teacher and administrator employment. The two areas of Title VII employment discrimination analysis are disparate treatment and disparate impact. Disparate impact deals with employment discrimination against a specific individual. Disparate treatment deals with employment discrimination against a general classification of employees. *Griggs v. Duke Power Co.* (1971) is the classic case dealing with disparate treatment.

## Affirmative Action

Title VII does not specifically address affirmative action. Affirmative action is a voluntary plan whereby a school district tries to remediate past discrimination. Providing a preference, even to a protected classification, is not allowed under Title VII, which tries to make hiring procedures neutral. School districts, even those with a history of discriminatory practices, must exercise care when practicing affirmative action because white applicants might allege "reverse discrimination." *Wygant v. Jackson Board of Education* (1986) held that any affirmative action plan must be carefully tailored and is only appropriate in the absence of a less-intrusive method to remediate past discrimination.

## Sexual Discrimination

Sexually discriminatory practices may be challenged under the equal protection clause of the Fourteenth Amendment, the Equal Pay Act of 1964, and Title IX of the Educational Amendments of 1972. Each of these protective enactments prohibits gender-based discrimination. If a teacher establishes a prima facie case of sex discrimination, the school board must prove that its hiring decision was based on nondiscriminatory reasons.

Title IX was drafted to protect the rights of everyone and to prohibit gender discrimination. Initially, Title IX did not cover employees, but successor legislation included sex discrimination as grounds to withhold federal financial assistance from an entire university. Later, *Franklin v. Gwinnett County Public Schools* (1992) allowed both compensatory and punitive damages to be recovered against a school district.

Sexual harassment ranges from verbal suggestions to overt acts and demands. Further, either Title IX or Title VII may serve as a plaintiff's cause of action. Classically, under Title VII, the two legal theories used to classify sexual harassment are "quid pro quo" and "hostile environment." Quid pro quo sexual harassment results when an employer (or his agent, usually a man) uses his superior status and power to force a subordinate (usually a woman) to provide sexual favors in exchange for some job enhancement. This is often called "put out or get out" harassment. "Hostile environment" sexual harassment is unwelcome, hurtful conduct by an employer and/or co workers that creates a "hostile environment," which causes a resentment and unpleasantness in the workplace.

## Retaliation

Individuals who inform the employer that an unlawful employment practice under Title VII occurred are entitled to protection from retaliatory termination. The employee must show a "causal connection" between the retaliation and the claim of sexual harassment. This standard has come under much scrutiny, with no clear and manageable standard to follow. *Meritor Savings Bank, FSB v. Vinson* (1986), while providing guidance, has not been the bright line that many predicted.[27] In a recent case, *Jackson v. Birmingham Board of Education* (2005), the Court provided more guidance to clarify whether Title IX's private cause of action includes claims of retaliation.[28] Here, the Court held that the party claiming the retaliation did not have to be the party against whom the sex discrimination was perpetrated. Furthermore, retaliation is discrimination "on the basis of sex" because it is an intentional response to the nature of the complaint, an allegation of sex discrimination.

## Equal Pay Act

The Equal Pay Act was intended to eliminate pay and wage differences based on sex when equal effort, skill, and work are involved. Differential pay is allowed only when the work is based on a seniority system, a merit system, and unit price payments based on quantity or quality (piecework). School districts may run afoul of the Equal Pay Act when female coaches earn less than their male counterparts for equal work.[29] Even private schools have to be careful to avoid sexual discrimination because the Fair Labor Standards Act provides similar protections against gender discrimination.

## Age Discrimination

The Age Discrimination in Employment Act (ADEA) protects from discrimination workers who are at least 40 years old. Originally, people over 70 were not protected, but this was changed in 1968 to eliminate the age limit. However, when there is a bona fide occupational qualification, such as the rigorousness of job responsibilities for firefighters or law enforcement personnel, the law does not apply. Of course, an employer *may* discriminate between employees based on "reasonable factors other than age." For example, an employer may discriminate by paying more to new hires than is paid to incumbents, for the purpose of luring better-qualified new employees. Here, the employer is discriminating on the basis of skill, not age—a "reasonable factor other than age." This would be age discrimination if the employer merely paid more to younger employees.

When an employer lays off more expensive (as opposed to older) employees in order to reduce expenses and operate more effectively, it has been held to not violate ADEA, even when this layoff adversely impacts older employees.[30] This is also a "reasonable factor other than age," and it was upheld even though the impact fell far heavier on older employees.

## DISCRIMINATION AGAINST PERSONS WITH DISABILITIES

In Chapter 8, IDEIA was the primary statute providing protection for special needs children. The Americans with Disabilities Act (ADA) and § 504 of the Rehabilitation Act of 1973 were also discussed. These latter two statutes provide more protection to special needs adults. Section 504 provides protection when the employer receives federal funds, while ADA covers all employees in both public and private sector companies with 15 or more workers. ADA, which was modeled after the Education for All Handicapped Children Act, covers almost all aspects of the American enterprise. Most recent legislation has involved § 504. However, because of ADA's comprehensiveness and because with ADA a state's Eleventh Amendment immunity from being sued does not apply, the ADA will likely eventually be the leading protective statute for those with special needs. In a case with AIDS implications, a teacher with tuberculosis was held to have a physiological handicap covered by Section 504.[31] The question then turned on whether she was "otherwise qualified" and, if so, whether she could be "reasonably accommodated." With no testimony regarding these issues, the case was remanded for a determination. Interestingly, when considering a disability such as blindness, the Court held that the appropriate equal protection analysis was not strict scrutiny. It found that a handicapping condition was not a suspect classification entitled to heightened analysis, but merely called for the application of the rational basis test.[32] This failure to provide suspect class status further emphasizes the need for § 504 and ADA statutory protection.

The Supreme Court in *School Board of Nassau County v. Arline* (1987) refused to consider whether AIDS (a less hardy virus that is far more difficult to transmit and acquire than tuberculosis) was a physical impairment protected by the ADA. In *Chalk v. United States District Court Central District of California and Orange County Superintendent of Schools* (1988), the Court held that a teacher with AIDS cannot be prevented from returning to the classroom solely because of the fear and apprehension of parents. This led to schools having to take universal precautions (e.g., use of rubber gloves) whenever any blood or similar potentially contagious fluid was present. The decision to remove a student with AIDS or allow him to remain in school is a medical decision, and almost every school district has a medical panel to advise it regarding these types of difficult situations.

Remaining unresolved was the issue of when a "physical impairment" was established and, thereby, ADA protection would attach. In *Bragdon v. Abbot* (1998), the Court held that the human immunodeficiency virus (lowest level of AIDS contagion) was a "physical impairment" and was thereby covered by ADA from the moment of infection through the various stages of the disease.[33] It should be noted that, at any time, the medical team might determine that a dangerous condition exists and the teacher must be removed.

## Case Study

### Private and Public

You are principal of a private school, Traditional Academy, which operates under a state charter but is not affiliated with any public school or school district. You charge tuition and enroll students who must conform to school standards established by your Academy's board of trustees. You hire teachers who sign term contracts of varying lengths that are renewable if both parties agree. These contracts require that the employee conform to Traditional Academy traditions and policies. One of your teachers, Mr. Clean, agreed to the rules, including one that prohibited teachers from wearing beards. He discussed with his class the wearing of a beard as an expression of his civil rights. Mr. Clean then grew a full beard, which he carefully groomed and which most thought made him look very distinguished. After conferring with the Academy trustees, you terminated his contract. Mr. Clean argued that he had the constitutional right to wear a beard and filed suit in federal court under Section 1983, claiming a federal tort violation. Your private school board argues that state law does not control private schools because you are not a state actor and are not required to conform to the indicated federal laws.

### Discussion Questions

1. Is there a difference between public and private schools? If so, what rights do private school teachers have, or not have, compared to public school teachers?

2. If the private school provided retirement benefits through the State Teachers' Retirement System, could this make them a public employer?

3. A private luncheon group with thousands of members wants to continue to limit its membership to men. Would this be seen as a private entity that does not have to admit women? Does the number of members and appearance of a public entity impact the decision?

4. What about a private golf country club, like Augusta National, where the Master's Tournament is played every year?

# CONLUSION . . . . . . . . . . . . . . . . . . . . . . . . . . . . . . . . . .

A teacher is protected by the Fourteenth Amendment from arbitrary and unfair dismissal. Dismissal involves termination of a teacher who is either tenured or probationary (but under contract). Aside from affording a teacher the appropriate due process protections, a school board generally must be able to show good or justifiable cause supporting termination.

Nonrenewal of a teacher's contract occurs when, at the end of a nontenured teacher's contract, the school board elects not to renew the teacher's contract. A probationary teacher, with a contract for a specific term, is not entitled to procedural due process protections in connection with a school board's nonrenewal decision at the end of the contract term. However, when the decision to not renew is based on unconstitutional reasons, such as racial animus, the teacher may then be entitled to a hearing.

Teacher retirement plans are established through two types of contributions: employer and employee contributions. The former come from state coffers, while the latter is deducted from the teacher's paycheck and is often called an annuity. Because retirement plans are governed by statute rather than by contract law, a state legislature may make changes to existing teacher retirement plans as it sees fit.

Even a tenured teacher's employment contract may not be renewed, so long as the evidence relied upon to establish good cause is not arbitrary, irrational, unreasonable, or irrelevant to school board objectives. A teacher may not be dismissed for exercising constitutional rights, although he may be if this exercise of constitutional rights is incidental to the reasons for termination or is not expressive or communicative in nature.

Public employees are also protected by a variety of constitutional and federal laws that prohibit various types of discrimination. The equal protection clause and due process clauses of the Fourteenth Amendment specifically seek to thwart such discrimination. This protection was codified in a number of federal statutes, including the Civil Rights Act of 1964, the Age Discrimination in Employment Act of 1987, the Americans With Disabilities Act, and the Equal Pay Act of 1964, among others.

The following cases explore the avenues of hiring and terminating teachers. In some instances, you will notice that the cases distinguish between tenured and nontenured teachers. Many cases illustrate how much due process each teacher is afforded before being terminated. Hopefully, you will be able to determine in which situations a teacher may have been terminated for no cause.

# CASE BRIEFS · · · · · · · · · · · · · · · · · · · · · · · ·

# JACKSON V. BIRMINGHAM BOARD OF EDUCATION 2005 U.S. LEXIS 2928 (2005)

**GENERAL RULE OF LAW:** Title IX's private right of action encompasses claims of retaliation against an individual because he has complained about sex discrimination.

**PROCEDURE SUMMARY:**

**Plaintiff:** Roderick Jackson (P), public school teacher

**Defendant:** Birmingham Board of Education (Board) (D)

**U.S. District Court Decision:** Dismissed Jackson's (P) cause of action

**U.S. Court of Appeals Decision:** Affirmed

**U.S. Supreme Court Decision:** Reversed and remanded for lower court proceedings

**FACTS:** Roderick Jackson (P), a teacher in Birmingham, Alabama, brought suit against the Board (D) alleging that the Board (D) retaliated against him because he had complained about sex discrimination in the high school's athletic program. Jackson (P) claimed that the Board's (D) retaliation violated Title IX of the Education Amendments of 1972. In December, 2000, Jackson (P) began complaining to his supervisors about the unequal treatment of the girls' basketball team, but to no avail. Jackson's (P) complaints went unanswered, and the school failed to remedy the situation. Instead, Jackson (P) began to receive negative work evaluations and ultimately was removed as the girls' coach in May, 2001. Jackson (P) is still employed by the Board (D) as a teacher, but he no longer receives supplemental pay for coaching. After the Board (D) terminated Jackson's (P) coaching duties, he filed suit in the United States District Court for the Northern District of Alabama. The Board (D) moved to dismiss on the ground that Title IX's private cause of action does not include claims of retaliation. The district court granted the motion to dismiss. The Court of Appeals for the Eleventh Circuit affirmed. The Supreme Court reversed the judgment, and the case was remanded for further proceedings.

**ISSUE:** Does Title IX's private cause of action apply when the person wasn't the victim of sexual discrimination, but was retaliated against for complaining of sexual discrimination?

**HOLDING AND DECISION:** (O'Connor, J.) Yes. Title IX of the Education Amendments of 1972 broadly prohibits a funding recipient from subjecting any person to discrimination on the basis of sex. Retaliation against a person because that person has complained of sex discrimination is another form of intentional sex discrimination encompassed by Title IX's private cause of action. Retaliation is, by definition, an intentional act. It is a form of "discrimination" because the complainant is being subjected to differential treatment. Moreover, retaliation is discrimination "on the basis of sex" because it is an intentional response to the nature of the complaint: an allegation of sex discrimination. The Court concluded that when a funding recipient retaliates against a person because he complains of sex discrimination, this constitutes intentional discrimination on the basis of sex in violation of Title IX.

**COMMENT:** In many instances, an individual may not sue unless he or she is directly affected by discriminatory behavior. Here, the Court declared that Title IX of the Education Amendments of 1972 can be utilized with respect to discriminatory behaviors that do not have a direct impact on the employee personally. When a school employee complains of discriminatory behavior, he or she cannot be punished for this complaint. A teacher is protected from retaliation by a school district that doesn't want to rectify its discriminatory behavior. The Court recognized the retaliatory efforts of the school district due to the coach's complaint. It is apparent from this decision that the Court will not tolerate discrimination based on sex.

## Discussion Questions

1. If the school does not receive public funds, could it retaliate against an employee for complaining of sexual discrimination?

2. Is firing an employee who complains of sexual discrimination the only form of retaliation?

3. In what ways can a school deal with employee sexual discrimination claims to help alleviate any problems of retaliation?

# VIEMEISTER V. BOARD OF EDUCATION OF BOROUGH OF PROSPECT PARK
# 5 N.J. SUPER. 215, 68 A.2D 768 (1949)

**GENERAL RULE OF LAW:** A tenured principal may not be replaced by another without bringing charges and conducting a hearing.

**PROCEDURE SUMMARY:**

**Plaintiff:** Viemeister (P), a tenured principal

**Defendant:** Board of Education of Borough of Prospect Park (Board) (D)

**State Superior Court Appellate Division Decision:** Held for Viemeister (P), upholding state board order of reinstatement

**FACTS:** Viemeister (P) was a tenured principal who performed no teaching duties and was employed by the Board (D). For economic reasons, the Board (D) adopted a resolution abolishing the position of principal and creating the position of teaching principal. As a result, Viemeister (P) was terminated, without any charges ever being made against him, and a tenured teacher was appointed teaching principal. Viemeister (P) appealed his termination to the Commissioner of Education, who directed his reinstatement. The State Board of Education sustained. The Board (D) appealed.

**ISSUE:** May a tenured principal be terminated and replaced without charges being brought against him and without a hearing being conducted?

**HOLDING AND DECISION:** (Jacobs, J.) No. A tenured principal may not be terminated and replaced without bringing charges and conducting a hearing. School laws expressly state that tenured teachers and principals are only subject to dismissal for cause after charges and a hearing. The Board's (D) argument that this rule has no application here because the Board (D) eliminated the office of principal was not substantiated by any applicable law. As the Commissioner of Education correctly found, the office of principal was not actually eliminated. Rather, it still existed, though under the guise of the newly created office of "teaching principal." Sustaining the Board's (D) action would contravene the policy behind the tenure laws of providing principals and teachers with a measure of security in the ranks they hold.

**COMMENT:** *Viemeister* is unusual because most states do not provide principals with tenure. Courts tend to be skeptical of school board attempts to circumvent state tenure laws. Two questions arise in such situations: Has the position been eliminated for a legitimate reason, and has the position actually been eliminated? Here, the court only had to address the latter question. If the position has been eliminated, the court must then determine whether the position was eliminated for a legitimate reason. Most states do not allow principal tenure and instead grant "teacher tenure" to the principal. Thus, if the principal qualified for tenure as a teacher, a teaching position would need to be provided, if available.

## Discussion Questions

1. What needs to take place in order to terminate a tenured teacher or principal?

2. What reasoning does the court give for not accepting termination of the position as a basis for the tenured principal's termination?

3. Do you think this ruling is only applicable to tenured principals?

# PERRY V. SINDERMAN
# 408 U.S. 593, 92 S. CT. 2694 (1972)

**GENERAL RULE OF LAW:** A formal tenure system is not a prerequisite to a teacher possessing a due process interest in continued employment.

**PROCEDURE SUMMARY:**

**Plaintiff:** Sinderman (P), a teacher

**Defendants:** Perry (D) and various other officials of the Texas state college system

**U.S. District Court Decision:** Dismissed

**U.S. Court of Appeals Decision:** Reversed

**U.S. Supreme Court Decision:** Affirmed

**FACTS:** Sinderman (P) was a teacher in the Texas state college system. The system had no official tenure system, although there allegedly was an informal "understanding" that teachers would not be terminated except for cause. Sinderman (P) was employed for four successive years by Odessa Junior College, under one-year contracts. During the 1968–1969 academic year, he was elected president of the Texas Junior College Teachers Association. In this capacity, he left his teaching duties on several occasions to testify before Texas legislative committees. He also became involved in public disagreements with the policies of Odessa Junior College's board of regents. At one point, the state declined, without explanation, to review Sinderman's (P) contract. Sinderman (P) sued for reinstatement, contending that the termination was in retaliation for certain political stands he had taken. The district court granted summary judgment dismissing the action, holding that since Sinderman (P) did not have tenure, he had no right to a hearing. The court of appeals reversed, and the Supreme Court granted review.

**ISSUE:** Is a formal tenure system a prerequisite to a teacher's due process interest in continued employment?

**HOLDING AND DECISION:** (Stewart, J.) No. A formal system is not a prerequisite to a teacher's due process interest with respect to employment. The jurisprudence of due process with respect to employment is not so simple as a tenured/not-tenured dichotomy. Rather, what gives rise to a due process interest is an interest in continued employment sufficiently concrete as to be considered a property interest. While tenure is a situation that would almost certainly indicate such an interest, it is not the only situation indicating this interest. If an informal understanding regarding continued employment exists, this may also give rise to a property interest. Here, as this was the nature of Sinderman's (P) interest, a hearing on this issue was required. Reversed.

**COMMENT:** This action involved matters of both procedural and substantive due process. The procedural due process issue was that discussed above. The substantive due process issue related to the First Amendment. A state may not-terminate an employee in a manner that abridges his right of free speech; Sinderman (P) alleged that Texas had done that very thing. This case, announced at the same time as *Board of Regents of State Colleges v. Roth* (1972), clarified the contract rights of teachers.[34] In *Sinderman,* as in its companion case, the plaintiff had no formal tenure or contractual interest in being rehired. Rather, the plaintiff relied on de facto tenure based on administrative policy enunciated in the college's official faculty guide and the guidelines promulgated by state colleges and universities. A teacher's public criticism on matters of public concern is constitutionally protected.[35] The college's basis for termination of employment could, therefore, not be upheld (regardless of tenure status). The First Amendment prohibited the impairment of the teacher's freedom of speech and expression. Furthermore, the "objective" expectation of tenure provided the teacher with procedural protections prior to termination. Here, the state refused to afford a pre-termination hearing.

## Discussion Questions

1. In your opinion, why does the Court think that continued employment is a property interest?

2. What facts indicate that this could have been a violation of the teacher's First Amendment rights?

# VANELLI V. REYNOLDS SCHOOL DIST.
# NO. 7 667 F.2D 773 (9TH CIR. 1982)

**GENERAL RULE OF LAW:** The midyear termination of a teacher without a pre-termination hearing deprives the teacher of property and liberty without due process.

**PROCEDURE SUMMARY:**

**Plaintiff:** Vanelli (P), a teacher

**Defendant:** Reynolds School Dist. No. 7 (District) (D)

**U.S. District Court Decision:** Held for the District (D), upholding the termination but assessing damages against the District (D) for failure to hold a pre-termination hearing

**U.S. Court of Appeals Decision:** Affirmed

**FACTS:** Vanelli (P), a probationary teacher employed by the District (D), was charged with immoral conduct. Some female students complained that Vanelli (P) stared at their "physical attributes" and made statements with "sexual overtones." He was dismissed by the District (D) without a pre-termination hearing at the midpoint of a one-year contract. One month later, the District (D) conducted a full evidentiary hearing and affirmed its earlier dismissal decision. Vanelli (P) was represented by legal counsel, and four of the five girls who had filed a complaint testified and were cross-examined by Vanelli's (P) counsel. Vanelli (P) brought a civil rights action under 42 U.S.C. § 1983, alleging that the dismissal, without a pre-termination hearing, infringed his property and liberty interests and thus constituted a denial of due process. The district court disagreed, finding that the posttermination evidentiary hearing was sufficient to sustain the termination. Vanelli (P) appealed.

**ISSUE:** Is the midyear dismissal, without a pretermination hearing, of a teacher with a one-year contract an impermissible infringement of the teacher's property and liberty interests that violates due process?

**HOLDING AND DECISION:** (Kennedy, J.) Yes. The midyear dismissal, without a pre-termination hearing, of a teacher with a one-year contract is an impermissible infringement of the teacher's property and liberty interests that violates due process. Public employees are presumptively entitled to some form of notice and opportunity to be heard before being deprived of a liberty or property interest. Vanelli's (P) liberty interest was implicated because the immoral conduct charge might seriously damage his standing in the community; his property interest was implicated because the one-year contract gave him a right under state law to employment for that period of time. Though, as the district court correctly found, the subsequent evidentiary hearing was sufficient to sustain the dismissal, the failure to hold a pre-termination hearing was, nevertheless, a due process violation.

**COMMENT:** There is a difference between dismissal and nonrenewal in most states. Dismissal applies to a teacher who has tenure or a permanent contract; the board must show good cause and afford the individual opportunity to refute the reasons for dismissal. Nonrenewal applies to a probationary teacher or a teacher with a contract for a specified period. To refuse renewal, a board needs only to provide the teacher with notice of nonrenewal by a specific date. The key in *Vanelli* is that while Vanelli (P) did not have tenure, he had a contract for one full year, which, under state law, created the right protected by the Fourteenth Amendment's due process clause. Termination in the middle of the contract term, if unsupported by due cause and carried out without the required procedural safeguards, is not unlike a simple breach of contract. Accusations of sexual misconduct by teachers are a growing concern. For example, child abuse charges against teachers that prove groundless may still result in adverse publicity and great community concern. Often, there are various legal standards involved. All that is required for a report of child abuse is merely a suspicion. The level of proof is far less rigorous for the school to report a suspicion of abuse than for a court conviction for sexual misconduct. The intent is to protect the child from abuse such as that which occurred in *Deshaney v. Winnebago Cnty. Dep. Soc. Serv.* (1989).[36] The burden in a criminal case, to sustain a guilty verdict, would be proof "beyond a reasonable doubt," while "a preponderance of the evidence" is all that is required if civil charges were filed by a plaintiff.

## Discussion Questions

1. Do you think the result would be different if there was no formal contract? Why or why not?

2. What liberty interests in the employment did Vanelli have?

3. What is the difference between this case and the cases of tenured professors described above?

# BARCHESKI V. GRAND RAPIDS PUBLIC SCHOOLS 412 N.W.2D 296 (MICH. APP. 1987)

**GENERAL RULE OF LAW:** A teacher's taking a young, intoxicated female student home alone in his car constitutes grounds for discipline.

**PROCEDURE SUMMARY:**

**Plaintiff:** Robert Barcheski (P), a teacher

**Defendant:** Grand Rapids Public Schools (Board) (D)

**State Tenure Commission Decision:** Reversed school board decision to discharge Barcheski

**Kent Circuit Court Decision:** Reversed Tenure Commission's decision

**State Appellate Court Decision**: Upheld circuit court decision

**State Supreme Court Decision:** Reversed both circuit and appellate court decisions, in part. Remanded the case to the Tenure Commission "for reconsideration and issuance of a new opinion" in conformity with its order

**State Tenure Commission Decision:** Reversed itself, ruling that petitioner's discharge was based on reasonable and just cause

**State Appellate Court Decision:** Upheld Tenure Commission decision

**FACTS:** Robert Barcheski (P), a tenured teacher employed by the Grand Rapids Public Schools (D), was charged with impropriety with a student. The Board (D) brought charges against him for the following reasons: (1) he invited two female members of his drivers' education class to a Friday night party; (2) at the party, the two students drank beer and smoked pot in his presence; and, (3) while taking a 15-year-old student home in his car, he had sex with her. After evaluating the evidence, the Board (D) concluded that the first two charges were proven, while the evidence concerning the third charge was conflicting. Barcheski (P) was discharged based on reasonable and just cause because he "exhibited extremely poor judgment and invited charges and claims of improper conduct." Barcheski (P) appealed the decision to the Tenure Commission, which then voted to reinstate him. The Board (D) requested a review in local circuit court, where the Tenure Commission's decision to reinstate was reversed. The Michigan Supreme Court, in lieu of granting leave to appeal, remanded the case to the Tenure Commission for "reconsideration and issuance of a new opinion." This time, the commission held that the dismissal was based on reasonable and just cause. A petition for review was filed, the circuit court affirmed, and the case went back to the court of appeals.

**ISSUE:** Did the Tenure Commission exceed the scope of the supreme court's remand instruction by issuing a wholly new decision and not merely reconsidering the testimony of one of the students?

**HOLDING AND DECISION:** No. The remand order required the Tenure Commission to issue a "new opinion" after taking the unchanged testimony of one of the students at the party. The commission then determined that based on substantial, material, and competent evidence, Barcheski (P) did indeed invite at least one female student to the party, and that substantial evidence supported the fact that the two female students did drink beer and smoke marijuana in Barcheski's (P) presence. Furthermore, Barcheski (P) admitted in his testimony that he took one student home alone. The court also ruled that based on Barcheski's (P) testimony, he was, or should have been, well aware that taking a young intoxicated female student home alone in his car was, alone, grounds for discipline. The testimony of both students was also at issue. Little credence was given to one student, who recanted and changed her testimony in Barcheski's (P) favor after having many meetings and conversations with him. Although known to have problems with drugs and alcohol, the other student who accompanied Barcheski (P) in the car was believed to be a credible witness. Barcheski (P) claimed that when the Board (D) dropped the sexual intercourse charge in the first hearing and added the sub silentio charge (the just cause charge), he did not receive proper notification. This position was not supported.

**COMMENT:** This case further supports the position that a school board has the right to dismiss a tenured teacher under particular circumstances. In a situation such as this one, where the conduct is reprehensible, a school board's dismissal authority is not abusive so long as it is used wisely and the board does not abuse its discretion. It is interesting that this case took 11 years to reach a final conclusion. Also of note is the court's consideration of what constitutes reasonable behavior and judgment on the part of a teacher. Reasonable behavior is not a static concept, but rather may be a "slippery slope." For example, in this case, the court stated, "Whether driving a student home is innocuous depends on the circumstances."

## Discussion Questions

1. Do you think the remand from the Michigan Supreme Court was a polite instruction to the Tenure Commission that it they erred in its opinion?

2.  Does this further the notion that tenured teachers are "untouchable"? In what situations may a tenured teacher be terminated?

3.  In your opinion, did the commission get it right in its first decision or the final opinion? Why?

# SCHOOL BOARD OF NASSAU COUNTY, FLORIDA V. ARLINE 480 U.S. 273, 107 S. CT. 1123 (1987)

**GENERAL RULE OF LAW:** A person with a contagious disease may be a handicapped person for purposes of § 504 of the Rehabilitation Act.

**PROCEDURE SUMMARY:**

**Plaintiff:** Arline (P), a fired elementary school teacher with tuberculosis

**Defendant:** School Board of Nassau County, Florida (Board) (D)

**U.S. District Court Decision:** Held for the Board (D), finding that Arline (P) was not handicapped for purposes of § 504 of the Act

**U.S. Court of Appeals Decision:** Reversed, holding for Arline (P) that persons with contagious disease come within § 504

**U.S. Supreme Court Decision:** Affirmed

**FACTS:** Section 504 of the Rehabilitation Act provides that no otherwise-qualified handicapped individual shall, solely by reason of his handicap, be excluded from participation in any program receiving federal assistance. Arline (P) had been hospitalized for tuberculosis. The disease then went into remission for 20 years, during which time she taught elementary school. In 1977 and 1978, she had a relapse. The Board (D) suspended Arline (P) for the remainder of the school year and then discharged her, citing continued recurrence of the disease. Arline (P) filed suit, alleging that the discharge was a violation of § 504 of the Rehabilitation Act. The district court held that the Act did not apply because Arline (P) was not a "handicapped person" for purposes of the Act. The court of appeals reversed, and the U.S. Supreme Court granted review.

**ISSUE:** Is a person with a contagious disease a handicapped person for purposes of § 504 of the Act?

**HOLDING AND DECISION:** (Brennan, J.) Yes. A person with a contagious disease may be considered a handicapped person under § 504 of the Act. Section 706 of the Act defines handicapped individuals as any person who has a physical impairment that substantially limits one or more of his major life activities, has a record of such impairment, or is regarded as having such impairment. Further, Department of Health and Human Services regulations define "physical impairment" as any physiological disorder affecting the respiratory system and "major life activities," including working. The fact that Arline (P) was hospitalized in 1957 for tuberculosis, which then and now substantially limited her ability to work, clearly places her within § 504. That the disease happens to be contagious does not remove her from § 504's coverage. [The Court cannot determine whether Arline (P) was otherwise qualified to work because the district court failed to properly inquire into the nature of the risk, the duration of the risk, the severity of the risk, and the probability that the disease would be transmitted and cause harm.] Affirmed and remanded.

**COMMENT:** The case demonstrates just how broadly the term "handicapped" will be interpreted under § 504 of the Act. One can be handicapped, for example, if one has tested positive for HIV, the virus that causes AIDS, without yet exhibiting any symptoms of AIDS. Of greater controversy is the question of when one should come under the scope of § 504 if the handicapped is "perceived" rather than actual.

## Discussion Questions

1. How is Arline protected under § 504 of the Rehabilitation Act?

2. What precautions need to be taken in a school building to protect teachers and students?

3. If the defendants had argued not on the qualification of special needs, but rather the severity of the risk to others, would the ruling remain the same?

# CHALK V. U.S. DISTRICT COURT, CENTRAL DISTRICT OF CALIFORNIA 840 F.2D 701 (9TH CIR. 1988)

**GENERAL RULE OF LAW:** A person with AIDS is considered "otherwise qualified" under § 504 of the Rehabilitation Act of 1973 and is therefore afforded full protection under the Act.

**PROCEDURE SUMMARY:**

**Plaintiff:** Vincent L. Chalk (P), a teacher of hearing-impaired pupils

**Defendant:** U.S. District Court, Central District of California (D)

**U.S. District Court Decision:** Motions for preliminary injunctions denied

**U.S. Court of Appeals Decision:** Reversed and remanded

**FACTS:** Chalk (P), a certified teacher of hearing-impaired pupils in Orange County Schools, taught in that district for approximately six years. While hospitalized for pneumonia in February of 1987, Chalk (P) learned he had contracted Acquired Immune Deficiency Syndrome (AIDS). Chalk's (P) physician, Dr. Siskind, declared Chalk (P) fit to return to work April 20, after nearly eight weeks of treatment and recuperation. However, after learning of the diagnosis, the Orange County Department of Education barred Chalk (P) from teaching in the classroom and reassigned him to an administrative position. Chalk (P) agreed to remain in the administrative position until an opinion could be submitted by Dr. Prendergast, the director of Epidemiology and Disease Control for the Orange County Health Care Agency, regarding the degree of risk Chalk (P) posed to his students. On May 22, Dr. Prendergast reported to the Department that Chalk (P) did not present any risk of transmitting HIV, the virus believed to cause AIDS, to students or to anyone else at the school. Chalk (P) then agreed to stay at his administrative post for the remaining weeks of the school year.

Chalk (P) met with Department representatives on August 5 to discuss Chalk's (P) permanent return. The Department offered Chalk (P) another administrative position with the option of working at home or in the office and at the same salary and benefit level that he was currently entitled to. Chalk (P) refused. The Department informed him it would file an action for declaratory relief if he demanded to be returned to the classroom. The Department filed the action on August 6 in state court. Meanwhile, Chalk (P) filed in federal district court (D), where he requested a preliminary and permanent injunction to prevent the Department from excluding him from classroom duties. Chalk (P) claimed that the Department's action violated the Rehabilitation Act of 1973, which prohibits recipients of federal funds from discriminating against otherwise qualified handicapped persons. Chalk (P) contended that he was "otherwise qualified" under the Act, and could not be transferred because he posed no risk to the health of persons around him.

After some discussion, the Department dropped its state court action and filed a counterclaim in district court (D). The district court (D) denied Chalk's (P) motion for a preliminary and permanent injunction, finding that he had not shown sufficient monetary loss and therefore had not proven irreparable injury, one of the prerequisites for an injunction. As a result, the Department reassigned Chalk (P) to an administrative position. Chalk (P) filed a **writ of mandamus** and a motion for an expedited appeal with the court of appeals, which granted the latter. Pending the appeal, Chalk (F) filed an emergency motion for an injunction. On November 18, the court of appeals reversed, remanding the case to the district court (D). [Procedurally, the district court (D) was the named defendant (for purposes of this case) in the motion for an emergency injunction to order the district court (D) to act.]

**ISSUE:** Is a person with AIDS considered to be "otherwise qualified" under § 504 of the Rehabilitation Act of 1973 and therefore entitled to full protection under the Act?

**HOLDING AND DECISION:** (Poole, C. J.) Yes. Section 504 of the Rehabilitation Act of 1973 is applicable to a person with AIDS. This conclusion is compelled by application of the standard formulated in *School Board of Nassau County v. Arline* (1987). In the *Arline* decision, the Supreme Court held that a person with a contagious disease could be excluded from the "otherwise qualified" provision of § 504 of the Act only if reasonable accommodation by an employer could not eliminate the transmission risk presented by the contagious person. To determine this, the Supreme Court required that four specific findings of fact be made, based on reasonable medical judgments with deference to public health officials' judgments.

The fact findings included determining how the disease was transmitted (nature of the risk), the length of time the individual was infectious (duration of the risk), the potential harm the person presented (severity of the risk), and the probability of transmission. In this case, the district court (D) neglected to follow the legal standards in *Arline* when it improperly relied on unsupported scientific speculation instead of deferring to the public health officials' reasonable medical judgments entered into evidence. In addition, Chalk (P) had met the burden of proving one of the elements necessary for granting a preliminary injunction. The two elements were (a) showing that the motion would probably succeed on the merits of the case and that a denial of the motion had the possibility of inflicting irreparable injury to him, or (b) showing that the motion raised serious questions that tipped the balance of hardships sharply against Chalk' (P). In assessing the possibility of irreparable injury, both monetary loss and nonmonetary deprivation must be taken into account. Chalk (P) successfully demonstrated that the motion would probably succeed on the merits of the case. Thus, the district court (D) erred in focusing solely on monetary loss when making its determination. Accordingly, the district court (D) erred when it denied Chalk's (P) motion for a preliminary injunction. Reversed and remanded.

**COMMENT:** The court noted that a person with AIDS could be reevaluated under the "otherwise qualified" clause contained in § 504 of the Rehabilitation Act if the person developed a contagious disease. Administrators must balance the rights of an employee with AIDS against the risk presented to other employees and to students who come within the infected employee's presence; however, the balancing test must rest on the best medical knowledge and not on irrational fear and prejudice. As HIV cannot be transmitted casually, mere infection with the virus is not enough to justify reevaluation. Moreover, development of symptoms of AIDS (i.e., specific secondary infections that are typical of the disease) will not necessarily justify reevaluation. For example, Kaposi's sarcoma, a rare cancer, poses no risk of casual transmission, whereas tuberculosis, an airborne lung infection, does. The former would not justify reevaluation, but the latter probably would. School administrators, when transferring a teacher with a contagious disease such as AIDS, are best protected against suit by obtaining the written permission of the employee to be transferred. This case is a warning to school administrators that they cannot deal with personnel without exercising caution. Great care must be taken when transferring a teacher with a contagious disease such as AIDS. Regardless of the community pressure that may be generated for an administrative transfer, unless permission is secured from the person, an arbitrary transfer could result in a tortious situation.

## Discussion Questions

1. Under what circumstances may a person handicapped with a contagious disease be "otherwise qualified" within the meaning of § 504 of the Rehabilitation Act of 1973?

2. Based on *School Board of Nassau County v. Arline* (1987), on what four factors does the court base its determination whether one "poses a direct threat" to himself or herself or others due to the nature of his or her job? How did the district court fail to follow the legal standards?

3. Under what circumstances may an employer investigate whether an employee poses a direct threat to himself or herself or others due to the nature of his or her job?

4. Do employees have a duty to disclose HIV/AIDS status to their employer?

---

Additional case briefs can be found on the SAGE Web site at the following address:
http://www.sagepub.com/aquilacasebriefs

---

# NOTES

1. Knox County Board of Education v. Willis, 405 S.W.2d 952 (1966).
2. Vanelli v. Reynolds School Dist. No.7, 667 F.2d 773 (9th Cir. 1982).

3. Barcheski v. Grand Rapids Public School, 412 N.W.2d 296 (Mich. App. 1987).

4. See Board of Regents of State Colleges v. Roth, 408 U.S. 564 (1972).

5. Griggs v. Duke Power Co., 401 U.S. 424, 91 S. Ct. 849 (1971).

6. Wygant v. Jackson Board of Education, 476 U.S. 367 (1986).

7. Franklin v. Gwinnett County Public Schools, 503 U.S. 60 (1992).

8. School Board of Nassau County v. Arline, 481 U.S. 1024 (1987).

9. See Gurmankin v. Costanzo, 556 F.2d 184 (3d Cir. 1977).

10. Chalk v. United States District Court Central District of California and Orange County Superintendent of Schools, 840 F.2d 701 (9th Cir. 1988).

11. See Knox County Board of Education v. Willis, 405 S.W.2d 952 (1966); see also Penasco Independent School District No.4 v. Lucero, 86 N.M. 683 (1974).

12. See Vanelli v. Reynolds School Dist. No.7, 667 F.2d 773 (9th Cir. 1982).

13. See Barcheski v. Grand Rapids Public School, 412 N.W.2d 296 (Mich. App. 1987), for an example of the dismissal of a tenured teacher based on poor judgment and improper conduct.

14. See Keefe v. Geanakos, 418 F.2d 359 (1st Cir. 1969).

15. See Fisher v. Snyder, 476 F.2d 375 (8th Cir. 1973).

16. See Erb v. Iowa State Board of Public Instruction, 216 N.W.2d 339 (1974).

17. See Viemeister v. Board of Education of Borough of Prospect Park, 5 N.J. Super 215 (1949).

18. See Board of Regents of State Colleges v. Roth, 408 U.S. 564 (1972).

19. See Kingsville Independent School District v. Cooper, 611 F.2d 1109 (5th Cir. 1980).

20. See Palmer v. Board of Ed. of City of Chicago, 603 F.2d 1271 (7th Cir. 1979).

21. See Perry v. Sinderman, 408 U.S. 593 (1972).

22. See Gosney v. Sonora Independent School District, 603 F.2d 522 (5th Cir. 1979).

23. See Gillett v. Unified School District No. 276, 227 Kan. 71 (1980).

24. See Pickering v. Board of Education of Township High School District 205, 391 U.S. 563 (1968).

25. See Mt. Healthy City School District Board of Education v. Doyle, 429 U.S. 274 (1977).

26. See Fowler v. Board of Education of Lincoln County, 819 F.2d 657 (6th Cir. 1987), in which the court determined that a teacher was properly terminated for showing an objectionable movie to her class when this was done without the requisite communicative intent.

27. Meritor Savings Bank, FSB v. Vinson, 477 U.S. 57 (1986).

28. Jackson v. Birmingham Board of Education, 2005 U.S. LEXIS 2928 (2005).

29. See E.E.O.C. v. Madison Community Unit School District No. 12 818 F.2d 577 (7th Cir. 1987).

30. Davidson v. Board of Governors, 920 F.2d 441 (7th Cir. 1990).

31. School Board of Nassau County v. Arline, 481 U.S. 1024 (1987).

32. Gurmankin v. Costanzo, 556 F.2d 184 (3d Cir. 1977).

33. Bragdon v. Abbot, 524 U.S. 624 (1998).

34. Board of Regents of State Colleges v. Roth, 408 U.S. 564, 92 S. Ct. 2701 (1972).

35. See Board of Regents of State Colleges v. Roth, 408 U.S. 564, 92 S. Ct. 2701 (1972).

36. Deshaney v. Winnebago Cnty. Dep. Soc. Serv., 489 U.S. 189 (1989).

# Part IV

# Legal Aspects of Schools

# 13

# Local School Boards
# and Contract Liability

*The powers not delegated to the United States by the Constitution, nor prohibited by it to the States, are reserved to the States respectively, or to the people.*

—Amendment X, 1781

## OVERVIEW

The "reserve" clause of the Tenth Amendment of the U.S. Constitution makes education a state responsibility, similar to a state's sovereignty in its exercise of police powers, power to tax, and obligation to provide for the welfare of its citizens. Therefore, the local school board is a creature of state government, and, as such, its members are considered state, not local, officers. A state legislature typically enacts legislation providing for the creation of local school boards and the selection and retention of board members. The authority delegated to local board members is sovereign in nature and is broadly interpreted by the courts. As with most elected or appointed officials, board members are forbidden to delegate their discretionary (as opposed to ministerial) authority to other entities or parties. In this context, discretionary authority refers to their decision-making authority, that is, their exercise of judgment or discretion. Thus, while pro forma **ministerial authority** may be delegated to other agents or agencies, the decision-making authority of a school board may not be delegated.

Just as the Tenth Amendment reserves powers not delegated to the federal government to the state, when there is a conflict between a state law and a federal law, the U.S. Constitution is paramount. Thus, when there is a conflict between the U.S. Constitution and a local school board action, the school board's preference must, obviously, give way to the Constitution. For example, an Arkansas school board's prohibition of the teaching of Darwin's theory of evolution in schools was held to be unconstitutional as a violation of the

First Amendment. The reasoning was that neither a state nor a local school board may forbid the teaching of evolution because doing so promotes a religion (in this case, the board-approved Genesis creation theory).[1] Another example was a Nebraska statute prohibiting the teaching of a foreign language to a child before the eighth grade. This violates the Fourteenth Amendment's liberty guarantees. Among these guarantees are the rights of teachers to teach and students to acquire knowledge.[2]

School board members are state officers rather than employees. An officer is one who holds an office and carries out a sovereign function for the public. School board members, as state officers, acquire their sovereign position by appointment or election. As a rule, an officer may not exercise her public position in a manner that leads to her private gain. School board meetings must be conducted within the school district, and, usually, the deliberations must be public. Board members sometimes adjourn public meetings in order to consider sensitive matters in a private, executive session. However, no formal actions may be taken in an executive session; such meetings are for purposes of discussion only. If a local board wishes to take action based on executive session discussions, it must reconvene in open session and thereafter make its action official. A quorum, usually defined as a majority of board members, is required for action to be taken. Finally, the official or legal record of school board action is contained in the minutes of its meetings, which are public records available for review.

Local school boards frequently enter into contracts for a wide range of services that are necessary for the planning and operation of a regional school system. However, there is no inherent authority on the part of the local board to enter into contracts. Rather, such authority exists only insofar as it has been expressly or implicitly granted by the state legislature. Questions often arise as to the nature and extent of the authority that has been granted.

In most instances, the general law of contracts applies to school board actions. The contract law discussed in this chapter involves contract actions of school boards apart from those contractual relationships involving faculty and staff (see Chapters 9 through 12 for a discussion of contract issues concerning teachers). The law of contract requires certain basic elements, such as mutual assent, consideration, legally competent parties, legal subject matter, and agreement in a form accepted in law. Mutual assent is often referred to as a "meeting of the minds," and includes an offer and acceptance whereby parties agree on essential elements such as price, subject involved, and terms of performance. Essentially, it is the basis of the bargain—that which is bargained for (a purchased good and the currency used to make the purchase constitute the consideration of most commercial transactions). Modification of an offer constitutes a counteroffer that must be accepted by the first party for it to be binding. Thus, a counteroffer is a rejection of the original offer, and in its place, a new offer with modified terms is made. Consideration is something of value (often money) that one side pays for performance. Gifts and gratuitous services do not constitute contracts because no consideration is provided. In education, legal competence requires that the parties are authorized to enter into the contract. For example, only the school board, not an individual member, can enter into a contract. Further, when a school board enters into a contract that exceeds the board's power, that contract is **ultra vires** and not enforceable. The final element is form. A contract must follow the correct form (e.g., it must be in writing), although even this can sometimes be waived.

There are three types of contracts: express, implied in fact, and implied in law. An express contract is characterized by a precise declaration of the rights and duties of the parties, either orally or in writing. Implied-in-fact contracts are suggested by the conduct of the parties, meaning that the parties' actions clearly indicate that they intended a contract to exist, even though they did not enter into an express contract. If an implied-in-fact contract is found to exist, its terms will be no less binding than those of an express contract.

In contrast, an implied-in-law contract (or quasi-contract) is created by courts in order to promote equity and to remedy injustice. A party will be bound by an implied-in-law contract if failing to create such a contract would result in his "unjust enrichment" at the expense of another.[3]

## Case Study

### Should the School Board Pay?

The Scholarly Book Company, a textbook publishing company, provided the Happy Hearts School Board with thousands of volumes of books for use in each of its school libraries. The Scholarly Book Company textbook sales agent, eager to make a sale, recommended books that the Happy Hearts School District librarian deemed unsuitable. Further, the Scholarly Book Company textbook agent also ignored information that indicated federal funds would not be available to pay for the books. Of course, the Happy Hearts School District superintendent told the sales agent that the school district anticipated paying for the books with Title II funds. The school superintendent also approved the purchase, even though the superintendent should have known that he needed school board approval to do so. The parties signed a "purchase-lease" agreement under which Happy Hearts School District would pay for the books in installments. Soon thereafter, Happy Hearts took possession of the books, distributed the books to the libraries, and used the books for a year. At the end of the year, the school district then collected all of the books and held them for Scholarly Book Company's pickup after it became clear that federal funds were not available, and would not become available, for such a purchase. Happy Hearts School District made no attempt to pay for the books and refused to make payment when Scholarly Book Company requested payment. Scholarly Book Company then sued for breach of contract and demanded the full purchase price.

### Discussion Questions

1. What are the arguments on both sides?

2. Should the court decide differently if there is a statute expressly denying reimbursement?

3. Should a school district be legally required to pay a reasonable amount for school materials it has ordered and used, even if it intended to buy them only if federal funding became available?

4. Do quantum meruit principles apply here?

# IMPORTANT CONCEPTS

- **Legislature-delegated authority:** State legislatures delegate to local school boards the authority to govern their respective districts.

- **Board jurisdiction:** Local boards are generally empowered to take action with respect to local curricula, revenue generation, and personnel issues, among other functions.

- **Distinct entities:** Local school boards and local government are separate, distinct entities.

- **Nature of authority:** Authority delegated to local boards may be express or implied and discretionary or ministerial. Implied authority is commonly upheld by courts as a necessary and practical means of effectuating express authority. Discretionary authority, which involves judgment, generally cannot be delegated to subordinate personnel.

- **State officers:** Local school board members are state, not local, officers.

- **Member selection and limitations:** Generally speaking, board members are elected or appointed, but they may not use their sovereign positions for their private gain and may be removed only for cause.

- **Board elections:** School board elections are set by statute; the "one person, one vote" principle predominates, and members may be elected from subdistricts or "at large."

- **Invalid election standard:** A school board election will not be declared invalid unless the disputed conduct of the election renders the results uncertain.

- **Collective board action:** School board members must act collectively; individual members may not act on behalf of the entire board.

- **Board rules and regulations:** Local boards are generally free to set their own procedural rules and regulations in connection with board meetings.

- **Board meeting requirements:** Board meetings must be held within school district territory, must be open to the public, and must be recorded in official minutes.

- **State grant of authority:** Each local school board receives its authority to contract from the state legislature.

- **Competitive bidding:** A competitive bidding selection process is generally required by statute in order to ensure that local school boards make efficient expenditures of public funds.

- **Lowest responsible bidder:** Most competitive bidding statutes provide that contracts must be awarded to the "lowest responsible bidder." However, school boards that are required by law to award contracts to the "lowest responsible bidder" must conduct thorough investigations into the financial standing, reputation, experience, resources, facilities, efficiency, and judgment of a lowest bidder before accepting a bid.

- **Statutory bidding requirements:** Many states require that school districts enter into contracts whenever the total cost of needed goods or services exceeds a set dollar amount. When the amount is less than the statutorily set amount, a school district may still enter into any contract, if doing so leads to a more "efficient and economical" system.

- **Performance by mistaken bidder:** A bidder who discovers a mistake in the bid after it has been accepted may nonetheless be required to perform under the terms of the contract that has been created, unless it can be shown that the school board reasonably should have suspected bidding error and investigated prior to accepting the bid.

- **Contract amendments and modifications:** Generally speaking, the parties to a contract may amend or modify it unless doing so contravenes statutory guidelines.

- **Recovery for part performance under a voided contract:** When a contract is declared void, the contracting party who has performed in part may be able to recover the reasonable value of services rendered if the underlying contract was initially a proper subject of the school board's contracting authority.

- **Invalid contracts entered into by school board's agent:** While a school board will not be bound by an invalid contract entered into on its behalf by its agent, it may, however, choose to ratify such a contract by accepting the benefits of the contract.

- **Conflicts of interest:** A school board member may not maintain a personal financial interest in a contract that comes before the board.

# AUTHORITY OF THE LOCAL SCHOOL BOARD

While education in this country is the responsibility of the states, portions of it must necessarily be administered at the local level. State legislatures generally delegate the responsibility of administering local school districts to local school boards. Please note, however, that in some cases, a state board of education, itself a creature of legislative delegation, may oversee various functions or aspects of local school districts. Nevertheless, a local school board is empowered to make a wide range of operational decisions affecting its district.

## The Local School Board

Because education is a unique state function, a state government may delegate, but not distribute, its authority to govern the state school system to local school boards. Authority is commonly delegated by way of legislative enactments or regulations. Therefore, state laws and administrative codes direct the management of schools by local school boards.

State legislatures frequently empower local boards to do part or all of each of the following specific functions:

*Establish Curriculum.* Local boards may oversee and respond to specific curriculum-related needs of the local district. Curriculum includes all aspects of the instructional program that provide content knowledge to students.

*Conform to Federal Law and the U.S. Constitution.* Federal law may be controlling with regard to the curriculum-setting practices of the local board. For example, a group of Chinese-speaking students challenged the San Francisco school board's refusal to provide them either with instruction in the English language or with classes in their native language. The U.S. Supreme Court held that the local board's inaction in this regard was a violation of the federal Civil Rights Act of 1964.[4] The U.S. Constitution is also controlling. Therefore, when there is a conflict between the U.S. Constitution and a local school board action, the school board's preference must, obviously, give way to the Constitution. For example, an Arkansas school board prohibited the teaching of Darwin's theory of evolution in schools. This was held to be unconstitutional: Neither a state nor a local school board may forbid the teaching of evolution because doing so promotes a religion (as embodied in the board-approved Genesis creation theory), in violation of the First Amendment to the Constitution.[5] A Nebraska statute prohibited the teaching of a foreign language to a child before the eighth grade. This was held to be a violation of the Fourteenth Amendment's liberty guarantees. Among these guarantees are the rights of teachers to teach and students to acquire knowledge.[6] Florida state courts would not entertain Section 1983 claims against school boards, on the ground that doing so would violate **sovereign immunity**. Such an interpretation would lead to a rule that state agencies are not subject to liability under Section 1983. This state court failure to enforce a federal law is a violation of the supremacy clause.[7]

*Raise School Revenues.* Local boards may raise revenues for school construction and maintenance by passing local school bond issues. Local boards may also pass operating levies, which support the day-to-day costs of operating a school district.

*Employ and Discharge Personnel.* Local boards may hire and fire personnel, such as teachers and administrators. While the specific procedures are established in law or by codes, the authority to do so is delegated by the state to the local board.

*Establish Policy.* Local boards may set and implement other policies necessary to the operation of the school district, such as rules and regulations pertaining to student conduct, athletic activities, and competitive examinations. These rules and regulations must not, of course, violate constitutional guarantees and protections. For example, a student's First Amendment right to refrain from reciting the pledge of allegiance was upheld by a federal court of appeals in *Goetz v. Ansell* (1973).[8] Specifically, a local school board's rule was declared unconstitutional because it required that all students who chose not to take the pledge had to leave the classroom or stand in silence during the recitation. Further, a student's constitutional right to a public education does *not* prohibit a state (and by delegation, a local school board or state athletic association) from restricting access to athletic activities. In *Albach v. Odle* (1976), a rule barring newly transferred students from participating in athletics was upheld because the court ruled that athletic participation was not a protected part of the broader right to a public education.[9] In *Debra P. v. Turlington* (1984), a federal court of appeals held that a state law requiring successful completion of a competency exam prior to high school graduation could not be challenged when the students challenging the exam requirement had received sufficient instruction in the skills tested and the exam helped remedy, rather than perpetuate, past discrimination.[10]

*Manage School Affairs.* Local school boards have wide discretion in the management of school affairs. Nevertheless, this discretion is not unlimited. For example, a local school board may not remove selected books from the library simply because it dislikes the ideas conveyed in the books.[11]

## Express or Implied Local Board Authority

*Express Power.* An express power is one that is stated in state laws or administrative regulations.

*Implied Power.* An implied power generally flows from an express power; it is "implied" in the grant of an express power such that if it was not assumed, the express power could not be exercised. Generally, courts are not disposed toward recognizing implied powers. However, with regard to local school boards, most courts construe implied powers broadly, perhaps in recognition of the practical need for them.

## Discretionary or Ministerial Authority

Authority delegated to local boards is either "discretionary" or "ministerial" in nature.

*Discretionary Powers.* Powers are referred to as "discretionary" when they call for an exercise of judgment or discretion on the part of the person to whom they have been delegated. Such discretionary powers generally cannot be delegated by local board members to subordinate employees, such as superintendents and other administrators. Typical nondelegable discretionary powers include the powers to transfer or reassign teachers, close schools, and raise revenues.

*Ministerial Powers.* Powers are referred to as "ministerial" if they are more or less perfunctory or administrative in nature, that is, they involve little or no discretion and are a necessary means of carrying out a particular policy (e.g., the development—as opposed to the adoption—of a district budget). Such powers can be, and are often, delegated by local board members to district employees. As a rule, courts will not interfere with a local school board's exercise of its ministerial authority unless in doing so the board violates the law or in some manner abuses its authority. Thus, soundness of judgment is not a criterion considered by a reviewing court.

## Separate and Distinct Nature of Local School District and Local Government

The local school district and local government are separate, distinct entities. Local school districts and municipal government functions are rarely, if ever, merged. Although many urban areas are discussing joining a failing school district with the local government, usually the city, this is rarely done because of the local politics and the complexity of the undertaking. Similarly, regional government is being advocated in many urban areas. Sometimes the development of a regional governmental authority is accomplished, but this reorganization, which makes good sense from the perspective of economy of scale, rarely includes school districts. An example of such a regional design is greater Indianapolis, Indiana, which has a regional government that includes all governmental bodies with the exception of the area school districts.

## SCHOOL BOARD OFFICERS AND ELECTIONS

*State Officer Status of Board Members.* School board members are state officers, as opposed to employees.

*Sovereign Functions.* One who holds an office carries out a sovereign function on behalf of the general public.

*Appointment or Election.* An officer, in this case a school board member, acquires her sovereign position by appointment or election.

*Private Gain Prohibited.* As a rule, an officer may not exercise her public position in a manner that leads to her private gain.

*Acceptance of Resignation.* In some cases, an officer may not resign without the approval of the sovereign (in the case of a school board member, this means the state legislature).

*Removal for Cause.* An officer may be removed for cause only—unless the law provides otherwise. Notice and some sort of a fair hearing are generally required.

*School Board Election Requirements.* School board elections are set by statute.

*One Person, One Vote.* School board members are generally elected according to the "one person, one vote" principle. Board members may be elected from geographical subdistricts of the school district by the voters of their respective districts. As an alternative to district elections, board members may be elected "at large" (i.e., by the voters of the entire school district). In such cases, the candidates with the highest number of votes become school board members.

*Collective Board Action.* Once elected, the school board must act collectively. Individual board members may not set policies on behalf of the entire board, nor may they alone represent the interests of the full board.

*Standard for Invalidation of Irregular Election.* Irregularities in the conduct of a school board election will not result in the invalidation of the election so long as the results are reasonably certain.

## SCHOOL BOARD MEETINGS

*Procedural Rules and Regulations.* Generally speaking, each local school board is free to set its own procedural rules and regulations. In some cases, state legislatures prescribe by statute pertinent rules and regulations. In other cases, where no statutory requirements exist and the local board has not adopted its own rules, common parliamentary procedure will control.

*Meeting Location.* All meetings must be conducted within the territorial jurisdiction of the local school board.

*Open and Public Deliberations.* Most courts, and a large number of state statutes, require that local school board meetings be conducted in a manner that is open to the public (i.e., deliberations must be conducted and official actions must be taken in public). These provisions are often described as Sunshine Laws.

*Executive Session.* Board members sometimes adjourn public meetings in order to consider sensitive matters in private (or in executive session, as this type of meeting is commonly termed). Sensitive matters include those that would adversely affect the public interest if presented at an open meeting, such as the board's intended posture in connection with specific ongoing litigation. However, no formal actions may be taken in executive session; such meetings are for purposes of discussion only. If a local board wishes to take action based on executive session discussions, it must reconvene in open session and thereafter make its action official.

*Proper Notice of Meetings.* Proper notice as to the time and place of each scheduled board meeting must be provided to each board member, as well as to the public. Notice is proper if it is likely to be considered reasonable by a court of law.

*Voting Procedures.* Local school boards are free to establish their own voting procedures, if they have not been preempted in this area by state law. A quorum, usually defined as a majority of board members, is required for action to be taken.

*Minutes.* The official (i.e., legal) record of the local school board is contained in the minutes of its meetings, to which the public must be allowed access once they have been transcribed.

## GENERAL PRINCIPLES OF STATUTORY CONTRACT LIABILITY

*Contracting Authority Is Statutory in Origin.* A local school board's authority to contract is granted to it by the state legislature.

*Determining Nature and Extent of Statutory Authority.* Generally accepted principles of statutory construction provide a method for defining the nature and extent of the authority granted local school boards by way of statute.

*Effect of Specific Authority.* If the legislature has been specific in its delineation of the authority granted to a local school board, additional authority not granted in the same manner may not be assumed by the board. This principle will be upheld even where a local board in good faith enters into a contract that later is deemed invalid by reason of the board's failure to follow explicit statutory guidelines.

*Effect of Nonspecific Authority.* If the legislature has not been specific in its statutory grant of authority, the local board has some latitude in interpreting the nature and extent of its contractual authority. For example, if the manner in which a local board is to execute a particular function is not expressly or implicitly provided for by statute, a board may choose to "contract out" a particular service (i.e., enter into a contract with a private company to provide a particular service for the school district that might otherwise be provided by the district's own personnel).

# THE COMPETITIVE BIDDING PROCESS

Most states, by statute, require that local boards entertain competing bids from would-be contractors prior to selecting the best and most economical contract. Such contracts generally involve more than a certain minimum dollar amount. As a rule, the "lowest responsible bidder" is chosen from among those who compete for the contract award.[12] This process is designed to prevent favoritism and influence peddling from entering into the contractor selection process. The goal is the most cost-efficient expenditure of public funds possible. It is not always easy to determine which bidder is the lowest *responsible* bidder; the bidder who submits the lowest bid may not be as "responsible" as other bidders or sufficiently responsible to be worthy of a particular contract award. Generally, courts will not intervene in the bid selection process unless the selecting entity has acted wholly arbitrarily. Responsible bidder statutes are designed to protect taxpayers, not grant rights to bidders.

## Miscellaneous Considerations Regarding the Submission and Acceptance of Bids

School boards often require that bidders submit financial statements with their bids; failure to do so is grounds for rejection of a bid. School boards often reserve the right to reject all bids if none is considered suitable. In most states, competitive bidding is not required if the dollar amount of a contract is below a certain statutory minimum. Courts will not permit school boards to circumvent the bidding process by breaking a contract up into smaller subcontracts, each below the minimum bidding dollar amount.[13]

## Withdrawn and Mistaken Bids

### Before Acceptance

Before a bid has been accepted, the bidder may wish to withdraw it for various reasons, such as the discovery of an error in the calculation of the bid amount. Many states have set procedures that allow for the withdrawal of bids in legitimate circumstances (such as those involving error) but prevent withdrawal when it is sought as a means of manipulating the bidding process. Generally speaking, the benefit of the bidding process would be circumvented if bidders could unilaterally withdraw their bids prior to their acceptance/rejection but after all bids have been opened and made public.

### Post-Acceptance Discovery of Bid Amount Error

The discovery of an error in the calculation of a bid amount after it has been accepted presents a different problem. Under the principles of contract law, the acceptance of the bid has created an obligation to perform on the part of the bidder (as well as on the entity accepting the bid). On the one hand, it may be argued that the bidder should be required to perform because she alone was in the best position to control for error. However, if it can be demonstrated that the entity accepting the bid *knew* of the error, most courts will not permit it to benefit thereby. In some such cases, knowledge will be attributed to the acceptor if it is determined that a reasonable person would have suspected the bid error and investigated it prior to accepting the bid.

## Modified or Amended Bids

Ordinarily, the parties to a contract are free to modify or amend its terms. Since competitive bidding laws exist to benefit the public, the parties to a competitively bid agreement may not be permitted to modify or amend the agreement unless doing so is clearly in the public interest. As a rule, modifications or amendments that alter a contract to the point of abandoning it in favor of creating a new one are not permissible. Changes aimed at updating the contract in light of new and unexpected circumstances will generally be permitted by the courts.

# RECOVERY UNDER THE VARIOUS FORMS OF CONTRACT

It is not always clear what a contractor will be permitted to recover under a contract that has subsequently been declared void, assuming the contractor has performed all or a portion of his obligations. Recovery depends upon various factors, including the type of contract, the nature of the parties' obligations under the contract, when the contract was breached, and who was responsible for the breach.

## Types of Contracts

*Express Contracts.* Express contracts are characterized by a precise declaration of the rights and duties of the parties, either orally or in writing.

*Implied-in-Fact Contracts.* Implied-in-fact contracts are suggested by the *conduct* of the parties (i.e., the parties' actions clearly indicate that they intended a contract to exist, even though they did not enter into an express contract). Note that an implied-in-fact contract can only be created in those instances in which the school district possessed the authority to enter into an express contract with regard to the subject matter in the first place. If an implied-in-fact contract is found to exist, its terms will be no less binding than those of an express contract.

*Implied-in-Law Contracts (or Quasi-Contracts).* Implied-in-law contracts are created by courts in order to promote equity and remedy injustice. A party will be bound by an implied-in-law contract if failing to create such a contract would result in his "unjust enrichment" at the expense of another.[14]

## Measures of Recovery

When a plaintiff brings an action for damages for breach of contract, the method the court will use to "measure" or determine the amount of damages to be awarded will depend on the type of contract breached.

*Express Contracts.* Recovery under an express contract depends on the provisions of the contract (regardless of whether the recovery is viewed as equitable or just) and the nature of the breach (e.g., failure to deliver goods, failure to deliver goods of contracted-for quality, failure to perform services, or failure to complete partially performed services). Generally, recovery is called "expectancy damages." In other words, the breaching party is liable to put the nonbreaching party in the position it would have been in had the contract been fully performed.

*Implied-in-Fact Contracts.* Recovery under an implied-in-fact contract is based upon the *reasonable value* of goods or services rendered, which may not be the same as the actual price of the goods or services rendered.

*Implied-in-Law Contracts.* Recovery under an implied-in-law contract is based upon the value of the *benefit conferred* upon the party to whom the goods or services have been rendered. Under the theory of quantum meruit, the benefited party is required to pay an amount equal to the benefit it has received to the party who conferred the benefit at its expense.[15]

*Note.* The "reasonable value" and "benefit conferred" tests are separate and distinct, yet many courts confuse them by using them interchangeably.

## Recovery Under Invalid or Unauthorized School Contracts

A contract can be declared invalid when school officials have entered into it without following statutory guidelines (e.g., the local school board president orders items from a provider without any authorization from the full board of education). A contract that a school board is unauthorized by law to enter into is said to be ultra vires, or "beyond the powers" granted to the board. Complicating matters is the fact that it is not always easy to determine which contractual actions or subject matters are within the power of the school board. Statutory authority will govern in most instances, but statutes are sometimes quite difficult to construe.

*Express Contracts.* A contractor whose express contract with a school board has been declared invalid will be able to recover the value of the obligations performed, in whole or in part, to the benefit of the school board as of the date of invalidation.

*Implied-in-Fact Contracts.* In most cases, the courts will hold the school district liable under an implied-in-fact contract for the reasonable value of the goods or services it received, so long as the contract does not in some other way violate public policy (a public good). Because an implied-in-fact contract can only be found if a school board could have entered into an express contract with the aggrieved party, recovery for breach of an implied-in-fact contract is treated similarly to breach of an express contract. An aggrieved party will be denied recovery when the school district did not have the authority to enter into an express contract for the same obligation, but mistakenly did so anyway.[16]

For example, a contract that runs afoul of competitive bidding requirements will probably be deemed ultra vires insofar as school boards generally have no authority to enter into agreements circumventing such statutory procedures. The hardships to the aggrieved party denied recovery on an ultra vires contract are no different than if the underlying contract had merely been invalid but within the contracting authority of the school district.

## Recovery Under Invalid Contracts Entered Into by Agents of the School Board

School boards can authorize one or more people, such as a school superintendent, to enter into contracts on behalf of the board. A person who has been granted such authority acts as an agent of the board, and the board will be bound by its agent's agreements made within the scope of the agent's authority. However, a board is not bound to a contract when its agent has entered into it without authority (i.e., the agent acts outside the scope of her authority), and the contract is invalid.

*Ratification.* Although a board will ordinarily not be bound to a contract entered into by its agent without authority, it may choose to be bound after the fact by ratifying the agreement. The board may ratify an unauthorized contract either by voting to approve it or by signaling its approval through accepting the benefits of the contract (with full knowledge it was not originally authorized). Note, however, that if it is impossible for the board to reject the benefits flowing from the contract, retention of the benefits will not signal ratification. Ratification renders the contract as valid as if it had been entered into with the proper authority in the first place. In effect, ratification is a retroactive authorization of the agent to enter into the contract.

*Ratification of Ultra Vires Contracts.* Note, though, that an ultra vires contract cannot be ratified because the school board itself lacks the authority to commit to such an agreement.

## CONFLICTS OF INTEREST

Occasionally, a school board member will find herself with the following conflicting interests: sitting on the school board as a representative of the people of the school district and being a private party with a stake in a contract to which the board is also a party.

## Statutory Prohibitions

Most state statutes provide that a person may not officially represent two or more competing interests. A school board member (a public officer) may not maintain a financial interest in a contract on which she may be required to vote as a board member, lest the contract be declared void.

## Nature of Conflicting Interests

A board member's direct private participation in a contract with the board creates a sufficient conflicting interest. Some courts go even further: A school board contract entered into by a corporation, of which a board member is a stockholder, may be declared void in light of the potential, though less probable, conflict.

---

### Case Study

### Variable School Boundaries?

You are the principal of a high school in an affluent suburban district that shares a border with an urban school district. This urban district has encountered many scholarly difficulties and has extremely poor student academic performance. Additionally, it has developed a reputation for school violence resulting from the number of youth gangs operating in the city schools. A problem that concerns many of the parents of students with the ability and willingness to learn is the poor performance of these urban students on the state's high-stakes testing program required by No Child Left Behind. Some parents who live on the common border pay a special tuition so their children can attend your suburban high school. Others illegally attend your school by claiming that they live in the district when, in fact, it is their friend or relative who resides in the district. One of your teachers has brought to your attention the fact that a student who is attending the high school actually lives outside your building's attendance boundaries. This student is well-mannered and bright. He has passed the state tests and plans to attend college. The teacher wants you to know, but she, and several other of this student's teachers, want you to allow the student to remain without having to pay special fees.

### Discussion Questions

1. What action should you take? Why?

2. If this student is disruptive, would you do anything differently? (For your information, your school district does not have an open enrollment option.)

3. If you decide to send the student back to his home school, what do you say to these teachers?

4. Is there a personal problem created if you decide not to notify school officials and begin the de-enrollment process?

# CONCLUSION . . . . . . . . . . . . . . . . . . . . . . . . . . . . . . . . . . . . . .

This chapter discussed the scope of school boards' authority to enter into contracts. Notably, the school board has no innate authority to enter into contracts of any kind. Rather, any such authority must be specifically delegated to it by the state legislature.

In determining the extent and scope of a statutory delegation of power to the board to enter into contracts, the court will apply general statutory construction principles. If the statute is specific, it is assumed that the board has no more authority than is explicitly given by the language of the statute. However, when the statute is not specific, boards are afforded more latitude.

In most states, if a contract exceeds a certain dollar amount, boards are required to contract with the lowest responsible bidder. This process is designed to prevent favoritism and influence peddling. However, it is possible to imagine a situation in which a low bidder is sufficiently responsible, but not nearly as responsible as a slightly higher bidder. Situations such as this create difficulty. Generally, courts will not intervene in the bid selection process unless the board has acted in a wholly arbitrary or capricious manner.

When contractors make bids, states only allow withdrawal of bids if they were based on a good faith mistake in calculation. Otherwise, the benefit of the bidding process would be circumvented if bidders could unilaterally withdraw their bids prior to acceptance but after all bids from competitors have been disclosed. If, however, the board discovers an error after it has accepted the bid, courts generally only allow withdrawal if the board knew or should have known of the error. The parties may not amend bids unless doing so benefits the public interest. However, changes aimed at updating the contract in light of new and unexpected circumstances will generally be permitted by the courts.

These contracts, like any contracts, are subject to recovery by the nonbreaching party on the basis of a variety of contract theories. These include violation of express contracts, implied-in-fact contracts, or implied-in-law contracts. Also, a contract can be declared invalid when the board has entered into it without statutory authority. These are called ultra vires, or "beyond the powers," contracts.

School boards can authorize one or more people, such as a school superintendent, to enter into contracts on behalf of the board. However, a board is not necessarily bound to this person's contracts if she acted beyond the scope granted to her as an agent of the board. The board may choose to ratify such an agreement by voting to approve it or by signaling approval by accepting the benefits of the contract.

If a board member has a significant financial interest in one of the competing contractors, a conflict of interest will likely arise. Most state statutes prevent a person from officially representing two competing parties to a contract. Such board members may not participate in the bidding process.

The cases below explore these concepts and the evolution of the powers granted to boards via statute to enter into and break contracts. The cases are meant to give the reader a sense of the impact of contract law on education. Refer to these cases as you read the textbook. As you become more familiar with how the law affects school boards, educators, students, and local governments, you may be able to more fully appreciate the heated controversy that contractual disputes can generate.

# CASE BRIEFS  ....................................................

## GOETZ V. ANSELL
## 477 F.2D 636 (2D CIR. 1973)

**GENERAL RULE OF LAW:** The state may not compel students to participate in the pledge of allegiance by requiring them either to say it or to stand while it is being said.

**PROCEDURE SUMMARY:**

**Plaintiff:** Goetz (P), a senior high school honor student and class president

**Defendant:** Ansell (D), president of North Colonie School District Board of Education

**U.S. District Court Decision:** Held for Ansell (D)

**U.S. Court of Appeals Decision:** Reversed

**FACTS:** Goetz (P), a senior high school honor student and president of his class, refused to participate in the pledge of allegiance. The president of the Board of Education, Ansell (D), gave Goetz (P) the option to either leave the classroom or stand silently during the recitation of the pledge. Goetz (P), contending that he had a First Amendment right to stay quietly seated, sued Ansell (D) in federal district court. He alleged that Ansell (D) violated his First Amendment right of free speech. The district court did not reach the merits of Goetz's (P) case, preferring to dismiss it because Goetz (P) had not gone first to the Board of Education for a hearing or to the New York Commissioner of Education. Goetz (P) appealed this dismissal to the Second Circuit Court of Appeals.

**ISSUE:** May the state compel students to participate in the pledge of allegiance by requiring them either to say it or to stand while it is being said?

**HOLDING AND DECISION:** (Feinberg, J.) No. A state may not, consistent with the First Amendment of the Constitution, compel a student to stand during recitation of the pledge of allegiance or make the student utter its words. Standing is part of the pledge as much as saying it and is a gesture of acceptance and respect. Thus, boards of education must allow silent, nondisruptive expressions of belief, such as sitting down. Nor can boards of education compel students to leave the classroom while the pledge is being said, as this could be interpreted by other students as punishment for nonparticipation and could subject the student to reproach and contempt among his classmates. Goetz (P), by sitting silently during the pledge, was legitimately asserting his First Amendment rights, and Ansell (D) had no basis for asking him to leave the room or stand during its recitation. Reversed.

**COMMENT:** In reaching this decision, the Second Circuit heavily emphasized that Goetz's (P) refusal to stand did not disrupt or interfere with the rights of other students to say the pledge. Obviously, if Goetz (P) had been disruptive, Ansell's (D) command to leave the room would have rested on stronger ground because Goetz (P) would then be interfering with the First Amendment freedoms of others. Although not addressed in this decision, Goetz's (P) claim had a legitimate basis in another aspect of the First Amendment: the right to free exercise of religion. Because the pledge explicitly refers to "one nation under God," Ansell's (D) directive that Goetz (P) stand could have also signaled acquiescence to belief in a deity or supernatural being.

## Discussion Questions

1. What other historical events were happening in the United States at the time of this decision?

2. Did the court believe that stating "one nation under God" was a public statement that a student believed in a supreme being?

3. Why was it important that Goetz's refusal to participate was nondisruptive?

# ALBACH V. ODLE 531 F.2D 983 (10TH CIR. 1976)

**GENERAL RULE OF LAW:** A student's constitutional right to a public education does not prevent appropriate state boards from regulating access to interscholastic athletics.

**PROCEDURE SUMMARY:**

**Plaintiff:** Albach (P), a high school transfer student

**Defendant:** Odle (D), Executive Secretary of New Mexico Activities Association

**U.S. District Court Decision:** Held for Odle (D)

**U.S. Court of Appeals Decision:** Affirmed

**FACTS:** The New Mexico Activities Association, of which Odle (D) was executive secretary, barred students from interscholastic high school competition for one year if they had recently transferred between a boarding school and a home district school. Albach (P) was a student covered by the rule, but he wanted to participate in school athletics. Therefore, he sued Odle (D), claiming that the rule barring him from participation was unconstitutional because he had a protected property right in a public education. The district court found for Odle (D), and Albach (P) appealed to the Tenth Circuit Court of Appeals.

**ISSUE:** Does a student's constitutional right to a public education prevent a state from regulating or restricting access to interscholastic athletics?

**HOLDING AND DECISION:** (Per curiam) No. A student's constitutional right to a public education does not prevent a state from regulating or restricting access to interscholastic athletics. Appropriate state boards have the discretion to supervise and regulate high school athletic programs, and their rules governing access will not be invalidated unless constitutionally protected "suspect classes," such as aliens or members of certain races, are excluded as a result. Although the right to a public education is constitutionally protected, its many components, including participation in athletic activity, are not individually or separately protected. Affirmed.

**COMMENT:** The court's decision here appears to be based on the fact that Albach's (P) exclusion from school was not complete and did not last for an unreasonable period of time. Albach (P) had based his claim on the U.S. Supreme Court decision of *Goss v. Lopez* (1975), which recognized a student's property interest in public education.[17] The student in the *Goss* case had been suspended for 10 days without a hearing and thus had been denied any and all access to public education for a defined period of time. The Supreme Court in *Goss* held that this deprived him of property without due process. It also held that this right of public education is not limited to classroom attendance but includes all activities, such as athletics and school clubs and social groups, which combined to provide an atmosphere of intellectual and moral advancement.

## Discussion Questions

1. Would the case result have been different if the student were a member of the chess club and the school had banned the student from attending meetings for one year because his grades did not meet a minimum standard?

2. Same question as above, but the student was required by his math teacher to join the chess club to receive credit for math class.

# BOARD OF ED. OF ISLAND TREES UNION FREE SCHOOL DIST. NO. 26 V. PICO 457 U.S. 853 (1982)

**GENERAL RULE OF LAW:** A local school board may not remove certain books from the library simply because it dislikes the ideas conveyed in the books.

**PROCEDURE SUMMARY:**

**Plaintiff:** Pico (P), a high school student

**Defendant:** Board of Education of Island Trees Union Free School Dist. #26 (Board) (D)

**U.S. District Court Decision:** Granted summary judgment for Board (D)

**U.S. Court of Appeals Decision:** Reversed and remanded

**U.S. Supreme Court Decision:** Affirmed the appeals court

**FACTS:** At a conference sponsored by a politically conservative organization of parents, certain members of the Board (D) obtained a list of books described as "objectionable" for allegedly being anti-American, anti-Christian, and anti-Semitic. Subsequently, it was discovered that the local high school library contained nine of the books on the list. Later, the Board (D) appointed a committee, made up of parents and school staff, to read the books and recommend whether they should be removed from the library. The committee recommended that most of the books not be removed. Despite the committee's recommendation, the Board (D) ordered the books removed. Pico (P), a high school student, then filed suit under Section 1983, alleging the removal violated his rights under the First Amendment. The Board (D) moved for summary judgment, which the district court granted. Pico (P) appealed, and the court of appeals reversed, holding that a triable issue of fact existed. The Board (D) appealed, and the U.S. Supreme Court granted review.

**ISSUE:** May a local school board remove certain books from a school library simply because members of the board dislike the ideas conveyed in the books?

**HOLDING AND DECISION:** (Brennan, J.) No. A local school board may not remove certain books from a school library simply because members of the board dislike the ideas conveyed in the books. To do so would violate students' rights under the First Amendment. Local school boards have wide discretion in the management of school affairs. This discretion, however, is not unlimited. Whether removal of the books denied Pico (P) his First Amendment rights depends upon the Board's (D) motive for doing so. If the motive was to prescribe what is "orthodox in politics, nationalism, religion, or other matters of opinion," the action infringed the students' rights. This is a question of fact to be determined at trial. The court of appeals, therefore, was correct in reversing the district court's grant of summary judgment for the Board (D). Affirmed.

**COMMENT:** Prior to *Pico,* the courts of appeals were divided on whether and under what circumstances a school board could remove certain books from public school libraries. The Second Circuit, in *President's Council, Dist. 25 v. Community School Board* (1972), held that a board could remove books that were without artistic or scientific merit.[18] The Sixth Circuit, in *Minarcini v. Strongesville City School District* (1976), held that removal simply because the board found the books objectionable violated the First Amendment.[19] The Court's ruling in *Pico* appears to be an adoption of the Sixth Circuit's position. The Court found that the board's motive for removal is the determinative factor. This **plurality decision** does allow school boards significant discretion in determining content. But this discretion cannot be exercised in a partisan or political manner so as to establish an official orthodoxy. A school board's rights need to be balanced with the First Amendment rights of students. Thus, if a board's motivation is to remove educationally unsuitable and vulgar books, this would not constitute an official suppression of ideas. Furthermore, when purchasing materials, school boards have the responsibility and duty to decide and exercise this very discretion. When the materials have been purchased and are in the library, a board's discretion is more limited (although various child-protective actions have been justified). When books are used in the classroom, the board's discretion is even more limited because of a teacher's academic freedom.

## Discussion Questions

1. Would the result in this case have been different if the board-appointed committee had recommended that all of the suspect books be removed?

2. Under this case, could a principal refuse to authorize the purchase of a specific book on the grounds that it was objectionable?

# DEBRA P. V. TURLINGTON 564 F. SUPP. 177, AFF'D, 730 F.2D 1405 (11TH CIR. 1984)

**GENERAL RULE OF LAW:** Students may be required to pass a competency examination in order to receive a high school diploma if the students have received sufficient instruction in the skills tested and if the test remedies, rather than perpetuates, the effects of past segregation in the high school district.

**PROCEDURE SUMMARY:**

**Plaintiffs:** Debra P. (P) and other Florida high school students

**Defendant:** Turlington (D), Florida Commissioner of Education

**First U.S. District Court Decision:** Held for Debra P. (P), enjoining use of test until 1982–1983 school year; held for Turlington (D), finding test valid

**First U.S. Court of Appeals Decision:** Affirmed as to injunction; reversed as to holding that test was valid and remanded to determine whether test covered materials actually taught and whether test intentionally discriminated against African Americans

**Second U.S. District Court Decision:** Held for Turlington (D) on remand questions

**Second U.S. Court of Appeals Decision:** Affirmed

**FACTS:** In 1978, Florida began to require that public high school students pass a functional competency exam, the SSAT-II, in order to receive a diploma. The test covered both communication skills and math skills. The failure rate was 10 times higher for African Americans than for whites in the test's first administration in 1979. By 1983, 99% of African American students passed the communication part and 91% passed the math part. High school students (P) challenged the constitutionality of the examination, alleging that it denied them due process in requiring them to demonstrate competency in skills they had not been taught. They also claimed it violated the Civil Rights Act because it discriminated against African Americans. During a first trial in the U.S. district court, surveys were introduced that showed that most students believed Florida taught what it tested; expert witnesses also testified that each student received an average of 2.7 opportunities to learn skills tested. Further, the schools made extensive remedial efforts to help students who initially failed the test to pass it before graduation. The district court held that the SSAT-II's content was valid but also held that the test violated the equal protection clause and the Civil Rights Act by perpetuating past discrimination against African Americans who had attended segregated schools for the first four years of their education. Because only students in the high school class of 1983 would be the first to have attended physically integrated schools for all of their 12 years of education, the test could not be administered until 1983. The U.S. Court of Appeals upheld the injunction but remanded to the district court to determine whether the exam was a "fair test of that which is taught" and whether the test reflected present effects of past discrimination or actually helped remedy past discrimination. On remand, the district court held that the test was "instructionally valid" and that although it had a racially discriminatory impact, the disproportionate rate of failure among African Americans was not caused by past segregation. The students (P) appealed.

**ISSUE:** May students be required to pass a competency examination in order to graduate from high school?

**HOLDING AND DECISION:** (Anderson III, C. J.) Yes. Students may be required to pass a competency examination in order to receive a diploma from high school if sufficient instruction has been provided for a student to master the skills tested and if the examination helps remedy, rather than perpetuate, any history of segregation in the school district. Here, most of the Florida students surveyed (90%–99%) believed they had been taught the skills tested, and evidence showed they had 2.7 opportunities to learn the material and were provided many chances for help if they failed the test. Further, although proportionately more blacks than whites fail the test, this failure rate is probably caused mostly by other factors, including remaining biases among teachers that African American students do not learn as well as whites. In fact, the African American passing rate had improved dramatically between 1979 and 1983, indicating that the test helped African Americans overcome the effects of past segregation. Affirmed.

**COMMENT:** The court here was most concerned with whether "vestiges" of past discrimination against African Americans caused poor performance on the SSAT-II, and it concluded that they had not. It emphasized the district court's finding of other facts that contributed to the higher African American failure rate, such as frequent suspensions of African American students, teacher stereotyping and bias, absence of African American administrators, and more frequent assignment to EMR ("educable mentally retarded") classes—practices unrelated to the administration of the test. The court found that the use of the test as a "diploma sanction" actually helped motivate African American students by creating a "climate of order" (which one expert testified was successful in Catholic schools). African American students' improvement in test scores over a four-year period actually reflected progress in battling discrimination. The result has been that competency examinations, which must be instructionally valid, are an accepted educational practice. They are now common as a high school graduation requirement.

## Discussion Questions

1. According to *Debra P. v. Turlington,* what two criteria must be met by a competency test before it can be used as a graduation requirement?

2. Why did Florida postpone using the SSAT-II test as a graduation requirement until 1983?

3. In this case, how was it determined that the SSAT-II test helped to remedy the effects of past segregation? How did the court explain the discrepancy in passing rates that existed between blacks and whites?

# HOWLETT V. ROSE
# 496 U.S. 356, 110 S. CT. 2430 (1990)

**GENERAL RULE OF LAW:** A state court's refusal to entertain a Section 1983 claim against a school board on sovereign immunity grounds violates the supremacy clause.

**PROCEDURE SUMMARY:**

**Plaintiff:** Howlett (P), a former high school student

**Defendant:** Rose (D), Superintendent of Schools for Pinellas County

**State Appeals Court Decision:** Held for Rose (D), dismissing on grounds the state court lacked jurisdiction over the Section 1983 claim

**State Supreme Court Decision:** Affirmed

**U.S. Supreme Court Decision:** Reversed

**FACTS:** An assistant principal searched Howlett's (P) car while it was parked on school premises. Based on the search, Howlett (P), then a student, was suspended for five days. Howlett (P) filed suit in state court under Section 1983 of the Civil Rights Act of 1871, arguing that the search and suspension violated his rights under the Fourth and Fourteenth Amendments of the U.S. Constitution. Rose (D), the school's superintendent, moved to dismiss the action, arguing the state court lacked jurisdiction to hear the Section 1983 claim because the state waiver of immunity statute did not apply to federal claims. The circuit court agreed and granted Rose's (D) motion. The state's high court affirmed. The U.S. Supreme Court granted review.

**ISSUE:** May a state court refuse to entertain a Section 1983 claim against a school board on grounds that to do so would violate sovereign immunity?

**HOLDING AND DECISION:** (Stevens, J.) No. A state court may not refuse to entertain a Section 1983 claim on grounds that to do so would violate sovereign immunity when the court otherwise has jurisdiction and the defense could not have been raised had the claim been brought in federal court. Absent a valid excuse, a state court's failure to enforce federal law according to the court's normal procedures is a violation of the supremacy clause. The refusal to entertain a Section 1983 claim against the school board directly violates federal law if the refusal amounts to a rule that state agencies are not subject to liability under Section 1983. Reversed.

**COMMENT:** *Howlett* was a unanimous decision clearly indicating that state infringement of the supremacy concept of federalism would not be tolerated. State courts may not deny a right guaranteed by the U.S. Constitution based upon a state law or practice that is in conflict with the federal right. However, the case may have a chilling effect on school boards and officials. The decision makes clear that their actions must pass federal civil rights protection standards even when federal law is more stringent than any similar state protections.

## Discussion Questions

1. Are school districts immune from liability for violating a student's civil rights?

2. What do you think is meant by "a chilling effect on school boards and officials"?

# HIBBS V. ARENSBERG
# 276 PA. 24, 119 A. 727 (1923)

**GENERAL RULE OF LAW:** School boards required by law to award construction contracts to the lowest "responsible" bidder must conduct a thorough investigation into the financial condition and practical experience of the lowest bidders before making the award.

**PROCEDURE SUMMARY:**

**Plaintiff:** Hibbs (P), an unsuccessful bidder for a construction contract

**Defendants:** Arensberg (D), the successful bidder; Fayette County School (School Board) (D)

**State Trial Court Decision (Pennsylvania):** Held for Arensberg (D) and Fayette County School Board (D)

**State Supreme Court Decision (Pennsylvania):** Reversed

**FACTS:** The Fayette County School Board (D) began to have a school built. It advertised for bids for component materials, including "vitrified, wire-cut face brick . . . to cost no more than $34 per thousand"; however, the ad did not refer to the deadline for completion of the school. Many bids were received, but all were rejected as "too high" at an initial meeting of the School Board (D). Nonetheless, at a second meeting, the fourth-lowest bid, submitted by Arensberg (D), was accepted during a vote. Although Pennsylvania state law required that school boards award contracts to the lowest "responsible" bidder, the Fayette County School Board (D) did not investigate whether any of the low bidders were financially safe and possessed the experience and technical resources to do the job well. Hibbs (P), a bricklayer and supplier who bid lower than Arensberg (D), challenged the School Board's (D) action in court as an improper exercise of discretion. The Pennsylvania trial court censured the Fayette County School Board (D) for not conducting this investigation, but it found that the School Board (D) had enough general knowledge of the quality of Arensberg's (D) work to award the contract to him. Hibbs (P) appealed.

**ISSUE:** Must school boards, which are required by law to award construction contracts to the lowest "responsible" bidder, conduct a thorough investigation into the financial condition and practical experience of the lowest bidders before accepting a bid?

**HOLDING AND DECISION:** (Kephart, J.) Yes. School boards, which are required by law to award construction contracts to the lowest "responsible" bidder, must conduct a thorough investigation into the financial standing, reputation, experience, resources, facilities, efficiency, and judgment of the lowest bidders before accepting a bid. Although boards may exercise their sound discretion and are not required to accept the lowest bid submitted if their investigation reveals the bidder to be financially irresponsible, it is not enough for boards merely to rely on the bidder's posting of a bond or the bidder's general reputation for good work. Furthermore, boards must include in their ads for bids the deadline for completion of the bid project and must furnish copies of the project specifications to all prospective bidders; not to do so encourages collusion by local bidders and the exclusion of outside bidders. Here, the Fayette County School Board (D) did not investigate Arensberg's (D) financial condition, experience, or resources. Instead, the board relied generally on his reputation. In addition, the School Board did not include in its ads completion deadlines or provide specs to all bidders. Therefore, it improperly exercised its discretion in accepting Arensberg's (D) bid. Reversed.

**COMMENT:** Because the appropriate use of public funds was at stake, the court here was particularly worried about the school board's obtaining the most information it could about the low bidders. It was also concerned that the school board, in turn, provided enough information to all prospective bidders, through spec sheets, in order to preempt two pervasive practices that restrict competition in bidding: first, the "hoarding" of a limited number of spec sheets by one bidder and second, the submission of an inflated bid by a contractor who has agreed in advance with other potential local bidders to "rake off" some of his excess profit to them in exchange for their "holding off" from submitting lower bids.

## Discussion Questions

1. When a school board investigates a "low bidder," may the school award the contract after acquiring positive reputation feedback only?

2. What details does a school board need to provide the bidders? Why?

3. Would it make more sense for a school board to ask for all the additional information as part of a bid submission?

---

# UTAH PLUMB./HEAT. CONTRACTOR ASSN. V. BD. OF ED. WEISER CNTY. SCH. DIST.
# 19 UTAH 2D 203, 429 P.2D 49 (1967)

**GENERAL RULE OF LAW:** A state statute that requires local school boards to advertise for bids "whenever schoolhouses are to be built" does not prevent them from exercising discretion in economizing when making improvements to a school once it is already built.

**PROCEDURE SUMMARY:**

**Plaintiff:** Utah Plumbing and Heating Contractors Association (P)

**Defendant:** Utah County Board of Education (School Board) (D)

**State Trial Court Decision:** Held for Utah County Board of Education (D)

**State Supreme Court Decision:** Affirmed

**FACTS:** The Utah Plumbing and Heating Contractors Association (P) sued a local Utah school board (D) to enjoin it from using its regular maintenance personnel to install a football field sprinkler system and from advertising for bids for "materials only" for the job. In doing so, it relied on a Utah statute that required the local school boards to advertise for bids for both labor and materials "whenever a schoolhouse is to be built." The School Board (D) had decided to use its personnel because it was short of funds and had long put off this and other desirable improvements, such as tennis courts. The trial court ruled that the Utah statute granted local school boards discretion to economize when construction of the school had already been completed and improvements to an existing facility were being made; therefore, if a school district was short of funds, it was entitled to determine the least expensive way of acquiring the system, and using its own personnel was one such legitimate way. The Utah Plumbing and Heating Contractors Association (P) appealed.

**ISSUE:** If a state statute requires local school boards to advertise for bids "whenever schoolhouses are built," are they thereby prevented from exercising discretion in economizing when making improvements to a school once it is already built?

**HOLDING AND DECISION:** (Crockett, C. J.) No. A state statute that requires local school boards to advertise for bids "whenever schoolhouses are to be built" does not prevent them from exercising broad discretion in cutting costs while making improvements to a school once it is already built. Here, the Utah school district

(D) was short on funds and had long put off installation of such things as sprinklers and tennis courts. It was entitled under the statute to determine the most efficient and economical way of carrying out its mission of providing a well-equipped facility for its students. The use of regular maintenance personnel during their off-hours promoted these objectives, saved money, and was well within this discretion. Affirmed.

**COMMENT:** Although the state supreme court noted that the board's action was in line with its efforts in administering the school system in the most "efficient and economical" manner possible, this decision should not be construed to allow a school board to divide a contract into parts in order to avoid statutory bidding requirements. State bid laws usually indicate the maximum amount that may be expended without requiring competitive bidding. Many states also allow for "alternative" bidding on public contracts. This procedure allows for bid submissions on alternative kinds or qualities of work and materials. While the board may select one of the alternatives (even if the bid is higher than another), it is bound to select the lowest responsible bidder in the category selected.

## Discussion Questions

1. Does this decision mean that school boards can avoid the bidding process for any work to be done on school grounds by hiring on-site personnel to do the job?

2. Do you think this lawsuit would have been filed if the school district had at least opened up bidding and prepared a cost analysis that showed using on-site personnel was the best option?

3. Why do you think Utah would have a statute requiring school boards to advertise for bids?

# RESPONSIVE ENVIRONMENTS CORP. V. PULASKI CNTY. SPECIAL SCHOOL DIST. 366 F. SUPP. 241 (E.D. ARK. 1973)

**GENERAL RULE OF LAW:** Under the theory of quantum meruit, a school district may be legally required to pay a reasonable amount for school materials it has ordered and used but refused to pay for, even if it intended to buy them only if federal funding became available.

**PROCEDURE SUMMARY:**

**Plaintiff:** Responsive Environments Corp. (P), a schoolbook dealer

**Defendant:** Pulaski County, Arkansas, Special School District (D)

**U.S. District Court Decision:** Held for Responsive Environments Corp. (P)

**FACTS:** Responsive Environments Corp. (P), a schoolbook publishing company, sold Pulaski Special School District (D) thousands of volumes of books for use in its school libraries. The Responsive Environments (P) agent, eager to make a sale, recommended books that the Pulaski District (D) librarian deemed unsuitable. He also ignored information indicating that federal funds would not be available to pay for the books. The Pulaski District (D) superintendent, in turn, told the sales agent that the district anticipated paying for the books with Title II funds and approved the purchase, even though he needed school board approval to do so. The parties signed a "purchase-lease" agreement, under which Pulaski (D) would pay for the books in installments. Pulaski (D) took, distributed, and used the books for a year, but collected them and held them for Responsive Environments' (P) pickup when it became clear that federal funds were not forthcoming. Pulaski (D) made no payment for the books, and when it refused Responsive's (P) demand for the full purchase price, Responsive (P) sued for breach of contract.

**ISSUES:** Under the theory of quantum meruit, may a school district be legally required to pay a reasonable amount for school materials it has ordered and used but refused to pay for, even if it intended to buy them only if federal funding became available?

**HOLDING AND DECISION:** (Williams, D. J.) Yes. Under the theory of quantum meruit, a school district may be legally required to pay a reasonable amount for school materials it has ordered and used but refused to pay for, even if it intended to buy them only if federal funding became available. The theory of quantum meruit applies when no real or implied contract exists between the parties but one party has, nevertheless, received a benefit from the other which is unjust for him to retain without paying for it. Here, despite the "lease-purchase" agreement, there was no contract between Responsive Environments (P) and Pulaski School District (D) because the Pulaski (D) superintendent had not obtained the approval of the school board before agreeing to buy the library books, nor did the Pulaski (D) superintendent intend to pay for them if the district did not receive federal funding. However, Pulaski (D) used the books for a year, and therefore Responsive Environments (P) deserves them back or a payment of $13,000 (somewhat less than their sale price), at its election.

**COMMENT:** The court here was mindful that neither party was blameless and that both were, in the words of the court, "seeking the pot of gold at the end of the federal rainbow." It points out the dereliction in duty by the school superintendent, whose actions on behalf of the district were not enforceable absent approval of the school board and who carelessly (and somewhat successfully) attempted to spend public funds for books his own librarian deemed unsuitable for adolescent consumption.

## Discussion Questions

1. What is "quantum meruit"?
2. Do you think a school should be permitted to enter into contracts before federal funding has been approved?
3. Does the opinion seem fair? Why or why not?

# JUNEAU ACADEMY V. CHICAGO BOARD OF EDUCATION 122 ILL. APP. 3D 553, 78 ILL. DEC. 13,461 N.E.2D 597 (1984)

**GENERAL RULE OF LAW:** If private special education schools accept transfer students from state facilities without first obtaining required state approval, they will not be reimbursed for tuition on an implied contract theory.

**PROCEDURE SUMMARY:**

**Plaintiff:** Juneau Academy (P), a private special education facility for the handicapped located in Wisconsin

**Defendants:** Chicago Board of Education (D) and several Illinois school districts

**State Trial Court Decision:** Held for Chicago Board of Education (D)

**State Court of Appeals Decision:** Affirmed

**FACTS:** Juneau Academy (P) was a residential facility in Wisconsin for the treatment of mentally handicapped adolescent boys. Under Illinois law, Juneau Academy's (P) tuition rates had to be approved by the Purchased Care Review Board of the Illinois governor's office prior to placement of transfer students from Illinois public facilities; without such prior approval, Juneau Academy's (P) costs of care and education would not be reimbursed. An official with the Chicago Board of Education (CBE) (D), however, requested that Juneau Academy (P) accept the students even though rate approval was still pending; a representative from Illinois School District 108 (108) (D) also requested placement for one of its students. However, after Juneau Academy's (P) rates were approved, both CBE (D) and 108 (D) refused to reimburse Juneau Academy (P) for rates incurred ($2,000 per month each) for the six students prior to the rate approval. Juneau (P) sued both the state and regional boards of education, alleging that the requests of their agents for placement of special education students from public facilities and Juneau's (P) acceptance of such students amounted to implied contracts under which the boards agreed to reimburse Juneau (P) for tuition for those students. The trial court found, as matters of fact, that CBE's (D) representative had agreed to pay for tuition incurred prior to rate approval but that 108's (D) representative had not; however, even CBE (D) had no authority from the state to make such a promise. Therefore, no implied contracts for tuition reimbursement ever arose. Juneau (P) appealed.

**ISSUE:** If private special education schools accept transfer students from state facilities without first obtaining required state approval, will they be reimbursed for tuition on an implied contract theory?

**HOLDING AND DECISION:** (Stamos, J.) No. If a state requires prior approval by one of its agencies before a student is transferred from a public school to a private special education facility and/or requires approval of the school's rate schedule prior to placement, then the private school will not be reimbursed for tuition costs incurred for students placed before such approval is granted. No contract for reimbursement for costs of education in return for acceptance, care, and schooling of such students will be implied, even if agents of the state or local school boards make such a promise to reimburse. Here, Illinois state approval was required by statute both for Juneau's (P) rate structure and for placement of students. Because the costs for these students were incurred prior to Illinois' approval of Juneau's (P) rates, Juneau (P) is not entitled to tuition reimbursement. Affirmed.

**COMMENT:** A contract is "implied in fact" by a court if the facts and circumstances surrounding the "negotiations" suggest that even though one party did not say, "I will pay you X amount if you do Z," the other party agreed to accept "X for Z." In this case, however, the problem for Juneau Academy (P) was that Illinois law expressly deprived state officials of the power to reimburse Juneau (P) for tuition for transfer students prior to the approval of its rates; any such promise to reimburse, as in fact made by the CBE (D) official, would then be ultra vires (i.e., beyond the power), and thus illegal. Obviously, no court will imply a contract that would have one of the parties perform an illegal act, so the court here did not find one.

## Discussion Questions

1. Compare this case with the previous case. Why do you think the court decided against the reimbursement here?

2. Do you think students are adversely affected when they need to remain in public school pending approval of transfer?

---

Additional case briefs can be found on the SAGE Web site at the following address:
http://www.sagepub.com/aquilacasebriefs

---

## NOTES

1. See Epperson v. Arkansas, 393 U.S. 97, 89 S. Ct. 266 (1968).
2. See Meyer v. Nebraska, 262 U.S. 390 (1923).
3. See Oracle Sch. Dist. #2 v. Mammoth High School District No. 88, 130 Ariz. App. 41 (1981).
4. See Lau v. Nichols, 414 U.S. 563, 94 S. Ct. 786 (1974). This case is discussed in Chapter 7.
5. See Epperson v. Arkansas, 393 U.S. 97, 89 S. Ct. 266 (1968).
6. See Meyer v. Nebraska, 262 U.S. 390 (1923).
7. See Howlett v. Rose, 496 U.S. 356 (1990).
8. Goetz v. Ansell, 477 F.2d 636 (2d Cir. 1973).
9. Albach v. Odle, 531 F.2d 983 (10th Cir. 1976).
10. Debra P. v. Turlington, 564 F. Supp. 177, *aff'd*, 730 F.2d 1405 (11th Cir. 1984).
11. See Board of Ed. of Island Trees Union Free School District No. 26 v. Pico, 457 U.S. 853 (1982).
12. See Hibbs v. Arensberg, 276 Pa. 24 (1923).
13. See Utah Plumb./Heat. Contractor Assn. v. Bd. of Ed. Weiser Cnty. Sch. Dist., 19 Utah 2d. 203, 429 P.2d 49 (1967).
14. See Oracle Sch. Dist. #2 v. Mammoth High School District No. 88, 130 Ariz. App. 41 (1981).
15. See Responsive Environments Corp. v. Pulaski Cnty. Special School Dist., 366 F.Supp. 241 (E.D. Ark 1973).
16. See Juneau Academy v. Chicago Board of Education, 122 Ill. App.3d 553 (1984).
17. Goss v. Lopez, 419 U.S. 565, 95 S. Ct. 729 (1975).
18. President's Council, Dist. 25 v. Community School Board, 457 F.2d 289 (2nd Cir. 1972).
19. Minarcini v. Strongesville City School District, 541 F.2d 577 (6th Cir. 1976).

# 14

## Tort Liability of School Districts, Officers, and Employees

*A tort is an act or omission which unlawfully violates a person's right created by the law, and for which the appropriate remedy is a common law action for damage by the injured person.*

— Keeton, Dobbs, Keeton, & Owen (1984, p. 2)[1]

## OVERVIEW . . . . . . . . . . . . . . . . . . . . . . . . . . . . . . . . . . . .

Civil and criminal law are the two fundamental areas of law. A tort is a civil wrong, as opposed to a criminal wrong. The law of torts is based on the theory that people are liable for the consequences of their conduct that results in injury to others. Thus, a person commits a tort when he violates a duty, imposed by law (rather than contract), that he owes to another. If his breach of duty has caused injury to the other party, he generally will be required to offer compensation in the form of money damages. Essentially, one has harmed another in a way that makes another "less than whole." Thus, one must compensate another to make the other "whole" again.

There are three categories of torts: negligence, strict liability, and intentional torts. Negligence, which involves the breach of a legal duty to protect an individual from the risk of foreseeable harm, is by far the most common category of tort in the context of the school system. Intentional torts are far less common, and strict liability torts are almost absent in school situations. Strict liability applies to injuries resulting from the establishment of an unusual hazard, and because of the seriousness of the injuries, liability is imposed without fault needing to be established. If another is hurt as a consequence of a strict liability—regardless of who is at fault—he is entitled to compensation. Intentional torts such as

**assault**, **battery**, false imprisonment, intentional infliction of emotional distress, and defamation involve some affirmative action by an accused, and each tortious action has specific elements that must be proven before liability is established for the act. Since negligence is the most common cause of action in the school system context, the cases and discussions that follow will mainly focus on the tort of negligence.

A tort action involves four specific elements. A tort action based on negligence may result from an improper act—or a failure to act—that causes injury to another. To permit recovery, a court must determine that each of the four elements of a tort is present. These elements are (1) duty of care, (2) breach of that duty of care, (3) **proximate cause**, and (4) actual injury.

When considering the liability of an actor representing the school system, one first must ascertain the nature and extent of the duties that the law requires of school district officers and employees as well as the duties and responsibilities of the school district itself. The process requires that if a duty of care has been breached, it must be determined whether an injury has resulted. If that is the case, the court next must determine whether the parties or entities that have committed torts may avail themselves of any special defenses, privileges, or immunities from suit. Absent some immunity or special defense, liability will attach and the court will endeavor to determine the appropriate remedy to make the plaintiff whole.

Historically, at common law, school boards were not liable for torts committed by their employees or agents. This nonliability, or immunity, is based on the theory that the state is sovereign and should not be sued without its consent. The principle was that the "King can do no wrong." Furthermore, taking funds from everyone (i.e., the King) to pay a single individual would injure the general good. This application of English common law in America—nonliability though sovereign immunity—led to dissatisfaction, and most states have modified this immunity doctrine through legislative enactment or judicial action. Even in early American history, liability was, at times, imposed on school boards for torts associated with their proprietary functions, but not for their governmental functions. The rationale is that when boards act as a private sector entity might act, they should also be held liable for their actions. For example, a Michigan school district was held immune when it acted in its governmental, not proprietary, role. As poorly as the school district administered and supervised its speech therapy program, this action was a governmental function, thereby entitling the school district to immunity from tort liability to the injured child.[2] But if a school district conducts a summer recreation program that is open to the general public, it is taking on a proprietary function, serving as a private provider, and would be liable for injuries sustained while children participated in the program.[3]

The relatively modern ability to purchase liability insurance has created some difficulty with the immunity and liability of school districts. Courts have not agreed on whether school boards waive their governmental immunity from tort liability by purchasing insurance. Some states even permit immunity up to the limit of the district's insurance coverage, to limit the school district's loss of school funds. When a legislature has refused to take a position, some courts have repudiated the immunity doctrine in personal injury suits, thus placing school boards in the same legal position as private corporations, which can be sued for injuries caused by their negligence. Other states have modified immunity secondarily through "save harmless" statutes. Here, a school board must defend at its own expense. Usually, costs may be recovered against the employee who caused the injury outside the scope of his duties.

## Case Study

### Drinking in School

Three tenth-grade female students whose performance and attitude had previously been excellent were suspended for violating the school rule about providing alcoholic beverages at a school function. The girls had organized and directed an extracurricular club activity at which parents and students were present. The students later told the teacher-sponsor that they "spiked" the punch by adding two 12-ounce bottles of malt liquor. No one noticed and nothing was done until the teacher-sponsor informed you, the principal, that the girls admitted to adding the alcohol to the punch. The teacher also informed you that she told the girls that she would handle the discipline herself, if they told the truth. When the teacher later encouraged the girls to tell the principal, they were suspended for the maximum two-week period, subject to the school board's decision. The principal told the girls not to tell their parents, and that he and the teacher would advocate for them at the board meeting. At the board meeting that evening, both recommended that the board act leniently. Prior to the decision of the board, the administration received a phone call indicating that one of the girls had been involved in a fight at the basketball game. The school board then voted to expel all the girls for the remainder of the semester. The school board provided another hearing within a short time and upheld its previous decision. The parents took their case against the school board to federal court, using Section 1983 as a cause of action. The board argued that it had legal immunity from any damages, based on the common law tradition.

## Discussion Questions

1. Should the qualified good-faith immunity of school board members from liability for damages apply in this situation? Why? Why not?

2. Regardless of the right and wrong of the board's action, did the board deny these students their procedural due process rights?[4]

3. You must not—even when acting sincerely and in good faith—act in "ignorance . . . of settled, indisputable" law. What does this imply for the use of lawyers at school board meetings?

4. What is meant by the statement that the *Wood v. Strickland* decision (upon which this case study is based) is a full-employment bill for school lawyers?

# IMPORTANT CONCEPTS

- **"Tort" defined:** A tort is a civil wrong, based in law rather than contract, which occurs when a person violates a duty that he owes to another, thereby causing injury.

- **Tort of negligence:** Negligence, the most common tort, involves the breach of a legal duty to protect another person from the unreasonable risk of harm.

- **Duty to protect:** For liability to attach, the party being sued must have a duty to protect the suing party from unreasonable risks. There can be no liability absent duty.

- **Standard of care:** A party breaches its duty to another when it fails to exercise a proper standard of care with respect to its conduct.

- **Causal connection:** No recovery in negligence will be permitted unless it can be said that the party who is being sued was the legal cause of the injury suffered by the suing party. The term "nexus" is used to describe this causal connection.

- **Injury suffered:** There is no recovery in negligence unless the suing party has suffered an injury, translatable into an actual monetary or comparable loss.

- **Common duties in the school setting:** School personnel are commonly held to duties and appropriate standards of care in connection with the supervision, instruction, and punishment of students and the administration and maintenance of school buildings and grounds.

- **Common defenses to liability:** Defenses to liability commonly asserted by school personnel include the contributory negligence of the suing party, the assumption of an unreasonable risk by the suing party, and the failure of the suing party to establish each of the elements of negligence.

- **School board members immune from certain suits:** School officers, such as board members, commonly enjoy immunity from lawsuits that charge them with negligence in the exercise of their discretionary, as opposed to ministerial, functions. Ministerial tasks are those in which school officials do not exercise discretion, but simply conform with board policy and practice. It is with discretionary functions that school board members exercise judgment.

- **Vicarious liability of school districts:** School districts are fictional entities and, as such, can only be assessed liability vicariously, based on the conduct of district employees and officers.

- **Doctrine of governmental immunity (no liability):** The old common law rule is that governmental agencies, such as school districts, cannot be held liable for the negligent acts of their officers, employees, and agents.

- **Exceptions to doctrine:** In recent years, courts and state legislatures have waived governmental immunity, thereby permitting recovery against school districts, in connection with suits concerning nuisances, proprietary activities on school property, administrative functions, violations of safety statutes, and injuries to school employees.

# ELEMENTS OF THE TORT OF NEGLIGENCE

A tort action based on negligence may result from an improper act, or a failure to act, which causes injury to another. However, existence of injury does not necessarily impute liability to the actor. Before it will permit recovery, a court of law must determine whether each of the four elements of this tort is present. The elements are (1) duty of care, (2) breach of that duty of care, (3) proximate cause, and (4) actual injury.

## Duty of Care

For a duty to be imposed, the individual or entity that is being sued must have been held to some responsibility to protect another party from unreasonable risks. In most states, education professionals are under a duty to their students to provide adequate instruction and supervision, to keep school facilities and property in good repair, and to warn of known dangers, **inter alia**.

## Breach of Duty of Care

After establishing that the party being sued (the defendant) owed a duty to the injured party, it must then be proven that the defendant breached the duty owed. The defendant must have breached its duty by failing to exercise the degree of care that a reasonably prudent person would exercise in the same or similar circumstances.[5] A child need only exercise the degree of care that is appropriate according to the child's age, experience, and mental capacity.[6]

### Standard of Care

Reasonableness is a critical concept. The standard of care that will be required in the school setting is based on the reasonableness of a person's actions in fulfilling his duty to another. Courts assess the reasonableness of a party's actions by determining whether a prudent person would have acted in the same manner under similar circumstances.[7]

The extent or level of care that may be owed another will vary based on factors such as the age of students, the condition of facilities, and so on. For example, greater care may be required when instructing younger students (who have limited attention spans), just as greater care may be required when supervising student activities in older school buildings (where harm is more likely to occur). Further, a school district's duty of care is heightened when a child has a disability that may hinder the ability to protest. However, a school district may not have a duty to supervise and control activities unrelated to school functions.[8] The traditional concept was that when an educator fails to perform an act when there is a duty to act, this is **nonfeasance**. When educators act improperly when there is a duty to act, this is **misfeasance**.

## Proximate Cause

Keep in mind that although the defendant may have breached the duty owed to the injured party, a defendant may still not have actually caused the injuries sustained.

Proximate (legal) cause requires that the individual or entity being sued be the proximate or legal cause of the conduct which has resulted in injury. In other words, there must be a legally recognized causal connection between the actions of the party being sued and the injury of the suing party. "Foreseeability" is the critical concept in determining whether an action proximately caused injury, just as "reasonableness" is critical in determining whether an actor upheld or breached his required duty of care.

Assessing whether the injury was a foreseeable consequence of a party's improper conduct is one means of determining whether the party proximately caused the injury. If an injury is a foreseeable consequence of the conduct in question, this conduct will generally be found to have proximately caused the injury. However, sometimes events "intervene" between an action and an injury. If an intervening act is not a foreseeable consequence of the original action, then the intervening act breaks proximate cause. Thus, the actor will not be held liable for injury (rather, the intervening act will be found to have proximately caused the injury).[9] However, a court or jury may choose to disregard an intervening event in order to hold a school district liable for a plaintiff's injuries.[10]

## Actual Injury

Actual injury must occur. This means that the party who is bringing suit must have suffered some kind of injury, whether physical or mental, resulting in a measurable loss. Physical injuries may be defined by the financial losses that they have occasioned (e.g., medical expenses, lost wages). Mental injuries may be defined by the less easily quantifiable "pain and suffering." The goal of tort litigation is to make the injured party "whole again." More specifically, the goal of damage awards in tort litigation is to return the injured party to the state he was in before the injury occurred.

# DEFENSES TO THE TORT OF NEGLIGENCE

Even when an injured plaintiff establishes all the elements of negligence, there may be defenses that preclude recovery from the school board. These defenses are (1) immunity, (2) contributory/comparative negligence, and (3) assumption of risk. Immunity has been discussed above. Both contributory and comparative negligence assume that the injured party played some part in causing his injuries.

The concept of contributory negligence, which can be traced back almost to our founding fathers, completely bars individuals from any recovery for their injuries if they, in any way, contributed to the harm they suffered. Contributory negligence often led to iniquitous results, and most states have enacted comparative negligence legislation as an alternative defense.

The concept of comparative negligence allows a jury to apportion blame, and therefore liability, based on a percentage of relative fault. Usually, plaintiffs are allowed to recover for the harm they have suffered if they are less than 50% liable. The traditional standard used to determine whether a student could contribute to his injuries was the "rule of seven." Courts would hold that children under the age of 7 were incapable of negligence for their own behavior, while those over the age of 14 could be accountable, on a case-by-case basis. More recently, jurisdictions have used "reasonableness, under the circumstances" as the controlling standard. This is a more flexible standard based on factors such as age, intelligence, training, conditions, and so on. Essentially, did the child act as a reasonable child would with the same characteristics and under the same circumstances? If not, then there may be liability.

The final defense of assumption of risk is similar to comparative negligence because it is based on comparative fault. A party's recovery can be reduced by the degree that the plaintiff voluntarily exposed himself to a known and understood risk of harm. Nevertheless, negligence can never be waived. For example, the permission slips that students sign are merely notification. If the school officials act negligently, they still may be liable. Of course, standards for assumption of risk will vary depending upon the jurisdiction.

# DEFENSES AGAINST LIABILITY IN THE SCHOOL SETTING

## Liability of School District Personnel

Teachers, administrators, and other employees who make up the school system may be sued for tortious conduct that occurs in the school setting. Below are the common duties and standards of care that are required of various school personnel, followed by the defenses they commonly assert to reduce or negate liability.

### Adequacy of Supervision

The lion's share of negligence claims in the school setting involves allegations of failure to supervise students adequately. One who adequately supervises is aware of the activities to be supervised, the conditions that surround those activities, and the potential dangers that could arise during activity periods. In some classes, mere general supervision is sufficient to protect students from reasonably foreseeable dangers. In some classes, more specific supervision may be warranted, such as the heightened supervision a vocational instructor provides in a welding class. The student activity, rather than the time of day or where it occurs, determines the type of supervision and supervisor required.

### Instruction

Teachers may be liable for failing to provide appropriate instruction to students prior to engaging in risky activities. Courts may infer a teacher's failure to provide appropriate instruction from the harm a student suffers after undertaking an unreasonable risk. For example, the fact that a student sustained a broken jaw after engaging in an authorized boxing match in physical education class implies that the instructor failed to properly instruct the student in the principles of self-defense. However, a teacher may not be held liable in negligence if he can establish that he properly instructed his students, but these instructions were later disregarded. The doctrine of due process protects everyone, including students. Here, a student must have knowledge of the rules as a matter of simple due process. Although discussed in chapters dealing with student rights (*Goss v. Lopez,* 1975 is the controlling case), it is worth noting here that school rules should be read and explained to all students (and documented) to ensure that appropriate punishment can be administered.[11]

## Corporal Punishment

The common law rule, which is in effect in most states today, is that educators will not be liable for administering *reasonable* corporal punishment to students. School boards generally are empowered to regulate methods and procedures for administering corporal punishment. A greater sensitivity to students' rights has led many school districts to require (1) each school principal, as opposed to a specific teacher, to determine where, when, and how such punishment will be administered and (2) another adult to be present at the time of the punishment. It should be noted that many school districts no longer allow any corporal punishment. Thus, a teacher who administers corporal punishment may be supported in state law but may risk serious action from the local school board.

## Maintenance of Property and Facilities

As a rule, those who own or possess property and buildings have a duty to maintain them in a reasonably safe condition. Negligence lawsuits frequently arise when unsafe conditions are not corrected and result in harm to an unsuspecting user. An owner or possessor will be liable for an unsafe condition even if he is unaware that it exists, so long as a proper inspection would have revealed its existence. Essentially, if he knows or should have known of the risk, he may be held liable. However, owners or possessors may not be held liable in negligence if it is apparent that the conduct of the injured party, rather than the unsafe condition, was the primary cause of the injury.

## Administration

As a rule, administrators are not liable for negligent acts of a staff member so long as the staff member is qualified to perform the function in question and the administrator has developed sufficient guidelines for proper staff conduct.

# Common Defenses to Negligence

The following defenses are frequently asserted by teachers and other school personnel when attempting to avoid or reduce their liability:

## Establishing Lack of an Essential Element of Negligence

A school employee may seek to demonstrate that one or more of the elements that are required in order to establish negligence (breach of duty, proximate cause, etc.) is not present.

## Contributory Negligence

A school employee may seek to prove that the injured party's own conduct contributed to the injury. If contributory negligence is found, the injured party will be precluded from recovering. Note, however, that in assessing whether contributory negligence exists, the court will not hold children to the same standard of care as adults. In most cases, contributory negligence will prohibit recovery if it can be proven that a student was aware of, or should have been aware of, the consequences of his actions but undertook a dangerous activity anyway.

### Assumption of Risk

Like contributory negligence, the assumption of risk defense prohibits recovery if it can be demonstrated that the injured party knowingly assumed a risk of harm. Once again, the age of the injured party is crucial to the determination of whether voluntary consent to participate in a dangerous activity existed.

### Comparative Negligence

This defense, when permitted, apportions fault among the negligent parties, including the injured party. In most states, a negligent injured party may not recover unless the negligence of the party he is suing is greater than his own. Comparative negligence has replaced contributory negligence in most states. As a matter of fairness, this allows an injured party to recover for the negligence that he did not cause.

## Liability of Officers

School board members, like their school district employees, may be the subject of lawsuits arising from acts and omissions undertaken in the course of their official duties. Unlike their employees, however, school board members are immune from suit under certain specified circumstances. School officers, therefore, enjoy "official immunity." Official immunity extends only to discretionary (policy making), as opposed to ministerial (administrative), actions of school officers. Also, it is doubtful that an officer will be immune from suit if he has undertaken discretionary duties with malicious or injurious intent. In recent years, some state legislatures have extended a similar immunity to teachers and administrators for acts and omissions undertaken in the course of their employment.

## Liability of School Districts

The liability of school districts is necessarily *vicarious* because a fictional entity can only act through the individuals whose conduct may be imputed to it.

As a rule, school districts benefit from the common law principle, extended by the courts, that a government agency cannot be held liable for the negligent acts of its officers, agents, or employees.[12] However, in recent years, some state legislatures and courts have eroded the doctrine of governmental immunity under the following circumstances:

*Nuisance.* A school district may be held liable for the creation and maintenance of conditions that unlawfully invade the property rights of others.

*Proprietary Functions or Activities.* A school district may not be immune from lawsuits in connection with proprietary activities that it permits on school premises. Proprietary activities are more commercial than governmental in nature, such as extracurricular profit-making events.

*Ministerial Functions.* Some courts have rejected the proprietary/governmental functions distinction in favor of granting immunity for discretionary functions and waiving immunity for ministerial functions.[13]

*Violations of Safety Statutes.* Most states waive school district immunity in connection with lawsuits arising from defective school buildings and grounds.

*Workers' Compensation Statutes.* Most legislatures waive school district immunity for employee injuries.

### Defenses to Liability

When governmental immunity is not applicable, school districts frequently assert the following defenses to liability. The school district may claim that its officer or employee did not commit the tort in question. The district may assert that the officer or employee whose conduct is in question acted outside of the scope of his authority or employment. Pursuant to the common law doctrine of respondeat superior, a master may be held responsible only for the *authorized* acts of his servants. The district may claim that the officer or employee whose conduct is in question is himself immune from liability. The district may also assert that the party bringing suit has failed to provide it with a timely written notice of the alleged tort claim, which is required by law. This is often described as a statute of limitations defense.[14]

# FEDERAL TORT LIABILITY

## Section 1983 Actions

Tort actions are generally matters of state law and thus are generally heard in state court. However, a series of federal tort actions have been of major benefit for plaintiffs who want their tort actions adjudicated in federal and not state court. After the Civil War, a series of Civil Rights Acts were enacted to protect the rights of newly freed former slaves. These Acts allowed all Americans, including newly freed former slaves, to take their qualifying tort actions into federal rather than Reconstruction state courts, which might discriminate against them (particularly in former Confederate states). Essentially, the Civil Rights Act of 1866, codified as Title 42, United States Code, § 1983, now provides the broadest avenue for private suits. Over 38,000 cases are filed annually using Section 1983 as the avenue into federal court for tort actions in which private citizens claim injury involving state actors.

Section 1983, unlike other civil rights statutes, creates no substantive rights; rather, it is purely remedial in nature. Section 1983 subjects any person to liability who, while acting under "color of state law," deprives another person of a federal constitutional or statutory right. Thus, a state actor must be acting under his or her legal authority (i.e., "under color of law") for a plaintiff to bring a Section 1983 cause of action. Public school employees are "persons" under Section 1983 and are acting under color of law even if their conduct is contrary to school policy or unauthorized.[15] Private schools and their employees are not state actors and thus are not subject to Section 1983 liability.[16] Those federal rights established by federal law are remedied by Section 1983. State law violations are not corrected through Section 1983 actions. An act of negligence by a public figure will not automatically be converted into a federal tort.[17]

Initially, a "person" under Section 1983 referred only to the actual tortfeasor; a municipality was not considered to be a "person" and was therefore immune.[18] The concept of "person" was then expanded to include municipalities as well as individuals. Specifically, the Supreme Court has held that a municipality may be liable under Section 1983 for the acts of its employees, if such acts reflect municipal policy.[19] "Persons" was then expanded to include individual school board members, thus limiting their past absolute immunity. At present, school board members are immune from liability under Section 1983 if they neither knew nor had reason to know that their actions (which caused improper injury) amounted to a civil rights violation.[20] This limited immunity is provided to encourage school officials to perform effectively without fear of litigation.

Nevertheless, board members are still exposed to potential liability. Thus, if the school official knows or should know that an action violates a protected right, that school official is liable in his or her individual (nonofficial) capacity. After *Wood v. Strickland* (1975), school board members had to rely far more on the opinions of school district legal counsel, who are now usually at board meetings or available by phone. Additionally, state statutes often authorize the purchase by the school district of acts and omission insurance, to protect board members.

Money damages may be recovered only for *actual* damages, not for deprivations of federal rights that have no fiscal consequences.[21] Without proof of actual harm, an aggrieved plaintiff will recover only nominal damages, often no more than one dollar. Actual damages include out-of-pocket losses and emotional distress suffered as a consequence of the plaintiff's being deprived of a federal right. The Supreme Court has allowed exemplary or "punitive" damages[22] under Section 1983 for willful or wanton deprivations of civil rights by individuals, but it has disallowed the recovery of such damages from school districts for the wanton or willful misconduct of their employees.[23] Only the prevailing party may recover attorney fees.[24] A prevailing party is a party that is successful on a significant issue.[25]

Section 1983 also covers federal rights not created by a specific statute, such as when a state agency has a "special relationship" to an injured party and when a state actor exhibits a "deliberate indifference" to the injured party's need. A special relationship (which is defined by the court) creates a duty to protect the victim from third party harm. Absent a "special relationship," there is no duty under Section 1983 to protect individuals from harm by others.[26]

# OTHER TORT CONCERNS

## Monetary Recovery for Sexual Abuse Under Title IX

Title IX prohibits gender-based discrimination in federally supported educational programs. In an important decision, the Supreme Court held that Title IX created a private right to recover monetary compensation for intentional violations of Title IX.[27] In the *Franklin* case, a high school student proved that her school district failed to protect her from sexual abuse perpetrated by one of the district's teachers. The Court held that (1) Title IX provided a damages remedy for the student because the Court presumed the availability of all appropriate remedies unless the United States Congress had expressly indicated otherwise, and (2) when liability was created by statute without a remedy, common law governs the enforcement of the remedy.

This type of situation exposes the school district to liability that teachers and administrators must address. Because of the many situations in which abuse can occur, it is important that district officials consider providing inservice programs as well as providing written policies and procedures to guide personal actions.

## Educational Malpractice

The tort of educational malpractice is a recognizable cause of action, but its application has been very limited. Courts have avoided establishing any liability for failure of school authorities to exercise due care in testing, evaluation, and placement, or for failure to bring a student up to satisfactory levels of achievement in basic skills. The reason courts have steered clear of finding liability in this area is they have been unable to arrive at an objective standard of care that could be used to measure the liability of educators.[28] While cognizable, an educational malpractice action is very difficult to establish. Recoveries are also limited by the courts' reluctance to expose already financially strapped schools to excessive liability. When the Supreme Court eventually upholds an educational malpractice claim, it will probably be in the area of negligent evaluation and placement.[29]

## Case Study

### A Terrible Reaction

A reliable informant tells Principal Hardnose that an eighth-grade student, Juan Gomez, has cigarettes at school. Hardnose searches Juan's locker and finds a pack of cigarettes. The principal calls Juan to the office and informs him that he has a three-day suspension. While Hardnose is leaving a voice-mail message for Juan's mother about the suspension, Juan says that Linda Thomas has cigarettes hidden in a tennis shoe in her locker.

After Linda denies the allegation, Hardnose's locker search uncovers one cigarette. She claims that it is not hers; she is merely holding it for another student. The principal explains that possession of the cigarette is a violation of school policy. He thereafter suspends her for three days. Linda cries and protests her suspension. Although Hardnose explains that this is not a serious violation, Linda remains upset.

Hardnose asks Linda where her parents work. She tells him that her father will come to school the next day to discuss the suspension. While in the office, Juan's mother comes to school to take him home. Hardnose asks and learns that Linda has to go home by bus. Hardnose asks whether she wants him to call her mother, but Linda, in tears, says that she will take the bus home. The principal then calls her home, leaving a message about Linda's suspension on the family's answering machine. Unfortunately, when Linda's mother arrives home, she finds Linda dead in the basement, where she hanged herself.

Linda's parents sue Hardnose, other school administrators, and the school district in federal district court for violating Linda's procedural due process, substantive due process, and equal protection rights under the Fourteenth Amendment. The procedural due process claim is based on the principal suspending Linda without notifying her parents and holding a hearing first.

### Discussion Questions

1. What are the arguments supporting Linda's parents?

2. What arguments support Hardnose and the school district?

3. Who will prevail? Why?

# CONCLUSION . . . . . . . . . . . . . . . . . . . . . . . . . . . . . .

A tort is a civil wrong, based in law rather than contract, which occurs when a person violates a duty that he owes to another, thereby causing injury. Negligence, the most common tort, involves the breach of a legal duty to protect another person from unreasonable risk of harm. In order to sue, a plaintiff must show that the four elements of a negligence tort are present.

First, the plaintiff must show that the defendant owed a duty of care to the plaintiff. Second, the plaintiff must show that the defendant breached that duty of care. The critical question in determining whether the defendant acted negligently is whether a reasonable person, in the defendant's position, would have acted this way. Third, the plaintiff must show that the defendant's action proximately caused injury. Whether the conduct could "foreseeably" cause injury is the critical question addressed when determining proximate cause. And, lastly, the plaintiff must show that he suffered an actual injury sufficient to warrant recovery from the defendant.

Defendants may assert a variety of defenses, including immunity, contributory or comparative negligence on the part of the plaintiff, or that the plaintiff assumed the risk that the injury would occur.

The most common tort actions against a school include claims of inadequate supervision, inadequate instruction, unreasonable corporal punishment, inadequate maintenance of property and facilities, and inadequate administration.

These tort actions are generally matters of state law. However, a series of tort actions have provided plaintiffs an avenue to seek tort damages in federal court. The most common of these is Section 1983 of the Civil Rights Act of 1866, which allows private citizens who claim injury involving state actors to bring their claims to federal court. Generally, under this statute, a municipality may be held liable for the actions of one of its employees if this action reflected a municipal policy. This statute also creates liability when a state agency has a "special relationship" to an injured party or shows a "deliberate indifference" to the injured party's needs. Also, under this statute, plaintiffs may recover for sexual abuse perpetrated by a school employee when the school grossly fails to protect the plaintiff from such abuse. Lastly, the tort of educational malpractice is a recognizable cause of action, but its application has been very limited.

The doctrine of sovereign immunity generally renders school officers free from tort liability. This immunity doctrine is generally applied when a school is acting in its governmental capacity. However, if a school acts in a proprietary role, such as when it charges participants to attend a summer camp, the sovereign immunity doctrine usually does not attach. In addition, courts have not agreed whether school boards and their officers waive their governmental immunity by purchasing insurance. Some states even permit liability up to the policy's limit. When the legislature has refused to take a position, some courts have ruled that an insured school loses sovereign immunity and is as liable as any private entity would be for tort actions.

The Case Briefs in this chapter examine tort liability of teachers, school administrators, and students; school officials have a duty to protect those under their supervision from foreseeable dangers. These cases examine the failure of teachers to adequately teach students and to take steps to protect their students from foreseeable harm at home and on school grounds. They examine tort liability from various positions and include causes of action at the federal and the state level.

# CASE BRIEFS ·····························

# LAWES V. BOARD OF EDUCATION OF THE CITY OF NEW YORK 16 N.Y.2D 302, 266 N.Y.S.2D 364, 213 N.E.2D 667 (1965)

**GENERAL RULE OF LAW:** A school is not liable for injuries a student suffers on school property as a result of the activity of other students when there is no notice of the special danger or previous occasions of dangerous activity.

**PROCEDURE SUMMARY:**

**Plaintiff:** Lawes (P), an injured student

**Defendant:** Board of Education of the City of New York (Board) (D)

**State Court Trial Division Decision:** Held for Lawes (P), awarding $45,000 in damages

**State Court Appellate Division Decision:** Affirmed

**State Court of Appeal (New York's highest court) Decision:** Reversed

**FACTS:** Lawes (P), an 11-year-old student returning to school after having lunch at home, was struck by a snowball thrown by another student as she proceeded to her classroom. She suffered a serious eye injury as a result. The school had prohibited snowball throwing, and Lawes' (P) teacher had warned her students not to throw them. Lawes (P) filed a personal injury action for damages, alleging the Board (D) failed to adequately supervise the students' activities. The trial court held for Lawes (P), awarding her $45,000 in damages. The Board (D) appealed, contending that it could not be responsible for an unforeseeable injury.

**ISSUE:** Is a school liable for injuries sustained by a student from student activity on school premises when there is no notice of a special danger or previous dangerous activity?

**HOLDING AND DECISION:** (Bergan, J.) No. A school is not liable for injuries sustained by a student on school premises from student activity when there is no notice of the special danger or previous dangerous activity. In supervising students, school personnel must act as a parent of ordinary prudence would in comparable circumstances. Such a parent would not invariably prohibit her child from throwing snowballs; she would simply prohibit dangerous throwing if she were aware that the circumstances made the activity dangerous. Similarly, the school need only prohibit play when it is on notice that such play is dangerous. There is no evidence of such notice here. The record did not reveal that teachers knew of any other snowball throwing on the day of the incident, nor was there sufficient evidence of other occasions of snowball throwing to show the requisite notice. Accordingly, the threat of injury by snowball throwing was not reasonably foreseeable. Thus, no duty of care was owed Lawes (P) to protect her from such injury. Reversed.

**COMMENT:** *Lawes* clarifies the standard of care to which school officials will be held when supervising students. It was long believed that school officials owed students some type of special duty (without a clear definition of the scope of that duty). The standard of care in this type of situation is that of a parent of ordinary prudence. Nevertheless, the standard adopted not only makes schools liable for their acts of omission, but also places upon them a duty to take affirmative action to protect students in some instances.

## Discussion Questions

1. If, in fact, the school is not liable for the student's injuries under the general rule of law, who is liable?

2. Does the act of prohibiting snowball throwing by the school and a warning to students by the teacher constitute the event/injury being reasonably foreseeable?

3. How can the assumption be made that a parent would act as the school did in this situation? Was there adequate supervision?

# TITUS V. LINDBERG 49 N.J. 66, 228 A.2D 65 (1967)

**GENERAL RULE OF LAW:** School personnel are liable for injuries sustained by students entrusted to the school's care when such personnel fail to exercise reasonable supervisory care for the students' safety.

**PROCEDURE SUMMARY:**

**Plaintiff:** Titus (P), an injured student represented by his guardian

**Defendants:** Smith (D), the Fairview principal; Lindberg (D), the student who shot the paper clip

**State Trial Court Decision:** Held for Titus (P), finding Lindberg (D) and Smith (D) negligent

**State Court of Appeal Decision:** Affirmed

**State Supreme Court Decision:** Affirmed

**FACTS:** Titus (P), a 9-year-old student at Fairview School, arrived on the school grounds at 8:05 A.M. As he headed toward the bicycle rack, he was struck by a paper clip shot by Lindberg (D), a student at Thompson School. Five minutes prior, Lindberg (D) had struck another student with a paper clip. Lindberg (D) was at Fairview awaiting a bus to transport him to Thompson. Fairview classes did not begin until 8:15 A.M.; however, Smith (D), the Fairview principal, supervised children who arrived early. Titus (P) filed a personal injury action for damages, alleging Lindberg's (D) negligent shooting and Smith's (D) negligent failure to supervise caused his injuries. The trial court found for Titus (P) and awarded him $44,000 in damages. Smith (D) sought review.

**ISSUE:** Are school personnel liable for injuries sustained by students entrusted to the school's care when such personnel fail to exercise reasonable supervisory care for the students' safety?

**HOLDING AND DECISION:** (Jacobs, J.) Yes. School personnel are liable for injuries sustained by students entrusted to their care when such personnel fail to exercise reasonable supervisory care for the students' safety. Though school did not officially begin until 8:15 A.M., Smith (D) was not relieved from this duty. It was expected that children would arrive a little early; they customarily did, and Smith (D) was well aware of this. Furthermore, Smith (D) affirmatively assumed responsibility for supervising the school grounds beginning at 8:00 A.M. However, he did not announce any rules regulating conduct before class, assign any teachers or other personnel to assist him in supervising, or take sufficient measures himself to oversee the students' presence or activities. Thus, the finding that Smith (D) failed to supervise adequately cannot be said to lack reasonable foundation. Affirmed.

**COMMENT:** *Titus* illustrates the rule followed in most states that imposes a duty on teachers to supervise students. Under this duty, a teacher must take reasonable steps to protect students. Further, the amount of care required of the teacher increases or decreases with the relative maturity or immaturity of the students. This principle of supervision is one which is often disregarded by school personnel. Defendants incorrectly assume that notifying parents that they should not send their children to school before it starts releases the school from liability. This practice is clearly wrong and exposes the school district and school personnel if an injury occurs as a result of negligent supervision.

## Discussion Questions

1. A group of students remain after school to participate in a club. Must the teacher or principal supervise their departure from school?

2. Does this case imply that a teacher can leave any students unsupervised?

3. Do you believe the definition of "reasonable care" should change with the age of the students? Why or why not?

# VIVEIROS V. HAWAII 54 HAW. 611, 513 P.2D 487 (1973)

**GENERAL RULE OF LAW:** A child is only required to use the degree of care appropriate to her age, experience, and mental capacity.

**PROCEDURE SUMMARY:**

**Plaintiff:** Viveiros (P), a 15-year-old high school student

**Defendant:** The State of Hawaii (D)

**State Circuit Court Decision:** Held for Viveiros (P), but (in a comparative negligence decision) found Viveiros (P) 25% negligent (and thus reduced her award by 25%)

**State Supreme Court Decision:** Reversed

**FACTS:** Viveiros (P) attended a light show in a lecture hall at Kailua High School. There were no teachers present to supervise the show. The only staff member present, an education assistant, left the hall shortly after the show began. Viveiros (P) could not find a seat and had to stand in an aisle. A few moments later, a group of students about 35 feet from Viveiros (P) became noisy. A student running the show told them to be quiet or the teachers would come in. Shortly thereafter, Viveiros (P) was struck by a metal object apparently thrown by a member of the noisy group. She suffered permanent damage to her left eye. Viveiros (P) filed a negligence suit for damages against Hawaii (D) under the State Tort Liability Act. She claimed that Hawaii's (D) failure to supervise the show caused her injuries. The trial court found Hawaii (D) negligent but also found Viveiros (P) to have been comparatively negligent for 25% of her injuries for failing to leave the scene. Viveiros (P) appealed, arguing that the damages should not have been reduced.

**ISSUE:** Is a child only required to use that degree of care appropriate for her age, experience, and mental capacity?

**HOLDING AND DECISION:** (Richardson, C. J.) Yes. A child need only use that degree of care appropriate for her age, experience, and mental capacity. The trial court's finding that Viveiros (P) was 25% negligent must be reversed if the supreme court finds that her conduct was reasonable granted her age, experience, and mental capacity. At the time of the incident, Viveiros (P) was 35 feet from the noisy group of students. Further, the group was merely vocal. The record did not reveal that any threats were conveyed or objects thrown prior to the incident. In addition, none of her peers evinced fear of danger because none of them left the program out of concern for the noisy group. On these facts, Viveiros (P) could not have reasonably anticipated the danger she was in, and the trial court erred in finding otherwise. Reversed (full award of damages reinstated).

**COMMENT:** The standard of care applied here is the same as would be applied in any other case where the issue is whether a child was negligent. *Viveiros* represents the majority view. A few courts, however, attempt to establish varying standards depending upon the age of the child. For example, children under 7 are sometimes conclusively presumed incapable of negligence, while there is a rebuttable presumption that children ages 7 to 14 are incapable of negligence. Some jurisdictions hold children to the adult standard of care when the child has engaged in adult activities (e.g., driving a motor vehicle or piloting a boat).

## Discussion and Questions

1. Would Viveiros have been successful in a lawsuit against the student who threw the object?

2. Using your school, create a plan for supervising students during an assembly.

3. Using your school, create a plan for supervising students during a pep rally.

# WOOD V. STRICKLAND
# 420 U.S. 308, 95 S. CT. 992 (1975)

**GENERAL RULE OF LAW:** A school official is immune from liability under 42 U.S.C. § 1983 if he neither knew nor had reason to know that his actions amounted to a civil rights violation.

**PROCEDURE SUMMARY:**

   **Plaintiffs:** Strickland (P) and Crain (P), high school students

   **Defendants:** Wood (D), and other school board officials

   **U.S. District Court Decision:** Dismissed

   **U.S. Court of Appeals Decision:** Reversed

   **U.S. Supreme Court Decision:** Reversed and remanded for additional factual development

**FACTS:** Strickland (P) and Crain (P) were high school students who were found by the local school board (D) to have "spiked" the punch at a school function, in contravention of school rules. After a hearing in which they essentially admitted to the scheme, they were suspended for the rest of the year. The students (P) appealed to the school board. The board (D) upheld the administrative action suspending the students for the year, but it did not provide an adequate hearing. The lack of an adequate hearing was contrary to "settled" law, *Goss v. Lopez* (1975) having been announced by the Court. The students (P) filed an action under 42 U.S.C. § 1983, the federal law allowing a suit for violation of constitutional rights by state actors while acting pursuant to state law. The students contended that the punishment was unconstitutionally excessive and, thus, in violation of due process. Essentially, the federal district court dismissed and held that the school officials (D) were immune from Section 1983 for acts that the officials subjectively did not know would violate constitutional rights (i.e., if they did not personally know they violated constitutional rights, then they were immune). The court of appeals reversed, holding that the standard of liability was objective (i.e., officials would be immune only if a reasonable school official in their position would not know that his acts violated constitutional rights). Essentially, he is immune unless he should have known his acts violated constitutional rights. The issue of whether the school official in question personally knew the subjective standard would be immaterial. The Supreme Court granted review.

**ISSUE:** Is a school official immune from liability under Section 1983 if he neither knew nor should have known that his actions amounted to a civil rights violation?

**HOLDING AND DECISION:** (White, J.) Yes. A school official is immune from liability under Section 1983 if he neither knew nor should have known that his actions amounted to a civil rights violation. School officials, in exercising their duties, often have to make judgment calls based on information supplied by others. This being so, it is proper that they enjoy some immunity from Section 1983 liability, because to hold otherwise could chill their ability to properly fulfill their duties. The district court imposed a subjective actual malice standard; the court of appeals thought an objective implied malice standard was more appropriate. In fact, the proper standard is both objective and subjective—it is a "knew or should have known" standard. Since insufficient facts were **adduced** at trial to decide the issue, the matter was remanded. Reversed.

**COMMENT:** The school officials (D) argued in favor of an absolute immunity. The Court rejected this. First, no lower court has ever deemed it proper to grant such immunity. More important, to grant unqualified immunity might leave legitimately aggrieved students with no avenue of redress. At first, this case caused great consternation among school board members because it exposed them to liability if they acted improperly when they either "knew or reasonably should have known" that their action was improper. One result of this decision was the provision of additional insurance coverage. Another interesting result of this case is that school boards now rely more heavily on legal advice prior to taking action.

## Discussion Questions

1. Why was the precedent of *Goss* v. *Lopez* (1975) so important to *Wood*, in the opinion of the plaintiffs? How did it relate to due process in this case?

2. What determines whether a school official is liable for civil rights violations? How is the proper standard stated, and why is it significant?

3. What kind of precedent did this set for school board officials? What were the results of this precedent?

# PETER V. SAN FRANCISCO UNIFIED SCH. DIST. 60 CAL.APP.3D 814, 131 CAL. RPTR. 854 (1976)

**GENERAL RULE OF LAW:** A student in a public school system may not bring a tort cause of action for inadequate education against public authorities responsible for the administration and operation of a school system.

**PROCEDURE SUMMARY:**

**Plaintiff:** Peter (P), an 18-year-old high school graduate

**Defendant:** San Francisco School District (School District) (D)

**State Trial Court Decision:** Dismissed

**State Appeals Court Decision:** Held for defendant

**State Supreme Court Decision:** Affirmed

**FACTS:** Peter (P), an 18-year-old male, attended the schools of San Francisco Unified School District (D) for 12 years. He brought suit against the School District (D) and alleged that the School District (D) negligently failed to provide him with adequate instruction. According to Peter (P), this proximately caused him to graduate with only a fifth-grade reading level, thereby reducing his earning potential. Peter (P) also alleged that the School District (D) breached its mandatory duties. Peter (P) sought general and special damages. The School District (D) was granted judgment by the court, which allowed Peter 20 days leave to amend and re-file. The trial court dismissed after Peter (P) failed to amend. The court of appeals affirmed on the basis that the School District (D) did not owe a duty of care to Peter (P) and that Peter (P) failed to state a cause of action. Peter (P) appealed.

**ISSUE:** May a student in a public school system bring a tort cause of action for inadequate education against public authorities responsible for the administration and operation of a school system?

**HOLDING AND DECISION:** (Rattigan, J.) No. A student in a public school system may not bring a tort cause of action for inadequate education against public authorities responsible for the administration and operation of a school system. In order to establish a cause of action for negligence under California law, the plaintiff must show the defendant had a duty of care that he breached through his negligent acts, and this proximately caused the plaintiff's injury. The issue here is whether the School District (D) owed a duty of care to Peter (P) to educate him adequately. This is a question of law to be determined by the court. Such a determination requires the court to weigh policy considerations, including the foreseeability of harm, the relativity of the defendant's conduct to the plaintiff's injury, prevention of future injury, the burden on the defendant, consequences to the functioning of the community, and the burden of obtaining insurance. The supreme court stated that the test was whether the plaintiff is entitled to protection against the defendant's conduct. In finding tort liability based on new theories of negligence, the conduct and harm involved must fit within the framework of the law. In contrast, the determination of whether an injury has been sustained based on a theory of educational negligence is based on subjective determinations. Thus, there is no objective means of ascertaining whether the defendant breached its duty. Peter (P) failed to show that the School District (D) owed him a duty of care. Peter's (P) second **count** of misrepresentation against the School District (D) fails on the same basis. Affirmed.

**COMMENT:** A public entity may be held vicariously liable for the acts of its employees only if that employee could be held personally liable for his conduct. Governmental immunity in California is determined under the Tort Claims Act of 1963. That statute requires that in order to hold a public entity liable there must first be a finding of negligence.

## Discussion Questions

1.  How would public education today be different if Peter had been successful in his suit?

2.  Would it have been a just result if the jury had ruled that the school was negligent, but that Peter was also negligent, and therefore not entitled to recover any damages?

3.  If a school principal believes in the concept of social promotion, and socially promotes students in spite of poor performance, could that principal be found negligent?

# MONELL V. DEPARTMENT OF SOCIAL SERVICES OF THE CITY OF NEW YORK 436 U.S. 658, 98 S. CT. 2018 (1978)

**GENERAL RULE OF LAW:** A municipality may be liable under Section 1983 for the acts of its employees if such acts reflect municipal policy.

**PROCEDURE SUMMARY:**

**Plaintiff:** Monell (P), a private citizen

**Defendants:** The City of New York (City) (D), and various agencies thereof

**U.S. District Court Decision:** Dismissed

**U.S. Court of Appeals Decision:** Affirmed

**U.S. Supreme Court Decision:** Reversed and remanded

**FACTS:** Monell (P) brought a Section 1983 action against the City of New York (D) and various agencies based on acts of City (D) employees. Although the case turned on the issue of municipal liability under Section 1983, the facts of the case were as follows. Female employees (P) of the Department of Social Services and the Board of Education of the City of New York brought suit against the Department and Board (D) challenging the policies of those bodies that required pregnant employees to take unpaid leaves of absence before those leaves were required for medical reasons. The petitioners brought this class action against the department and its commissioner, the board and its chancellor, and the City of New York and its mayor. Petitioners sought injunctive relief and back pay under Section 1983 of the Civil Rights Act of 1871. Section 1983 provides that every "person" who, under color of a statute, ordinance, regulation, custom, or usage of any state, subjects or "causes to be subjected" any person to deprivation of any federally protected rights, privileges, or immunities shall be civilly liable to the injured party. The individual defendants were sued solely in their official capacities. The district court dismissed, holding that a municipality was immune from liability under Section 1983 for acts of employees. The court of appeals affirmed, and the Supreme Court granted certiorari.

**ISSUE:** May a municipality be liable under Section 1983 for the acts of its employees if such acts reflect municipal policy?

**HOLDING AND DECISION:** (Brennan, J.) Yes. A municipality may be liable under Section 1983 if such acts reflect municipal policy. An earlier case, *Monroe v. Pape* (1961), held that municipalities were absolutely immune from liability under Section 1983. This case was inconsistent with the legislative intent of Congress, as evidenced by the legislative history. Therefore, the Supreme Court overruled *Monroe*. Nonetheless, the Court declined to adopt a rule of respondeat superior/automatic liability on the part of a municipality for the misdeeds of its employees. Section 1983 speaks of damages being awardable against one "causing" a civil rights violation. "Cause" implies some affirmative act in bringing the violation about. An automatic liability rule would contravene this and hold that the municipality is liable whenever an injury manifests, regardless of the cause. Therefore, the better rule is that only a violation caused by either official or unofficial policy may result in municipal liability. The Supreme Court reversed and remanded to the district trial court to determine whether the municipality caused injury.

**COMMENT:** The Court took some pains to include unofficial as well as official policy within the scope of its decision. Seldom will a municipality have an official policy of committing civil rights violations. Unofficial policy may be demonstrated by a pattern of violations occurring without reprimand. In addition to expanding the definition of a "person" subject to a Section 1983 suit, this case makes school officials liable for their actions. As with other professionals, educators must be concerned with the potential liability attached to their professional acts and policies. Some may wonder about the facts of this case. The reason Monell was able to establish the important principle expanding the definition of "person" to a municipality (not just the individual actor who caused the injury) was the official policy of these government bodies that required pregnant employees to take unpaid leaves of absence before those leaves were required for medical reasons. This issue had been decided years before in the *LaFleur* case, and the state actors should have known this settled law. Their failure to correct their unconstitutional policy provided the plaintiffs with the legal opportunity to expand the definition of "person" subject to the application of Section 1983.

## Discussion and Questions

1. Create a policy that, while reasonable, violates the civil rights of a school employee or group of employees.

2. Create a policy that, while reasonable, violates the civil rights of a public school student or group of students.

3. Would a school district be automatically liable if a school administrator sexually harassed a teacher?

# DONOHUE V. COPIAGUE UNION FREE SCHOOL DISTRICT 47 N.Y.2D 440, 418 N.Y.S.2D 375, 391 N.E. 2D 1352 (1979)

**GENERAL RULE OF LAW:** Causes of action against a school district for educational malpractice and negligent failure to educate are not cognizable.

**PROCEDURE SUMMARY:**

**Plaintiff:** Donohue (P), a District (D) high school graduate

**Defendant:** Copiague Union Free School District (District) (D)

**State Trial Court Decision:** Held for the District (D), dismissing Donohue's (P) complaint for failure to state a cognizable claim

**State Appellate Court Decision:** Affirmed

**State Court of Appeals (New York's highest court) Decision:** Affirmed

**FACTS:** Donohue (P) attended Copiague High School from 1972 until his graduation in 1976. After graduation, he filed an action for damages against the District (D), contending it failed to educate him as was required. Donohue (P) claimed that, though he had a certificate of graduation, he was functionally illiterate. The complaint alleged that because of the District's (D) failure to properly teach him and evaluate his mental abilities, he was unable to even complete applications for employment. The District (D) filed a motion to dismiss the action for failure to state a claim. The trial court granted the motion, and the appellate court affirmed. Donohue (P) appealed.

**ISSUE:** Are causes of action for educational malpractice and negligent failure to educate cognizable against a school district?

**HOLDING AND DECISION:** (Jasen, J.) No. Causes of action for educational malpractice and negligent failure to educate are not cognizable against a school district. Though traditional notions of tort law may allow for an educational malpractice action against a school district, public policy cautions against this. To entertain such a claim would require the court to judge the validity of broad educational policies and review their day-to-day implementation. Such judgment and review would overly infringe upon duties clearly granted to the legislature and district in the Constitution. In addition, the legislature has provided aggrieved persons, such as Donohue (P), other statutory means of redress. The claim failed because though the state constitution requires the legislature to maintain and support public schools, it does not require that each student receive a minimum level of education. Affirmed.

**COMMENT:** This case illustrates the courts' long-held "hands off" policy toward educational policy issues. Only in cases of gross violations of public policy or deprivation of rights are courts compelled to intervene. Today, however, there are increasing efforts to require schools to provide a minimum level of education. Acceptance of such a standard could compel future courts to sustain an educational malpractice action when a plaintiff shows the school failed to provide the minimum level of education to a particular student. But whether mere negligence will sustain such a claim, even where a minimum education standard is recognized, is not yet settled. This case established that while educational malpractice can be pleaded (thus, it is a cognizable cause of action), because of public policy it will not be sustained. Should educational malpractice be recognized, it will probably occur in an area such as handicapped education (where accountability, testing, and placement are mandated). The general failure to educate argued in this case will not be the breakthrough area for an educational malpractice claim.

## Discussion Questions

1. Does the No Child Left Behind Act conflict with the statement "the state constitution . . . does not require that each student receive a minimum level of education?"

2. Would this suit have been successful if brought against a private school that charged the plaintiff tuition?

# HUNTER V. BOARD OF EDUCATION OF MONTGOMERY COUNTY 292 MD. 481, 439 A.2D 582 (1982)

**GENERAL RULE OF LAW:** School personnel entrusted with a child's care can be held liable for intentionally injurious conduct in evaluating, placing, and teaching the child, but not for merely negligent conduct.

**PROCEDURE SUMMARY:**

**Plaintiff:** Hunter (P), an elementary school student

**Defendant:** Board of Education of Montgomery County (Board) (D)

**State District Court Decision:** Held for the Board (D), sustaining its **demurrer** to Hunter's (P) complaint without leave to amend

**State Court of Special Appeals Decision:** Affirmed

**State Court of Appeals (Maryland's highest court) Decision:** Affirmed in part; reversed in part

**FACTS:** When Hunter (P) was in elementary school, he was forced to repeat first-grade material though he was physically placed in the second grade. The plaintiff alleged that this misplacement, which continued through grade school, caused the student embarrassment and led him to develop learning deficiencies and to experience depletion of ego strength. Hunter (P) filed suit, alleging two causes of action: first, that his being forced to repeat first-grade material was a result of the Board's (D) negligence in evaluating his learning abilities and second, that the Board (D) intentionally and maliciously furnished false information to his parents concerning his learning abilities in an attempt to conceal the Board's (D) negligence. The Board (D) demurred to Hunter's (P) complaint. The circuit court sustained the demurrer without leave to amend, holding that neither the negligent nor intentional conduct actions could be maintained. The court of special appeals affirmed, and Hunter (P) appealed.

**ISSUE:** May school personnel entrusted with a student's care be held liable for intentionally injurious conduct in evaluating, placing, and teaching the student?

**HOLDING AND DECISION:** (Digges, J.) Yes. School personnel entrusted with a student's care may be held liable for intentionally injurious conduct in evaluating, placing, and teaching the student. Mere negligence is not enough. This court adopts the rule of many other jurisdictions that an action for "educational malpractice," essentially Hunter's (P) claim, does not lie for merely negligent conduct in evaluating, placing, and teaching a child. To allow such a claim would contravene public policy by exposing already financially burdened schools to incalculable liability. This, however, by no means shields school officials from liability for intentionally injurious conduct. Such conduct greatly outweighs the policy considerations precluding liability in the negligence context. Thus, Hunter (P) was allowed the opportunity to proceed on the intentional conduct claim. Reversed in part and remanded.

**COMMENT:** Even if cognizable, an educational malpractice action would be difficult to establish. Classroom methodology affords no readily acceptable standard of care, as there are often conflicting theories of how and what students should be taught. These problems, combined with the courts' concern for exposing already financially strapped schools to excessive liability, also underlie the rejection of the education malpractice cause of action. A demurrer is the equivalent of a motion to dismiss filed with the court after the pleadings have been served but before trial has commenced. The court can sustain a demurrer only when the plaintiff has failed to state a cause of action (i.e., has failed to allege or have the ability to prove the required elements of the particular cause of action). Thus, there is no triable issue of fact, and thus the court may enter judgment based solely on an issue of law (there is a legal deficiency that precludes the plaintiff from ever winning—such as presenting no evidence that could be used to prove an essential element of a tort). This area of negligent evaluation and placement is the one which will first be sustained for educational malpractice.

## Discussion Questions

1. Was the Board of Education negligent in the case of *Hunter v. Board of Education of Montgomery County?*

2. Could suits of "educational malpractice" arise every time a student fails? What would the impact of such suits be on the court system and financially burdened school systems?

3. Why would a case of educational malpractice be difficult to establish in the court room?

# DESHANEY V. WINNEBAGO COUNTY DEPARTMENT OF SOCIAL SERVICES 489 U.S. 189 (1989)

**GENERAL RULE OF LAW:** A state's failure to protect a child from a parent's abusive behavior is not a violation of the child's rights under the due process clause of the Fourteenth Amendment.

**PROCEDURE SUMMARY:**

**Plaintiff:** DeShaney (P), an abused child

**Defendant:** Winnebago County Department of Social Services (WCDSS) (D)

**U.S. District Court Decision:** Held for WCDSS (D), granting summary judgment

**U.S. Court of Appeals Decision:** Affirmed

**U.S. Supreme Court Decision:** Affirmed

**FACTS:** DeShaney (P), a one-year-old baby, was placed in his father's custody when his parents divorced in 1980. From complaints made by the father's second wife, WCDSS (D) first learned in 1982 that DeShaney (P) was possibly a victim of abuse. The father denied any abuse, and WCDSS (D) did not pursue the matter. In January, 1983, DeShaney (P) was admitted to the hospital with multiple bruises and abrasions. The treating physician, suspecting child abuse, notified WCDSS (D). DeShaney (P) was placed in the protective custody of the hospital, a "Child Protection Team" was formed, and treatment for both DeShaney (P) and his father was arranged. DeShaney (P) was then placed back in his father's custody. One month later, the hospital notified WCDSS (D) that DeShaney (P) again had suspicious injuries. WCDSS (D) found no reason for action. On multiple occasions, a WCDSS (D) caseworker noticed suspicious injuries but took no action. Finally, in March, 1984, the father beat DeShaney (P) into a coma. DeShaney (P), by his appointed guardian, filed suit, alleging WCDSS (D) deprived him of his right to bodily integrity under the due process clause by failing to protect him from danger about which WCDSS (D) knew or should have known. The district court and court of appeals found that the clause did not require WCDSS (D) to protect citizens from private violence. The Supreme Court granted review.

**ISSUE:** Is a state's failure to protect a child from the abusive behavior of a parent a violation of the child's right to bodily integrity under the due process clause of the Fourteenth Amendment?

**HOLDING AND DECISION:** (Rehnquist, C. J.) No. A state's failure to protect a child from the abusive behavior of a parent is not a violation of the child's right to bodily integrity under the due process clause. That clause imposes no affirmative duty on a state to provide its citizenry with adequate protective services.

Textually, the clause is only a limitation on a state's power to act, not a mandate to act in a particular manner. Nor does the state's knowledge of a particular danger to an individual establish a special relationship between the state and that individual, thereby creating a constitutional duty to protect. Such a duty arises from state-imposed limitations on the individual's ability to protect himself, not merely from knowledge of a particular danger. Here, state action played no part in creating the danger, nor was the father a state actor. Thus, no duty arose. Affirmed.

**COMMENT:** The issues raised by this can easily be extended to the school board or district context. They are clearly state agencies, like the defendant in *DeShaney*. Thus, it would follow that the due process clause likewise places no affirmative duty on schools to act. Three dissenting justices, Brennan, Marshall, and White, however, strongly disagreed, arguing that the due process clause required a more active role of the state. The argument has both moral and emotional appeal, especially given the chilling facts of *DeShaney*, but is unlikely to succeed in the near future given that the three dissenting justices are no longer on the Court. The Court noted that the father was not a "state actor." Thus, there is no special duty for the state to prevent the father from acting. A special duty would be placed on the state to protect a prisoner in a state penal institution. The special duty or "special relationship" test is the key in determining whether the state would be liable under Section 1983. Here, the mere notice of severe child abuse by the custodial father did not trigger this special relationship. Such a special relationship is present when the state renders the person incapable of acting in his or her own defense.

## Discussion Questions

1. Why did the Court fail to recognize that the state's failure to protect a child from the abusive behavior of a parent was a violation of the child's right under the due process clause of the Fourteenth Amendment?

2. Does being a young child in an abusive relationship, when the child is incapable of acting in its own defense, constitute a "special relationship?"

3. Would a prisoner in a state correctional facility have more or less protection from abusive behavior than this child?

Additional case briefs can be found on the SAGE Web site at the following address:
http://www.sagepub.com/aquilacasebriefs

## NOTES

1. Keeton, W. P., Dobbs, D. B., Keeton, R. E., & Owen, D. G. (1984). *Prosser and Keeton on torts* (5th ed.). St. Paul, MN: West.
2. Brosnan v. Livonia Public Schools, 123 Mich. App. 377 (1983).
3. Ayala v. Philadelphia Bd. of Pub. Educ., 305 A.2d 877 (Pa.1973).

4. See Goss v. Lopez, 419 U.S. 565, 95 S. Ct. 729 (1975).

5. See Dailey v. Los Angeles Unified School District, 470 P.2d 360 (1970).

6. See Viveiros v. Hawaii, 54 Haw. 611 (1973).

7. See Titus v. Lindberg, 49 N.J. 66, 228 A.2d 65 (1967).

8. See Bartell v. Palos Verdes Peninsula Sch. Dist., 83 Cal. App. 3d 492 (1978).

9. See Lawes v. Board of Education of the City of New York, 16 N.Y.2d 302 (1965).

10. See Raleigh v. Independent School District No. 625, 275 N.W. 2d 572 (Minn. 1979).

11. Goss v. Lopez, 419 U.S. 565 (1975).

12. See Brosnan v. Livonia Public Schools, 123 Mich. App. 377 (1983).

13. See Rupp v. Bryant, 417 So. 2d 658 (Fla. 1982).

14. Each state has a statute that indicates the time the defendant has to bring a claim either after a cause of action arises or after the defendant should have known the cause of action arose.

15. See Monroe v. Pape, 365 U.S. 167 (1961).

16. See Johnson v. Pinkerton Academy, 861 F.2d 335 (1st Cir. 1988).

17. See Golden State Transit Corp. v. Los Angeles, 498 U.S. 103 (1989).

18. See Monroe v. Pape, 365 U.S. 167 (1961).

19. See Monell v. Department of Social Services of the City of New York, 436 U.S. 658 (1978).

20. See Wood v. Strickland, 420 U.S. 308, 95 S. Ct. 992 (1975).

21. See Carey v. Piphus, 435 U.S. 247 (1978).

22. Punitive damages are "awarded in addition to actual damages when the defendant acted with recklessness, malice, or deceit" (*Black's law dictionary,* 2001, p. 171). Punitive damages are awarded in part to punish egregious offenses and in part to further deter potential tortfeasors from engaging in these types of offenses, especially when a company or organization might find it economical to risk committing the tort and paying only regular compensation.

23. City of Newport v. Fact Concerts, Inc., 453 U.S. 247 (1981).

24. Civic Rights Attorneys Fees Award Statute, 42 U.S.C. § 1988.

25. See Texas State Teachers Assn. v. Garland Independent School District, 777 F.2d 1046 (5th Cir. 1985).

26. See DeShaney v. Winnebago County Department of Social Services, 489 U.S. 189 (1989).

27. See Franklin v. Gwinnett County Public Schools, 503 U.S. 60 (1992).

28. See Peter v. San Francisco Unified School Dist., 60 C.A.3d 814 (1976). See also Donohue v. Copiague Union Free School District, 47 N.Y.2d 440 (1979).

29. See Hunter v. Board of Education of Montgomery County, 292 Md. 481 (1982).

# 15

# Financing Public Schools
# and Use of Funds

*The most common and durable source of factions has been the various and
unequal distribution of property.*

—James Madison, *Federalist Papers*

## OVERVIEW . . . . . . . . . . . . . . . . . . . . . . . . . . . . . .

School funding in the United States is based on a combination of federal, state, and local
funds. In almost all states except Hawaii, the majority of public education funding is provided
by the state and local governments. The federal government usually only provides about
5–10% of the total school budget. The state share, which comes from state income and sales
tax revenues, is provided to school districts based on a foundation (or equal yield) formula
devised by the state legislature. The basic program cost for each district is calculated by mul-
tiplying the per-pupil foundation level (formula amount) adjusted with a regional cost factor
times the number of pupils in the school district. The state provides additional supplements
to compensate for the extra financial burden of costs associated with special education, gifted
student programs, vocational training, transportation, poverty assistance, and parity aid. The
purpose of state foundation funding is to equalize financial support to school districts to compensate for the disparity created by the local funding system, which is almost exclusively
based on property taxes. Local funds are received from taxes levied on real property in the
school district. When a school district wants to increase its local funds, it must place a levy
(or bond issue) on the ballot to be passed by the voters in that district.

States such as Ohio have a constitutionally mandated tax, levied without a vote of
the people (called inside millage), which is for the operation of local government and school
services. All other taxes must be approved by the voters in the school district. This system,

335

while seemingly effective, often leads to vast disparity in the number of dollars per child available to support the education of children in different school districts. While the state share in Ohio was 44% in the 2000 fiscal year, the local share was 50%. Over the past 10 years, even with additional state funding as a result of *DeRolph* litigation (explained below), the gap has increased. Furthermore, local property values vary widely across Ohio, resulting in varying property tax revenues. The Ohio School Foundation program has one fatal flaw: It does not work. It is woefully underfunded, and more affluent districts, because of their local property tax wealth, are able to spend far more per child than poorer Ohio school districts. In effect, the quality of children's education is, all too often, a function of where they are born.

Most state constitutions empower the state legislature to tax and distribute funds to support public education. Sometimes, legal challenges are filed in opposition to the methods used by state legislatures to regulate revenues and expenditures. Local school districts and other local-level entities may also have authorization to provide funds to support education. Similarly, local districts may be challenged in the courts by those who believe the districts are operating outside the limits of the powers conferred upon them by state government. Still another area of conflict involves the constitutional rights of students and the resulting impact on state school finance. Nationally, there is a long history of litigation concerning school finance issues. Nevertheless, until recent times, the number of cases regarding the constitutional rights of students and the resulting impact on state school finance has been quite small compared to the number of cases regarding other fiscal matters.

Since 1968, substantial litigation has been initiated challenging the methods that states use to distribute funds to public schools. This challenge to state aid formulas is a historic step in judicial expansion of constitutional protections. Courts that once considered education to be a privilege are treating education as a right—and now often support decisions based on state constitutional provisions that limit the power of the state to control and regulate education. A key issue is whether the quality of a child's education should depend on the property wealth of the local community. Another concern is an unwillingness to accept that all children do not have similar educational needs and, therefore, funding levels may need to be structured to provide more funds to some children (e.g., at-risk children, children with disabilities). The legal theory used to challenge these inequities is based on the equal protection clause of the Fourteenth Amendment.

In *San Antonio Independent School District v. Rodriguez* (1973), the Supreme Court addressed whether it was constitutional for a child's education to hinge on the wealth of the school district.[1] The Court concluded that education was not a fundamental right, and therefore the higher equal protection standard of "strict scrutiny" was not applied. Thus, because the Court concluded that education was not a fundamental right and allowed a "rational basis" test to be applied, the Texas finance system that relied on property taxes was found to be constitutional. This decision effectively halted any attempt in the federal courts to use the equal protection clause of the Fourteenth Amendment to correct the fiscal inequities of the property tax system.

Since *Rodriguez,* those who challenged school funding as unconstitutional were forced to attack the property tax system using state constitutional provisions as the basis for change. With the federal system closed to them, challengers took their claims to state courts, basing their arguments on state constitutional provisions that resulted in an inequitable effect for schools in property tax-challenged school districts.

For the first 20 years, these state cases seemed to follow the *Rodriguez* position, upholding the constitutionality of the property tax. In recent years, however, the trend has reversed. The first important case that led to a change in direction by state courts was *Robinson v. Cahill* (1973).[2] In this case, the court found that the current inequitable funding system based on the property tax violated the New Jersey constitution's requirement that education be funded by "thorough and efficient" means.

Some state courts found that education was a fundamental right under their state constitutions, and some found it was not. In the Kentucky school finance case, *Rose v. Council for Better Education, Inc.* (1989), whether education was a fundamental right was not even an issue.[3] Nevertheless, the state supreme court required a change in the financing of Kentucky schools because the legislature failed to provide an efficient system of common schools.

An instructive Ohio case is *DeRolph v. State* (1997).[4] There have been four *DeRolph* rulings, wherein the Ohio Supreme Court has tried to restructure the property tax system. The result of their efforts remains unclear. Initially, although education was held not to be a fundamental right, the Ohio Supreme Court found that the present school finance system did not meet the state constitution's "thorough and efficient" mandate. The second decision again held that the legislature had failed to meet its constitutional mandate. However, despite this decision, the legislature continued to provide additional funding to the foundation and relied on the property tax system that had been found unconstitutional. In its final *DeRolph* decision, the court restated its initial holding and again ordered the school financing system to be restructured. The legislature and governor did nothing to implement the court's decision, leaving the plaintiffs no way to obtain relief and clearly challenging the balance of powers theory underpinning government action. After the original judge who made the initial ruling in the Court of Common Pleas was held to not have standing because the case had been decided, the plaintiffs tried to get the Supreme Court to accept their writ. When the U.S. Supreme Court refused certiorari, the result was essentially an unenforceable decision.

## Case Study

### Breakdown in the Balance of Power

You are superintendent in a school district that is experiencing severe financial difficulties. You have discussed the problem with your school board and informed them that the problem is statewide and created by the state government's use of property taxes to fund school districts. Because the *Rodriguez* decision held that the property tax funding system did not violate the U.S. Constitution, your district joined with hundreds of others throughout the state to bring a challenge in state court to the use of the property tax as the basic source of funding for schools. You were victorious in your state's supreme court, which required that the legislature find a "thorough and efficient" way to fund education. Nevertheless, the legislature and the governor still failed to provide a financing method that eliminated the reliance on property taxes. One of your state's supreme court justices even stated that while "we are mindful of the difficulties facing the state, those difficulties do not

*(Continued)*

(Continued)

trump the constitution." In effect, he directed the state legislature to find a thorough and effective way to fund schools in spite of fiscal shortfalls. After making a fourth and final order, essentially restating the very first decision, the state supreme court withdrew from the case and refused to use its judicial power to take action against the governor and the state legislature. With the legislature and governor unwilling to change the dependence on the property tax, school districts in your state continue to experience financial distress. Finally, complicating the situation, your plaintiff coalition of school districts (about 90% of the state's school districts) asked the U.S. Supreme Court to hear the case. Certiorari was denied, thereby closing the case after more than a decade of legal entanglements. While further litigation will certainly ensue, it must be through new state actions, which will take years to move through the various state courts. You must make recommendations to the school board concerning the increasingly difficult financial condition that the district faces. What are you going to say and do?

## Discussion Questions

1. Do you really have any options? The state legislature and the governor have failed to follow the lead of the third branch of government. You cannot sue them, but should you force the state supreme court to act?

2. Your budget deficits have resulted from the state government's failure to act on the state supreme court's order. If you are unable to sue the state without its permission, why not send them a bill requesting that they pay for your financial shortfall? Could you then sue them to recover funds?

3. What are some other options for funding public education, other than the traditional reliance on local property taxes?

# IMPORTANT CONCEPTS

- **State taxing power:** The power to tax is an inherent power of the state, although it may be delegated to local bodies under certain specified circumstances.

- **No local taxing power:** Local school districts have no authority to tax, despite the fact that they are often charged with the responsibility of operating district schools.

- **Improper tax levies:** Taxes that have been levied improperly because of the taxing authority's failure to follow formal procedures will be declared invalid if the ignored procedures were mandatory. However, if the ignored procedures were merely **directory** and not mandatory, then the taxes will be declared valid.

- **No recovery for illegal taxes already paid:** Taxpayers may not recover taxes they have paid pursuant to a tax levy that is subsequently declared illegal if their payments were made voluntarily and not under duress or compulsion.

- **No authority to borrow or issue:** Local school districts have no inherent authority to borrow funds or issue bonds or similar negotiable instruments.

- **Limit on indebtedness:** The amount of debt that a local school district may incur is usually limited by statute or by state constitution.

- **Federal education spending:** Congress may spend on education throughout the various states, so long as the purpose of its expenditures is not to control local education programs.

- **Constitutional mandate:** Many state constitutions set forth specific plans for the distribution of education funds, while others merely set forth an intended purpose or goal of the distributions.

- **Limited to constitutional funds:** Only those funds contemplated within a state's constitution are subject to constitutional mandates concerning their distribution.

- **Unequal expenditures of funds:** Numerous lawsuits throughout the nation have challenged state school finance plans that are perceived as permitting uneven per-pupil expenditures of funds across the state's local school districts.

- **Unusual expenditure suits properly brought in state court:** Because the U.S. Supreme Court has ruled that education is not a fundamental interest warranting "strict scrutiny" analysis (see *San Antonio v. Rodriguez,* 1973), the appropriate forum for unequal expenditure suits is state court, not federal court, and the proper basis for unequal expenditure arguments is the state's own constitution and statutes, not federal law.

- **Choice plans:** The state may create "choice" plans, which permit the education-consuming public to select from a variety of educational services, in a variety of settings, at public expense. Choice plans, often implemented as voucher or choice schools, are increasing rapidly.

- **Variations of choice:** Choice plans can be set up to provide various options for students, allowing them to select from any open school in their existing district, to select from any open school in any other district within the state, to receive a voucher redeemable for approved educational services from various sources, and/or to obtain educational service from approved private sector providers.

- **Discretion in making education expenditures:** Local school boards are given considerable discretion in determining what constitutes a "public purpose," which many school fund expenditures are required to serve.

- **School property is state, not local, in nature:** School property is state property. It is merely held in trust by the local school district for the public's benefit.

*(Continued)*

(Continued)

- **Control may be vested in any agency:** The legislature could, conceivably, vest control of local school property in another local agency.

- **School property to be used for school-related purposes:** Some courts do not permit the use of school property for nonschool purposes. Where such uses are permissible, they must not interfere with school operations.

- **Discrimination not permissible:** When nonschool uses of property are permitted, local school boards cannot discriminate between users based on the content of their expressions.

- **Broad authority to acquire property:** Most school boards are delegated broad authority to purchase property for school-related purposes.

- **Power to take private property (eminent domain):** The taking of private property for public use is constitutionally permissible so long as it constitutes a necessity and the property owner receives just compensation for her loss.

- **Disposition of school property:** Courts may validate unauthorized dispositions of school property if it is determined that they have been made in the public interest.

- **Express authority required to transport students:** A school board must be authorized by statute to expend school funds in order to transport students to and from school. Even when this is the case, such authorizing statutes will be interpreted narrowly by the courts.

- **Implied authority to insure:** Most school boards are implicitly authorized to expend school funds for insurance coverage.

- **Short-term medical services permitted:** Most school boards are permitted to expend school funds for short-term (i.e., emergency or first aid) medical services, but usually not for services of a continuing nature.

- **Legal services:** Most local school boards are implicitly authorized to expend school funds in order to pay for legal services provided on behalf of district employees.

# PUBLIC SCHOOL REVENUES

## Revenues Raised Through Taxation

*Inherent Power.* The power of taxation is an inherent power of the state. This power suffers no limitation except that provided by the Fourteenth Amendment to the U.S. Constitution (and by any limitation that may be contained in a state's own constitution).

*No Inherent Power.* Local school districts have no inherent power to levy taxes. The state legislature must specifically confer such powers on a local entity.[5] School districts must strictly adhere to the express language of their statutory authority. Most courts are hesitant to imply greater taxing authority than is apparent on the face of the conferring statute. Even a statutory mandate to establish and operate a local school system does not, necessarily, give a local school board the authority to tax for funds to accomplish those purposes.

*Delegation of Taxing Authority.* The legislature may delegate its taxing power to subordinate bodies. This includes both the form and rate of taxation. The legislature need not set any limits on the delegation of its power if the subordinate body is composed of local elected officials. However, if the subordinate body is appointed rather than elected, clear limitations must be placed on the extent of the delegated power. This includes specifying the purpose for which the delegated taxing power may be exercised and setting maximum tax rates.

*State, Not Local, Taxes.* Even if the taxing authority is delegated to a local entity, the taxes that are imposed through the exercise of it remain state, and not local, in nature.

*Special Taxes.* Funds raised through special purpose taxation may be used only for that purpose. Funds remaining after distribution are usually returned to the voters or allocated as the legislature sees fit.

*Improper Levies.* When a school tax has been levied improperly, such as when a prescribed statutory procedure is not followed, courts will determine whether the statutory provision is mandatory or directory. Failure to follow a mandatory provision in levying a tax renders the tax invalid. Failure to follow a directory provision will not result in invalidation. Courts have not developed guidelines for determining the difference between mandatory and directory provisions, although they usually construe provisions liberally (i.e., as directory). This avoids invalidating taxes and thereby harming educational programs that are dependent on funds generated by the tax in question.

*Rate of Levies.* Before taxes are levied, the amount of revenue to be generated must be determined. As a rule, a school board may not use its taxing power to over-tax and thereby establish a surplus fund. There is no requirement that the distribution of the funds must benefit all the properties assessed. So long as the tax is assessed equally and for the public welfare, it need not be distributed equally.[6] Many states amended statutes during the inflationary 1970s, requiring the return of additional tax monies collected as a result of inflation (see, e.g., Ohio's House Bill 920). Essentially, as the value of school property increases with periodic property tax re-evaluation, the school district collects only the original tax dollars requested, not the additional dollars from the inflated property values. School districts are strongly in opposition to such state laws because their cost of doing business increases with inflation while the dollars they receive from the tax levy remain constant.

## Taxpayers' Remedies Against Illegal Taxation

In certain situations, a taxpayer may pay taxes in accordance with a law that is later held invalid because the law in some way contravenes the state or federal constitution, or for some other reason. The taxpayer, who will undoubtedly wish to recover payments made because of an illegal tax, does not necessarily have the right to a refund. As a general rule, if an illegal tax was paid *voluntarily,* it is presumed that the taxpayer knew the underlying tax law was invalid but paid anyway. Thus, no recovery will be permitted. The general rule of nonrecovery does not apply if payment of the tax was made under duress or compulsion. However, if the payment were made under mere *protest,* then the general rule of nonrecovery is usually applicable. A protest is usually not enough to make a payment involuntary, except in those jurisdictions that recognize it as such by statute. Whether a court rules in favor of a taxpayer may depend upon its characterization of what best serves the public interest. Public hardships may result if local agency funds are depleted by virtue of a court order requiring repayment to the taxpayer. Regardless of the foregoing rationale, the collection of an illegal tax may be enjoined prior to actual collection.

## Revenues Raised Through Bond Issues

*No Authority to Borrow Funds.* A local school board has no inherent power to borrow funds, despite the fact that it is usually charged with responsibility for the day-to-day management of its school system.

*No Bond-Issuing Authority.* No authority to borrow also means no authority to issue bonds or other similar negotiable instruments.

*Authority Conferred by Statute.* The state legislature confers the authority to issue bonds upon the local school board, which usually must follow elaborate procedures, including a vote of local citizens. Failure to follow the required procedures may result in the bond issue being declared invalid. Most courts will likely uphold the validity of the issue if it appears that the irregularity does not deprive taxpayers of significant rights.

*Illegal Bonds.* A bond issue that falls outside the law is void, and no recovery will be permitted. A difficult situation arises when the illegality is not discovered until after the school board has spent the funds derived from the issue. There is no hard and fast rule. However, some courts will permit the bondholder to recover the value of the benefit conferred upon the school district from the illegal issuance of bonds if the following are met: the board initially had the authority to issue valid bonds, and the issue would have been valid had the district exercised its authority properly.

## Debt Ceiling Limits

The amount of indebtedness that a local school district may incur is generally limited by statute or by state constitution. When a question arises as to whether the district's debt limit has been exceeded, a net indebtedness figure is determined by subtracting from all outstanding debts those assets that could be used to pay off the debts (such as cash on hand, taxes levied, etc.). A school district may resort to long-term leases and installment contracts for materials, services, or use of real estate in order to avoid debt creation because technically such leases and contracts create a succession of separate obligations in the nature of current expenses (i.e., to be paid when due from current revenues).

# Federal Funds

Pursuant to the general welfare clause of the U.S. Constitution, Congress is authorized to spend money to further the education of U.S. citizens. The purpose of the funds spent, however, may not be to regulate or control educational programs within the states. Before Congress offers education dollars to the states, it may attach conditions to such grants, but a state will not be bound to a condition unless it was fully aware of Congress's intent to impose it.

# ALLOCATION OF STATE FUNDS

## State Constitutional Mandates

In some states, the exact manner in which state school funds are to be distributed is set forth in the state's constitution. In other states, the state constitution merely sets forth a goal or purpose of the intended distribution. A state constitution's funding distribution requirements establish a mandatory level of education spending. Other funds may be earmarked and distributed by the state legislature, at its discretion, to fund other areas of education, so long as such funds do not become a part of the "constitutional fund."

## Equalization of Resources

A matter of continued controversy, over which a good deal of litigation has arisen, is the constitutionality of those state school finance plans that permit uneven per-pupil expenditures of funds among the state's local school districts. Under such plans, school districts with a strong tax base receive more tax dollars than school districts with a weak tax base. The wealthier districts thus receive more money to spend per pupil than the poorer districts, and it is not unusual for neighboring districts to have significantly disproportionate budgets. The obvious consequences include profound differences in facilitates, equipment, programs, and class size, all affecting the quality of education provided for each district's students.

*No Fundamental Right to Education.* The United States Supreme Court held that education was *not* a fundamental right. Consequently, a rational basis analysis—rather than strict scrutiny—via the equal protection clause may be applied when specific laws appear to be unconstitutional.[7] The result is that decisions concerning the legality of state school financing plans are left to each state's constitution, its legislature, and its courts for interpretation. Most state constitutions contain a prohibition against "unreasonable classifications," the state equivalent of the U.S. Constitution's equal protection clause. Those attacking state school finance plans often contend that such plans result in the creation of unreasonable classifications among pupils from different local school systems.

*Landmark.* In a historic state court opinion that preceded the U.S. Supreme Court's decision in the *Rodriguez* case, the California Supreme Court stated, in dicta, that a state funding plan that permitted the quality of students' education to vary according to the wealth of their respective school districts discriminated against the poor and thus violated the equal protection clause and a similar provision in the California constitution. Interestingly, while the California funding plan failed to equalize the discrepancies between districts with high property valuations and those with low valuations, the court did not find it violated the state constitution.[8]

*Post-Rodriguez State Court Decisions.* Because of differences in the various state constitutions and statutory financing plans, state court opinions responding to challenges to state financing plans have not been uniform. When such courts have struck down financing plans, they have generally done so in response to significant disparity among various local school districts' per-pupil expenditures.

## "Choice" Plans

Choice plans permit the education-consuming public to select from a variety of educational services, in a variety of settings, at public expense. Supporters believe that providing the public with a choice will do away with a socialist education bureaucracy and lead to increased competition among the various educational alternatives. The plan's supporters hope it will elicit free market and competition-derived benefits not present in a regulated system. Those in opposition argue that choice will destroy the current egalitarian, "melting pot," diverse atmosphere within the public school system.

*Choice Within and Between Public School Systems.* Students are allowed to attend the school of their choice in their own school district or any other district in their state, so long as there is space for them at the school they desire and their choice does not upset existing desegregation plans.

*Choice Within a Public School System.* Students are allowed to attend a school within their school district other than the one they would normally attend.

*Voucher Plan.* Parents receive a voucher, redeemable for a specific dollar amount per year per child, which may be spent on approved educational services (such as those provided in public or private schools). The government would ensure that each approved program met certain minimum educational standards. Voucher plans that allowed a significant number of students to attend religious schools have survived constitutional challenges.

*Services From Private Firms.* Public school systems sometimes contract with outside firms to provide specific educational services. The performance level of the students is the standard by which the outside firm is judged.

# LOCAL SCHOOL DISTRICT BUDGETS AND EXPENDITURES

## Public Purpose Rule Regarding Expenditures

Local school boards are given considerable discretion in determining what constitutes a "public purpose" in connection with school fund expenditures. Courts will not intervene in a school board's exercise of its discretion to spend unless it is apparent that expenditure has been made for an improper purpose, such as one that is contrary to a state statute or constitutional provision. In the case of a school system that is fiscally dependent upon its local municipal government, the courts construe board powers liberally. The board will not be restricted to the particularities of its budget so long as it does not attempt to spend more than it has been allocated.

## Budgetary Itemizations

Most states require local school boards to prepare budgets of proposed expenditures. State statutes may also regulate the manner in which the budgets are prepared, published, and presented to the public. Occasionally, taxpayers bring suit, contending that a local school board has failed to provide a sufficient itemization of expenditures within its budget. Such suits rarely prevail.

# PROPERTY AND FUND USE

Taxpayers and citizen groups occasionally challenge the use that a local school board makes of the funds and property that are entrusted to its care by the state. Lawsuits may arise in connection with arguably "nonschool" uses to which school property may be subjected or, more frequently, in connection with the sale or other disposition of such property. Questions about the use of school funds generally arise when it is perceived that funds are not used for a school purpose or are used in violation of a particular statutory or constitutional provision.

## School Property

### Nature of School Property

School property is state property, held in trust by the local school district, as trustee, for the benefit of the public at large. A state legislature does not relinquish its control over school property when it vests a local district with the power to acquire and hold property. A state legislature could conceivably vest control of local school property in an agency other than the local school district. Or, it could reorganize smaller districts into one large district, thereby removing the local districts as trustees in favor of the new, larger district.

### Permissible Uses of School Property

The general public may use school buildings for education or school-related purposes. Fees may be charged for usage. The use of school property for nonschool purposes has been forbidden by some courts. In other cases, nonschool uses have been permitted so long as they do not interfere with the school's programs and operations. The California legislature has provided for a wide variety of nonschool uses on state school property. By statute, each state school is designated a civic center, which is available for local organizations to use for a variety of community purposes. When broad nonschool uses of property are permissible, local school boards must be careful not to distinguish based on the content of their respective expressions.[9]

*Expression of a Religious Nature.* In 1981, the U.S. Supreme Court determined that religious groups could not be denied the same opportunities that were provided to nonreligious groups who routinely sought and were given permission to use school property. More recently, however, the U.S. Supreme Court, while holding that when a school creates a limited public forum, it cannot deny access to religious groups, held that a church's use of school district property for all religious purposes may be banned so long as the school district's exclusion is reasonable and viewpoint-neutral.[10]

*Prohibitions Against Loitering and Solicitation.* Loitering on school grounds may be prohibited, provided that the enabling statute or ordinance is not so vague that it makes it difficult to determine what type of conduct is prohibited. Blanket prohibitions against solicitations likely infringe upon freedom of speech rights.

## Purchase of Property by Local Districts

Taxpayers sometimes question a local school board's use of tax money to purchase property when the purchase does not appear to advance a generally accepted school purpose. Examples of questionable purchases include acquisitions of property for playgrounds, athletic fields, and recreational centers. Courts interpret the local board's authority broadly in this regard. This comports with the trend that most courts have established in expanding the definition of "educational purpose." This allows school boards wide latitude in making decisions they believe will somehow benefit education. In rare situations, a school board may allow a proper authority to use the power of eminent domain. Eminent domain refers to the expanding power of government to take private property for public use.

*Local School Board Use.* When authorized to do so by statute, local school boards may condemn and take for public use property that is needed for public school purposes.

*Constitutional Requirements.* A taking by eminent domain must satisfy state and federal constitutional requirements of procedural due process, equal protection of the laws, and just compensation. The question of what constitutes "just compensation" has led to a good deal of litigation, although in most cases the fair market value of the property satisfies this requirement.

*Necessity Requirement.* In taking property for public use, a school board must demonstrate that the taking was out of necessity. This means that it cannot condemn any more property than it actually needs.

*Property Held by Another Public Agency.* Generally, a school board cannot condemn property that is being held by another public agency. However, if two public agencies seek to condemn the same private property, the agency with the greater need will prevail.

## Disposal of School Property

The disposition of school property is usually governed by statute. Grants of authority to manage and control school property do not imply authority to sell it or give it away. Where no statutory authority exists, courts will review sales of property by local boards in order to determine whether there has been an abuse of discretion (i.e., whether the board has taken an action that is not in the best interest of the school district).

# Use of School Funds for Particular Purposes

## Student Transportation Services

Authority to transport students to and from school must be expressly conferred on local school boards by the state legislature. Even a statute authorizing a local board to take necessary steps to maintain its schools and educate its students does not confer upon it the authority to spend district money on transportation services. Even when a local board has the responsibility to transport, it temporarily may withhold transportation services as a means of controlling improper student bus behavior. However, when such a suspension of services would result in the denial of educational opportunities or bring harm to students' reputations, suspension will not be permitted because it violates the students' Fourteenth Amendment due process rights.[11] Most courts narrowly interpret legislative grants of authority to transport students. They view transportation of students as the responsibility of the parents and not of the local school system. In some states, school boards are empowered to pay a mileage rate to parents of students who live at considerable distances from public schools. This discharges the school's statutory obligation to provide transportation.

## Insurance Coverage

The power of a local school board to insure school property is generally implied from the board's mission. Occasionally, school boards seek to insure school property by joining associations that do not require premium payments but do pro-rate losses among all association members. Joining an association with shared and uncertain potential liability may subject the district to large, uncertain losses. Because this may amount, in effect, to a loan of public funds to other agencies that sustain losses, litigation has arisen in connection with the constitutionality of this alternative. A pooled risk plan that sets no specified limit on the district's liability is probably invalid because of this rationale. Of course, local school boards generally may purchase group health, life, and disability insurance for employees, such as teachers and administrators.

## Professional Services

*Medical Services.* The implied powers of local school boards usually do not include authority to pay for long-term or extended medical services for students who are injured on school property. Implied authority does exist to pay for short-term emergency medical services, such as first aid.

*Legal Services*

a. *Implied authority to fund.* In most jurisdictions, the authority to pay for legal services is implied.

b. *Statutory authority under certain circumstances.* In some jurisdictions, local school boards are authorized, by statute, to avail themselves of government attorneys when they need legal services.

c. *Defense of school officials.* Public school funds may be spent to defend a school official who has been sued in his *individual* capacity, so long as the official was fulfilling the duties of his position in good faith. (A suit against an official in his *official* capacity will almost certainly be funded.) Knowing that legal defense costs will be borne by the school district under appropriate circumstances permits school officials to perform their duties freely, without the inhibitions that sometimes result from fear of lawsuits.

### Use of Funds for Other Purposes

Implied powers may not extend to specialty items. Courts may not find that local board's implied powers include purchasing arguably nonschool items for special segments of the student population. Examples include, in some instances, athletic gear and supplies and band uniforms. However, the courts have found that a board's implied powers allowed it to use school funds to "buy out" a superintendent's contract, even though taxpayers challenged this action as an unauthorized gift of public funds.[12]

## Case Study

### Can School Property Use Be Refused to Religious Groups?

You have received another request from the local church group almost demanding that you allow them use of the high school auditorium to show a series of films with follow-up lectures and discussions. These films deal with family and child-rearing issues faced by parents today and are, admittedly, for religious purposes. This evangelical group is led by an aggressive pastor, John Steigerwald, who has made this and similar requests in the past. The emphasis of the film series and the lectures and discussion is to help us return "to traditional, Christian family values instilled in us in our early youth and being lost in the decadent morality of modern life." There have been few other request for use of the schools by religious groups in recent years. You would like to recommend that this group not be allowed to use school facilities, but you are not sure of your position.

### Discussion Questions

1. Whose opinion should you solicit?

2. Is there a problem if you deny use of any school facilities to all religious groups?

3. Will you have to deny access to all outside groups if you want to deny use of school facilities to this religious group?

# CONCLUSION · · · · · · · · · · · · · · · · · · · · · · · · · · · · · · · · · · · · · · ·

Generally, public schools are funded through a combination of federal, state, and local funding. Because the federal government provides very little funding, it is the states' responsibility to provide nearly all educational funding. Primarily, the states raise revenues through taxation.

Though the state has an inherent power to tax, local school districts must be conferred that power by the state. Sometimes, a district imposes an improper school tax levy. Failure to follow a mandatory provision will invalidate the tax, although failure to follow a directory provision does not necessarily invalidate it. Unfortunately, the courts have been unclear in distinguishing between the two. A school district may not tax to the point of creating a surplus; all funds must be immediately needed. If a citizen is illegally taxed, he is not necessarily entitled to reimbursement. Rather, if the court deems that the tax was voluntarily paid, absent coercion or similar circumstances, the citizen is generally presumed to have known the tax was invalid and to have voluntarily paid it.

School boards have no inherent ability to borrow, though the state legislature may statutorily confer authority. If a school board borrows outside the scope of its authority, the lender may not be entitled to recovery. Some courts will permit the lender to recover the value of the benefit conferred on the school district if the board initially had authority to borrow and the authority would have been valid had the district exercised it properly.

Some states' constitutions prescribe the exact manner in which state school funds are to be distributed, while others are much less specific. A matter of continued controversy is whether uneven per-pupil expenditures are constitutional. Obviously, richer districts are able to spend more than poorer ones. The United States Supreme Court has held that education is *not* a fundamental right. The result is that decisions concerning the legality of state school financing plans are left to each state's constitution. Because of differences in various state constitutions and statutory financing plans, state court opinions responding to challenges to state financing plans have not been uniform.

Choice plans publicly fund a variety of schools from which a student may choose. Proponents of this plan believe that free market principles associated with competition and choice will benefit the educational system. Opponents argue that this plan will destroy the egalitarian and diverse atmosphere of the public school system. A variety of plans exist, spanning from student choice of any public school within the state to a voucher program allowing students to use public funding to pay to attend private schools.

Local school boards are given significant discretion in determining what constitutes a "public purpose" in connection with school expenditures. Courts will refrain from intervention absent a clear statutory violation. Most states require schools to prepare and publish their budgets and expenditures.

School property is state property, held in trust by the local school district for the benefit of the public at large. The general public may use school buildings for education or school-related purposes. Some courts have forbidden the use of school property for nonschool uses. In most states, by statute, each state school is designated a civic center, which is available for local organizations to use for a variety of community purposes. When broad nonschool uses of property are permissible, boards must carefully avoid content-based discrimination.

Authority to transport students to and from school must be expressly conferred on local school boards by the state legislature. Transportation is viewed as a parent and not a school responsibility. A school with the authority to fund transportation may suspend these services as a means of controlling student behavior, though courts may invalidate such attempts if they result in denial of equal educational opportunities or harm students' reputations.

A school board, under its implied powers, may usually insure school property and pay for legal services. Also, provision of medical services is usually included under these powers. However, schools generally may not use implied powers to fund specialty items, such as athletic equipment and band uniforms.

The following cases illustrate the competing interests of students, taxpayers, and state and local governments. The powers vested in state governments may be conferred to local school districts, so long as those powers are clearly defined by the state legislature. In distributing taxes, a state assessed tax does not need to benefit each taxpayer equally. The Court in *Sawyer v. Gilmore, State Treasurer* (1912) stated that when a state tax is collected for public welfare, the benefit elicited need not be distributed equally amongst the taxpayers. School districts are free to decide which services to provide for schoolchildren so long as those decisions do not deny schoolchildren the right to an education. Finally, taxpayers are not powerless against the spending powers of local school districts. The Court held in *Ingram v. Boone* (1983) that taxpayers have a right to challenge payments that appear to be unauthorized gifts of public monies. After reading these cases, you should better understand the roles of state and local governments and their control over the funding of school districts.

# CASE BRIEFS · · · · · · · · · · · · · · · · · · · · · · · · · · · · · ·

# DEROLPH V. STATE (DEROLPH I)
## 78 OHIO ST. 3D 193, 677 N.E.2D 733 (1997)

**GENERAL RULE OF LAW:** The Ohio Constitution provides that the state shall establish a thorough and efficient system of common schools throughout the state. When school district funding relies primarily on local property taxes, the effect is a substandard school system in some districts. Therefore, the entire statewide system needs to be overhauled. This is not a job for the court but the job of the legislature.

**PROCEDURE SUMMARY:**

> **Plaintiffs:** Dale R. DeRolph (P), along with five other school districts (Coalition for Adequacy and Equity and over 500 Ohio school districts were later added)

> **Defendant:** State of Ohio (D)

> **Court of Common Pleas Decision (Perry County, Ohio):** Found that several provisions of school funding violated the Ohio Constitution

> **State Fifth District Court of Appeals Decision (Ohio):** Reversed

> **State Supreme Court Decision (Ohio):** Affirmed the trial court's ruling

**FACTS:** Dale R. DeRolph (P), on behalf of his son Nathan, a high school student in Northern Local School District in Perry County, filed a lawsuit, along with five school districts, against the state of Ohio (D). They sought a determination that Ohio's system of funding public education was unconstitutional. The Coalition for Adequacy and Equity and numerous other school districts later joined as plaintiffs. After the initial state supreme court decision for the plaintiffs, there were three later rulings by the Ohio Supreme Court because the plaintiffs challenged aspects of the implementation of the remedy attempted by the state of Ohio (D). These various decisions are discussed below in a historical narrative format.

**ISSUE:** Is Ohio's public elementary and secondary school finance system thorough and efficient, as mandated in Article VI, Section 2 of the Ohio Constitution?

**HOLDING AND DECISION:** No. Ohio's elementary and secondary public school financing system violates Article VI, Section 2, of the Ohio Constitution, which mandates a thorough and efficient system of common schools throughout the state. The following specific provisions were found unconstitutional: the provisions granting borrowing authority to school districts, the emergency school assistance loan provisions, the School Foundation Program, and the Classroom Facilities Act (to the extent that it was underfunded).

At the heart of this controversy is Ohio's School Foundation Program. The revenue available to a school district comes from two primary sources: state revenue (the majority of which is provided through the

School Foundation Program) and local revenue (consisting primarily of revenue from local school district property taxes). Federal funds play a relatively minor role in this financing system. Contrary to the national trend, Ohio relies more on local revenue than on state revenue. Additionally, the court found that a school system would not be operating in a "thorough and efficient" manner if "a school district was receiving so little local and state revenue that the students were effectively being deprived of educational opportunity." The court found extensive evidence establishing that the appellant school districts were in great need of funds, teachers, buildings, and equipment. Further, the court found that these school districts had sub-standard educational programs and their pupils were deprived of educational opportunity. Moreover, the court found that the General Assembly had failed its constitutional obligation to structure school financing to ensure a thorough and efficient system of common schools. As the court stated, "Clearly, the current school financing scheme is a far cry from thorough and efficient. Instead, the system has failed to educate our youth to their fullest potential."

Although the court found the school financing system to be unconstitutional, it did not instruct the General Assembly to enact specific legislation. However, it did admonish the General Assembly that it must create an entirely new school financing system while keeping in mind that the Ohio system of public education is a statewide system. Therefore, it was the state's responsibility to establish, organize, and maintain its public education system. Furthermore, because of its importance, education should be placed high in the state's budgetary priorities. A thorough and efficient system of common schools would have facilities in good repair, proper funding for necessary supplies and materials, and maintenance of these facilities to keep them safe and in compliance with all local, state, and federal mandates.

## DeRolph II: 89 Ohio St.3d 1, 728 N.E.2d 993 (2000)

**ISSUE:** Is the revised system of school funding thorough and efficient, pursuant to Article VI, Section 2, of the Ohio Constitution?

**HOLDING AND DECISION:** No. The court stated that *DeRolph I* did not require a specific funding scheme, but it did not instruct the General Assembly as to what legislation should be enacted because it feared violating the "separation of powers" doctrine: "The legislature has the power to draft legislation, and the court has the power to determine whether that legislation complies with the Constitution." However, while it is the job of the General Assembly to legislate a remedy, courts possess the authority to enforce their orders. The court's power to declare a particular law unconstitutional includes the remedial power to require a revision of that enactment. "If it did not, then the power to find a particular Act unconstitutional would be a nullity." The court determined that the Governor and General Assembly have made progress and allowed them more time to comply with Article VI, Section 2, of the Ohio Constitution. The court declined to appoint a special master to oversee the state's further efforts to comply with Article VI, Section 2, but it stated that it would maintain jurisdiction over the matter. The court set a June 15, 2001 deadline, at which time the court established a briefing schedule.

## DeRolph III: 98 Ohio St.3d 309, 754 N.E.2d 1184 (2001)

**HOLDING AND DECISION:** The supreme court, by a 4–3 vote, ruled that Ohio's school funding system was still unconstitutional. However, the court stated that if the legislature adjusted the new school finance system by accelerating some funding goals and fully implemented these modifications, the funding plan adopted by the General Assembly would meet the test for constitutionality created in *DeRolph I* and *DeRolph*

*II.* The supreme court then ended the case. When the defendants realized the extent of the financial liability (because foundation adjustments were retroactive to September), they petitioned for reconsideration of the settled decision.

## DeRolph IV: 97 Ohio St.3d 434, 780 N.E. 2d 529 (2002)

**HOLDING AND DECISION:** After being asked to reconsider the decision in *DeRolph III,* the court decided to vacate it. Its new and final ruling held that *DeRolph I* and *II* still controlled. Additionally, the court held that the current school funding system was still unconstitutional. The court found that the principal legislative response to *DeRolph I* and *DeRolph II,* an increase in funding, was not enough. It ordered the General Assembly again to focus on the core constitutional directive of *DeRolph I*: "a complete systematic overhaul" of the school funding system. The majority stated: "Today we reiterate that that is what is needed, not further nibbling at the edges. Accordingly, we direct the General Assembly to enact a school funding scheme that is thorough and efficient, as explained in *DeRolph I, DeRolph II,* and the accompanying concurrences."

The court stated that it is mindful of the difficulties facing the state, but those difficulties do not trump the constitutional mandates. In conclusion, the court added, "We realize that the General Assembly cannot spend money it does not have. Nevertheless, we reiterate that the constitutional mandate must be met. The Constitution protects us whether the state is flush or destitute."

**COMMENT:** The series of *DeRolph* opinions tackle the constitutionality of funding in Ohio's schools. The courts are reluctant to fashion their own remedy for fear of violating the separation of powers. This series of cases resembles the decision making in *Brown v. Board of Education* (1954).[13] Recall that in *Brown* the court established that the concept of "separate but equal" was unconstitutional and ordered the violating districts to fashion a remedy. *Brown* called for district courts to oversee the desegregation process. The courts here have not taken any role in overseeing the process of "overhauling" school funding in Ohio. Thus, the multiple opinions are needed to rule on the constitutionality of the various attempted corrections. The plaintiffs were granted a favorable ruling that called for the implementation of a financing system that did not rely on property taxes. The Ohio legislature and the governor refused to provide for such a plan. This left the plaintiff without a means to implement the remedy provided by the judiciary. First, the plaintiffs asked the original trial court judge, Linton Lewis, to implement the remedy. The plaintiffs immediately asked for a ruling from the newly elected Ohio Supreme Court. However, that court found that the case was over, and thus Judge Lewis had no jurisdiction. As a last-ditch measure, the plaintiffs requested certiorari from the U.S. Supreme Court. Certiorari was denied. As of this writing, the Ohio legislature and the governor have taken no action on the state's educational system, though the supreme court has three times found it unconstitutional.

## Discussion Questions

1. Do you agree with the court's opinion that the school funding system is unconstitutional? Why or why not?

2. Do you think the court should oversee the legislature in "overhauling" school funding in Ohio? Would it eliminate the need for several more opinions on this issue?

3. If the court offers guidance to rule makers in this process, do you think it violates the separation of powers?

# MARION & MCPHERSON RY. CO. V. ALEXANDER
# 63 KAN. 72, 64 P. 978 (1901)

**GENERAL RULE OF LAW:** The authority to assess a tax to fund schools is extraordinary and must be clearly given by the legislature.

**PROCEDURE SUMMARY:**

**Plaintiff:** Marion & McPherson Railway Co. (Marion) (P)

**Defendant:** Alexander (D), county treasurer

**State District Court Decision:** Held for Alexander (D), that tax was authorized by legislature and constitutional

**State Supreme Court Decision:** Reversed

**FACTS:** Various provisions of a Kansas statute gave counties the power to levy a property tax that did not exceed 2% annually. It was to be used for school purposes. Pursuant to these provisions, Alexander (D), the county treasurer, levied a 2% tax. Marion (P), a property owner, sought to enjoin enforcement of the tax. He contended that this tax caused the total district assessment to exceed 2%, in violation of the provisions. Alexander (D) countered that the provisions, when read together, allowed the district to levy a 2% tax in addition to and separate from the other levies permitted by the provisions. Finding for Alexander (D), the district court sustained the tax assessment and denied an injunction. Marion (P) appealed.

**ISSUE:** Is the authority to assess a tax to fund and support schools extraordinary, and thus must be clearly given by the legislature?

**HOLDING AND DECISION:** (Cunningham, J.) Yes. The authority to assess a tax to fund and support schools is extraordinary and must be clearly given by the legislature. Such authority can never be found by implication, as Alexander (D) suggests, unless it is a necessary implication. Any other rule would lead to great wrong and oppression. Thus, where there is a reasonable doubt of the existence of such authority, as is the case here, it must be denied. Reversed.

**COMMENT:** The rule in most states is that school districts have no power to tax absent clearly expressed legislative authority. State statutes, however, vary in the extent that they grant the school board power to raise and collect school taxes. In some states, school boards are fiscally independent, meaning that they have the power to set the tax and distribute the funds collected as they desire. Other boards are fiscally dependent; they receive only a portion of funds collected, and some other local entity has the actual power to assess the tax and collect and distribute funds.

## Discussion Questions

1. Why is authority to fund schools considered extraordinary?

2. If funding is the only way to support the schools, why wouldn't the legislative branch allow school districts to assess taxes without its authorization?

3. If the Kansas law gave counties the power to levy a property tax not to exceed 2%, and Alexander levied a tax of 2%, what was the basis of Marion & McPherson's lawsuit?

# SAWYER V. GILMORE, STATE TREASURER
## 109 ME. 169, 83 A. 673 (1912)

**GENERAL RULE OF LAW:** A tax assessment to fund public schools is not necessarily invalid when the funds are distributed in a manner that does not benefit all the properties assessed.

**PROCEDURE SUMMARY:**

**Plaintiff:** Sawyer (P), a taxpayer in an unorganized township

**Defendant:** Gilmore (D), state treasurer

**State Supreme Judicial Court Decision:** Held for Gilmore (D), finding the tax assessment constitutional

**FACTS:** To fund public schools, Maine enacted a law assessing a tax on all real property. Real property in unorganized townships was subject to the tax; however, such townships received no portion of the tax benefits. Sawyer (P), a taxpayer who lived in an unorganized township, sought to enjoin Gilmore (D), the state treasurer, from enforcing the tax assessment. He contended that it violated the state constitution and the equal protection clause of the U.S. Constitution's Fourteenth Amendment.

**ISSUE:** Must the funds raised by a tax assessment to fund public schools be distributed in a manner that benefits all the properties assessed?

**HOLDING AND DECISION:** (Cornish, J.) No. A tax assessment upon all that does not benefit all does not necessarily violate the equal protection clause of the Constitution. So long as the tax is assessed equally and is for the public welfare, it need not be distributed equally. The manner in which the funds are distributed is within the legislature's discretion and is valid so long as there is no positive constitutional restriction. Here, the tax is assessed equally and is intended to fund public schools, a purpose clearly benefiting the public welfare. Further, no positive constitutional restriction prohibits the manner in which the legislature has decided to distribute the funds. The assessment is therefore constitutional. Injunction denied; dismissed.

**COMMENT:** This case is a forerunner of the Supreme Court's landmark decision in *San Antonio Independent School District v. Rodriguez* (1973). Both *Sawyer* and *Rodriguez* demonstrate the judiciary's unwillingness to hamper the legislature's judgment in dealing with local education funding problems. The legislature's wide discretion to distribute funds is rarely disputed nowadays. Today, the claim is that a particular method of distribution is an abuse of that discretion.

## Discussion Questions

1. Why do you think a tax assessment upon all that does not benefit all is not a violation of the equal protection clause of the Fourteenth Amendment?

2. Why is funding schools considered a benefit for the public welfare?

3. Up until this point, was there an amendment mandating how the legislature must distribute the funds?

# SAN ANTONIO INDEPENDENT SCHOOL DISTRICT V. RODRIGUEZ NO.411 U.S. I, 93 S. CT. 1278 (1973)

**GENERAL RULE OF LAW:** So long as no suspect class or fundamental right is implicated, the state need only show a rational basis for implementing a tax assessment plan to benefit public schools.

**PROCEDURE SUMMARY:**

**Plaintiff:** Rodriguez (P), a Mexican American and parent of students attending public elementary and secondary schools

**Defendant:** San Antonio Independent School District (District) (D)

**U.S. District Court Decision:** Held for Rodriguez (P), finding the assessment system invalid

**U.S. Supreme Court Decision:** Reversed

**FACTS:** The District (D) supplemented state funds received to support its schools with an ad valorem tax on property within the district. Rodriguez (P), a Mexican American and parent of children attending District (D) schools, filed suit, alleging that the reliance on the tax base within a district favored the more affluent districts over the poorer districts. He argued that this disparity violated the equal protection clause of the Fourteenth Amendment. The district court held that "wealth" was a suspect classification and education a fundamental right. Under an equal protection analysis, this would require the District (D) to demonstrate a compelling state interest for the assessment system using the property tax as its basis. The lower court held that the District (D) failed to show such a compelling interest or even a rational basis for the system and invalidated it. The District (D) appealed.

**ISSUE:** Need a state demonstrate only a rational basis for adopting an assessment system if no suspect classification or fundamental right is implicated?

**HOLDING AND DECISION:** (Powell, J.) Yes. So long as no suspect classification or fundamental right is implicated, a state need only establish a rational basis for the implementation of a tax assessment system to fund public schools. Though education is one of the most important services performed by the state, it is not a fundamental right. Furthermore, "wealth" is not a suspect classification. The system has not been shown to discriminate against any definable class of "poor" people. The local taxation, fiscal, and education policy matters at issue caution this Court to take a more restrained review. Therefore, though not perfect, the tax system cannot be said to bear no rational relationship to a legitimate state purpose, which is all the Constitution requires. Reversed.

**COMMENT:** This is a landmark case in that it establishes that education is not a fundamental right. It also clearly demonstrates the Court's unwillingness to interfere with states' attempts to deal with local fiscal and educational problems. The group alleged to be suspect, in this case "poor" people, did not satisfy any of the traditional indicia of a suspect class. It was large, diverse, amorphous, and not clearly definable. Furthermore, it had not been subjected to a history of purposeful unequal treatment. It should be noted that this decision does not prevent state courts from determining on the basis of their state constitution that the kind of tax system the state operates violates the state constitutional rights of its citizenry. (Remember that states can extend individual rights but cannot diminish them beyond federal minimum requirements.) In fact, dozens of cases have been initiated in state courts challenging the constitutionality of similar "foundation formulas" to finance a state's public schools. State court decisions have been split, some validating the property tax and others holding it to be an unconstitutional violation based on state law. The trend of the last 10 to 15 cases has been to find unconstitutional those property tax assessment systems that give affluent districts more money per student and poorer districts less money per student. It seems clear that the Supreme Court will need to review this issue to determine whether *Rodriguez* should be upheld or overturned.

## Discussion Questions

1. Does *San Antonio Independent School District v. Rodriguez* (1973) find education to be a fundamental right?

2. Do states have the right to implement a property tax assessment system to fund public schools as long as they do not violate any fundamental rights or have suspect classifications? Is a rational basis needed for the implementation of a tax assessment system?

3. Do you feel that the court system is willing to interfere with states' attempts to deal with local fiscal and educational problems in funding public schools?

# ROSE V. NASHUA BOARD OF EDUCATION
# 679 F.2D 279 (1ST CIR. 1982)

**GENERAL RULE OF LAW:** If school board policy merely inconveniences its students but does not deny them educational opportunity or harm their reputation, it does not violate their due process rights.

**PROCEDURE SUMMARY:**

**Plaintiffs:** Rose (P), and other parents of children subject to the suspension rule who had not been identified as "troublemakers"

**Defendant:** Nashua Board of Education (Board) (D)

**U.S. District Court Decision:** Held for Board (D), denying claim of civil rights violations

**U.S. Court of Appeals Decision:** Affirmed

**FACTS:** New Hampshire required its school districts to provide free school bus transportation to pupils under 14. However, vandalism and disruptive conduct, such as slashing seats, making noise, and throwing objects, began to threaten the safety of bus service in Nashua. The bus drivers could not identify which students were responsible because they had to keep their eyes on the road. The Nashua Board of Education (D) met to determine the best policy for preventing such student disruption. After deciding that alternatives such as seat assignments, ID cards, and monitors were too expensive or ineffective, it decided to suspend certain routes for up to five days if prior warnings failed. In the policy's first two years of operation, disruptions decreased dramatically, and only 12 suspensions occurred the first year and four the next. The Board (D) also made accommodations for students who could not get to school any other way. However, it left no alternatives for the others, who had to hitch a ride with their parents, walk, or carpool. Rose (P) believed that his child was not one of the "troublemakers," and he and other parents whose children were equally blameless sued the Board (D). They claimed that suspending their children without a prior hearing on their child's culpability deprived them of due process. The U.S. district court held that the policy did not offend the students' due process rights. Rose (P) and the other parents appealed.

**ISSUE:** If a school board policy does not deny its students an educational opportunity or harm their reputation, does it violate their due process rights?

**HOLDING AND DECISION:** (Breyer, C. J.) No. A school board policy that merely inconveniences students but does not deny them educational opportunity or injure their reputation does not violate their due process rights. Here, Rose (P) and the other parents did not allege sufficient property rights violations to warrant due process scrutiny. A five-day bus suspension is merely an inconvenience, not a deprivation of education, educational opportunity, or reputational injury. A post-suspension hearing, which was provided for the students in question, was sufficient protection of their due process rights. Thus, this minimal loss of bus service did not warrant pre-suspension due process protection, and a hearing to determine student guilt or innocence was not required. Affirmed.

**COMMENT:** In this case, the court held that the students' property interest in a bus route was not as strong as the state's interest in maintaining safety and discipline. The Board's (D) suspension of service on the bus route had been preceded by sufficient notice regarding the action to be taken to limit student misbehavior and vandalism. This case involved the court in deciding the proper exercise of judgment in a due process case. In *Rose,* the court not only had to decide if due process applied, but also how much "process is due."

## Discussion Questions

1. How does this case compare to one in which a teacher threatens an entire class with punishment if one student refuses to cooperate?

2. Why is denying bus service to a handicapped student a violation of rights, but it is not a violation of rights to deny denying bus service to a nonhandicapped student who has not been provided a hearing?[14]

3. Would the holding in this case allow the school district to force all of the disruptive students on the bus to take turns cleaning it?

# INGRAM V. BOONE
## 458 N.Y.S. 2D 671, 91 A.D.2D 1063 (1983)

**GENERAL RULE OF LAW:** Taxpayers in school districts may sue their school boards in order to challenge payments that appear to be unauthorized gifts of public money.

**PROCEDURE SUMMARY:**

**Plaintiffs:** Ingram (P), and other resident taxpayers and parents of children attending public school in Nassau County, New York, school district

**Defendant:** Boone (D), chairman of Union Free School District, Hempstead, New York

**State Trial Court Decision:** Held for Ingram (P)

**State Court of Appeals Decision:** Affirmed

**FACTS:** Union Free School District in Nassau County, New York, hired a superintendent by written contract for a four-year term. However, after becoming displeased with his performance after only a year, the Union Free school board voted to buy out the remaining three years under the contract for a lump-sum payment of $65,000 and the continuation of the superintendent's insurance benefits through the expiration of the contract term. Ingram (P) and other resident taxpayers and parents of children attending school in the district filed suit in New York state court challenging the settlement as an unconstitutional gift of public funds; however, the initial issue decided by the court was whether Ingram (P) and the others had "standing," or the right, to maintain the suit. The trial court answered affirmatively, and Boone (D), chairman of the Union Free school board, appealed.

**ISSUE:** May taxpayers in school districts sue their school boards in order to challenge payments that appear to be unauthorized gifts of public money?

**HOLDING AND DECISION:** (Memorandum Opinion) Yes. Taxpayers residing in school districts may sue their school boards in order to challenge payments that appear to be unauthorized gifts of public money. School boards may not merely assert in defense of such payments that they properly exercised their discretion and judgment; a hearing is required in order to fully flesh out and test the validity of an agreement that appears to make an improper transfer. As residents who directly contributed to the school district's financing through payment of property taxes, and as parents whose children's quality of education may be affected by the decrease in funds attributable to an improper gift, Ingram (P) and the other parents have a direct interest in this constitutional challenge to the school board's settlement with the superintendent. Affirmed.

**COMMENT:** This case is an important precedent for citizen review of decisions of their school boards. Although school boards are endowed by their residents with broad latitude and discretion in making financial decisions, this discretion is not unlimited, and taxpayer **standing to sue** can provide an important "check" upon a school board's allocation of public moneys. Such school boards act in quasi-fiduciary capacities with regard to taxpayer money.

## Question and Discussion

1. If the superintendent had resigned, believing that the school board would honor the agreement, and the agreement was later invalidated, would he be permitted to rescind his resignation?

2. Assume you live in the Nassau County school district. Construct an argument (as a citizen, not a teacher or administrator) for approving the agreement between the board and the superintendent.

3. Assume you live in the Nassau County school district (as a citizen, not a teacher or administrator). Construct an argument for not approving the agreement between the board and the superintendent.

Additional case briefs can be found on the SAGE Web site at the following address:
http://www.sagepub.com/aquilacasebriefs

## NOTES

1. San Antonio Independent School District v. Rodriguez, 411 U.S. 1 (1973).
2. Robinson v. Cahill, 70 N.J. 465 (1973).
3. Rose v. Council for Better Education, Inc., 790 S.W.2d (1989).
4. DeRolph v. State, 78 Ohio St. 3d 193 (1997).
5. See Marion & McPherson Ry. Co. v. Alexander, 63 Kan 72 (1901).
6. See Sawyer v. Gilmore, State Treasurer, 109 Me. 169 (1912).
7. See San Antonio Indep. School Dist. v. Rodriguez, 411 U.S. 1 (1973).
8. Serrano v. Priest, 5 Cal.3d 584, 487 P.2d. 1241 (1971).
9. See Board of Education of the Westside Community School v. Mergens, 496 U.S. 226 (1990); see also Resnick v. East Brunswick Township Board of Education, 77 N.J. 88 (1978).
10. See Lamb's Chapel et al. v. Center Moriches, 1135 S. Ct. 2141 (1993).
11. See Rose v. Nashua Board of Education, 679 F.2d 279 (1st Cir. 1982).
12. See Ingram v. Boone, 91 A.D.2d 1063 (N.Y. App. 1983).
13. Brown v. Board of Education, 347 U.S. 483, 74 S. Ct. 686 (1954).
14. See Hurry v. Jones, 734 F.2d 879 (1st Cir. 1984).

# 16

# School Violence and Internet Issues

*We must make as certain as possible that we do not permit criminality to begin with juveniles in schools. We do not have police officers in our classrooms. We do not have parents in our classrooms. Therefore we must give to teachers and principals all the tools they reasonably need to preserve order in classrooms and school grounds.*

—Judge Stanley Mosk, 1985

## OVERVIEW · · · · · · · · · · · · · · · · · · · · · · · · · · · · · · · · · · · · · · · · · · · ·

When violence in the schools—whether student-to-student or student-to-teacher—was confined to the nation's troubled inner-city schools, violent assaults in suburban schools were interpreted as atypical and not part of any pattern. The notion of school violence as a purely inner-city phenomenon was put to rest in the 1990s. In fact, media reports of school violence resulting in serious injury and even death suggest that these events are not only underreported, but are on the rise. In addition, acts of violence occur in all schools and all school districts regardless of location. The reported emergence of acts of school violence across all schools—urban, rural, and suburban—has been associated with a parallel increase in reports of the possession of guns and other weapons of violence by students inside our nation's schools.

The rise in violence is occurring while there is a widespread reluctance on the part of school boards and school administrators to acknowledge the extent and the consequences of violent behavior in schools. This reluctance to report injuries to students and teachers has been linked to concerns that reporting these events would erode local support for schools already perceived as violence prone. A secondary concern preventing the reporting of violence is the potential damage to the local school district's reputation. The unwillingness of school boards to accurately report school violence has resulted in related agencies, such as teacher unions, gathering and trying to disseminate this information.

361

To deal with this crisis of escalating violence, school boards have utilized more sophisticated surveillance systems and student and faculty identification cards, as well as increased security personnel in the schools. Interestingly, the responses to the potential dangers are of mixed benefit and may be taking away from the educational effort. Nevertheless, these measures appear to be on the rise as school districts try to protect children while limiting districts' potential liability. The cases in this chapter are intended to illustrate the problem, not to provide answers. When looking at school violence, the legal rules regarding liability, elements of a tortious or criminal act, issues such as foreseeability, and related concerns still apply. The general principle is that if a public school is aware of a risk of violence, it is not liable for depriving a victim of his procedural due process rights, unless the school acted with a "deliberate indifference" toward the victim's safety. Hopefully, the discussion below will provide a better perspective on the extent and depth of the issue of school violence.

The Internet has created a series of entirely new problems for school personnel. While free speech has always been a treasured American value, special concerns have emerged with the Internet. Even traditional school policy statements have been refined to remedy concerns about vagueness and overbroadness.[1] Because the number of computers in the home and school has greatly increased, students' inappropriate use of these computers has become an issue. The answers are never clear cut because many of the questions have previously never been addressed. Obviously, school boards need to be very careful to craft board policies that are not overbroad, vague, or ambiguous. The results from court actions regarding threatening student expression on the Internet have been mixed. One of the most discussed cases has been *J. S. v. Bethlehem Area School Dist.* (2002), in which a student unsuccessfully challenged his expulsion for derogatory remarks he made about his algebra teacher and for seeking money from other students to pay a hit man to kill her.[2]

Can a school restrict the use of the Internet, or will denying this access be a violation of a student's rights? The general rule that seems to be emerging is that schools can legally limit use of school computers if the restrictions are for a legitimate educational purpose. Past Supreme Court cases dealing with censorship would support reasonable school censorship of controversial materials. In *Board of Education of Island Trees Free School District No. 26 v. Pico* (1982), the Court held that school officials could not remove controversial books from the library simply because they disagreed with certain ideas, but they could remove books that were pervasively vulgar, educationally unsuitable, or not age appropriate.[3] In *Hazelwood School District v. Kuhlmeier* (1988), the Court also allowed censorship of the content and style of a school newspaper as long as the restrictions were related to "legitimate educational concerns."[4]

## Case Study

### School Violence on the Internet

A middle school student at Paul Dunbar Middle School created a Web site on his home computer without the knowledge or involvement of school authorities. On his Web site, which he titled "Screw Teachers," he made derogatory, offensive, profane, and threatening comments about his teachers, especially his science teacher, Ms. Smyth. This commentary took the form of pictures, written words, and animation, as well as sound clips. Among these comments were suggestions that "Ms. Smyth must die!" and "Donate a dollar to the fund to pay for a hit man." Students quickly learned about the Web site; it took longer for school authorities to learn about it. The school district adopted a board resolution that a student could be expelled for using the Internet to harass and cause harm to school personnel. They then suspended this student with the intent of expelling him.

### Discussion Questions

1. What are the arguments supporting the student?

2. What are the arguments supporting the school district?

3. Does the date the board resolution was adopted have any significance?

4. Who will prevail? Why?

# IMPORTANT CONCEPTS

- **School violence is pervasive:** Violence in the schools, both student-to-student and student-to-teacher, is not confined to urban inner-city schools. Suburban schools are experiencing the same type of violent assaults as well as related drug and alcohol problems.

- **Legal analysis remains the same:** The traditional legal applications and rules apply in school violence situations. Thus, when considering liability, elements of a tortious or criminal act, issues such as foreseeability and related concerns still apply and must be used when reviewing school violence cases.

- **Ostrich syndrome:** At the same time as there is a rise in violence, there is a widespread reluctance on the part of school boards and school administrators to acknowledge the extent and the consequences of violent behavior in schools. The probable rationale for such action is the concern about the reputation of and support for schools.

- **Various responses to deter school violence:** School boards have responded to the increase in violence by introducing more sophisticated surveillance systems, requiring students and faculty to wear identification cards, and increasing the number of security personnel in the schools.

*(Continued)*

(Continued)

- **Changing view of purpose of juvenile court:** Rehabilitation of youths before they became hardened criminals was the original intent in the development of juvenile courts. This early twentieth-century intent to help a youth to change lasted until the latter part of the century. With the rapid development of youth gangs and the dramatic increase in juvenile violence, the change in attitudes of the public led to a change in practice in most juvenile courts. With an intent to control and regulate violent behavior of youth, the administration of juvenile justice changed its focus to punishment and retribution for the escalating violent acts committed by youth.

- **Internet and free speech:** Even though free speech is a treasured American value, the advent of the Internet has created special and unique concerns. School boards have had to re-craft traditional speech rights policies in light of the Internet, to avoid concerns about vagueness and overbroadness.

- **Courts supporting schools:** Although the results from court actions regarding threatening student expression on the Internet have been mixed, the trend has been to support school districts. Nevertheless, the key to being supported is the development and adoption of school policies that protect the school, faculty, staff, and students without severely limiting the free speech rights of students.

# SCHOOL VIOLENCE

## Emerging School Violence

Throughout the 1980s, it was customary to regard violence in the schools—whether student-to-student or student-to-teacher—as a phenomenon confined to the nation's troubled inner-city schools. Assaults in suburban schools were interpreted as atypical, not part of a pattern of violence. The 1990s challenged these interpretations of school violence as a purely inner-city phenomenon. Recent reviews of media reports of school violence resulting in serious injury and even death suggest that these events have been underreported. Acts of school violence across all schools—urban, rural and suburban—have been associated with a parallel increase in the possession of guns and other weapons of violence by students inside the nation's schools. One in five high school students, and almost one in three boys, now routinely carries a gun, knife, or some other weapon. Furthermore, this pattern of weapon carrying by students has become a national phenomenon applicable to schools in all regions.

An altercation between an African American and a white student resulted in one student firing three gunshots that fatally wounded the other. The court examined whether adequate school supervision could have prevented the occurrence. The court record indicated a history of serious crime on the school campus. The history included an attempted robbery and battery of a white student by two African Americans in the school parking lot, an assault with a knife in the loading zone, an on-campus threat with a knife by a nonstudent directed toward a student, and an attack on a student by four nonstudents in front of the school. Witnesses also testified about other fights and riots between African Americans and whites. The court held that a school district, after being put on notice of foreseeable criminal acts, owes a duty to make its premises safe. Here, if a criminal attack is reasonably foreseeable, a duty may arise between a school district and its students.[5]

## Reporting School Violence

These developments are occurring in a context of widespread reluctance on the part of school boards and school administrators to acknowledge the extent and the consequences of violent behavior in schools. This reluctance has been linked to concerns that the reporting of such events would erode local support for schools perceived as violence prone. The unwillingness of school boards to accurately report school violence has resulted in related agencies, such as teachers' unions, gathering and disseminating this information.

## School Reactions to Increased Violence

Among the responses of school boards has been the introduction of more sophisticated surveillance systems, student and faculty identification cards, and increased security personnel in the schools. These responses to the potential dangers are of a mixed benefit because they often detract from the educational effort. Yet, they appear to be on the rise as school districts try to protect students while limiting the district's potential liability.

A student dance on school grounds was sponsored by the school. This dance resulted in violence and injury. After the dance, a number of teenagers met in the school partking lot. Some of these individuals began to fire handguns randomly and recklessly into the air, which resulted in the accidental but fatal shooting of a student. The issue was whether the school's decision to sponsor the dance, despite its knowledge of the danger of just such an occurrence, violated the student's constitutional rights. The court ruled that the student's rights had not been violated. Importantly, it was not enough to show that the state's action increased the danger of harm from third persons. A state plaintiff (or a Section 1983 federal plaintiff) must show that the state acted with the requisite culpability in failing to protect the plaintiff from danger. Here, for a substantive due process claim, a plaintiff must prove "deliberate indifference."[6]

# JUVENILE COURTS

## Procedures

The original intent in the development of juvenile courts in the early part of the twentieth century was to provide youth with an opportunity to change. The state's purpose was rehabilitation. This was the practice until the latter part of the century. As gangs and juvenile violence continued to escalate, the attitudes of the public led to a change in practice in many juvenile courts. In an attempt to control and regulate the violent behavior of youth, the administration of juvenile justice changed its focus. Nevertheless, even today, juveniles are usually not "bound over" to an adult court (where they would be treated as adults and could serve time in an adult prison) for the criminal acts that they commit while they are juveniles. These status offenses are handled in a juvenile court (some states use a family court).

Not surprisingly, under FERPA (the Family Educational Rights and Privacy Act) parents have the right to access school lawyers' records regarding juvenile court actions involving the student because discoverable records include not only records created and retained by the school, but also information maintained by a person acting for the school.[7] Below, in a short outline, is a breakdown of juvenile court procedure using the Ohio Juvenile Court system as the model. Procedures and standards differ from state to state, but the Ohio Juvenile Court system is an appropriate model that can be compared to other states.

1. Jurisdiction of a Juvenile Court
   a. Age Jurisdiction
      i. A "child" is a person who is under the age of 18 years, except that any person who violates a federal or state law or municipal ordinance prior to attaining age 18 shall be deemed a "child" irrespective of his age at the time the complaint is filed or hearing is held.
      ii. Jurisdiction of juvenile courts terminates once the child reaches the age of 21.
   b. Subject Matter Jurisdiction
      i. Children's Cases
         (a) Delinquent Child
             Definition: Any child who violates any law of Ohio, the U.S., or any ordinance or regulation in a city or county in Ohio, which would be a crime if committed by an adult, or violates a lawful order of the juvenile court.
             Only a delinquent felon may be committed to the legal custody of the Ohio Department of Youth Services, and only a child charged with a delinquent **felony** may be transferred to a criminal court for prosecution as an adult.
         (b) Juvenile Traffic Offender
             Definition: Any child who violates any traffic law, ordinance, or regulation (not including parking violations) of Ohio or the U.S.
             The distinction between a traffic offender and a delinquent child becomes gray when dealing with a death resulting from the operation of a motor vehicle.
         (c) Unruly Child
             Definition: Any child who
             (1) Does not subject himself to the reasonable control of his parents, teachers, guardian, or custodian, by reason of being wayward or habitually disobedient
             (2) Is a habitual truant from home or school
             (3) So deports himself as to injure or endanger the health or morals of himself or others
             (4) Attempts to enter the marriage relation in any state without the consent of his parents

            (5) Is found in a disreputable place, visits or patronizes a place prohibited by law, or associates with vagrant, vicious, criminal, notorious, or immoral people

            (6) Engages in an occupation prohibited by law, or is in a situation dangerous to life or limb or injurious to the health or morals of himself or others

            (7) Has violated a law applicable only to a child

    (d) Neglected Child

    Definition: A neglected child is one

            (1) Who is abandoned by his parents, guardian, or custodian

            (2) Who lacks proper parental care because of the faults or habits of his parents, guardian, or custodian

            (3) Whose parents refuse to provide him with proper and necessary subsistence, education, medical care, or other care necessary for his well-being

            (4) Whose parents neglect or refuse to provide the special care made necessary by his mental condition

            (5) Whose parents have attempted to illegally place him for adoption

            (6) Who, because of the omission of his parents, suffers physical or mental injury that harms or threatens to harm the child's health or welfare

            (7) Who is subjected to out-of-home-care child neglect

    (e) Dependent Child

    Definition: A dependant child includes any child

            (1) Who is homeless or destitute through no fault of his parents, guardian, or custodian

            (2) Who lacks proper care by reason of the mental or physical condition of his parents, guardian, or custodian

            (3) Whose condition is such as to warrant the state to take custody of the child

            (4) Who resides in a home where a parent, guardian, or custodian has abused or neglected another sibling and the child is in danger of also being abused or neglected

    (f) Abused Child

    Definition: Any child who

            (1) Is the victim of "sexual activity" as defined under Chapter 2907 of the Ohio Revised Code

            (2) Is endangered

            (3) Exhibits any evidence of or suffers from physical or mental injury inflicted other than by accidental means

            (4) Because of the acts of his parents, suffers physical or mental injury that harms or threatens to harm the child's health or welfare

            (5) Is subjected to out-of-home-care child abuse

ii. Other Cases

    (a) Abortion Notification Cases

            (1) A pregnant, unmarried, unemancipated, minor female who wishes to have an abortion without parental notification may request authorization from juvenile court to consent to the abortion without parental notification.

(2) **Venue** lies in the county of residence or legal settlement, or in any bordering county, or in the county in which the hospital is located.

(3) Parents are not notified of hearing, but a guardian ad litem and attorney must be appointed for the child.

(4) The court shall authorize the child to consent to the abortion without parental notification if it finds any of the following:

(i) The child is sufficiently mature and well enough informed to decide intelligently whether to have an abortion.

(ii) There is a pattern of abuse of the child by one or both of her parents.

(iii) Parental notification is not in the best interest of the child.

(5) Alternatively, the requisite notification may be given to a specified adult brother or sister, stepparent, or grandparent if the minor female and specified relative file affidavits in the juvenile court that the minor is in fear of parental abuse and that this fear is based on a pattern of abuse.

(b) Consent to Marry

(1) A male may marry at age 18, and a female may marry at age 16 with parental consent.

(i) If a female age 16 or 17 has no parent or guardian, the consent of the juvenile court must be obtained.

(2) If a female is pregnant or has delivered a child out of wedlock, and she and the father wish to marry, even though she is under 16 and/or he is under 18, they may marry if they receive the consent of the juvenile court and consent of the parent of the minor.

(i) If either party is under age 18, both must receive marriage counseling prior to marrying.

2. Reporting of Abuse and Neglect

a. General Rules

i. Known or suspected abuse or neglect of a child must be immediately reported to the Department of Human Services or Police Department by any of the following, acting in official or professional capacity:

(a) Attorney
(b) Physician
(c) Dentist
(d) Podiatrist
(e) Limited practitioner
(f) Registered nurse
(g) Licensed practical nurse
(h) Visiting nurse
(i) Other health-care professional
(j) Licensing psychologist
(k) Licensed school psychologist
(l) Speech pathologist or audiologist
(m) Coroner
(n) Administrator or employee of child care agency

(o)   School teacher, employee, or authority

(p)   Social worker

(q)   Person rendering spiritual treatment through prayer

(r)   Professional counselor

   ii. Attorneys or physicians are not required to make a report concerning any communication made by client or patient unless both of the following apply:

(a)   The child or patient is under age 18.

(b)   The attorney-client or physician-patient relationship does not arise out of the child's attempt to have an abortion without parental notification.

  iii. Any person required to report abuse or neglect may take color photographs of the areas of trauma and perform radiological examinations of the child.

  iv. The Department of Human Services must investigate each report within 24 hours, in cooperation with the law enforcement agency.

   v. All reports are confidential.

3.  Immunity

a.  Anyone mandated to report who participates in the making of the reports, and anyone else not mandated to report who participates in good faith in the making of the reports, and anyone participating in good faith in a judicial proceeding resulting from the reports is immune from any civil or criminal liability.

4.  Penalties

a.  Anyone mandated to report who fails to report, and anyone who permits or encourages the unauthorized dissemination of a report, is guilty of a fourth-degree misdemeanor.

## STUDENT FREE SPEECH AND THE INTERNET

The Internet has created a series of new problems for school personnel. Free speech has always been a treasured American value. With the advent of the Internet, special concerns have emerged. Even traditional statements in school policy manuals have had to be recrafted due to concerns about vagueness and overbroadness.[8]

The number of computers, both at home and in schools, has raised the question about students inappropriately using them for commercial, pornographic, and other inappropriate reasons. The answers as well as the questions regarding appropriateness are not clear cut because many involve issues of original review. Can a school review the use of the Internet, or will this be a violation of a student's constitutional rights if access is denied? This is especially difficult when a school punishes a student for violating a school rule and that violation involves the student's inappropriate use of his home computer. The general rule that seems to be emerging is that schools can legally limit use of school computers if the restrictions are for a legitimate educational purpose. In all states, the use of the computer to transmit indecent material to those under 18 years of age would be a criminal offense. Nevertheless, it appears that adults using the Internet have the same First Amendment protection as those using books and newspapers. Although the issue has not been resolved, it would appear that when dealing with a school situation, the criminal statute will not apply.

Past Supreme Court decisions dealing with censorship would support the notion that a school can reasonably censor controversial materials. In *Board of Education of Island Trees Free School District No. 26 v. Pico* (1982), the Court held that school officials could not remove controversial books from the library simply because the school disagreed with certain ideas contained in the books. However, the school *could* remove books that were pervasively vulgar, educationally unsuitable, or not age appropriate. Similarly, in *Hazelwood School District v. Kuhlmeier* (1988), the Court allowed censorship of content and style of a school newspaper as long as the restrictions were related to "legitimate educational concerns." The natural parallel, while not exact, is that computers can be compared to curriculum-related projects or to use in a school library. Obviously, school boards need to be very careful to craft board policies that are not overbroad, vague, or ambiguous.

The results from court actions regarding threats by students on the Internet have been mixed. The most discussed case has been *J. S. v. Bethlehem Area School Dist.* (2002), in which a student unsuccessfully challenged his expulsion for derogatory remarks he made on a Web site about his algebra teacher and for seeking donations to pay a hit man to kill her. The student created the Web site on his own computer while at home. Nevertheless, the school board permanently expelled the student for violating the school code of conduct by threatening, harassing, and showing disrespect to the teacher. The appellate court affirmed in holding that school officials had not violated his First Amendment rights.

## Case Study

### Are School Lawyers' Records Protected in a Juvenile Court Proceeding?

Using the authority of FERPA, the mother of a special education student requested all of the school records of her child. The student was involved in a juvenile court action initiated by the school district because of a problem at school. The school district's attorney had been involved with the child when the school asked for a consultation regarding the boy's individualized educational plan. Based on FERPA, the school district agreed to and did provide the mother access to her child's cumulative file containing all school records. When asked to provide the lawyer's records from the juvenile court proceeding, the school district and lawyer refused.

### Discussion Questions

1. Does this mother need access to this information in order to protect the interest of her child?

2. Does it matter whether the juvenile court record was created by the school or by outsiders?

3. If another law firm were acting for the school district in the juvenile court action, would this have made a difference? Or, would these be records available to the parent under FERPA?

# CONCLUSION .............................................

Prior to the 1990s, school violence was seen as primarily an inner-city problem. However, schools in more affluent suburbs became increasingly violent. This increase in violence parallels the increase of the number of guns or other weapons in schools. Today, it is sad to say, nearly one out of every five students in schools carries some type of weapon.

School boards, however, have been reluctant to report the prevalence of violence in their schools. They are afraid that dissemination of such information will reflect negatively on schools already seen as troubled. The unwillingness of school boards to accurately report school violence has resulted in related agencies, such as teachers' unions, gathering and disseminating this information.

In response to increased violence, schools have implemented various protective measures, such as installing sophisticated surveillance systems, requiring student and faculty identification cards, and increasing security personnel. Schools are usually only liable for violent acts on campus when the school is found to have acted with "deliberate indifference" toward the victim's safety.

Juvenile courts were founded on a principle of rehabilitation. However, with the increase in adolescent violence in schools, the focus has shifted to also include deterrence and incarceration of potentially dangerous children. Juvenile courts generally have jurisdiction only over children under the age of 18 who could be deemed delinquent, a traffic offender, unruly, neglected, dependent, or abused.

The Internet has also created a series of new problems for school personnel. Just what may students post on the Internet, and do these students have a right to unfettered Internet access while they are in school? These questions implicate many First Amendment concerns.

The cases in this chapter are selected to illustrate the problem, not to provide answers. When looking at school violence, the legal rules regarding tort liability, elements of a tortious or criminal act, issues such as foreseeability, and related concerns still apply. The Case Briefs will help familiarize educators with the potential for liability, the extent of their powers to prevent it, and the various rights issues that may arise while trying to deflect a potentially dangerous situation. As with many other chapters, here lies another "balancing of the equities" between the rights of the individual, the education community, and the state and local governments.

# CASE BRIEFS ......................

## THE SCHOOL BOARD OF PALM BEACH COUNTY V. ANDERSON 411 SO. 2D 940 (1982)

**GENERAL RULE OF LAW:** If a criminal attack by a third party is foreseeable on school grounds, then the school district owes its students a duty to take reasonable precautions to ensure their safety.

**PROCEDURE SUMMARY:**

**Plaintiff:** William Anderson (P), father of the deceased Brian Anderson

**Defendant:** Palm Beach School Board (D)

**State Court Trial Decision:** Jury verdict in favor of the deceased's father (D)

**State Court Appellate Division Decision:** Affirmed

**FACTS:** In May of 1976, two former students of Palm Beach Gardens High School (D), Brian Anderson, a white student, and Gregory Ransom, an African American student, went to the school during lunchtime. Anderson was in the parking lot talking with a group of his friends when Ransom approached him. An altercation ensued, resulting in Ransom firing three shots and fatally wounding Anderson. Adequate school supervision, according to Anderson (P), could have prevented the occurrence. The record in the present case reflects a history of serious crime on the school campus. Prior incidents included an attempted robbery and battery of a white student by two African Americans in the school parking lot on October 22, 1975; an assault with a knife in the loading zone on November 19, 1975; an on-campus threat with a knife by a nonstudent directed toward a student on March 3, 1976; and an attack upon a student by four nonstudents in front of the school on May 11, 1976. Witnesses also testified about other fights and riots between African Americans and whites.

**ISSUE:** After being put on notice of foreseeable criminal acts, does a school district owe a duty to make its premises safe?

**HOLDING AND DECISION:** (Glickstein, J.) Yes. If a criminal attack is reasonably foreseeable, a duty may arise between a school district and its students. But it must be borne in mind that the school district is not an ensurer of the students' safety, and it is not required to take precautions against a sudden, unanticipated attack from a third person. Given the history of racial incidents, there was sufficient evidence to raise a jury question of notice of prior, similar attacks upon students. Accordingly, the trial court's denial of appellant's motions was affirmed.

**COMMENT:** In this case, the court held that after being put on notice of foreseeable criminal acts, a school district owed a duty to make its premises safe. Therefore, if school officials believe that a criminal attack is reasonably foreseeable, a duty may arise between a school district and its students. In such a situation, a school district is exposed to potential liability. Of course, a school district is not a guarantor of the safety of its students, and, as discussed in the holding, it is not required to take precautions against a sudden, unanticipated attack from a third person absent some foreknowledge. Applying this logic, in this case, with the school's history of racial incidents, there was sufficient evidence to raise a jury question and require a trial to determine whether notice of prior similar attacks upon students existed that was sufficient for recovery.

## Discussion Questions

1. Should a school that has had prior incidents of violence have a security guard working in its parking lot?

2. What are some steps a school district can take to guard against violence on its campus?

3. Why should a school have to guard against the actions of others?

# LOGAN V. CITY OF NEW YORK
# 148 A.D.2D 167, 543 N.Y.S.2D 661 (1989)

**GENERAL RULE OF LAW:** A school board owes a duty to exercise the same degree of care and supervision over the pupils under its control as a reasonably prudent parent would exercise under the same circumstances.

**PROCEDURE SUMMARY:**

**Plaintiff:** Darlene Logan (P)

**Defendant:** City of New York (D), where school district is located

**State Court Trial Decision:** Motion for summary judgment granted in favor of the City of New York (D)

**State Court Appellate Decision:** Reversed summary judgment and re-instated claim

**State Supreme Court Decision:** Reversed, reaffirming summary judgment for City of New York (D)

**FACTS:** On December 17, 1981, Darlene Logan (P), then a 12-year-old student enrolled at Intermediate School 88 on West 114th Street in Manhattan, went to her art class on the fifth floor. While she was there, Darlene's social studies teacher arrived and obtained the art teacher's permission to take Darlene (P) back to the social studies classroom to clean up papers the student (P) had left behind. When Darlene (P) completed the task, the social studies teacher directed her to return to the art classroom. As Darlene (P) approached the fifth floor, she was accosted by three boys who also attended Intermediate School 88. The boys forced Darlene (P) to accompany them to a locked ceramics room on the first floor where, after opening the door with a key, one of them raped her. The three boys were subsequently arrested and found guilty in a family court proceeding. The district court's decision that granted the school board's (D) motion for summary judgment was modified, and Darlene's (P) complaint was reinstated.

**ISSUE:** Can the school board be held liable for a sexual assault on school grounds during the school day?

**HOLDING AND DECISION:** (Kassal, J.) Yes. Negligence was defined here as the Board's failure to exercise the same degree of care and supervision over its students that a reasonably prudent parent would exercise under the same circumstances. If the court finds that a reasonably prudent parent would have required supervision here and that the Board had actual or constructive notice of a dangerous condition for a sufficient length of time, then the court will find that the Board was negligent.

**COMMENT:** In most respects, this case follows the traditional rules and applications of tort law. For example, note that the school in which this incident took place had established careful security measures, which included the posting of two security guards and at least two school aides on each floor. The question these measures raise—*and that is not to be confused with whether there was a special duty to protect Darlene*—is whether the Board had notice, actual or constructive, that a child was at risk of attack if left unescorted to travel the stairwells of this school at a time other than the scheduled change-of-class intervals. Another traditional question that was raised regarded the adequacy of the supervision of the three boys, also students at the school, who were apparently roaming the building during class hours. They, as well as the plaintiff, fall within the well-settled rule that a school district is obliged to adequately supervise the activities of its students.

## Discussion Questions

1. How can schools monitor their students at all times?
2. Do parents follow their children at all times? Why does a school need to constantly monitor its children?
3. Should there be a faculty member in the hallways at all times? Or should a faculty member be roaming around a school at all times of the day to deter such behaviors?

# LEFFALL V. DALLAS INDEPENDENT SCHOOL DISTRICT 28 F.3D 521 (5TH CIR. 1994)

**GENERAL RULE OF LAW:** When a public school is aware of a danger of violence, it is not liable for depriving a victim of his procedural due process rights unless the school acted with a "deliberate indifference" toward the victim's safety.

**PROCEDURE SUMMARY:**

**Plaintiff:** Dameon Steadham (P)

**Defendant:** Dallas Independent School District (D)

**U.S. District Court Decision:** Dismissed the complaint

**U.S. Court of Appeals Decision:** Affirmed

**FACTS:** On or about the evening of April 17, 1992, Dameon Steadham attended a dance held at Lincoln High School in Dallas, Texas. The dance was sponsored by Lincoln High School and an organization identified only as the "Parent Teacher Association." After the dance, a number of teenagers congregated in the Lincoln High School parking lot. Several individuals began to fire handguns randomly and recklessly into the air. In the course of the shooting, 16-year-old John L. Cofield, a student at Bryan Adams High School, accidentally and fatally shot Steadham in the head.

**ISSUE:** Did the decision of the public school district and the high school principal to sponsor the dance, despite their knowledge of potential danger, violate Steadham's constitutional rights?

**HOLDING AND DECISION:** (King, J.) No. Under the rationale of the cases recognizing a state-created danger theory using 42 U.S.C. § 1983 liability, it is not enough to show that the state increased the danger of harm from third persons. Courts have consistently required a Section 1983 plaintiff who relies on a substantive due process claim to show that the state actors are guilty of "deliberate indifference" toward the victim of the deprivation.

**COMMENT:** This case follows the tort rules that apply equally to both state and federal tort actions. Here, only intentional or reckless conduct violates the due process clause and would result in liability for the school district. "Reckless" conduct is reckless in the criminal sense—conduct that reflects complete indifference to a risk. Generally, the actor does not care whether the other person lives or dies, despite knowing that there is a significant risk of death. Assuming, for the purpose of argument, that the decision of the school district to sponsor the dance at Lincoln High School—despite an awareness of the dangers posed—was negligent, perhaps even grossly so, the court would still probably conclude that this conduct did not rise to the level of deliberate indifference. Thus, despite its knowledge of potential danger, a school is not liable for depriving a student of his procedural due process rights unless the school acted with a "deliberate indifference" toward the student's safety.

## Discussion Questions

1. What are instances that might constitute a "deliberate indifference" toward a student's safety?

2. In your opinion, was knowing that there was a safety risk, and holding the dance anyway, acting recklessly toward the students?

3. If the school wasn't violating the victim's constitutional rights, are there other areas where a school might be vulnerable as a result of this person's death?

# J. S. V. BETHLEHEM AREA SCHOOL DISTRICT
# 569 PA. 638; 807 A.2D 847 (N.D. OHIO 2002)

**GENERAL RULE OF LAW:** Consistent with the First Amendment, a school district may discipline a student for creating and posting from home onto the Internet a Web site that contained derogatory, profane, offensive, and threatening statements directed toward one of the student's teachers and his principal.

**PROCEDURE SUMMARY:**

**Plaintiff:** J. S. (P) was an eighth-grade student at Nitschmann Middle School, which is part of Bethlehem Area School District

**Defendant:** Bethlehem Area School District (School District) (D)

**Court of Common Pleas of Northampton County Decision:** Held for School District (D) that expulsion of J. S. (P) for the Web site was not a violation of his First Amendment rights

**Commonwealth Court of Appeals Decision:** Affirmed

**Commonwealth Supreme Court Decision (Pennsylvania):** Affirmed

**FACTS:** Sometime prior to May of 1998, J. S. created a Web site on his home computer and posted it on the Internet. The Web site was compiled on his own time and at his own home. The site was not created as part of a school project and was not sponsored by the school district. The site was entitled "Teacher Sux." It consisted of a number of Web pages that made derogatory, profane, offensive, and threatening comments, primarily about the student's algebra teacher, Mrs. Kathleen Fulmer, and middle school principal, Mr. A. Thomas Karsotis. The comments took the form of written words, pictures, animation, and sound clips. After the end of the school year, on July 30, 1998, the School District (D) sent a letter to J. S. (P) and his parents, informing them that it was aware of the Web site and that it intended to suspend the student for three days. The letter asserted that J. S. (P) violated School District (D) policy and committed three Level III infractions: threat to a teacher, harassment of a teacher and principal, and disrespect to a teacher and principal. Each of these infractions resulted in actual harm to the health, safety, and welfare of the school community. After a hearing on the suspension, the School District (D) opted to extend the suspension to 10 days, effective the beginning of the 1998–1999 school year. Shortly thereafter, the School District (D) began expulsion proceedings against the student. The School District (D) concluded that (1) the student's statements, "Why Should [Mrs. Fulmer] Die?" and "Give me $20 to help pay for the hit man" constituted a threat to a teacher and were perceived as a threat; (2) the statements regarding the teacher and the principal constituted harassment; (3) the statements constituted disrespect to a teacher and principal resulting in actual harm to the health, safety, and welfare of the school community; (4) the School District Code of Conduct prohibited such student conduct, and engaging in such action could result in expulsion; and (5) the statements caused actual harm to the teacher, as well as to other students and teachers. As a result of these findings, the School District (D) voted to expel J. S. (P). The plaintiff challenged the expulsion through the courts.

**ISSUE:** May a school district discipline a student for creating and posting from home onto the Internet a Web site that contained derogatory, profane, offensive, and threatening statements directed toward one of the student's teachers and his principal?

**HOLDING AND DECISION:** (Cappy, J.) Yes. The Web site posted by J. S. in this case disrupted the entire school community—teachers, students, and parents. This posting was directly and indirectly related to the teacher's emotional and physical injuries. Aside from the immediate effects of the site on the teacher, she was also unable to complete the school year and took a medical leave of absence for the next year. Mrs. Fulmer's absence for over 20 days at the end of the school year necessitated the use of three substitute teachers that unquestionably disrupted the delivery of instruction to the students and adversely impacted the educational environment. Students were also adversely impacted. Certain students expressed anxiety about the Web site and about their safety. Some students visited counselors. The Web site was a "hot" topic of conversation even prior to faculty discovery. Finally, among the staff and students, there was a feeling of helplessness and low morale. The atmosphere of the entire school community was described to be as if a student had died. Additionally, the disruption also involved parents. Certain parents understandably voiced concerns about school safety and questioned the delivery of instruction by substitute teachers.

**COMMENT:** As this case demonstrates, these Internet situations create significant controversy and difficulty for school authorities. Even before the district became aware of the situation, there were problems because the Web site was a "hot" topic of student conversation. As noted in the case, the situation created was a feeling of helplessness and low morale among the staff and students, with what was described as an atmosphere similar to a student having died. The Web site created disorder and significantly and adversely impacted the delivery of instruction. Indeed, this Web site was specifically aimed at this particular school district and seemed designed to create precisely this sort of turmoil. Based upon these facts, most courts would find that the Web site created an actual and substantial interference with the work of the school, to a magnitude that satisfies the requirements of *Tinker*. Thus, when sufficient potential for disruption is created, a school district's disciplinary action will be upheld as not violating students' First Amendment right to freedom of speech.

## Discussion Questions

1. Summarize what authority a school district has over the actions of its students while in their homes.

2. Think of two examples of material that would fall within the school's power and two that would fall outside the control of school officials.

3. Why do you think that this type of material isn't subject to the protections of the First Amendment?

---

Additional case briefs can be found on the SAGE Web site at the following address:
http://www.sagepub.com/aquilacasebriefs

---

## NOTES

1. See Flaherty v. Keystone Oaks School Dist., 247 F.Supp. 2d 698 (W.D.Pa.2003).
2. J. S. v. Bethlehem Area School Dist., 807 A.2d 847 (N.D. Ohio 2002).
3. Board of Education of Island Trees Free School District No. 26 v. Pico, 457 U.S. 853 (1982).
4. Hazelwood School District v. Kuhlmeier, 484 U.S. 260 (1988).
5. See The School Board of Palm Beach County v. Anderson, 411 So. 2d 940 (1982).
6. See Leffal v. Dallas Independent School District, 28 F.3d 521 (1994).
7. See Belanger v. Nashua, New Hampshire, School District, 856 F.Supp. 40 (D.N.H. 1994).
8. Flaherty v. Keystone Oaks School Dist., 247 F.Supp 2d 698 (W.D. Pa. 2003).

# Appendix A
# Selected Provisions of the
# Constitution of the United States

We the People of the United States, in Order to form a more perfect Union, establish Justice, insure domestic Tranquility, provide for the common defence, promote the general Welfare, and secure the Blessings of Liberty to ourselves and our Posterity, do ordain and establish this Constitution for the United States of America.

## Article I

Section 8.

[1] The Congress shall have Power to lay and collect Taxes, Duties, Imposts and Excises, to pay the Debts and provide for the common Defence and general Welfare of the United States; . . .

[3] To Regulate Commerce with foreign Nations, and among the several States, and within the Indian Tribes; . . .

[18] To make all Laws which shall be necessary and proper for carrying into Execution the foregoing Powers, and all other Powers vested by this Constitution in the Government of the United States, or in any Department or Officer thereof . . .

Section 10.

[1] No State shall . . . pass any . . . Law impairing the Obligation of Contracts . . . .

* * *

## Article III

Section 1. The judicial Power of the United States, shall be vested in one supreme Court, and in such inferior Courts as the congress may from time to time ordain and establish. The Judges, both of the supreme and inferior courts, shall hold their Offices during good Behaviour, and shall, at stated Times, receive for their Services, a Compensation, which shall not be diminished during their Continuance in Office.

379

Section 2. [1]

The Judicial Power shall extend to all Cases, in Law and Equity, arising under this constitution, the Laws of the United States and Treaties made, or which shall be made, under their Authority; . . . . to Controversies to which the United States shall be a Party; — to Controversies between two or more States; — between a State and Citizens of another State; — between Citizens or different States; — between Citizens of the same State claiming Lands under Grants of different States and between a State, or the Citizens thereof, and foreign States, Citizens or Subjects.

\* \* \*

## Article VI

[2] This Constitution, and the Laws of the United States which shall be made in Pursuance thereof; and all Treaties made, or which shall be made, under the Authority of the United States, shall be the supreme Law of the Land; and the Judges in every State shall be bound thereby, any Thing in the Constitution or Laws of any State of the Contrary notwithstanding.

## Amendment I [1791]

Congress shall make no law respecting an establishment of religion, or prohibiting the free exercise thereof; or abridging the freedom of speech, or of the press; or the right of the people peaceably to assemble, and to petition the Government for a redress of grievances.

\* \* \*

## Amendment IV [1791]

The right of the people to be secure in their persons, houses, papers, and effects, against unreasonable searches and seizures, shall not be violated, and no Warrants shall issue, but upon probable cause, supported by Oath or affirmation, and particularly describing the place to be searched, and the persons or things to be seized.

\* \* \*

## Amendment V [1791]

No person shall be . . . compelled in any criminal case to be a witness against himself, nor be deprived of life, liberty, or property, without due process of law; nor shall private property be taken for public use, without just compensation.

\* \* \*

## Amendment IX [1791]

The enumeration in the Constitution, of certain rights, shall not be construed to deny or disparage others retained by the people.

\* \* \*

## Amendment X [1791]

The powers not delegated to the United States by the Constitution, nor prohibited by it to the States, are reserved to the States respectively, or to the people.

\* \* \*

## Amendment XIII [1865]

Section 1. Neither slavery nor involuntary servitude, except as a punishment for crime whereof the party shall have been duly convicted, shall exist within the United States, or any place subject to their jurisdiction.

Section 2. Congress shall have power to enforce this article by appropriate legislation.

\* \* \*

## Amendment XIV [1868]

Section 1. All persons born or naturalized in the United States, and subject to the jurisdiction thereof, are citizens of the United States and of the State wherein they reside. No State shall make or enforce any law which shall abridge the privileges or immunities of citizens of the United States; nor shall any State deprive any person of life, liberty, or property, without due process of law; nor deny to any person within its jurisdiction the equal protection of the laws.

\* \* \*

## Amendment XXVII [Proposed]

Section 1. Equality of rights under the law shall not be denied or abridged by the United states or by any State on account of sex.

Section 2. The Congress shall have the power to enforce, by appropriate legislation, the provisions of this article.

Section 3. This amendment shall take effect two years after the date of ratification.

# Appendix B

## Table of Authorities

# Glossary

**Absolute**  Unconditional; complete and perfect in itself; without relation to or dependence on other things or persons.

**Act**  A law passed by the Congress or a state legislature; a statute.

**Action**  A judicial proceeding in which one party prosecutes another for the enforcement or protection of a right, for the redress or prevention of a wrong, or for punishment of a public offense.

**Adduced**  Presented as evidence.

**Admission**  A voluntary acknowledgment by a party of the truth of certain facts that are inconsistent with his claims in an action.

**Advocate**  To speak in favor of.

**Affidavit**  A written or printed declaration of statement of facts made voluntarily and confirmed by the oath or affirmation of the party making it, taken before an officer having authority to administer such an oath.

**Affirmed**  In the practice of appellate courts, to affirm a judgment, decree, or order, is to declare that it is valid and right and must stand as rendered below.

**Amicus Curiae**  Latin: Friend of the court. A person with strong interest in or views on the subject matter of an action, but who is not a party to the action, may petition the court for permission to file a brief, ostensibly on behalf of a party but actually to suggest a rationale consistent with his or her own views.

**Appeal**  The complaint to a superior court of an injustice done or error committed by an inferior court, whose judgment or decision the court above is called upon to correct or reverse.

**Appellant**  The party who takes an appeal from one court or jurisdiction to another.

**Appellate Court**   A state or federal court that may review the judgment of a lower court. In a trial de novo, the appellate court may also hear new evidence or redetermine the facts that appear in the record of the original trial. In the United States, the U.S. Supreme Court is the final court of appeals.

**Appellee**   Party against whom an appeal is taken.

**Assault**   Any intentional display of force or a movement that could reasonably give the victim reason to fear or expect immediate bodily harm.

**Battery**   Intentional and wrongful physical contact of a person without his or her consent that entails some injury or offensive touching.

**Bill**   The draft of a proposed law.

**Bill of Rights**   The first 10 amendments to the U.S. Constitution.

**Brief**   A written statement prepared by the counsel arguing a case in court. It contains a summary of the facts of the case, the pertinent laws, and how the laws apply to the facts supporting counsel's position.

**Case**   An action, cause, suit, or controversy; a question contested before a court of justice.

**Certiorari**   Writ issued by a superior to an inferior court requiring the latter to produce a certified record of a particular case tried therein. The Supreme Court of the United States uses the writ of certiorari as a discretionary device to choose the cases it wishes to hear.

**Challenge**   To object or take exception to.

**Citation**   The system used to identify the law report in which a court case is published. The citation includes the title, volume, and page number of the law report and the year of the decision.

**Cite**   To read or refer to legal authorities in support of propositions of law.

**Class Action**   The means by which one or more persons interested in a matter may sue or be sued as representatives of a class without needing to join every member of the class.

**Clause**   A subdivision of a legal document, such as a contract, deed, will, constitution, or statute.

**Code**   See Statutes.

**Common Law**   A body of law derived from usages and customs of antiquity or from court judgments affirming and enforcing such usages and customs, as distinguished from legislative enactments.

**Complaint**   The original or initial pleading by which an action is commenced under codes or Rules of Civil Procedure.

**Concurring Opinion**    A judge's decision that agrees with the result reached by the majority, but disagrees with the precise reasoning leading to that result.

**Constitutional**    Consistent with or authorized by the Constitution.

**Construe**    To ascertain the meaning of language by arranging and interpreting the words of an instrument, statute, regulation, court decision, or other legal authority.

**Count**    A charge; one of the offenses in the plaintiff's stated causes for an action.

**Court of Appeals**    See Appellate Court.

**Decide**    To arrive at a determination. To "decide" includes the power and right to deliberate, to weigh the reasons for and against, to see which preponderate, and to be governed by that preponderance.

**Declaratory Judgment**    Statutory remedy for the determination of a justiciable controversy in which the plaintiff is in doubt as to his legal rights.

**De Facto**    In fact; actually; a reality.

**Defendant**    The person against whom the case is brought. Essentially, the person who must make a response to the complaint that the plaintiff has initiated and put on the record.

**De Jure**    Of right; legitimate; lawful.

**De Minimis**    Under this doctrine, the law does not care for, or take notice of, very small or trifling matters.

**Demurrer**    An objection made by one party to his opponent's pleading, alleging that he ought not to answer it for some defect in law. It admits the facts but argues they do not warrant legal action.

**Dicta**    From the Latin Obiter Dicta: Remarks by the way. Statements and comments in a judge's opinion concerning some rule of law or legal proposition not essential to the determination of the case in hand.

**Directory**    A provision in a statute, rule, procedure, or the like that is mere direction of no obligatory force and involves no invalidating consequence for its disregard. See also Mandatory.

**Dissenting Opinion**    A judge's decision that disagrees with the result reached by the majority and thus disagrees with the reasoning and/or the principles of law used by the majority in deciding the case.

**Distinguished**    Pointed out an essential difference; proved a case is inapplicable.

**Diversity Jurisdiction**    Diversity jurisdiction applies when there is a conflict between a citizen of one state and a citizen of a different state. When such diversity occurs, the case goes into a federal court, which will apply the laws of the relevant state.

**Doctrine**   A rule, principle, theory, or tenet of the law.

**Due Process**   A course of legal proceeding designed to safeguard the legal rights of the individual.

**En Banc**   Full bench. Refers to a session where the entire membership of the court will participate in the decision rather than the regular quorum. Only occurs when the issues involved are unusually novel or of wide impact.

**Equal Protection of the Laws**   The constitutional guarantee that no person or class of persons can be denied the protection of the laws that is enjoyed by other persons in similar circumstances.

**Equity**   Concept from English common law that empowers a court to remedy a situation in which rights are being violated but existing law does not provide a remedy.

**Error**   A mistake of law, or false or irregular application of it, that vitiates the proceedings and warrants the reversal of judgment.

**Et al.**   Latin: And others.

**Express Authority**   Authority delegated to an agent by words that expressly authorize him to do a delegable act. That which confers power to do a particular identical thing set forth and declared exactly, plainly, and directly within well-defined limits.

**Ex rel.**   From the Latin Ex Relatione: On the relation. Legal proceedings that are instituted by the attorney general (or other proper person) in the name and on behalf of the state, but on the information and at the instigation of an individual who has a private interest in the matter.

**Federal Courts**   The principal federal courts are the District Court, a trial court of general federal jurisdiction, and the U.S. Court of Appeals, intermediate appellate courts sitting in 11 numbered circuits, the District of Columbia, and the Court of Appeal for the Federal Circuit and having jurisdiction over most cases decided by District Courts. The decisions of the Court of Appeals are reviewable on appeal only by the U.S. Supreme Court.

**Felony**   Generally, a crime punishable by death or imprisonment for a term exceeding one year.

**Finding**   A court's decision as to the facts in a case, an interpretation of the facts, or the case as a whole.

**Implied**   This word is used in law in contrast to "express," that is, the intention is not manifested by explicit and direct words, but is gathered by implication or necessary deduction from the circumstances, the general language, or the conduct of the parties.

**Injunction**   A court order prohibiting someone from doing some specified act or commanding someone to undo some wrong or injury.

**In Loco Parentis**   Latin: In the place of a parent.

**In Re**    Latin: In the matter of. In the title of a case, usually indicates that it is not an adversarial proceeding, but is merely asking for a judgment about some matter.

**Inter Alia**    Latin: Among other things. A term used in pleading, especially in reciting statements in which the whole statute is not set forth.

**Jurisdiction**    The power and authority of a court to hear and determine legal proceedings. Presupposes the existence of a duly constituted court with control over the subject matter and the parties.

**Justice**    Title given to judges, particularly to judges of U.S. and state supreme courts, as well as to judges of appellate courts.

**Liable**    Legally responsible; usually applies in a civil matter.

**Libel**    One of the twin torts of defamation; this is defamation by printed or written communication.

**Majority Opinion**    The majority opinion in a case is usually written by one judge and represents the principles of law that a majority of his or her colleagues on the court deem operative in a given decision; it has more precedential value than any other type of decision.

**Mandatory**    Containing a command; perceptive; imperative; peremptory; obligatory. Failure to follow a "mandatory" provision in a statute renders the proceedings to which it relates void, while following a "directory" provision is not necessary to the validity of the proceeding.

**Ministerial Authority**    Authority regarding which nothing is left to discretion. A simple and definite duty imposed by law.

**Misfeasance**    The improper performance of some act that a person may lawfully do (a misdeed).

**Moot**    A case is "moot" when a determination is sought on a matter that, when rendered, cannot have any practical effect on the existing controversy.

**Negligence**    The omission to do something that a reasonable man, guided by those ordinary considerations that ordinarily regulate human affairs, would do, or the doing of something that a reasonable and prudent man would not do. The failure to use ordinary care.

**Nonfeasance**    Nonperformance of some act that a person is obligated or has a responsibility to perform; omission to perform a required duty at all; or, total neglect of duty.

**Opinion**    The statement by a judge or court of the decision reached in regard to a cause tried or argued before either of them, expounding the law as applied to the case, and detailing the reasons upon which the judgment is based.

**Ordinance**    A municipal law.

**Parens Patriae**    Latin: Parent of the country. Refers traditionally to the role of the state as sovereign and guardian of persons under legal disability, such as juveniles or the insane.

**Per Curiam**    Latin: By the court. Used to distinguish an opinion of the whole court from written opinions of one judge.

**Petition**:    Written application or prayer to the court seeking redress of a wrong or requesting the grant of a privilege or license.

**Plaintiff**    A person who brings an action; the party who complains or sues in a civil action and is so named on the record.

**Plurality Decision**    A decision that is agreed to by less than a majority of the court with respect to the reasoning of the decision, but is agreed to by a majority with respect to the result.

**Police Power**    A state's power to make and enforce laws for the general welfare of the public, including regulation of education, both public and nonpublic.

**Precedent**    A decision by a higher court providing an authority for an identical or similar case later arising on a similar question of law.

**Prima Facie**    Latin: At first view, on its first appearance, on its face. Evidence supporting a conclusion unless it is rebutted.

**Proceeding**    Any action, hearing, investigation, inquest, or inquiry in which, pursuant to law, testimony can be compelled to be given; also called judicial proceedings.

**Proximate Cause**    That which, in a natural and continuous sequence, unbroken by an efficient intervening cause, produces the injury and without which the result would not have occurred.

**Punitive Damages**    An award in a civil case that is intended to punish.

**Quid Pro Quo**    Giving one valuable thing for another.

**Remand**    To send back. The act of an appellate court when it sends a case back to the trial court and orders the trial court to conduct limited new hearings or an entirely new trial or to take some further action.

**Reports**    Published volumes of case decisions by a particular court or group of courts, for example, *Supreme Court Reporter*.

**Res Judicata**    Latin: A thing decided. The final outcome in a case.

**Respondent**    The party who makes an answer to a bill or other proceeding in an equity. In appellate practice, the party who contends against an appeal; the appellee.

**Reversed**    To overthrow, vacate, set aside, make void, annul, repeal, or revoke; to reverse a judgment, sentence, or decree of a lower court by an appellate court, or to change to the contrary or to a former condition.

**Sect**    As applied to religious bodies, a party or body of persons who unite in holding certain special doctrines or opinions concerning religion, which distinguish them from others holding the same general religious belief.

**Sovereign Immunity**    A judicial doctrine that precludes bringing suit against the government without its consent.

**Standing to Sue**    The right to take the initial step that frames legal issues for ultimate adjudication by a court or jury.

**Stare Decisis**    Latin: Stand by what has been decided. Adhering to precedent, applying a previous decision to the present case; the previous decision has become the rule.

**Statutes**    Laws enacted by the legislative power of a country or state.

**Strict Scrutiny**    This standard is applied to suspect classifications in an equal protection analysis as well as to fundamental rights in a due process analysis; essentially, the state must establish that it has a compelling interest that justifies and necessitates the law being challenged.

**Subpoena**    A command to appear at a certain time and place to give testimony upon a certain matter.

**Summary Judgment**    Procedural device available for prompt and expeditious disposition of controversy without trial when there is no dispute as to either material fact or inferences to be drawn from undisputed facts, or if only a question of law is involved.

**Supra**    Above; upon. This word occurring by itself in a book refers the reader to a previous part of the book.

**Term**    When used with reference to a court, signifies the space of time during which the court holds session. A session signifies the time during the term when the court sits for the transaction of business, and the session commences when the court convenes for the term and continues until final adjournment, either before or at the expiration of the term.

**Theory**    See doctrine.

**Tort**    A private or civil wrong or injury for which the court will provide a remedy in the form of money damages.

**Trial Court**    A court of original jurisdiction; the initial court to consider litigation.

**Ultra Vires**   An act performed without any authority to act on the subject. Acts beyond the scope of the powers of a corporation, as defined by its charter or laws of state of incorporation.

**Unanimous**   To say that a proposition was adopted by a "unanimous" vote does not always mean that everyone present voted for the proposition, but it may, and generally does, mean when a *viva voce* vote is taken, that no one voted in the negative.

**Venue**   A neighborhood, place, or county in which an injury is declared to have been done or a fact declared to have happened. Venue does not refer to jurisdiction.

**Warrant**   A written order of the court that is made on behalf of the state, or United States, and is based upon a complaint issued pursuant to statute and/or court rule and commands a law enforcement officer to arrest a person and bring him before a magistrate.

**Writ of Mandamus**   Latin: We command. A writ that issues from a court of superior jurisdiction, directed to a private or municipal corporation or any of its officers or to an executive, administrative, or judicial officer or to an inferior court, commanding the performance of a particular act therein specified.

# Index

Regional reporters, xxxii
Rehabilitation Act of 1973, 166, 173–174,
    261, 271–274
Religious clubs or associations, 31–32, 35, 44,
    53–54, 57–58, 107, 111
Religious dress, 33, 42
Religious Freedom Restoration Act, 30
Religious holidays, 31, 42, 203–204
Religious instruction or related activities,
    33, 35, 41, 47–48, 348
Religious issues, 29–31, 41–43
    accommodating teachers'
        religions, 197, 214
    Bible study, 33, 41–42
    case briefs, 47–61
    child benefit doctrine, 35–37
    compulsory education exemption,
        30, 43, 86, 90, 96–97
    conflicts with religious beliefs, 43
    equal protection clause and, 37
    excessive entanglement test, 32, 34
    First Amendment and government neutrality,
        29–30, 32, 33–35
    important concepts, 32–33
    "In God We Trust" motto, 42
    invocations at graduation ceremonies, 42–43
    *Lemon* tests, 30, 33, 34, 45, 50–51
    prayer in public school, 33, 35, 41, 42
    private or parochial schools. *See* Private
        religious schools
    reasonable accommodation policy, 31, 45
    religious beliefs versus union
        membership, 235
    special school districts, 40
    Supreme Court balancing test, 34
    tension between establishment and
        free exercise clauses, 34–35
    true private choice programs, 59–60
    *See also specific issues*
Religious literature distribution, 32, 42
Religious requirement for employment,
    214, 228–229
Remand, defined, 396
Remedial education services, 39, 46
Report cards (school performance),
    64, 66, 69–70
Res judicata, xxxv, 396
Reserve clause (Tenth Amendment),
    xxxiv–xxxv, 279

Residency requirements, 86, 88, 91, 214, 218
Respondent, defined, 396
*Responsive Environments Corp. v. Pulaski Cnty.
    Special School Dist.*, 303–304
Retirement, 258
Reverse discrimination, 252, 259
Reversed, defined, 397
*Reynolds v. United States*, 30
*Roberts v. City of Boston*, 4
*Robinson v. Cahill*, 337
*Rose v. Council for Better Education, Inc.*, 337
*Rose v. Nashua Board of Education*, 357–358
Rule of seven, 312

San Antonio Independent School District v.
    Rodriguez, 336, 355, 356–357
*Santa Fe Independent School District v. Doe*, 41
Save harmless statutes, 309
*Sawyer v. Gilmore, State Treasurer*, 355–356
School attendance. *See* Compulsory education
*School Board of Nassau County v. Arline*,
    261, 271–272, 273
*School Board of Palm Beach County v. Anderson*,
    372–373
School boards. *See* Local school board(s)
School choice issues, 31, 59–60, 339, 344
    No Child Left Behind Act and, 71, 77
    voucher programs, 31, 40, 69, 89, 344
*School Dist. of Abington Township v.
    Schempp*, 42
*School Dist. of the City of Grand Rapids v. Ball*,
    55, 56
School district budgets and expenditures,
    344–345. *See also* School fund allocation
School district liability. *See* Local school board
    contract liability; Tort liability
*School District of the City of Pontiac et al. v
    Spellings*, 64, 66, 80–81
School districts:
    affirmative duty vs. segregation, 7, 11
    federal desegregation oversight,
        5–6, 8, 13, 23–24
    indebtedness limitations, 339, 342
    local governments and, 285
    no independent funding authority,
        338, 339, 340–341, 342
    religious communities within, 40
    report cards for, 64, 66, 69–70
    residency requirements, 86, 88, 91

# About the Author

**Frank D. Aquila** is a professor of educational administration at Cleveland State University. Aquila received his doctoral degree from Kent State University and his law degree from Cleveland-Marshall College of Law. In addition to his graduate teaching and direction of several grant programs, he has served as a teacher, coach, principal, supervisor, and central office administrator. In addition to over 100 journal articles and research studies and several books focusing on school administration, he has published two books of education law cases. Aquila serves as a hearing officer for several school districts. His legal practice has focused on youth and he has participated in over 200 guardian ad litem cases in both juvenile court and domestic relations court. He presently serves as of-counsel with McGown & Markling Co., LPA where he concentrates on special education law, collective bargaining, and issues related to civil rights.